Bitter Prerequisites

Bitter
Prerequisites

A Faculty for Survival
from Nazi Terror

WM. LAIRD KLEINE-AHLBRANDT

PURDUE UNIVERSITY PRESS
WEST LAFAYETTE, INDIANA

05   04   03   02   01   5   4   3   2   1

⊖ The paper used in this book meets the minimum requirements of American National Standard for Information Sciences—Permanence of Paper for Printed Library Materials, ANSI Z39.48-1992.

Designed and composed by inari information services, inc.

Printed in the United States of America

Library of Congress Cataloging-in-Publication Data
Bitter prerequisites ; a faculty for survival from Nazi terror / Wm. Laird Kleine-Ahlbrandt.
  p. cm.
  ISBN 1-55753-214-1 (alk. paper)
  1. Jews—Germany—History—1933–1945—Interviews. 2. Jewish refugees—Indiana—Interviews. 3. Jews, German—Indiana—Interviews. 4. Holocaust survivors—Indiana—Interviews. 5. Indiana—Interviews. 6. Purdue University—Interviews.
  I. Kleine-Ahlbrandt, W. Laird (William Laird)

DS135.G3315 .B58 2000
943'.004924—dc21
                                                    00-062782

FOR SHEILA
who inspired this book

AND

FOR STÉPHANIE AND E.J.
whose occupation with human rights reinforces its purpose

The human spirit can prevail as long as there are those who struggle against injustice and intolerance, as long as there are those who search for excellence and beauty, and as long as there are two people who will hold each other's hand in the darkness of the night.

Contents

The author gratefully acknowledges the contributions to this book of Joseph Haberer, who was there at its birth, helped shape its themes and dimensions, and participated in its interviews.

Preface

This book originated in the course of a relaxed after-dinner conversation with Joe Haberer who with his wife Rose was visiting my spouse Sheila and me at our home in Oak Park. Joe and I were discussing the Second World War in the context of its impact on our lives when we were children.

For me the conflict had been remote in distance and psychology. Raised in Cincinnati, I had followed the conflict from articles in the Times-Star and film snippets from Movietone News. I had also been involved in various patriotic projects in school and in the Cub Scouts. My limited participation in the war effort came through scrap metal drives, filling little books with savings stamps, and helping cultivate a Victory Garden—one of those small leased plots of public land at Lunken Airport on which patriots grew radishes, potatoes and green beans. Our government told us that these efforts would relieve wartime shortages, and I suppose they did in some small way, but it later became apparent that this activity was not really essential to defeating the Germans. The Americans had plenty of food and really did not need the extra tin from food cans or the lead from used tooth paste tubes. Of course, the government encouraged these activities more for propaganda purposes than for material benefits. The aim was to mobilize public opinion to better sustain the war effort. In sum World War II seemed to me a gigantic movie serial at a Saturday matinee, something on the big screen rather than an immediate struggle of life and death.

Joe Haberer had memories of a dramatically different sort. He experienced the conflict in a much more realistic, more terrifying way. Joe was a direct victim of Nazi racial politics who survived only because his parents, who subsequently were killed in the Holocaust, had the foresight and strength to part with him and send him to safety on the Kindertransport. Joe came of age in an English boarding school for refugees. There he struggled with the shock of losing his family as well as the shock of life among strangers, many of whom were well-intentioned but lacked the ability to relate to such trauma suffered by those so young. The war years were to him not ones of high purpose and fun, but of desperation, fear, and mourning.

From contrasting our vastly different experiences, Joe and I shifted to talking about various colleagues on the Purdue faculty who had Holocaust experiences akin to Joe's. We began to speculate on how these experiences might have affected their lives, their values, their careers, their sense of purpose and identity. Sheila, who had been listening to our conversation, suggested that we do more than talk about these people. She suggested we turn our speculations into a more active inquiry and make a serious effort to preserve the history of Holocaust survivors which existed in the Purdue academic community.

I had never done oral history. But being a historian I knew that the meaning and importance of each age is the product of personal experiences, whose particular and general aspects contribute to an overall historical structure. People constantly change, especially so in modern times, often with a rapidity that defies the efforts of historians to accurately distill, synthesize, and otherwise make sense of what has happened. From research I knew that the facts of certain events could often be established easier than the motives, fears, and effects behind them. The study of official documents, newspaper reports, and treaties has a certain frozen quality like butterflies pinned on a display board, but life as it is lived is fluid and not easy to compartmentalize. Only by monitoring the reaction to daily events can we truly recreate what has happened. In this way interviews can become living artifacts, the ultimate primary source.

My attraction to a project of this sort went beyond professional interest, however. I was a member on the faculty of the same university as people about whose survivorship experiences I was completely ignorant. Many I had known only superficially, either socially or by reputation. I wanted to find out for myself who these colleagues were and I wanted to make their stories as important for a larger public as they were for me. I thought it would be unfortunate if these experiences were allowed to vanish with the lives of those who had lived them.

Before being asked to be part of this book, these colleagues had not intended to make their lives public. And even after agreeing to participate, they were modest about the importance of what they might contribute to such a study of history. Many had to overcome the feeling that past unpleasantness was best left repressed. They also did not see themselves as "victims" as that term is commonly used today, meaning objects of sympathy, or pity, or worthy of special treatment. They had not lived their lives as victims because they had made successful lives and careers. I was impressed by and curious about their ability to transcend their own cruel histories.

More than fifty years separates these twelve colleagues from the Holocaust period, half a century in which the generation which had formulated and implemented those despicable Nazi racial policies has all but disappeared. However, even after all that time, they often found it difficult to recall painful experiences, believing that those who had not been through similar trauma would not understand or even be interested. Thus, many of the memories revealed here had not been previously shared with friends or even, in some cases, with their own families.

My initial fear that people with such painful memories would want to keep them within themselves proved unfounded. Once committed they gave of their time graciously and even thankfully, no matter how intrusive the nature of the investigation became. Despite that intrusion, their reasons for participating varied. Some expressed a desire to pass on something of their experiences to future generations, particularly to the members of their own families. Others manifested a desire to become reconciled with a traumatic past for which they had understandably kept compartmentalized. A decade or so before, they might not have been as willing to reveal so much of themselves. But most now recognized the necessity of keeping the memory of what had happened to them alive, voicing an obligation to bear personal witness if only to counter those who would prefer to forget, or even worse, acknowledge that history as horrendous as the Holocaust had happened at all. All these motives, and others not stated, resulted not only in a story of harassment and dislocation but also one of definition of identity, religious beliefs, and personal and professional values.

Instinctive sympathy with the plight of the victim is inevitable, but the horrendous nature of the events in which these participants were involved compounded the normal problems associated with objectivity. Yet the participants, as academics, understood the author's need to maintain critical distance, and did not evidence suspicion of my efforts to maintain that professional standard. Each participant sat through a series of lengthy sessions answering what may have seemed tedious, repetitive and painful, undoubtedly at times embarrassing, questions. Then each willingly read over and approved the edited copy of his or her interview, making corrections, additions and further suggestions. From this process, based on hundreds and hundreds of pages of transcribed dialogue, the final record was assembled. Unless people are making speeches, they usually do not generate final copy-ready prose. In conversation, subordinate clauses take the place of complete sentences, clarification produces thoughts within thoughts, phrases upon phrases, there is backtracking, repetition, a mixing of thoughts and impressions, making a truly verbatim account unfeasible. I have been extremely touched by and grateful for the willingness of the participants to expose their lives and thoughts for publication, and I hope I have done their stories justice.

I want to thank Peggy Quirk, Judy McHenry, Jan Whitehead, and Mary Wenger of the Purdue University Department of History staff for their constant and patient assistance in the preparation of this manuscript. And Diane Carlson and Sue English bore the major responsibility in transcribing the many, many hours of tape whose auditory quality was not always, if ever, state of the art. In addition to the inconsistent sound quality, they were inundated with French, German, Italian, Polish, Hungarian, Italian, and Russian place names, to say nothing of other unfamiliar words and expressions, including references to Jewish customs and rituals. They handled it all in stride, many coming to feel that they knew as more than acquaintances those whose lives they were hearing about for the first time. I deeply appreciate the friendly and professional help that Sherry Swank, Gail Garrison, and Chip Morrison gave me in the production of the maps. Further, I want to express my gratitude to Thomas Bacher, director of the Purdue University Press, who was enthusiastic about this project from the beginning and has given it sustained support and encouragement. I also want to recognize the immense importance of Margaret Hunt in putting the not-so-ready copy into publishable shape. She is not only a great editor but also a great opera lover.

I especially want to give credit to Professor Emeritus Joseph Haberer, who participated in practically all of the interviews. As stated, Joe Haberer's memories and my memories of the Holocaust could not have been more diverse. Our different experiences also showed in our different interview techniques. Inevitably the social scientist brings to his or her work a configuration of experiences, beliefs, biases, and assumptions which shapes the investigatory process.

I thought Joe and I made a sort of good-cops-bad-cops team. I asked more factual and historically analytical questions, trying to relate personal accounts to the age in which they were experienced. Joe Haberer zeroed in on matters of religious identity and personal introspection as these related to fundamental values. Our differences shaped the methodology of this book, whose shape would have been far less defined without Joe Haberer's participation. As well as doing the interviews together, we also had intended to write the book together. But Joe's other commitments precluded his participation in the process of verifying and editing the tapes and writing the book. Nonetheless, his stamp is clearly on this work from start to finish, and it would have been a different, less psychological, study without his cooperation. For my part, this book is in a very real sense a tribute to Joseph Haberer because without his story and our relationship as colleagues and friends over the years, I am sure it would probably never have been brought to press.

I would also like to give special thanks to Rose Haberer, Joe's spouse and Sheila's and my dear friend. Rose has always been ready with her encouragement, helpful advice, and analysis. Her interest in the progress of the work remained constant, her help consistent.

Finally, I want to pay tribute to my spouse, Sheila Hegy, whose dedication to preserving this wealth of history which existed in the Purdue Community was as strong as mine. She gave this project birth and has contributed sustained editorial advice. Not only throughout the project but in many aspects of my life she has acted as advisor and confidant, and always a friendly and incisive critic and helper.

Introduction

People do not die; they are always there, somewhere in the past. But the journeys of the past do not come alive by themselves. They have to be recreated. The biographies in this book are journeys of a special kind. They are not the kind found on the Grand Tour or in literature, like the kind spoken about by Shelley in his poem about the traveler from an antique land.

These survivors of Hitler's war against the Jews can speak about past civilizations and broken monuments, but they did not move from place to place to collect vignettes to enrich and entertain others. They hoped merely to survive and find a new way of life and identity, and they had no expectation of returning home at all.

Wherever possible, their parents tried to shield them from the trauma of rejection and exile. To the degree they succeeded, their children could board ship at Hamburg or Rotterdam more with a spirit of anticipation than rejection, feeling that they were beginning a great adventure, looking forward to a new home and new friends because their father had changed jobs or because they could now fulfill some childhood fantasy.

> I had always wanted to go to America, it was my dream. I had read Karl
> May and I wanted to be a cowboy. Going there would be pretty much of
> a lark and now I could see that I was going to get my wish.[1]

But this was hardly typical. Most of the émigrés, certainly old enough not

1

to be fooled, were surrounded with anxiety. They knew they were headed for an uncertain future. Moreover, without any schedules or itineraries, they realized they faced a long journey. One came to New York from Munich via Ljubljana, Belgrade, Zagreb, Paris, and Le Havre. Another came to New York from Vienna via Trieste, Palermo, Rome, Paris, Nantes, La Rochelle, Luchon, Marseilles, and Trinidad. Another arrived in San Francisco via Berlin, Moscow, Pusan (Korea), Kobe (Japan), and Yokahama. Others were unable to escape from Europe at all. They survived through hiding and subterfuge or endured the camps.

These refugees came from a wide variety of backgrounds and from cities spread across Europe: from Frankfurt-am-Main, Stuttgart, Ronnenberg, Würzburg, Kassel, and Villingen in Germany; from Vienna in Austria; from Warsaw and Stanislau in Poland; and from Munkács and Rimvaska Sobota in Czechoslovakia, towns which later became part of Hungary. One was an American, a prisoner of war from New York City, who was sent to a concentration camp. They spanned more than a generation and made careers in a broad range of disciplines: political science, physics, foreign languages and literature, chemical engineering, mathematics, sociology, industrial engineering, and biological sciences. The Nazi racial policy touched them all directly, all differently yet similarly, and with a certain chronological predictability. It first affected those from Germany, then Austria, Czechoslovakia, Poland, and Hungary.

Devoid of any of the fundamental considerations of morality upon which modern states base their law, Hitler's war against the Jews was evolutionary and expansive, and its fury took many by surprise. To them, the kind of violent antisemitism that had frequently marked European society before Hitler came to power seemed a thing of the past. This assumption was particularly strong in Germany, where ever since the constitutional guarantees of 1871, the Jews had enjoyed complete civil, political, and religious rights.[2]

German Jews had actively promoted the vital interests of their homeland and contributed mightily to its science, industry, and culture. Discrimination had not disappeared. In the civil service, for example, Jews found it difficult to climb into the upper ranks despite qualifications and constitutional guarantees; and few managed to obtain university professorships or army commissions. However, by the beginning of the twentieth century, all major German political parties had eliminated antisemitism from their platforms, and as time went on, other barriers were dropping.[3] In 1914, Jewish young men had enthusiastically rushed to defend the *Heimatland,* their numbers greater than any other group's, and they served overwhelmingly in front-line units.

Foreign Jews, particularly those in Eastern Europe, regarded the Reich as a haven of tolerance and opportunity, a kind of Promised Land. And even though their presence was not always welcomed, many immigrated there. Of course, it did not help that many German Jews considered these immigrants backward and feared that their strong Orthodox beliefs and often Hasidic way of dress might rekindle the fires of antisemitism. As a result they usually kept to themselves:

> Our Jewish community was divided between the Eastern Jews and the as-similated German Jews, or *jeckes*. . . . The German Jews were the ones who were highly educated. They would go to synagogue in *zilenders* (top hats), which now only chimney sweeps wear. We [of Polish origin] were not really assimilated into this assimilated group.[4]

These *Ostjuden* had little chance of ever receiving German citizenship, no matter how great their degree of assimilation. They could live in Germany as foreigners, but most of them and their descendants would remain officially aliens.

By contrast, the *Deutschjuden* had it made. The 1913 nationality law recognized their citizenship by blood — *jus sanguinis,* a right that was theirs even should they leave the country and settle elsewhere. The law stated that unless *Auslandsdeutsche* took out citizenship in another country or refused to perform military service, they could always be citizens of the Reich, and so could their descendants.[5]

Nazi racial legislation was a radical departure from these guaranties. Adolf Hitler saw history not as a progressive movement of liberation and tolerance but as a contest between the organic and inorganic forces of nature. In this gigantic struggle, the Teutonic peoples, bound in a powerful synthesis of blood and soil, would defeat the forces of racial pollution and prepare the way for the salvation of civilization. They thus would prove themselves worthy of Hitler, their leader, whose right to command was given him by God:

> I am acting in accordance with the will of the Almighty Creator: by defending myself against the Jews, I am fighting for the work of the Lord.[6]

The Nazi Party program, drawn up in February 1920, ruled that only those of German blood could be members of the nation! By this it meant that no Jew could be a German. Hitler claimed he had arrived at this belief during his down-and-out days in Vienna before the First World War.

> Once, as I was strolling through the Inner city, I suddenly encountered an apparition in a black caftan and black hair locks. Is this a Jew? was my first thought.

For, to be sure, they had not looked like that in [my boyhood town
of] Linz. I observed the man furtively and cautiously, but the longer I
stared at this foreign face, scrutinizing feature for feature, the more my first
question assumed a new form.

Is this a German?[7]

The one enduring, commanding facet of Hitler's character was his hatred of
the Jews, whom he blamed for all the evils with which he thought Germany was
currently afflicted: pornography, prostitution, treason, incest, Marxism, cultural
decadence, disease, economic exploitation, and the collapse of social values. But
most Germans were not that extreme. Those who initially supported him did so
more for the Nazi program of economic recovery and positive sense of nationalism than for obsessive antisemitism. Hitler's racism seemed more at home in
the Viennese gutter than in the Reich. And many German Jews, because of their
strong patriotism and identification with German culture, found it difficult to
view such hatemongering as anything more than a product of the political lu-
natic fringe:

> We were respected members of the community . . . and involved in the
> community's philanthropic and artistic activities. The National Socialist
> period was, therefore, a total and complete turnaround.[8]

Besides, until 1932, Hitler was not even a German citizen.[9]

However, German democracy always carried with it the taint of bastardy.
The Weimar Republic had been born into a cruel world, and on June 28, the day
of its establishment in 1919, Germans hung black bunting from their houses
and public buildings. Thus, Weimar did not mark its existence with an official
holiday. The Germans saved their parades and fireworks to honor an earlier
event: January 18, 1871, the day Bismarck had founded the Second Reich.

Most of the center and right-wing German political parties favored the restoration of German territory lost at Paris in 1919, and they vigorously opposed
paying reparations. Many of these groups were also outspokenly antidemocratic.
The cohesion of the old German middle class began to collapse into extremism,
antisemitism, and *völkisch* nationalism. A series of fragile coalitions, which ran
the Weimar government, no longer seemed to give dynamic focus to the nation's
political life. Patriotic paramilitary groups, youth movements, and league-type
organizations, many of which were preoccupied with the concept of a "new"
awakening and the solution of problems through authoritarianism, rose to
prominence.[10]

Many Germans saw the great drama of the modern age not in the power of the individual over the government, but in the intensification of the power of the government over the individual. The constant squabbling among more than thirty political parties undermined stable government and prompted a longing for the security of the good old days. Increasingly, the German electorate turned to leaders with easy solutions to pressing problems.

Yet, not until the Great Depression of the early thirties did a majority of Germans vote for parties that opposed democracy. The Nazi Party, which had become the largest party in the Reichstag in the elections of 1930, drew support from a wide section of the electorate, especially in southern Germany, among the lower and lower-middle classes, and members of the professional and middle classes, the civil service, and traditional ruling elites. Many nationalists came to regard Hitler as the true heir of Frederick the Great and Otto von Bismarck. And women saw him as the protector of family values, even though he advocated their disenfranchisement. In the 1932 presidential elections, Hitler kept Paul von Hindenburg from winning on the first round. His impressive showing against that venerable war hero helped catapult him to the chancellorship the following year.

Hitler successfully synthesized capitalism and socialism, the two great movements of modern times, making it appear he was acting above classes for the welfare of all citizens and the nation. His idea of service was expressed in the *Führerprinzip,* the duty of all Germans to submit without question to his will, an article of faith his subordinates enthusiastically propagated.

> You are Germany. When you act, the nation acts; when you judge, the people judge. Our gratitude to you will be our pledge to stand by you for better and for worse, come what may! Thanks to your leadership, Germany will attain her aim to be the homeland of all Germans of the world. You have guaranteed our victory, and you are now guaranteeing our peace.[11]

Yet despite its pretensions of solidarity and unity, the Nazi government itself was a profusion of fiefdoms, confusing jurisdictions, and fierce bureaucratic competitiveness. Hitler preferred a divide-and-conquer style of leadership, as long as it was understood he was in overall charge. He was constantly on guard against anyone who might dare challenge his right to determine who should live and who should die.

Shortly after he became chancellor, Hitler began his campaign against the Jews with a boycott of Jewish businesses and offices. But other than appointing a central boycott directorate, he had yet to establish the agencies to direct Jewish policy. Moreover, what it meant to be Jewish had yet to be defined. While the necessary legislation was being prepared, Hitler drummed away at his main theme: the Jews had to be excluded from German society. He hoped to make it so uncomfortable for them that they would all leave Germany "voluntarily." His fear was that other nations might be reluctant to accept the Jews Germany did not want:

> America's own Immigration Laws [have] excluded from admission those belonging to races of which America [disapproves], while America [is] by no means prepared to open the gates to Jewish "fugitives" from Germany.[12]

And:

> In England people assert that their arms are open to welcome all the oppressed, especially the Jews who have left Germany. . . . But it would be still finer if England did not make her grand gesture dependent on the possession of £1000—if England should say: Anyone can enter—as we unfortunately have done for thirty or forty years. If we too had declared that no one could enter Germany save under condition of bringing with him £1000 or paying more, then today we should have no Jewish question at all.[13]

The German people were willing to accept, even support, Hitler's campaign against the Jews, provided it was carried out as "legal" policy. Such legitimization began in 1935 with a redefinition of German citizenship. Hitler had received his authority to enact racial legislation from the so-called Enabling Law, or *Gesetz zur Behebung der Not von Volk und Reich* (The Law for Removing the Distress of People and Reich), which the members of the Reichstag had passed on March 23, 1933, by the necessary two-thirds majority. In giving him the power to rule by decree, the Reichstag provided the constitutional basis for Hitler's entire regime.

Although Hitler now possessed the authority to exercise legislative, executive, and judicial power as he wished, the Weimar Republic technically, and necessarily, continued to exist. The Enabling Law did not give Hitler the authority to abolish the Weimar regime. And now there was no real need to do so. But to maintain the illusion that actions were constitutional, Hitler dutifully had his powers under the enabling legislation extended every four years, just before their official expiration. The last time his rubber-stamp Reichstag participated in this bizarre ceremony was one month before the end of World War II. Ironically, the exercise of arbitrary power, which the Germans had feared would come from Storm Trooper hooliganism, was now in the hands of one man constituting his own *Rechtstaat.*

The new Reich Citizenship Law, made public at the Nazi Party Rally at Nürnberg on September 15, 1935, distinguished between an empire citizen (*Reichsbürger*) and a state subject (*Staatsangehöriger*). The first category included a person of "German or kindred blood and who shows, through his conduct that he is both desirous and fit to serve faithfully the German people and the Reich."[14] Only a citizen of the Reich enjoyed full political rights. The second classification included a person who merely belonged "to the protective union of the German Reich."

A second piece of legislation, the Law for the Protection of German Blood and Honor, outlawed marriage or sexual intercourse between Jews and nationals of German or kindred blood. It also prohibited Jews from employing German female nationals or those of kindred blood in their homes, and it forbade Jews to hoist the national flag or display the colors of the Reich.

The Nürnberg Laws allowed the Jews to remain as members of the state, albeit not full citizens, but at least on paper entitled to state protection. But there still was no law that defined what it meant to be a Jew. This legislation came later with the Reich Citizenship Law of November 14, 1935, with the determination made primarily on religious, rather than racial, grounds.

Article 5

(1) A Jew is anyone who descended from at least three grandparents who were racially full Jews.

(2) A Jew is also one who descended from two full Jewish parents, if:

    (a) he belonged to the Jewish religious community at the time this law was issued, or who joined the community later.

    (b) he was married to a Jewish person, at the time the law was issued, or married one subsequently.

    (c) he is the offspring of a marriage with a Jew in the sense of Section 1, which was contracted after the Law for the protection of German blood and German honor became effective (15 September 1935).

    (d) he is the offspring of an extramarital relationship, with a Jew, according to Section 1, and will be born out of wedlock after July 31, 1936.[15]

Even when it came time to pass to a policy of extermination, the Nazis were always careful to cloak their actions with the outward trappings of legality. Thus before the Final Solution, the Nazis stripped the Jews of their status as "state subjects" to remove from them any vestiges of official protection that they had been accorded in the Reich Citizenship Law. They did this by classifying all Jews who had taken up residence abroad as officially "stateless," including those who had been deported to concentration camps. Thus, no German subjects were being murdered, only "stateless persons of Jewish descent."[16]

Prior to 1939 it is difficult to find any direct announcement of intent to murder the Jews. However, the entire aim of Hitler's racial policy was eradication of the Jewish presence from Germany one way or another. In his famous speech to the Reichstag on January 30, 1939, he publicly announced his intention to expand this policy to the rest of Europe:

> To-day I will once more be a prophet: If the international Jewish financiers in and outside Europe should succeed in plunging the nations of Europe once more into a war, then the result will not be the bolshevization of the earth, and thus the victory of Jewry, but the annihilation of the Jewish race in Europe.[17]

The speech was shown on newsreels and had wide distribution. But only in retrospect did its full face value become clear. In *Mein Kampf* Hitler had advocated the expansion of the German racial community into the Ukraine and western Russia, a goal of German foreign policy that was hardly traditional and one that could not be attained without plunging the continent into war. In the important meeting he held in the Reich's chancellery on November 5, 1937, he had revealed that "it was his unalterable resolve to solve Germany's problem of space [at] the latest by 1943–45."[18] No one at that meeting, which included the combined chiefs of staff, doubted that the Führer had meant what he said.

Hitler now moved forward with his plans to create a vast new German empire while leaving the execution of his Jewish policy primarily in the hands of Heinrich Himmler, lord of the SS and Reich Commissioner for the Consolidation of the German Nation. Himmler, who was efficient, mystical, and a racial-purity fanatic with no ambition to challenge Hitler's power, was a perfect candidate for the job. He dreamed of creating an SS state out of the old middle kingdom of the Burgundian dukes, where after the war he would rule as an independent sovereign.[19]

Himmler had no trouble finding subordinates who were eager to carry out Hitler's insane schemes. His chief associate, Reinhard Heydrich, the head of the SS security service, although no committed ideologue, could, among other acts of brutality and cruelty, suavely host the Wannsee Conference, where the last phase of the Final Solution was planned. For Heydrich the issue was not race, but power. Heydrich, according to one of his assistants, was "untouched by any pangs of conscience and assisted by an ice-cold intellect, he could carry injustice to the point of extreme cruelty."[20]

Men such as these helped fashion the political culture, which turned the people of an entire nation into accomplices. Those in positions of authority knew what was expected of them and had no need of signed orders to perform their duties. Hitler had set the course, he had passed the laws, and now it was the people's job to produce. There was never a man in German history so trusted, loved, worshipped, and followed as the Führer.

The brevity of the Boycott period had encouraged many Jews to believe that the Nazi pogrom, like repressions in the past, would eventually spend its fury. Until then, life would be uncomfortable, but not impossible. The Nürnberg Laws changed this, but not just because of what they said. What had by 1935 become clear was the extent to which the Nazi policy of *Gleichschaltung,* or coordination, had succeeded among the German people, often with little apparent prompting from the government. The broad mass of the German people not only accepted what was happening but also seemed to enjoy it and want to join in. The Jews found they could no longer go to their favorite restaurants, take their usual Sunday walks, or send their children to school without fear that they would be beaten up.

The rush of Jews to leave Germany became a torrent. Had other nations been as willing to take them in as they were to leave, most of Germany's Jews would have been saved. However, other countries at the very least wanted assurances that those pounding at their doors to enter would not become wards of the state.

> [My parents] were working on getting an affidavit. But they weren't able to assemble the necessary documentation. It seems that some of their records were lost during the burning and looting that was going on during Kristallnacht. It wasn't as though they wanted to stay in Germany. But, like so many others, they couldn't obtain an affidavit.[21]

As it was, a majority of Germany's roughly half a million Jews had left by 1938, about half of these finding refuge in the United States. Not so fortunate were the Jews of the rest of Europe. Most of those who survived, especially those in this book, did so largely through luck.

Studies that focus on human behavior emphasize the impact of experience on personality. This is especially true of Holocaust studies, the focus of which is on those threatened in their existing way of life. This book is an account of the experiences of twelve remarkable individuals in the context of the times in which they lived. But more importantly, it is an effort to show how personality, family, culture, experience, and contingency affected religious and cultural identity and contributed to building those values that have determined and influenced their careers in teaching and research.

Notes

1. Walter Hirsch interview.
2. Such emancipation was not new. Sixty years before, the Kingdom of Prussia had already recognized its Jews as full citizens and allowed them to settle where they chose and marry whomever they wanted. Other states in the German Confederation had also eased their restrictions. However, progress was frequently piecemeal and the results ambiguous until German unification settled the matter.
3. Thus Daniel Goldhagen's contention that "in the election of 1893, parties avowedly antisemetic gained a majority in the Reichstag" is inaccurate. *Hitler's Willing Executioners: Ordinary Germans and the Holocaust* (New York: Random House, 1997), p. 75.
4. Sol Gartenhaus interview.
5. Rogers Brubaker, *Citizenship and Nationhood in France and Germany* (Cambridge, Mass.: Harvard University Press, 1992), pp. 114–25.
6. Adolf Hitler, *Mein Kampf* (Boston: Houghton Mifflin, 1943), p. 65. The book supposedly sold over twenty thousand copies its first year, but the figure is undoubtedly an exaggeration. When Hitler became Führer, the sales figures soared, second in sales only to the Bible. Hitler became a multimillionaire from the royalties.
7. *Mein Kampf,* p. 56. It is doubtful whether Hitler's antisemitism sprang from this one encounter. Prejudice usually is an evolutionary process developed within a culture that condones intolerance. The most important facet of this personal history is not its Damascus-road aspect, but that Hitler had by then begun to view the Jews as an alien species.
8. Fritz Cohen interview.
9. In 1925 Hitler, fearing that he would be deported to Austria as an undesirable alien, renounced his Austrian citizenship. He therefore became officially *staatslos.* However, having German citizenship was essential to running for public office. On February 25, 1932, three days after he announced his candidacy for the presidency, Hitler took advantage of a loophole in the Reich's citizenship law by having himself appointed a *Regierungsrat* (senior executive officer) in the Brunswick legation in Berlin, a position that naturalized him ipso facto.

10. Wm. Laird Kleine-Ahlbrandt, *The Burden of Victory: France, Britain, and the Enforcement of the Treaty of Versailles, 1919–1925* (New York: University Press of America, 1995), p. 70.

11. Rudolf Hess, deputy leader of the Nazi Party, opening the Nürnberg Party Rally, September 4, 1934. In *Triumph of the Will,* filmed by Leni Riefenstahl, Universum Film Aktiengesellschaft (UFA), released March 1935.

12. Speech to the Doctor's Union, April 1933, in Norman H. Baynes, *The Speeches of Adolf Hitler,* 1 (New York: Howard Fertig, 1969), pp. 728–29.

13. Speech in Berlin's Sportpalast, October 24, 1933. Ibid., pp. 729–30.

14. *Reichsbürgergesetz* vom 15 Sept 1935, in John Mendelsohn, ed., *The Holocaust: Selected Documents* (New York: Garland Publishing, 1982), p. 23.

15. John Mendelsohn, ed., *The Holocaust: Selected Documents* (New York: Garland Publishing, 1982), pp. 31–32.

16. Brubaker, *Citizenship and Nationhood in France and Germany,* pp. 167–68. The same legalistic hairsplitting reserved for German Jews was not necessary for the Jews of other countries. The German jurists had already categorized them as alien peoples without rights.

17. Baynes, p. 741.

18. *Documents of German Foreign Policy,* series D, vol. 7, pp. 635–36.

19. Others than Himmler concerned themselves with Jewish policy, such as Hans Frank, head of the Government General, and Alfred Rosenberg, minister for occupied eastern territories. Also involved were officials in the labor, food, and agriculture ministries, the Special Planning Homestead Office, the High Command of the Armed Forces, and the Directorate of the Four-Year Plan. Many were involved at different stages, and all were thirsty to build their careers by playing a role in the decision-making process in the German East.

20. Walter Schellenberg, *Hitler's Secret Service* (New York: Harper and Row, 1957), p. 21. Schellenberg was head of the SS foreign intelligence department and Heydrich's direct subordinate. Like his boss, he joined the Nazi Party because it promised the best career oppportunities.

21. Joseph Haberer interview.

Part One
Germany

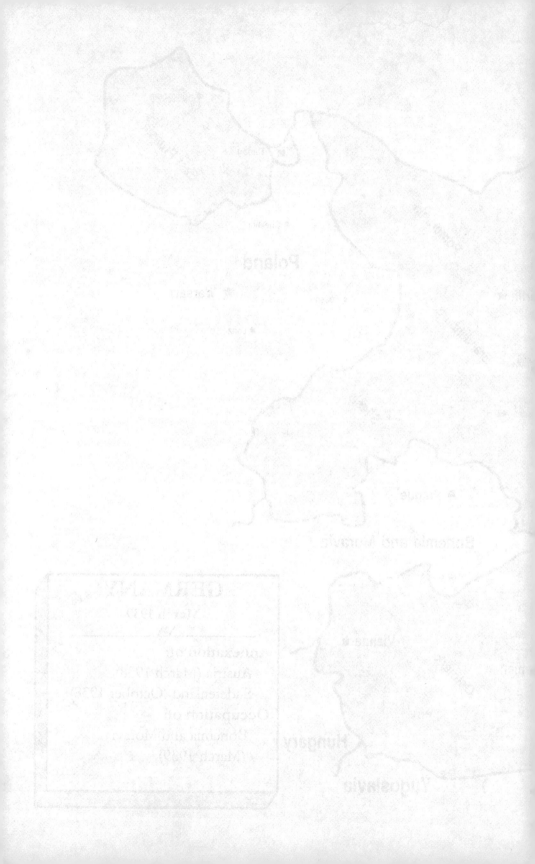

1
The Manner of Belonging

F ew German Jews were blind to the antisemitism that still existed
in their country. Some even recalled the fears of Heinrich Heine
of the German gods rising from their slumber and baring a soul of
boundless brutality. And after the First World War, psychiatrists
treating German Jewish patients reported a common dread of consumption by fire. But until the Nazis took power in 1933, the likelihood of many Jews' meeting a real fire-breathing bigot face-to-face
was remote.

Although Hitler's belief that he had a divine mission to wage a
holy war against the Jews had yet to gain universal acceptance, his
demand that the Treaty of Versailles be revised did. This "dictated"
peace, which rubbed Germany's nose in its World War I defeat, was
a national shame and, added to the rise of unemployment and the
collapse of the economy, gave weight to Hitler's demand that the
Weimar Republic be destroyed. Many Germans who questioned
whether the retention of democracy was worth the bother agreed.

In the July 1932 elections, more people voted for parties sworn
to destroy the Weimar Republic than for those parties that supported
it. These antidemocratic forces controlled 365 out of 608 seats in

the Reichstag, making legislative government impossible. The Nazis emerged the big winners, becoming the largest party in Germany, with 14 million popular votes (37.3 percent of the total) and 230 Reichstag seats. In districts like East Prussia, Pomerania, Frankfurt am Oder, East Hannover, Silesia, Chemnitz, and Schleswig-Holstein (areas mostly in the north and east) they had received almost half of the vote, the bulk of this support coming from an alarmed middle class, which regarded Hitler as a protector against Bolshevism and from bankruptcy.

After his appointment as chancellor in January 1933, Hitler lost no time putting his words into practice. He did not attempt to overturn the laws of the Weimar Republic. They continued to remain in force, but he did seek the authority to render them irrelevant. On February 28, 1933, the Reichstag passed the law for Terminating the Distress of the People and Nation *(Gesetz zur Behebung der Not von Volk und Reich)*, which gave Hitler the power to rule by decree.[1] Hitler proceeded to smash all political opposition. He appointed Reich commissioners in the place of the locally elected government officials and began a policy of denigration and intimidation against the Jews.

The Nazi-led government purged Jews from the civil service and other government-connected positions. And on April 1, 1933, it launched a boycott against Jewish businesses, department stores, physicians, lawyers, and civil servants. Julius Streicher, as head of the Central Committee for Deflecting Jewish Atrocity and Boycott Mongering, established local action committees to police the ban, organize meetings, and disseminate propaganda. Posters and graffiti warned the "Aryan population" to stay away from Jewish-owned businesses. To make sure they did, Brown Shirt sentries mounted guard outside the shops. The Nazis used this campaign as a means of consolidating public opinion against the common racial enemy. It reinforced their belief that the Jews were aliens whose influence should be excised from the life of the nation.

The *Judenboykott* alarmed some German Jews into making preparations to leave the country. However, many others could not believe that the rights they enjoyed under the German legal system would be destroyed by such antisemitic brutality. Even the most pessimistic could not imagine that within a few years they would lose their livelihoods and national identity, never mind the possibility of their lives in a Final Solution.

Indeed, the Boycott period did not last long. The Nazi leaders worried about the lack of control over Storm Trooper rowdyism. No matter what its stripe, vigilantism was dangerous. Furthermore, the Boycott had led to economic disruption at home and unpopularity abroad. The lid was put on and order returned. It was the calm before another, more ferocious storm.

Officially a Foreigner: Michael Golomb

"I was born in Germany and had never been outside the country until I emigrated."

A Question of Citizenship

Moses, the father of Michael Golomb, had been born in Lodz when it was part of the Russian Empire; his wife, Myriam, had come from the Austro-Hungarian village of Rymanov, fifty-five miles southeast of Tarnov, in the province of Galicia. They had met in Germany, the country to which they had been brought when they were both very young. They remained, married, Germanized their names (to Moritz and Maria), and raised a family. All of their five children attended German state schools. Their Orthodox ways gradually weakened.

But no matter how Germanized they became, the Reich still considered them foreigners. After 1919, they were listed as Polish, since their birthplaces were now part of that reconstructed country. Michael Golomb, born in Munich in 1909, was also considered Polish. The German citizenship laws did not recognize *jus soli*.

But even if the *Ostjuden* assimilated, they could not expect German citizenship for themselves or even for their offspring who were born in the country. Therefore they were legally aliens unless special circumstances, like service to the state, deemed otherwise. During the Weimar Republic period (1919–33), for example, only about 16,000 of the roughly 100,000 *Ostjuden* were judged to have qualified for citizenship.

MICHAEL GOLOMB: My grandfather was strictly Orthodox. Although my father's only formal education was in a *yeshiva* in Lodz and he observed *kashruth* [the dietary laws of being kosher], Sabbath, and the holidays, I cannot call him Orthodox. As long as he and my mother lived close to my grandparents, they kept a kosher household, but when they moved away, they gave it up. They still considered themselves religious, though. They believed in God, but one who had condemned Jews to live at the mercy of the *goyim.*

I wasn't very close to my father. For several years he ran a textile store, then became a traveling salesman, selling wines for a large company. [Many of the Eastern Jews who had come to Germany since the 1880s participated in German economic expansion by working in the factories or in some small retail trade.] He would spend the whole week traveling and came back home only on weekends. Therefore, my siblings and I had very little contact with him. But my father was also emotionally and intellectually distant from me, never appreciating what I was interested in. My mother and my grandfather were much warmer people.

With the help of my grandfather, who taught me to keep the holidays, the fast days, and to observe the Orthodox traditions, I was brought up in a strictly religious milieu. My grandfather's main occupation was studying the Talmud, but I don't believe he was a great scholar. He was a rather involuntary and inept peddler and brought in very little income. My grandmother was a resourceful woman and supported the family — eight sons and two daughters — by running a small but profitable store, while he spent most of his time studying the scriptures and their commentaries. Every Sabbath afternoon his teenage sons (my uncles) and myself — I was the oldest grandchild — would assemble around the long table in his dining room, and he would read us sections from the rabbinical commentaries in the Gemarah, then try to translate it from its original Aramaic.[2] None of us understood or had any interest in it, but we had to sit there and listen. And I think this really estranged me more than anything, because I had to spend hours there being bored, getting nothing from it. Even his own sons started considering their father a fool. So he relied more and more on me than on them to become a rabbi or a Talmud scholar. I eventually rebelled against this Orthodoxy, which I came to view as simply an all-embracing collection of rituals and prohibitions devoid of serious concern with positive values.

For example, when I met my grandfather in the street, when I was maybe six or seven years old, he would check to see if I was wearing my undergarment of prayer fringes, and when I said that I didn't have one on, he would ask, "So, what distinguishes you from a *goy* when you don't wear your *zizit?*"[3] And on another occasion he would touch my jacket and say, "This is not what a Jew wears." It seemed that there was some sort of law against the mixture of materials, like wool and linen.[4] And again, the question was always, "What distinguishes you from the *goyim?*" In this way, my grandfather always made me feel guilty. I was taught to watch out constantly, because I might do something wrong and commit another sin.

Even some of the greatest Jewish scholars and philosophers have tried to justify these absurd laws and prohibitions. Maimonides [1135–1204], in trying to rationalize them, came to the conclusion that the Jews would lose their identity if they did not impose these particular restrictions on themselves.

And your grandfather was afraid of losing that identity?

GOLOMB: That's right. He viewed many common practices as sins, making little distinction between minor missteps and serious sins.

During these formative years you identified strongly with this Orthodoxy?

GOLOMB: Only during early childhood. However, I felt strongly Jewish throughout my precollege years and was even much opposed to the assimilation of the German Jews. There was a discussion about the assimilation of the Jews in Germany when I was eighteen. One of my fellow students asked me, "How can you say you're a Jew first? When I happen to be in Paris, and I find somebody who is German, I would feel very close to him, but I would not feel close to some French Jew." I responded that I thought it despicable that he would identify himself first as a German and not as a Jew, that he had become so assimilated that he had severed his ties with his forefathers. I felt that the Eastern Jews were the only ones who preserved Jewish traditions and culture. Later, though, I could see no positive development in Judaism from the time of the prophets up to the time of the Enlightenment in the eighteenth century. The Jewish religion courses in the Gymnasium, taught by the local rabbi, did not help either. They were mainly apologetic, defending "nondogmatic" Jewish doctrine against Christian dogmatism.

What language did the family speak at home?

GOLOMB: My parents spoke Yiddish with my grandparents, but at home we spoke German. My father never really mastered the language grammatically, though. German was also an acquired language for my mother, and although she spoke it better than her husband, she was really not perfect either.

You then spoke German fluently?

GOLOMB: It's the only language that I grew up with. I never even learned Yiddish. I could understand Yiddish, but I never spoke it. I went to a religious elementary school, the *Israelische Volksschule*, which the Bavarian state financed, as it did the Catholic schools. (There were no secular elementary schools; they had to be either Catholic, Protestant, or Jewish. But in Würzburg, there were not enough Protestants for them to have a separate school.) The director of our school was a rabbi, but we followed the same curriculum as the other schools, except every day we read excerpts of the books of Moses in the original language followed by translations. From the first grade on, we learned the Hebrew alphabet and learned by osmosis the most common words in the scriptures and prayer books, but we did not learn Hebrew as a language.

Linguistically then, there was no difference between you and the other students?

GOLOMB: No, but there were differences nonetheless. Würzburg had as many as two hundred German Jewish families and maybe fifty Eastern Jewish families, but there was profound segregation, probably as profound as that in the U.S. South between the blacks and the whites. In Würzburg, the Eastern Jews had their own synagogue, *schul*. In our class at school we had about twenty-five students, five of them Eastern Jewish kids. And we sat on separate benches. The teachers knew who the *Ostjuden* kids were, and they went along with this separation.

You have a German birth certificate?

GOLOMB: I was born in Germany and had never been outside the country until I emigrated, but nobody in my family acquired German citizenship, even during the Weimar period. I don't think the policy applied only to Jews. Each of the states in Germany had a veto on citizenship admissions, and they made it so prohibitive that few foreigners even tried to become citizens.

The citizenship issue compounded the differences between the German Jews and the Eastern Jews?

GOLOMB: Of course. Later on, I learned that if I acquired an academic or other state position, I could acquire citizenship with the help of my employer.

Were you then staatenlos (stateless)?

GOLOMB: As long as we lived in Würzburg, we never thought about whether we had citizenship or not. It only became critical if you wanted to travel and you needed a passport. In 1930, when I went to study in Berlin, the city police there required that I register with them. They told me I was not a German citizen and asked me for my passport. I said I didn't know that I needed a passport. They asked where my father had come from, and when I told them, they said I was a Polish citizen and that I'd better produce a passport or I'd be in violation of the law.

I therefore went to the Polish consulate in Berlin and applied for a passport, showing them my birth certificate, which indicated my father's place of birth. They took down the information and said that before they could issue the passport, they would have to get verification from Lodz. That took an awfully long time, and in the meantime the Berlin police got very, very nasty. They took me to court and had me convicted of *Passvergehen* (passport violation), and I had to pay a fine.

Did the fact that you were officially a foreigner come as a shock?

GOLOMB: Definitely. I was born and grew up in Germany. I was very proud of German culture. I loved German literature and music. I also had developed an elegant German writing style. I have never learned to write English as well as I wrote German when I was nineteen.

Germany was your Heimat?

GOLOMB: Absolutely.

You started school in 1915, when the First World War was in its second year. What do you remember of that period?

GOLOMB: Not too much, but we had a pretty hard time. For example, we couldn't get milk, butter, or meat during the last years of the war. I sometimes went with my mother to one of the nearby village farms to buy potatoes, which we dug up ourselves, although this practice was considered illegal.

Was there much patriotism?

GOLOMB: When the Bavarian king visited Würzburg, all the kids stood along the street to salute him. We all wore the blue and white colors of the Wittelsbachers [the subjects of the royal house of Wittelsbach]. We didn't love the German emperor. Kaiser Wilhelm wasn't very popular in Bavaria. Neither were the Prussians. We used to call them *Saupreussen* (Pig Prussians). We loved Ludwig III, the Bavarian king [r. 1913–18]. I cried when I learned that he had abdicated.

Did your parents share those feelings?

GOLOMB: I can't say they did. My parents still thought of themselves as Jews and all the others as *goyim*.

A Passion for Mathematics

In Bavaria, students went to elementary school for four years and then to a Gymnasium for nine years. Only the best students, though, went to the Gymnasium. The entrance examination was very hard. Those who passed could choose between the "Classical Gymnasium," where the emphasis was on the humanities: Latin, Greek, literature, history; or the "Realgymnasium," where there was more mathematics, physics, and chemistry. Initially interested in languages, Golomb entered the Classical Gymnasium but transferred after three years when his passion for mathematics had developed.

GOLOMB: In the Gymnasium there was no longer a distinction between Eastern Jews and Western Jews, but between Jews and non-Jews.

How many Jews were there in your class at the Gymnasium?

GOLOMB: Out of about thirty students, there were only three Jews; I was the only Eastern Jew.

How did you decide that you wanted to go to the Gymnasium? Did your parents encourage you to go on?

GOLOMB: That is a good question. First of all, I was a top student in grade school, and my teachers noticed that. My mother was persuaded that I should go on, and she convinced my father. Also, by coincidence, the Classical Gymnasium happened to be directly across the street from our house. I think that helped a lot. It was so convenient, and there was no tuition.

What was the curriculum like at the Realgymnasium?

GOLOMB: They had a very comprehensive program of mathematics: algebra, analytic geometry, and trigonometry. They had subjects that the high schools here don't teach, such as descriptive geometry, spherical trigonometry, and much more advanced algebra. On the other hand, calculus was not covered at that time, although it is now. We had many more subjects than are given in the United States: geography, history, literature, art, Latin, French, English, physics, inorganic and organic chemistry, botany, zoology, and human anatomy.

What did they teach you in history?

GOLOMB: For several years we learned about ancient Greece and Rome.

How about the modern period?

GOLOMB: That was only in the last couple of years. We learned about wars and dynasties.

What were you taught about the Treaty of Versailles?

GOLOMB: I heard about the shameful *Kriegsschuldlüge,* the War Guilt clause.

Your teachers were no doubt holdovers from the old monarchy. What did they tell you about the new Weimar Republic?

GOLOMB: When I graduated from the Gymnasium, each student was handed a copy of the Weimar Constitution. The law mandated that the schools pass them out, but the rector, when he did this, told us that it was a shameful document.

Did you agree?

GOLOMB: At that time I was eighteen years old and a radical leftist. The Weimar Republic meant little to me. I didn't think that it was a stable regime. I thought it was a betrayal of the 1918 revolution.

To what do you attribute this radicalization?

GOLOMB: Early on, I was rebelling against the Jewish Orthodoxy of my grand-father and other members of the Eastern Jewish ghetto. Then, when I was twelve or thirteen, I had become a Zionist and joined the Jung Jüdischer Wan-derbund, an organization of the Zionist Youth Movement. In general the German Jews were not Zionist, and when I went out with my other comrades to collect funds for Zionist causes, you could tell that most of the Western Jewish people were very antagonistic to the Zionist ideal.

What made you join the Zionist movement?

GOLOMB: I felt strongly Jewish, but not religiously Jewish. I learned modern Hebrew and became pretty fluent at it. I started reading Hebrew, but mostly Yiddish literature. As a matter of fact, I was really opposed to using Hebrew as the language of the modern Palestine. I thought Yiddish was the language of the Jewish masses, and it should be preserved. I thought that Hebrew was an elitist development. And I got heavily involved in defending the culture of Eastern Jewry, primarily its literature and folk music. I became interested in the large Jewish socialist movement in Poland and lost interest in German politics. I read left-wing magazines, such as *Die Weltbühne.* I looked with sympathy on developments in the Soviet Union. My sympathies were all left-wing. I was an active member of the Borochov Jugend, the youth branch of the Mapai Party, the most left-wing organization in the Zionist movement.[5] I practiced a kind of populism and identified with the Jewish masses in Eastern Europe.

During my last years in Germany, I belonged to the Ha-Shomer ha-Za'ir.[6] I contemplated emigrating to Palestine, and during the summer of 1932, I worked on a farm to prepare myself for working on the land in Palestine. But then I started working on my dissertation and got deeply involved in mathematical research. Even before I got my Ph.D., I expected that I would find a position in academic life, probably starting as an assistant to a professor.

You joined the Zionist Youth Movement about six or seven years before Hitler came to power. In joining that movement, didn't you operate under the premise that there was no future for Jews in Europe, especially in Germany, because of endemic and systemic antisemitism?

GOLOMB: No. I became a Zionist not because of antisemitism, but because I thought that the Jews were living an unnatural life, a life unconnected to the soil, and that nowhere were they producers. Antisemitism was not a major concern of my personal life. I thought it was a scapegoat tool used by backward authoritarian governments, mainly those in Eastern Europe.

Golomb's reassessment of priorities, leading him toward a career in mathematics, was what the Ha-Shomer ha-Za'ir would have called "a crisis of individualism," since he was no longer interested in joining an agricultural collective in Palestine. Ha-Shomer ha-Za'ir demanded that an affirmation of Jewish identity, Jewish values, and commitment to the Jewish people come before any choice of career. Golomb also had difficulty reconciling the nationalistic bent of the Zionist movement's radical left wing with his own international, anti-imperialist, and antifascist principles.

Did you experience much antisemitism in the Gymnasium?

GOLOMB: I had very little social contact with non-Jews. Overt incidents were rare, but my experience at the Gymnasium was a mixed bag. I knew that some of my classmates were antisemitic, because they refused to speak to me. And once, when I was playing slideball during recess, a student deliberately threw the ball at my crotch from a short distance. It was so painful that I fainted momentarily. However, a teacher in my next class noticed my discomfort, inquired about the incident, and then addressed the class about the shamefulness of such behavior. Later he called me into his office and apologized that this could happen among the Gymnasium students, who should know better.

But another episode, which really made me aware of the existing antisemitism among my classmates, occurred when I was chosen to be the valedictorian in the Realgymnasium's graduation ceremonies—an honor accorded to the student with the highest academic standing. One of my classmates, whom I had long suspected of being a leading antisemite, circulated a petition protesting that a Jew should be allowed to speak on behalf of the class. It was signed by almost everybody in my class and came as such a shock that I withdrew as valedictorian. The result was that the organizer of the petition, Rudolf Schiedmaier, the son of the rector, replaced me as valedictorian. I mention his name because I found out that he later became a member of the Supreme Court, which validated the Nazi anti-Jewish legislation.

Did your parents ever mention antisemitism?

GOLOMB: They talked about the *goyim,* but they probably felt that it was much better in Germany than what they were used to in Eastern Europe. They really felt that the Germans were decent people. I think there's no doubt that even up to 1933, there was much less antisemitism in Germany than there was, say, in Poland, Romania, or Lithuania. And I myself went on proclaiming this to my political comrades. The German Jews did not consider antisemitism much of a threat.[7] They did not even form the equivalent of the American B'nai B'rith Anti-Defamation League.

The contention that antisemitism was not as pervasive and obvious in Germany as elsewhere has credence. However, it was also true that antagonism toward the Jews was on the increase in the 1920s. The *Protocols of the Elders of Zion,* a forgery based upon the German novelist Hermann Goedsche's satiric depiction of Napoleon III as a power-mad tyrant, appeared in a new German edition in 1919 and was immensely popular. The *Protocols* purported to reveal a Jewish plan for ruling the world through a supergovernment. The idea was to sow enough discord, confusion, and chaos among the *goyim* that organized society would turned into gladiatorial arenas:

We shall soon begin to establish huge monopolies, reservoirs of co-
lossal riches, upon which even the large fortunes of the goyim will
depend to such an extent that they will go to the bottom together
with the credit of the States on the day after the political smash.
(Protocol No. 6)

Even during the Great War, in which the Jews served with great
distinction (almost half who served being decorated), people ac-
cused them of draft dodging, goofing off, and subversion. Afterwards, Jews were blamed for Germany's defeat and for the current
political and economic confusion, including black marketeering,
profiteering, and hoarding.

The Germans loved Judeo-Bolshevik conspiracy theories and
sought international connections among Leon Trotsky in Russia,
Béla Kun in Hungary, Karl Liebknecht and Rosa Luxemburg in Berlin, and Kurt Eisner in Bavaria, all of whom were Jews. It made no
difference that the majority of the German Jews were against all rev-
olutions, either of the Left or the Right. While Nazis remained a
fringe group, parties like the German National Party and the right
wing of the People's Party favored the elimination of Jewish influence from the government and the economy. In short, the Jews
took the blame for a loss of national honor, pride, well-being, and
family values.

As a student in Berlin could you see the rise of political extremism?

GOLOMB: The university *Aula* [assembly hall] had political rallies all the time.
The left-wing radicals opposed the Nazis, but many students strongly sympa-
thized with them and actively participated in their functions. Increasingly, students appeared in class wearing Nazi uniforms. In 1932, when there were
presidential elections,[8] I spoke at a rally of the Centralverein Deutscher Staats-
bürger Jüdischen Glaubens (Central Organization of German Citizens of the
Jewish Faith), which was being held in Munich. Most of the organization's
members were from the upper middle class and a large part of these were determined to vote for the rightist Deutsche Volkspartei (German People's Party),
which strongly endorsed President Paul von Hindenburg's reelection.

Reconstructed after the 1918 defeat out of the old National Liberal Party, the monarchist and antisocialist People's Party

favored universal and secret suffrage, free enterprise, and nationalism. Despite its antirepublicanism, one of its most prominent leaders was Gustav Stresemann, who saw the practical necessity of working for the Weimar regime. Because of his "support," Stresemann was never fully trusted by the party's right wing, which, in addition to being strongly nationalistic, was antisemitic. However, this brand of conservatism seemed moderate when compared to that of the Nationalists and the National Socialists, both of whom were determined to destroy Jewish influence in Germany and bury all constitutional liberties.

GOLOMB: In the course of my speech I told them that by voting for the Volkspartei they were really voting for the Nazis. Of course I got pooh-poohed, but I believed that the center and the right-of-center political parties were undermining the Weimar Republic and promoting the triumph of fascism.

After Hitler became chancellor in 1933, I was asked to distribute some anti-Nazi leaflets — not hand them out, but go to the park and spread them out. It was risky, and dangerous if you were caught.

Were there any manifestations of antisemitism other than the demonstrations?

GOLOMB: Sometimes there was violence on university grounds, but at that time I didn't feel that it was mainly antisemitic. I thought that National Socialism was a fascist movement and antisemitism only a sideline, limited to a rather small number of members, that the leaders were only using it to stir up the mobs, and that they didn't take it seriously.

An Early Realization of Danger: Walter Hirsch

"The family stopped practicing religion by the time I grew up."

A Sense of Establishment

Hirsch grew up in Stuttgart. The family house was on the Botnangerstrasse, a comfortable middle-class street that led to the Kräherwald, one of the numerous forests that encircled the city's suburbs. Born in 1919, the year after the end of the First World War, he was the older of two sons. Walter's ancestors had lived in Württemberg for the past five generations, and both his parents, Eugene (1882–1953) and Fanny Wormser (1890–1990), were also born in Stuttgart. By the end of the First World War, Stuttgart had less than four thousand Jews, or 1.4 percent of the total population.

WALTER HIRSCH: Before the rise of National Socialism, we didn't feel at all different from anybody else. We had lots of friends who were Jewish. But somehow we did not feel different from the rest of the population in terms of religion. We felt different in terms of social class. We were middle class, but in terms of religion we didn't feel different or isolated.

Having been highly assimilated into the German community, the Hirsches were immediately affected by the exclusionary policies of the new Nazi regime. And they were among the first wave of Jewish emigrants to flee Germany.

Would you say your father was Jewish by tradition, rather than by religion?

HIRSCH: He had no feeling for the Jewish religion.

What about the rest of your family?

HIRSCH: They all came from the same tradition, but the family stopped practicing religion by the time I grew up.

Wasn't there a requirement in German schools that there should be some religious education?

HIRSCH: Yes, I had to attend religious classes. Once a week the rabbi came and gave us classes in religion and Hebrew, which I never managed to learn. I attended with a couple of other Jewish kids. Most of us resented being singled out and having to go to that special class.

Why was that? Was it because you just thought it was an intrusion on your life, or did you think other kids would think differently of you?

HIRSCH: I think both of those things. I think because we would be put down by the other kids for being Jewish. And I think it gave us a certain sense of inferiority.

If you had that feeling, then there was not really complete assimilation.

HIRSCH: That's right, that's one point where it was not complete. I think the Catholics also had the same feeling. They were also a minority in a Protestant majority.

Did you ever encounter antisemitic sentiments?

HIRSCH: Nothing explicit. I could occasionally sense some kind of antisemitism, but no real aggression.

No name-calling?

HIRSCH: Nothing like that.

Were there any incidents in the general area of Stuttgart that you knew about?

HIRSCH: Nothing that I was aware of.

Were you aware of the rising strength of the Nazi party?

HIRSCH: I could see they had more people being elected to the local legislature. But I don't think they packed a lot of influence, because they were a minority party. In Württemberg in 1932 and early 1933 there was no real Nazi upsurge yet. There didn't appear any real danger for the Jews.

But my father felt that it was not good for the family to remain in Germany. He said, "Hitler is going to do what he said he was going to do. So let's get out of here." He was very pessimistic about the Weimar Republic lasting.

When was this?

HIRSCH: It was in 1932. And as it turned out, of course he was right, and luckily we were in a position that we could do it. We could get out and still take some money that we had. It so happened that he had already given up his wine business, so he was not held back by economic entanglements, as was the case with my wife, Lotte's, father, who had all his money invested in his business.

So your father had a pretty good sense of what the National Socialists were capable of?

HIRSCH: Yes. People thought we were crazy to leave because it was going to blow over.

Unchallenged Credentials: Fritz Cohen

"Only after the Nazis came to power was the question of acceptability ever raised."

Service to the Country

The Cohen's house stood on Ronnenberg's town square, the doorstep giving out directly onto the crossing of the main streets. It was a large, three-storied dwelling, solid and permanent looking, in the modified baroque architecture of the Second Reich. Across the street to the right stood the *Gasthaus,* set back from the thoroughfare by a large parking area, while on the left was the First World War memorial, its sculpted soldiers facing outward. One of the names on it was that of Albrecht Cohen, Fritz's uncle.

Ronnenberg had no local newspaper. Items of local interest were shouted out by a man with a bell making the rounds. Any news of the outside world had to come from Hannover, the provincial capital, located about ten miles to the north.

FRITZ COHEN: We were respected members of the community. All the men of the family of my father's generation had served as German soldiers in the First World War. My father was wounded and decorated, and his brother was killed in November 1914 on the Russian front at the age of seventeen. No one felt more German than we did, and few had sacrificed more on the altar of patriotism than our family.

Such sacrifice and patriotism, albeit remarkable, was not unique among German Jews. Of the 100,000 Jews who served in that war, 80,000 had fought in frontline units, 35,000 had been decorated for bravery, and 12,000 killed in action.

COHEN: The issue of our belonging to the community never came up. My parents were involved in the community's philanthropic and artistic activities. We were never excluded from any municipal activities, although we, of course, didn't go to church. The National Socialist period was therefore a total and complete turnaround. Only after the Nazis came to power was the question of acceptability ever raised.

Michael Golomb's family at their home in Würzburg, circa 1915.

The Cohen family home in Ronnenberg.

Did your parents have any non-Jewish friends or associations?

COHEN: Oh, yes. My father belonged to the local *Turnverein,* a sort of gymnastics league. My mother was an excellent pianist and performed with the local theater group.

Where did you worship?

COHEN: We had a small synagogue in the attic of the house of one of my father's cousins, where we had Shabbat services. It was very informal, no rabbi, but usually one of the men, a *Forbeiter,* led the service and read from the Torah. I don't recall that we ever had a *minyon;* we never had more than seven or eight males. On high holidays, we went to the synagogue in Hannover. I did not understand the services very well, but they overwhelmed me. Still, my religious instruction was limited. When it would've been time to begin, the Nazis had come to power, and it simply became too complicated. I therefore did not have a bar mitzvah.

Ronnenberg had a population of four thousand. The Cohens were part of its small, well-established, and prosperous Jewish community, its six families all interrelated. The maternal Seligmann branch had lived here at least since the beginning of the eighteenth century, when Ronnenberg was part of the Kingdom of Hannover, then ruled by the British monarch George II. The Cohens, originally from Holland, had come in the middle of the following century when his grandfather had married a Seligmann, who were butchers and cattle traders. Fritz's father, Iwan, married Alice Leby, whose family came from Mecklenburg; Iwan owned Ronnenberg's only dry goods store.

COHEN: Apart from the fact that we had our own place of worship, the only thing that sensitized me to being a Jew was when we had religious instruction in primary school—one or two hours a week. The instruction was primarily New Testament, and the readings depicted the Jews as the people who had put Christ on trial. On those occasions, I felt uncomfortable and different. But I never recalled anyone saying, "You're one of *those* guys."

Although I wasn't aware of it then, in retrospect I suspect that despite our "credentials" in being long-time inhabitants of the village and having given service to the country, there still existed a barrier between us and the rest of the good, solid, church-going citizens.

Do you think this separation was due more to race or to religion?

COHEN: It's impossible to separate the two. But I'm inclined to think it was more religious, our not going to the same church, not being confirmed with the rest of the people, and not observing the same holidays. Whether or not it was verbalized, the difference, the separation, was still ingrained.

Did your father ever talk to you about being Jewish or about the family's tradition of being Jewish?

COHEN: My father was very well-educated in Hebrew and the religious traditions, but despite this background he did not preside over a very religious home. I think both my parents were agnostics. They came from very pious homes, but they rejected the faith totally, especially the emphasis upon ritual and custom as being central to being Jewish.

However, my grandmother, who lived with us, was very pious. She kept up the traditions, lit the candles, said *jahrzeit,* tried to keep kosher. She had her own set of dishes, but still had to make certain accommodations, since the rest of us did not keep kosher.

At what point did the family's assimilation process begin?

COHEN: It began in the nineteenth century and accelerated in the twentieth.

*It's amazing how this small group of people managed to maintain their
Jewish identity. Outwardly they are very assimilated, but they nonetheless
have a very strong idea of Jewishness, which survived from one generation to another. Was there any marriage between this Jewish community
and the Gentile community?*

COHEN: No. They either married among themselves or went outside, as was the case with my father's mother.

*Many German Jews had an ambivalent attitude toward the piety and rit-
ual of their eastern brethren. Did your parents share that feeling?*

COHEN: I think so.

Did some of that rub off on you?

COHEN: No doubt in my earlier years it did. In my home there even was an attempt to explain the Nazi antisemitism as a reaction against these strange-looking people from the east. But I wouldn't consider that at all valid anymore.

Before the Hitler period did your family ever talk about antisemitism?

COHEN: I don't think that the subject ever came up. If it did, I was not aware of it.

Did you sense any tension associated with the rise of National Socialism?

COHEN: I knew of the Storm Troopers, although we did not have a local group in our town. They were in nearby Hannover. And I knew that just before the Nazis took power that there were Nazis in our town. But then there were also communists. There was a mine in the district. The miners lived separately from everybody else in an area we called the *Kolonie*—a settlement built by the mining company. A good many of the miners were either socialists or communists.

Ingrained Restraint: Solomon Gartenhaus

"From my parents I got the idea that when I was in public, I should do nothing to attract attention."

The Wine Was Really Champagne

The Gartenhaus household was Orthodox. The father, Jacob, came from Przeworsk, a village in Galicia, which at the time of his birth in 1896 was part of the Austro-Hungarian Empire. Two months after World War I began, when he turned eighteen, he was inducted into the Austrian army. In 1919 Galicia became part of the newly reconstructed Poland. Although the Polish constitution guaranteed its ethnic minorities full civil liberties and freedom to foster their own national traditions, this promise withered under the exuberant intolerance of Polish nationalism.[9]

In April 1920, a Polish army invaded Russia in an attempt to restore Poland's eighteenth-century frontiers, thereby exposing the country again to destruction and pillage. In times of confusion, danger, and uncertainty, Jews were usually the first to suffer. Indeed, a reign of terror had already begun in 1918, and in 1919 massive pogroms had scarred Lvov and Vilnius. These outrages spread fear throughout the east and the south, both areas of high Jewish concentration.

Only four years before, the Russian invasion of Galicia had driven the Jews from their homes and led to thousands of them being executed. In no mood to wait and see what might happen this time, many decided that it was time to leave and seek protection in other countries, especially Germany.

In 1920, Jacob Gartenhaus left Poland for Germany, moving to Kassel, where he opened a men's clothing store. His wife, whom he married in 1923, had been born in the Russian part of Poland in the town of Woislawitz and, like her husband, had also migrated to Germany, settling with her family in the Hamburg suburb of Altona. Although the family prospered in Germany during the Weimar period, a sense of xenophobia and foreboding never really disappeared.

SOL GARTENHAUS: My father never liked to talk about his background. He was very *schmalstetl*. I always presumed Przeworsk to be the sort of place depicted in *Fiddler on the Roof*.[10] In the war he served as a medical orderly. His job was to pick up the wounded and bring them to the field hospitals.

My parents had six children, three boys and three girls; the oldest of the girls died in infancy. The last one, a son, was born in the United States, the rest in Germany. I was the oldest son.

We lived in the old Königsberg district of Kassel, where some of the streets in my neighborhood were named for animals: the Pferdegasse (Horse Street) the Entengasse (Duck Street), and the Ziegengasse (Goat Street). We lived on the Goat Street, but I couldn't find it when I went back there many years afterwards and took a look around. The old buildings were gone and an autobahn had taken away all remaining traces of the Ziegengasse. The Fulda River ran behind our apartment building, and I used to walk along its banks and cross over one of its bridges. I had all that in my mind when I later returned, and that's how I was able to pinpoint the area.

Shortly before we left Germany I couldn't go to the river anymore. Rows of barbed wire cut off access, and in the nearby fields the army used to hold maneuvers.

The old Königsberg district of Kassel no longer exists. It, with the rest of the central urban area, disappeared during the Allied bombardments of the summer and fall of 1943. The American Eighth Air Force struck first in July during its famous "Blitz Week," a time when it flew 1,672 sorties against all the major industrial cities in northern Germany. British bombers came calling three months later to complete the destruction of the city's aircraft and rocket production facilities, but in the process touched off a gigantic firestorm, which incinerated over 5,000 people and reduced the whole center of the town to a blackened ruin.

The city was rebuilt after the war, its famous parks and gardens were restored, and many of the old street names were retained, but otherwise few of the landmarks remain to remind former inhabitants of what had once been.

GARTENHAUS: My father had very little formal education and couldn't write or read anything but Yiddish and Hebrew. After his marriage, my mother taught him how to read and write German. He was a very Orthodox Jew, more Jewish than German. The Jewish community in Kassel was divided between the Eastern Jews and the more assimilated German Jews, or *jeckes*.[11] His associations were primarily with the Eastern Jews.

Did your parents talk about the German Jews in that derogatory manner?

GARTENHAUS: To some extent, but I don't think it was meant to be hostile. I think they used the term to designate a professional and moneyed class. The German Jews were the ones who were highly educated. They would go to synagogue in *zilenders* (top hats), which now only chimney sweeps wear. We were not really a part of this more assimilated group. But we went to the same Jewish parochial school, which was largely secular, but run by Jews for Jews.

The Polish Jews were not numerous enough to support their own synagogue, and they used to come to our apartment to worship on Rosh Hashanah and Yom Kippur.

Did this Eastern European community live in one area?

GARTENHAUS: I think it was spread throughout Kassel.

Who were your playmates?

GARTENHAUS: On the Ziegengasse there were no other Jews, so I used to play with the other kids on the street.

And there was no sorting out along religious lines?

GARTENHAUS: Not until the Nazis came into power and the anti-Jewish propaganda began. Then it became different.

What kind of a religious upbringing did you have?

GARTENHAUS: Even before I went to school at the age of six or so, I could read

Hebrew. My father taught me. He was a heavy smoker, and he would use a wooden matchstick to point to the places on the page where he wanted me to read.

Did you keep kosher? Go to the synagogue on Shabbat?

GARTENHAUS: Of course we ate kosher and we used to go to the main German synagogue every Friday night. When they made *kiddush* [the prayer of benediction before the evening meal], they would have all the kids come up at the end for a little cup of wine, which later on I realized was really champagne.

So you worshiped with the German Jews?

GARTENHAUS: Yes, the Polish Jews were mainly Orthodox, but they did not have their own synagogue. As I said, for the high holidays they came to our place, where one of the rooms was used as a synagogue. But even at the main synagogue on the Königstrasse, the service was in Hebrew and the prayer book was a traditional prayer book. However, the German Jews were acculturated insofar as their general outlook was mainly German.

The separation, of course, went farther insofar as the German Jews were citizens of the Reich and the Polish Jews probably never would be. In this respect the Gartenhauses were no different from the Golombs.

Did you have a choir and an organ in that synagogue?

GARTENHAUS: I don't recall if there was an organ.

Kassel had two main synagogues plus several private one-room places of worship organized by various communities and sects, a practice existing in most German cities. A main synagogue had been built in 1714 and continued as a separate building. In 1872, however, an Orthodox faction separated from the main group and sought its own quarters. In 1890 the liberal congregation began construction of an imposing building on the Königstrasse, which was completed in 1907. At that time the Jewish population of the city was over three thousand people, comprising about 1.5 percent of the overall population.

Wilhelmian Germany saw a rash of new synagogue construction as each Jewish community tried to show off its affluence and underscore its presence. Many of these places of worship were confidently built in the centers of town in a variety of architectural styles, including Near Eastern, Romanesque, Gothic, and Classical revival. A palazzo of the Italian Renaissance could have served as the inspiration for the facade of the main synagogue in Kassel.

The great period of monumental synagogue construction came, ironically, at a time of increased assimilation, intermarriage, and latitudinarianism. Many German Jews were "three-day Jews": they participated financially but showed up in the synagogue only on the high holy days. Prosperity and cosmopolitanism also brought changes to the style of religious service, which reflected many forms of Christian worship: organ music, hymn singing in German, sermons in German, and nonseparation of the sexes.

GARTENHAUS: All the Jewish kids went to the same parochial secular Jewish school, but the Eastern Jews were less likely to go to the university. Many Orthodox Jews were small shopkeepers and salesmen, like my father, others were workers, many of them in menial jobs. Had I not come to the United States, I probably would have followed my father into business.

Were you ever invited to the homes of the Deutschjuden?

GARTENHAUS: I had a friend named Gerhardt who invited me to his home at various times. (I once ran into him at the Bronx Zoo after we came to the United States.) Then there was another friend, Ludwig Seifel, who came from the more assimilated group.

Did these groups act differently in public?

GARTENHAUS: From my parents I somehow got the idea that I should do nothing to attract attention in public. Restraint was ingrained into me from a very early age. I guess they feared that the *goyim* were ready to pounce. *Rischus* (malice) was the Yiddish term for their antisemitism. There was a lot of *rischus* out there, and so we were taught to maintain a low profile.[12]

But weren't the indigenous German Jews fearful that the East European Jews, who were conspicuous because of their different customs, would create problems for them with the rest of the Germans?

GARTENHAUS: Yes, but in public we dressed like ordinary Germans. In that respect, there was no way you could tell we were Jewish. No one that I knew, in-

Jacob, Alfred, and Solomon
Gartenhaus, 1934.

Walter Hirsch's parents, Eugene
and Fanny.

Walter Hirsch, left, and his younger
brother.

cluding my father, had *payos,* or side curls; all shaved regularly. None of the Jews that I knew wore the traditional garb.

About 90,000 Jews came to Germany from Eastern Europe at the end of the nineteenth and beginning of the twentieth century, many fleeing the poverty and repression that had been their condition for generations. Assimilation usually followed. But Germany was nonetheless full of many such Jews who wanted to maintain their separateness. These attended a confusing array of synagogues with as many languages, doctrines, and dress as there had been definable communities. Most of Germany's large cities, like Berlin, Munich, Leipzig, Dresden, and Frankfurt am Main, had Jewish districts, where the men still wore Hasidic garb and spoke Yiddish and looked down on those who had abandoned their traditions. Such unreconstructed immigrants usually received little sympathy either from Gentiles or from German Jews, who feared that their backwardness would threaten their own well-being.

A Civil Service Position: Joseph Haberer

> "My parents hit me when I started saying 'Heil Hitler.' But I wanted to be like the other students. I wanted to be German. I wanted to be part of the excitement, but obviously I couldn't be."

An Emphasis on Cleanliness and Punctuality

Huddled behind its medieval fortifications, Villingen had withstood the assault of marauding armies three times, in 1525, 1625, and again in 1704. The city was situated in an area of rolling hills and farmlands in the southwest corner of Germany, sandwiched between the conifer-covered mountains of the Schwartzwald and the high limestone-clad plateaus of the Swabian Juras. This area, known as the Barr, is a fertile region with harsh winters and is famous for being the source of the mighty Danube, which is formed by the junction of the small streams of Breg and Brigach. Here also the Neckar begins snaking its way north past Stuttgart, Heidelberg, and Mannheim, where it merges with the waters of the Rhine.

During the Second Reich, Villingen was part of the Grand Duchy of Baden, one of its eleven administrative centers. Baden had an admirable record of liberal government, known especially for its enlightened treatment of its Jews. In 1807, the duchy began an emancipation process that protected Jewish religious beliefs, recognized Jewish organizations and congregations, and in 1862 granted the Jews complete civic equality with the right of participation in government.[13] In 1868 Grand Duke Frederick I appointed Moritz Ellstäter as his minister of finance—the first time a Jew had achieved cabinet rank in Germany.

The Haberers had come to Baden during the seventeenth century, their participation in the salt trade providing them with a comfortable living and the coveted distinction of *Schutzjuden,* an official protection granted to Jews who were recognized for their economic value. This status, however, came with a series of restrictions: no civil liberties, no recognition of the right to travel, and no permission to live and work where they pleased. Moreover, the status was extended only to the head of a household during his lifetime. It was renewable unto the next generation at the pleasure of the sovereign. The Jews also had to contend with special regulations adopted by the duchy's various municipalities. Villingen, for example, had expelled its Jews in 1510 and had not officially abolished this restriction until 1862.

Joseph Haberer's father, Bertold, had come to Villingen at the turn of the twentieth century. He had been born in Offenburg in 1882 and was one of nine brothers and two sisters, most of whom were to leave Germany before the First World War. Some went to South Africa, others to England, and others to the United States. Bertold joined the imperial civil service and worked in the Villingen *Finanzamt* (tax office). Although he never rose above the level of junior clerk, merely being part of the government service was no small accomplishment for a Jew.

Even during the more tolerant period of the Weimar Republic, Jews comprised about .5 percent, or 5,000, of the roughly one million people in government service, or less than half their relative numbers in the general population. Very few of these, only about 200, held senior positions.

Bertold married Georgine Seckels, who had come from Aurich

in West Friesland, that chunk of land between the Ems and Weser Rivers that jutted out into the North Sea. Joseph, their only child, was born in 1929, a time when the prosperous days of the Weimar Republic were coming to an end.

On October 29, 1929, the New York Stock Exchange experienced the worst day of losses in its history, with the value of its shares dropping by eighteen billion dollars. Over the next several days another forty billion — sums equivalent to the entire financial cost of American participation in World War I — also disappeared. American loans and investments, which had been crucial for the continuation of German prosperity, fell sharply. The Great Depression was at hand.

JOSEPH HABERER: Villingen had only ten Jewish families [about sixty people], and I was the only Jewish child. Most of the men were cattle dealers *(Viehhänd-ler)*, a sort of traditional occupation for Jews in that part of Germany. The congregation met in the house of one of these livestock merchants, one room serving as a synagogue. A rabbi came through once in a while, perhaps for the high holy days.

My mother was more observant than my father. He wasn't terribly religious, but he must have had some belief, because my most vivid recollection of him in a religious role was on Yom Kippur, when he'd wear a *kittel* [the white robe that Orthodox Jews wear on solemn occasions and in which they are buried]. So apparently he had had enough training to put on that consecrated garment. Had he been more assimilated, he probably would not have worn it.

But my father certainly didn't explain to me what it meant to be Jewish. Neither did my mother, although she did teach me the Hebrew alphabet. I don't remember having a seder. If we'd had it, I think I would've remembered. I remember looking at Jewish prayer books. I remember my mother had a prayer book, and I may have also. I do remember pictures of Moses and the Commandments and some Passover things, but they left no strong impression on me. But I don't think that was because my parents were on the road to assimilation. Part of the problem was that to be a Jew in the full sense of the word, you had to have a community in which to practice, and in Villingen there wasn't much of a community. Then by 1933 things became so rough and tough and difficult that my parents had other things on their minds.

My father had a lot on his mind. He was nervous, high-strung, and not very strong. He had problems with his lungs all his life. He was so physically unfit that he was not called up during the First World War and therefore didn't serve. But he seemed to have some interest in a variety of cultural things.

He liked operetta and told me about an operetta performance in which one of the characters is reading a newspaper and smoking a cigar, which he smokes right through the paper.[14] My father must have had a sense of humor, but as a general rule he was distant and somebody I had to be quiet around because of his nervousness and illness, which became worse when Hitler came to power and his job was put in jeopardy. This, plus his weak constitution, did not make him a very joyful person.

The Nazis first went after those Jews who held positions in municipal, district, regional, and national government agencies. The Law for the Reestablishment of the Professional Civil Service (*Gesetz zur Wiederherstellung des Berufsbeamtentums*), issued on April 7, 1933, decreed the immediate "retirement" of all non-Aryans. In the following weeks, the Nazis fleshed out the law to include jobs that had any relationship to the civil service or to state employment, for example, to manual laborers and blue-collar workers, clerical employees, doctors, notaries, lawyers, medical students, postgraduate assistants, laboratory technicians, university lecturers, and members of professional organizations.

There were some exclusions: World War I combat veterans, sons and fathers of those who had fallen in battle, and those with civil service status before August 1, 1914. Hitler agreed to these exemptions, apparently presuming the numbers would be relatively small because he believed that most of the Jews had been slackers during the Great War. In fact, the opposite was the case, and so great was the number of exemptions that about half of the Jews in the civil service were allowed to continue working. This situation lasted until 1935, when the Nürnberg Laws closed the loophole. Even so, those now fired were still allowed to collect pensions, albeit reduced ones, for another three years.

HABERER: The problem of Jewish identity became apparent when I started going to school in 1935. Antisemitic sentiments among some of the students were very strong. All the little Hitler Youths and others running around made my life unpleasant—and that's putting it euphemistically. They would throw stones, use slingshots, call me names, and harass me when I walked back and forth to school.

I don't recall the teachers abusing me by calling me names or making remarks like "there goes that Jew," but the German school system was extremely authoritarian and punitive. If they weren't satisfied with your performance, they would cane you. A couple of times I was caned because I was so nervous about everything that I couldn't do well.

Everybody else appeared to be having a good time. For the Aryans it was an exciting period: flags, marching, and all that National Socialist patriotic stuff. I wanted to be part of it. My parents hit me when I started saying "Heil Hitler." But I wanted to be like the other students. I wanted to be German. I wanted to be part of the excitement, but obviously I couldn't be. I was taunted and was also having a hard time learning.

Things were also very tense at home. My parents were not very emotive, no hugging or kissing, that kind of stuff. I can't honestly say, though, that my parents were temperamentally pessimistic or always saw the worst of everything in life.

We lived in a small apartment at the edge of town. My parents had one bedroom and there was this big living room with a stove in the middle and a small kitchen alcove. The toilets were very primitive. No lavatory. No running water.

We lived on my father's pension, and once a week I would walk with him to the office where he would collect the money. We were really poor, but we didn't go hungry. My mother, who was a seamstress, made all my clothes. There was nothing we could do except watch things getting progressively worse.

To help make ends meet, my parents took in Eric Gabler, a child from a Jewish social agency, who was about six months old when he came to live with us. He had been born out of wedlock, and his mother left him in Germany while she immigrated to the United States with his older sister. I was rather upset by this intruder, who was very noisy, probably suffering from colic, and who became a rival for my mother's attention. Add to this the tensions outside the house.

If you tried to walk in the park, there was a sign saying *Juden Verboten.* You couldn't go to the swimming pool. You couldn't do this and you couldn't do that—all of this raised the question: Why me?

Do you remember anything positive about those days?

HABERER: While the situation at school was increasingly unpleasant, the boys in the neighborhood did not persecute me. Quite the contrary, they were friendly and we played together in the fields. I was quite active, a typically rambunctious

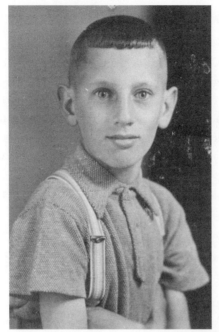

Joseph Haberer in Villingen, November 1938.

Sol Gartenhaus in Jewish school in 1936.

boy. Also, there were certain things in the German culture that I liked. There were the festivals and the holidays. The bell ringing, the songs, the stories, the fairy tales—not so pleasant, as a matter of fact, because Grimm's fairy tales are pretty grim.

Max and Morris is pretty chilling. Being ground up into sausage must surely be the ultimate revenge against kids.

HABERER: My parents were very German, and I had a very German kind of up-bringing. When my mother caught me telling a fib, she told me that famous German saying: *"Wer einmal lügt dem glaubt man nicht / Und wenn er auch die Wahrheit spricht"* (He who lies once is never again believed, even if he tells the truth). She always emphasized cleanliness and punctuality. My picture books contained a certain idealization of courage and patriotism. I was always moved at the singing of "Deutschland über Alles." (Just as later on when I heard the Israeli national anthem sung. On the other hand, "God Bless America" and "America the Beautiful" never got to me.)

Did you ever feel that because you were Jewish that somehow you had to constantly be better than everybody else to justify your position in society?

HABERER: No. A lot of the time I was having a pretty awful time. I wanted to be like the others, and it never occurred to me that I had to prove anything. I was just unhappy being what I was. At eight years old, I wasn't thinking about my responsibility or obligation to demonstrate to the Germans that Jews were as good, if not better, than they were. I wasn't conceptualizing in those terms at all.

A Stately Victorian House: Michael Rossmann

"My mother did not think of herself as being Jewish. She, like the other members of her family, was proud to be a German."

A Family Divided

The family of Michael Rossmann's father was non-Jewish; his mother's family, the Schwabachers, was Jewish. Wealthy and prominent, the Schwabachers came from Frankfurt am Main and could trace back their ancestry in the city to before the time of Napoleon.

In 1925, Frankfurt's Jewish population numbered 29,385 people, or 6.3 percent of the city's total population. Yet, despite what might seem like fairly small numbers, this Frankfurt community was second in size only to that of Berlin, with its Jewish population of 172,672. The third-largest was that of Breslau, with 23,240, followed by Hamburg, with 19,794. Since emancipation during the nineteenth century (a process which began with Napoleon's creation of the Confederation of the Rhine in 1806), many of Frankfurt's Jews had become increasingly assimilationist, despite the city's still remaining a strong intellectual citadel of Orthodoxy. The Jewish population, by and large, was becoming more wealthy, cultured, and civic-minded.

By 1842, the number of Orthodox had dwindled to 10 percent of the Jewish population. In that year the Friends of Reform rejected the authority of the Talmud, raised doubts about the necessity for circumcision and observance of dietary laws, and repudiated the Messianic faith and the return to Palestine. They claimed Germany as their Fatherland. In 1904, the Frankfurt Jews celebrated the hundredth anniversary of the founding of the famous Philanthropin, a progressive high school that had become the model for Jewish Reform education.

MICHAEL ROSSMANN: My parents divorced when I was about three years old. It had nothing to do with the religious differences, but in my father's family there was a very strange situation, since the family was divided between Nazi and non-Nazi.

His mother, Grandmother Rossmann, was an antisemite and so was my uncle, Bruno Rossmann, who was a committed National Socialist and obviously a member of the Party. In fact, after the [Second World] War, I had to go and see him because my Grandfather Rossmann, who had died during the war, had left all his property to me. My Uncle Bruno had been taking care of it in the meantime and when I was there, he showed me documents signed by Heinrich Himmler thanking him for his services as a biochemist. I really hate to think what that involved. He was quite nice to me, but I just felt uncomfortable to be associated with a guy like that.

After the divorce, what contact did you have with your father and his family?

ROSSMANN: I don't recall having met my father until after the Second World War, when he came to visit me in England. He had moved to France and then Switzerland, where he had remarried. But my mother occasionally took me to visit my father's parents in Wiesbaden, where they had a very stately Victorian-style house with servants—a very upper-middle-class lifestyle. My grandfather was a professor of French and the principal of the local Gymnasium, and he wrote textbooks. He had a little pointed beard and was physically quite imposing. When I went shopping with him, everybody greeted him, *"Guten Morgen, Herr Professor, Guten Morgen, Herr Professor!"*

He would spend time with me, and in one of our talks he asked me how many days there were in the year. I replied—I must have started school by that time, maybe about six years old—"Oh, there's so many you can't ever calculate that." "Well," he said, "let's sit down and see." He asked me to name and count the months of the year, then he asked me to help him put down the number of the days in each month, and then said, "Now let's add it up." I made a mistake in the addition, but he helped me correct it, and we came to 365 days. "Not so many really." I was very impressed.

Grandfather Rossmann was a very decent guy. He did a lot to support my mother, like giving her money for my upbringing. My father had left—he was working in Paris—and my grandfather was angry about his lack of support and later disinherited him.

And your grandmother?

ROSSMANN: She made a less favorable impression. When we arrived, it was as if the house were divided in two. My mother would talk to my grandfather, and grandmother refused to take part. She joined the others for meals, but afterwards she withdrew.

After her divorce, my mother returned to live with her parents in Frankfurt. They had a large house with servants. My grandfather was a well-known dealer in rare coins. He conducted his business in one part of the house.

My grandfather believed strongly in the education of women. My mother was educated at the Bauhaus.[15] She later worked as a feature writer for the *Frankfurter Zeitung,* doing commentaries about the city in the so-called *Stadtplatt* (city record) section of the paper. Her articles were illustrated with her own drawings.

The *Frankfurter Zeitung* was one of Germany's greatest liberal papers. It was founded in 1866 by Leopold Sonnemann, a Jew, who owned it until his death in 1909. Sonnemann also served in the Reichstag for eleven years (1871–76, 1878–84) and on the Frankfurt city council. In his will Sonnemann specified his newspaper continue to advocate freedom of political expression. Sonnemann was also involved in the establishment of the University of Frankfurt. Sonnemann with others, like Rudolf Mosse, founder of the *Berliner Tagblatt* (1871), and Leopold Ullstein, owner of the *Neues Berliner Tagblatt,* became known as the "Jewish press barons," proof enough to antisemites that Jews were controlling the German newspaper industry and exerting a malevolent influence on German society.

ROSSMANN: While my mother worked my grandmother looked after me. I also had a nanny, who lived upstairs.

Before I could read by myself, my grandmother read to me in the evenings from a child's Bible. Always from the Old Testament, because my grandmother didn't like to read from the New Testament.

My grandparents went to the synagogue on holy days, but they did not keep kosher and always had a Christmas tree. The more Orthodox members of the family used to complain about this. They also disapproved of my grandparents' eating ham.

My mother accompanied her parents to the synagogue on the holy days, but she did not relate well to the Jewish religion. She thought that many people who went to the synagogue were superficial in their beliefs and went primarily to show off their clothes.

My mother joined the Society of Friends. The religion's philanthropic aspects attracted her after the First World War, when she observed the Quakers helping to alleviate the German food shortages.[16] My mother was very idealistic and socially conscious. She was very much a pacifist and was involved in the emancipation of women movement in Weimar Germany.

My mother did not think of herself as being Jewish. She, like the other members of her family, was proud to be a German. My mother's brother had fought for Germany in the First World War. My grandmother's brother Ludwig had belonged to a dueling fraternity and boasted of the big scar on his cheek.

Jewish students, excluded from Gentile fraternities (as had indeed been the case in the United States), formed their own dueling societies, adopting similar uniforms, rules, and rituals, complete with banners, colors, flags, mottos, and William II mustaches. By 1896, there were five such corporations in Germany, formed into the Convention of Fraternities of German Students of the Jewish Faith. The Convention's constitution pledged to promote Jewish pride and fight against antisemitism. In addition, it declared itself "inextricably bound to the German fatherland by history, culture and a community of law."

How did your mother's association with the Quakers resonate with the rest of the family?

ROSSMANN: I don't know the exact answer. I do know that my mother wasn't very satisfied with the rituals of the Jewish faith. They didn't mean much to her, and Quakers are particularly strong in not having rituals.

You don't sense that she was ostracized in any way because of her conversion?

ROSSMANN: I think the family considered it a little bit extreme.

Notes

1. The law was passed by 444 to 538 votes, with only the Social Democrats voting against. The Communists, barred from participation, could not vote. This enabling act also gave Hitler the authority to change the present constitution.
2. The Gemarah, existing in both Palestinian and Babylonian versions, contains a series of commentaries and interpretations of the Mishnah—a collection of teachings from the classical period of rabbinic Judaism, 200–500 C.E. The Mishnah and Gemarah together comprise the Talmud. Transcription from the oral tradition and constant subsequent redaction have contributed to a multiplicity of conflicting opinions, which are subject themselves to further disagreement. Modern scholars are not even of one mind as to whether the Talmud is supposed to be primarily legal or pedagogical.
3. In fulfillment of the command in Deuteronomy 22:12: "You shall make twisted tassels on the four corners of your cloaks which you wrap around you" (New English Bible). Orthodox Jews wore these "fringes" on a four-cornered garment *(tallit)* as symbolic protection against immoral conduct and to remind them of observance of their religious duties.
4. "You shall not wear clothes woven with two kinds of yarn, wool and flax together." Deuteronomy 22:11 (New English Bible).

5. The Borochov Youth took inspiration from philosopher-politician Ber Borochov (1881–1917), who tried to reconcile "scientific socialism" with the needs of the Jewish people. Borochov believed that the Jewish masses, uprooted and nonproductive in the Diaspora, were driven to escape their precarious, exploited existence through migration to Palestine, where both economic and ethnic liberation would be achieved. Mapai, founded in Palestine in 1930, combined the ideal of national redemption with socialism in a Jewish homeland.

6. This organization, founded in 1916, attempted to combine Jewish cultural values and the establishment and defense of a homeland in Palestine with the resolution of the class struggle of the Jewish proletariat.

7. This, of course, is Golomb's opinion. In fact, many German Jews felt just the opposite and feared that National Socialism would lead to a virulent kind of political antisemitism.

8. It was a three-way race among Marshal Paul von Hindenburg, seeking a second term; Nazi leader Adolf Hitler; and Ernst Thälmann, the Communist candidate.

9. Over one-third of the people collected in this "new" state were ethnically non-Polish, being largely German, Ukrainian, White Russian, Lithuanian, or Jewish.

10. Actually Przeworsk had a population of around three thousand at the turn of the century.

11. Literally "jackets," in Yiddish, *yekkes*. The meaning can be anything from "uptight" to "reserved" to "snooty."

12. On a personal level this cautioned self-restraint: no loud talking, gesticulating, or wearing sloppy clothes. The concept also extended to the worship service, which had to be conducted with utmost decorum and bourgeois respectability, including the wearing of dark suits and top hats on the holidays. In teaching the avoidance of everything that might arouse *rischus,* Eastern European Jews were in part adapting the attitudes of the very *yekke* they criticized.

13. The Jewish population of Baden in that year was 24,000.

14. A very famous piece of business from act 3 of Johann Strauss's *Die Fledermaus.* Frank, the prison warden, returns to his office at the jail directly from an all-night party and falls asleep at his desk, the newspaper he was reading falling over his face, his lit cigar still clenched in his mouth.

15. The Bauhaus (Das Staatliche Bauhaus), founded at Weimar in 1919 by Walter Gropius (1883–1969), was an amalgamation of the School of Plastic Arts and the School of Arts and Trades, established eighteen years before by Henri Van de Velde (1863–1957). Gropius strove to form a new union of artists and artisans to construct "a future that will unite everything: architecture, painting, and sculpture in a single formation." At various times the Bauhaus had on its faculty such titans as

Marcel Breuer, Paul Klee, Josef Albers, Wassili Kandinski, and Lyonel Feininger. The student body, evenly balanced between men and women, was chosen on the basis of work presented, not diplomas. The rightist government of Weimar judged the school too revolutionary, forcing its transfer in 1925 to Dessau, which was more hospitable under its Social Democratic administration. However, by 1932 the National Socialists and their allies controlled the municipal government and voted 20 to 5 to throw this "Judeo-Marxist place" out of town. On April 1, 1933, Brown Shirts invaded the Bauhaus complex, arrested thirty-two students, and seized "a lot of illegal propaganda material." Such Nazi assaults on artistic freedom forced director Ludwig Mies van der Rohe (1886–1969) to dissolve the school that July. Although the Nazis denounced the Bauhaus style as being un-German, much National Socialist architecture reflected the Bauhaus's neat classicism.

16. The deprivations of wartime continued because the Allied blockade lasted until June 1919, when Germany signed the Treaty of Versailles.

2

The Process of Exile

E ven granting the debt Nazi racial legislation owed to the old tribal idea of a *Volksgemeinschaft,* the Nürnberg Laws were still a radical departure from the citizenship laws of the past, especially those of the Wilhelmine and the Weimar periods. The difference was not only in degree, but also in kind.[1] Between 1935 and 1943 some 250 anti-Jewish laws were enacted. These stripped the Jews not only of their citizenship and national identity, but also of their possessions, their security, and, for those who did not leave, their lives.

Eventually 330,000, over half of Germany's entire Jewish population, went into exile. Most of the 160,000 Jews who remained behind did not survive the war. Some died from natural causes or from deprivation, and there were suicides, but the overwhelming majority were murdered.[2]

Of the escapees, 102,000 made it to the United States, 63,000 went to Argentina, 52,000 to the United Kingdom, 33,000 to Palestine, 30,000 to France, 30,000 to the Netherlands, 26,000 to South Africa, 25,000 to Poland, 20,000 to Shanghai, and 12,000 to Belgium.[3] Those who had sought refuge in countries like France, the Netherlands, Poland, and Belgium were again threatened during the Second World War. Many of these refugees were rounded up and sent to the death camps.

For those fleeing to the United States, the first step was a visit to an American consulate for an immigration visa. American consuls had wide discretionary powers due to the system's characteristic of negative selection. Certain classes of aliens were excluded because of mental, physical, moral, or economic defects and thereby denied admission.[4] These included idiots, imbeciles, feebleminded, epileptics, paupers, professional beggars, vagrants, persons afflicted with loathsome or contagious diseases, physically incapacitated, felons, moral reprobates, polygamists, anarchists, prostitutes, pimps, contract laborers, and illiterates over sixteen years of age. In September 1930, President Herbert Hoover, in an executive order, added, "persons likely to become a public charge."

The immigrants first had to swear that they did not fit any of these categories. Then they had to submit two copies of a birth certificate, an unexpired copy of a passport (or other official document in the nature of a passport), and a police certificate attesting to their good character for the past five years. The burden of proof for demonstrating this clean bill of health was placed on the immigrant, and any consul looking for an excuse to avoid facilitating immigration could certainly have found it there. Consuls also had to keep immigration within its prescribed numerical limits. The number of visas they issued was supervised by a "quota control officer" assigned to each embassy. For this reason, many consuls insisted on full dossiers even if documents were unavailable.[5]

The current American quota system favored immigrants from northern and western Europe, at the expense of southern and eastern Europeans. During the 1930s the overall European total was approximately 150,00 a year, with 26,000 assigned to Germany. However, bureaucratic red tape, perceived lack of good character, fear of foreign contagion and indigence, and outright antisemitism kept the quotas routinely unfilled, despite increasing numbers of applicants.[6]

A Three-Month Visa: Michael Golomb

"I would never have believed that the Nazis intended to exterminate the Jews."

A Visa for Yugoslavia

Shortly after Hitler became chancellor in 1933, Michael Golomb was asked to distribute some anti-Nazi leaflets around the university and the immediately surrounding area. It was risky and dangerous business. Fortunately he was not caught.

Were there any manifestations of antisemitism other than the demonstrations?

MICHAEL GOLOMB: Sometimes there was violence on university grounds, but at that time I didn't feel that it was mainly antisemitic. I thought that National Socialism was a fascist movement and antisemitism was only a sideline, limited to a rather small number of members, that the leaders were only using it to stir up the mobs, and that they didn't take it seriously.

Were any of your professors Nazis?

GOLOMB: We had a famous mathematician named Ludwig Bieberbach. (He was the one who posed the famous "Bieberbach Conjecture," which many mathematicians at some time have worked on and which was proved just recently by one of my colleagues in the math department, Louis de Branges.)

Bieberbach became the editor of a new journal called *Deutsche Mathematik* (German Mathematics) shortly after Hitler came to power. No one had ever heard of such a concept before. But Bieberbach nonetheless had the "philosophy" that German and Nordic mathematicians thought differently from other mathematicians, especially Jewish mathematicians. He claimed that the Germanic and Nordic mathematical creativity was based on intuition (mainly spatial), while that of Jewish mathematicians was based on cold, analytical-logical manipulation. The publication did not outlast the Third Reich.

Bieberbach was definitely an outrageous antisemite, but he was more politically naive than an outright Nazi. He was a proud German nationalist and felt humiliated by the defeat of the First World War. He began coming to class in his brown SA (Storm Trooper) uniform and organized early-morning *Gepäckmärsche* (backpack marches) among his colleagues in the department in order to "harden them" for the defense of the Fatherland.

We know now that antisemitism and Nazism are absolutely inseparable. You apparently did not pick up on that dynamic. Did the Nazis hide it?

GOLOMB: No. I think it was not that prevalent in the first few months. I knew the first concentration camps were not filled with Jews, but with Communists, Social Democrats, trade union organizers, and other political opponents. Even many Nazis didn't like the anti-Jewish Boycott and opposed it.

Your perception was that antisemitism was peripheral.

GOLOMB: Yes. I would never have believed that the Nazis intended to extermi-nate the Jews. Between 1933 and 1935, many German Jews who could have emigrated did not want to leave Germany, including my parents and grandpar-ents. We all thought that the whole thing wouldn't last long.

So you based your interpretation on the notion that this was the old Left-Right, fascist-antifascist, elitist-democratic sort of struggle?

GOLOMB: That's right, that all the suppressive actions by the Nazis that took place in 1933 and in 1934 had nothing to do with Jews. In those years, I be-lieved that the main thrust was against the Communist and Socialist Parties and the trade unions. Hitler didn't become popular by espousing antisemitism, but because he appealed to nationalism and the solidarity of the German folk. He also denounced what happened to Germany under the despised Treaty of Ver-sailles. Besides, Germany was in a deep economic depression and had massive unemployment.

How did you manage to support yourself in Berlin?

GOLOMB: I lived with my uncle and aunt in an apartment on the Brückenalle in the Tiergarten district. Since the largest room of the flat served as a *schul* (syna-gogue), of which my uncle and aunt were the caretakers, they were able to live there rent-free. Otherwise they would have not been able to afford such a nice apartment.

I received no help from my parents. The little I needed for meals, transpor-tation, school supplies, toiletries, and occasional theater tickets came from part-time jobs, like tutoring and babysitting. (The part-time work that students do in the United States was not available to German students.) I also obtained a small loan from a state fund set up for the *Auslandsdeutsche,* in my case a "foreigner" who had been born and raised in Germany but had Polish citizenship. I never repaid the loan after I left Germany because the due notes were signed "Heil Hitler."

Golomb received his Ph.D. in mathematics from the University of Berlin in May 1933 with a dissertation entitled "Zur Theorie der nichtlinearen Integralgleichungen, Integralgleichungssysteme und allgemeinen Funktionalgleichungen" ("Systems of Non-Integral Equations").[7] The threatening political situation induced him to rush the work to completion despite the fact that he was producing less than perfect work. The thesis was approved within two weeks and accepted for publication without modification in the journal *Mathematische Zeitschrift*. Professors gave Golomb glowing recommendations. Bieberbach wrote "er est sehr begabt" (he is very talented) with "sehr" underlined twice. Golomb became confident that he would get a formal state academic position, his lack of German citizenship notwithstanding.[8] However, he soon discovered that no German university would hire a Jew, no matter what his qualifications.

The Nazis promulgated the Law for the Reestablishment of the Professional Civil Service (April 7, 1933), and began dismissing all Jews who were already on university faculties, starting with those without tenure. As civil servants, Jewish professors were lumped together with all "non-Aryan" employees of the national and local governments. At first an exception was made for those employed before August 1, 1914, those who had fought at the front for Germany during World War I, and those whose fathers or sons had fallen for the Fatherland. However, this proved no protection, and Jews, no matter what their status, could always be dismissed to further the "simplification of administration." Also *agents provocateurs* among the student body made it impossible for Jewish teachers to hold class.

Despite the handwriting on the wall, Golomb stayed in Berlin four more months. He attended seminars and colloquia and gave lectures on the results of his dissertation. He also wrote dozens of reviews for *Fortschritte der Mathematik,* a publication that continued to publish his reviews even after he had left Germany.

GOLOMB: I left Berlin in September for Munich, where my parents were then living. Because of the economic depression, my father's business had fallen off, and his sales territory had been shifted from northern Bavaria to the Munich area. On top of that, the man whom he had employed as a driver for his business travels had joined the Nazi Party. He denounced my father as a Jew and started taking customers from him. Of my five siblings, all younger than I, three were still living at home, and that caused further hardship. Now that I had finished my studies, I was expected to help keep them afloat. But the only way I could do this, with the Nazis now in charge, was to find work outside Germany. This was not easy. The depression prompted all nations to close their borders to immigration. And a Polish passport didn't add to one's chance of success.

The necessity of leaving the country was heightened when I was informed that the Gestapo had me blacklisted and that I might be arrested at any time. I didn't think that they were after me because I was a Jew, but because I was a political enemy.

Golomb left Munich for Yugoslavia on November 15, 1933, traveling on a three-month visa, ostensibly to visit his sister. But Golomb intended to stay longer. He had been promised an assistantship by a professor named Mitrinovitch at the University of Belgrade. Mitrinovitch, an astronomer, wanted Golomb to calculate the orbits of planetoids. Although Golomb did not think that the work was related to his own research interests, under the circumstances he could hardly be choosy and immediately accepted.

Your identity was German, but you could no longer become a mathematician in a German university. How did this rejection affect you?

GOLOMB: It certainly hardened my hatred of the Nazis, which, for political reasons, I had already. I had never imagined that because I was born a Jew, I could not build my career in Germany.

Apart from your emphasis on your career, did you have that feeling of being heimatlos—*a loss of your roots?*

GOLOMB: Well, I was strongly attached to Germany—the land of my birth, where I grew up and received my education—but not to the German political system and not to the German people.

Did any of your Jewish friends also feel that they were better off leaving?

GOLOMB: Those who had finished the university about the same time I did all felt they had to leave. They couldn't get positions. Some mathematicians older than myself stayed, at least for a while. But within two or three years they also were gone. For example, in our department at Purdue we had a Professor Rosenthal, who had been a member of the mathematics department at the University of Heidelberg. He was kept on because he had served in the First World War; and he left Germany only at the end of 1936.

Golomb arrived in Belgrade in December 1933, having spent some time in Ljubljana and Zagreb, the capital cities of Slovenia and Croatia. He registered at the Hotel Poshta, surrendering his passport to the concierge as required. The next day, a detective appeared at his door, even before he had gotten out of bed, and asked him to come with him to the police station.

GOLOMB: I asked, "What for?" "To pick up your passport," he said. I went with him to the station, and they immediately took me to see a supervisor, who asked me what I was doing in Belgrade. I said, "Well, I'm just sightseeing before I go to visit my sister." He said, "Your visa is just for a visit to your sister." From then on unbelievable things began to happen. They took my wallet. They took all my papers. A detective accompanied me back to the hotel and watched while I packed my stuff and gave me two choices: either I was to leave the country or go directly to my sister's. (She was living in Padej, a farm village in the northeast corner of the country, where her husband, who had studied medicine at the University of Würzburg, was the country doctor.)

The detective took me to the railway station and put me on a train. Another detective was with me the whole trip to Padej, never letting me out of his sight. We arrived at 4 o'clock in the morning, and he got my sister and brother-in-law out of bed and made them sign a receipt that I was now in their custody. I have never figured out why all this happened. Maybe I was on a black list for political radicals, or maybe they were afraid I was looking for work—not a minor thing at that time. I was reminded again that I had to leave Yugoslavia when my visa expired.

I stayed with my sister until February 1934, when I was summoned to the local police station to be issued an exit visa. "Which country do you want to go to?" they asked, saying I could go to any of the border countries of Yugoslavia—Italy, Albania, Austria, Hungary, Romania, Bulgaria, or Greece. I protested that I could get no entrance visa for any of those countries. They replied that

that did not concern them; they would simply put me across any border I chose. In my desperation I asked to be deported to Italy. I knew that the train would have to pass through Zagreb, where, during my short stay, I had made the acquaintance of some people who might help me.

Fortunately, this time no detective accompanied me on the trip. Since I figured that the police would be at the union station in Zagreb to prevent my getting off, I got off at one of the suburban stations. Then I took a streetcar to downtown Zagreb and telephoned one of my friends.

I thought my fugitive status would be of short duration, lasting only until my residence could be legalized; but this took time, and for the next ten months I remained undercover, receiving my first real residence permit only in December 1934 and then just for a year. It was a permit for Zagreb, not Yugoslavia. Thus, for the next five years, my tenure in Yugoslavia depended on the ability to get this permit renewed. This occurred six more times, each renewal for a shorter period.

The hostility of the Yugoslavs toward foreigners was nothing compared to the hatred that the country's various ethnic and religious groups had for each other. The country had emerged from the First World War and the subsequent Paris Peace Conference as the Kingdom of the Serbs, Croats, and Slovenes, an assemblage of south Slavic lands of the defunct Austro-Hungarian Empire together with Serbia and Montenegro. These areas had never before known unity.

In 1929, the dominant Serbs, led by King Alexander I, tried to centralize the country. They suspended parliament, outlawed political parties, and overhauled the administration. They changed the country's name to Yugoslavia. But the new royal dictatorship only succeeded in exacerbating the country's divisions and animosities. Each ethnic group became more determined not to surrender its identity to some vague, possibly insincere concept of nationhood.

On November 9, 1934, an agent of the Croatian terrorist organization, the Ustashi, gunned down King Alexander in Marseilles as he was on a state visit to France. The crime was so shocking that, for a time, people rallied to the monarchy, but this spirit of cooperation did not last long. Croatian nationalists continued to press for home rule and threatened to seek the help of Nazi Germany to obtain complete independence if their demands were not met.

GOLOMB: With the help of friends, I could maintain the fiction that I was a wealthy foreigner who did not need any employment and who freely spent his own money to the benefit of the local economy. In fact, I did not have enough money to pay for the rent of a room and barely enough to be able to pay for my meals. I got some income tutoring high-school students, and I taught Hebrew. I continued to write reviews for *Fortschritte der Mathematik,* and I sold a few articles to the local paper. I tried very hard to find more stable employment, preferably some work related to mathematics.

Mathematics was my lifeblood; I refused to give it up. I tried to find a position with various insurance companies. I asked the head of the mathematics department at the University of Zagreb what my chances were to teach in his department. He was sympathetic, but told me frankly, "First, you must be a citizen of Yugoslavia; second, you must be a native Croat; third, you must be a member of the Roman Catholic Church; and lastly you should be a member of the Croatian Nationalist Party." But, I protested, "What about my qualifications as a mathematician?" "Oh!" he replied, "Those come last on the list."

That I was able to subsist was due to the kindness of friends. And from 1937 to 1939, I lived with my fiancée, later wife, Dagmar, in her studio apartment.

The job with the astronomer never materialized?

GOLOMB: No. When I was having all that trouble with the Belgrade police, he filled the position with someone else.

Aside from the reviews you were writing, were you able to further your career in mathematics?

GOLOMB: That was not easy. At that time, Yugoslavia had some internationally known mathematicians, but none of them were in Zagreb. The local university sponsored no colloquia or advanced seminars, it brought in no outside speakers, and it had a woefully deficient library. None of the local mathematicians were interested in my work, and I had insufficient contacts with those outside the country who might have been interested. I published a thirty-one-page article in the *Publications Mathématiques de l'Université de Belgrade,* but that was hardly a prestigious journal. The article was a followup to my dissertation.

What kept me alive intellectually was my association with three outstanding intellectuals: Hrvoje Ivekovich, a chemical engineer; Rihard Podhorsky, a chemist; and, Zvonko Richtman, an engineer. All were professors at the local Technical Institute and all were committed Marxists who were interested in the application of dialectical materialism to modern science. The four of us usually had lunch together during the week. Many of our conversations were philosophical. For example, we talked about how epistemology could help emancipate the common people from superstition, religion, and false ideologies. Since we were refining logical empiricism as developed by the Wiener Kreis (Vienna Circle) along dialectical lines, we referred to ourselves as the Zagrebacki Krug (Zagreb Jug).[9]

The local Marxists condemned our ideas as heresy, however. None of these doctrinaires had any schooling in science, and they simply quoted Soviet hacks to discredit and dismiss us as revisionists and reactionaries. They were able to use their Stalinist connections to prevent any of our writing from being published.

The Threat of Expulsion

Golomb was eager to get out of Yugoslavia, but getting a visa to travel elsewhere seemed impossible. Golomb wrote to a variety of emergency committees — based in London, Zurich, Geneva, Stockholm, and New York — which were organized to help displaced German scholars, but he had no success.

The only offer he received was one from Ha-Shomer ha-Za'ir. But in return for its help, this Zionist youth organization wanted Golomb to organize a group of young pioneers from the Balkan countries to establish a *kevuzah* in Palestine.[10] Once there, he was told, he might obtain an actuarial position in the medical insurance office of the Histadrut trade union organization.[11] But the prospect of calculating insurance annuities and premiums and compiling life-expectancy statistics was not a fulfilling career for a theoretical mathematician. He refused the offer, whereupon Ha-Shomer ha-Za'ir wanted nothing to do with him.

At the beginning of 1938, Golomb's fiancée, Dagmar, came up with the idea that he should write to Bertrand Russell. Dagmar reminded him of the great respect he had for this famous British scholar's work in humanistic philosophy and in mathematical logic, and she thought that Russell might help him get a visa to go to England and work there.

GOLOMB: Many would have thought the idea of writing to such an illustrious person was crazy, but I was desperate. I told Russell that I was turning to him

The Hirsch family home in Stuttgart.

The Cohen family: from left, Fritz's grandmother; his father, Iwan; a neighbor; his aunt; Fritz; and his mother, Alice.

because I felt close to his work, and that I didn't have anybody else to whom I could apply for assistance. This was the first letter that I had ever written in English, and I'm sure it was stylistically very awkward.

At that time, Russell was touring the United States and the letter was forwarded to him from his address in England. It was many months before I received a response.[12]

At the end of April, the Zagreb chief of police notified Golomb that his temporary residence permit would no longer be renewed when it expired on May 31. The time came and passed, and Golomb embarked on a daily struggle to avoid deportation. In July, the minister of interior in Belgrade received a petition to grant Golomb political asylum from eight professors of the University of Zagreb who attested to Golomb's value as a scholar and to his good character. This intervention resulted in the date of expulsion again being put off, this time to November 30. But this, he was warned, was definitely the last such extension.

GOLOMB: I hit on a fantastic idea. I went to the Polish consulate with the intention of volunteering for service in the Polish armed forces. War with the fascist powers seemed inevitable, and I figured that Poland could not refuse me, since I was a Polish citizen. I thought that while doing my part in repelling the fascist onslaught, I would learn the language and customs of the country and eventually, if I survived, I might obtain an academic position there. When I told the consular official of my plan to return and serve my fatherland, he sneered at me and said, "Who wants you?" This cured me instantly of my delusion.

In those years, when I tried to obtain an immigration visa to a country more hospitable than Yugoslavia, America was not on my list. There was a common belief among German refugees that it was practically impossible to get permission to immigrate there because powerful circles in that country opposed an influx of Jews. Some officials were even openly sympathetic to the Nazis. Besides, mathematics had not developed there the way that it had in Germany and France or even Italy and England. So I wouldn't have chosen the United States. But I had nonetheless investigated the formal requirements for getting an American visa, and I had gone to the American consulate in Zagreb to find out what was required.

I was told that two American citizens had to guarantee that I would not become dependent on public assistance. These affidavits of support were usually provided by people of means, none of whom I knew in the United States. However, in 1938, a cousin living in New York had by chance written to my parents in Munich, offering to help a member of the family to come to the United States. I had never met this man—he was the son of my mother's brother—and I was only vaguely aware of his existence. He had visited the family in Würzburg when I was studying at the University of Berlin, so I had never met him. My parents gave me his address, and I wrote to him. The result was that I got an affidavit.

My cousin was a high-school teacher with a modest income and a small bank account; and to make sure I had the two required affidavits, he got the husband of his sister, also a high-school teacher, to act as the second guarantor. It took several months to assemble all this material, and it wasn't until the end of September that I was able to return to the American consulate to make a formal application for immigration.

The vice-consul who processed my application was not encouraging. He said that the United States had 13 million people unemployed and that Americans did not like foreigners coming in and taking jobs. But he told me to come back the next day to speak to the consul.

The reception with the consul was quite different. He began by asking me why he should believe that I was a mathematician engaged in research. I showed him the article that I had written for the University of Belgrade mathematics journal. He looked it over and said, "I must confess that these hieroglyphics impress me," and he began talking to me as if I were an old friend. "I myself took calculus in college, and I still remember the equations of the parabola and the ellipse, but I have forgotten that of the hyperbola." When I gave it to him, he was really pleased. From then on, I was sure he would approve my request for an immigration visa. He said he would ask Washington that I be given an entrance number and estimated that I should arrive in the United States no later than February 1939.

When I told the consul that my Polish passport would expire before then and that I probably could not get an extension, he told me not to worry, he would give me an identification card good for admittance. That was the first time in my life that a state authority did not require me to have a passport. It was my first lesson in American democracy.

The interview of fitness that Golomb had with the American consul in Zagreb was a test that Golomb fortunately passed. The consul did not even oblige him to furnish a police certificate.

Although Golomb, by German standards, was considered a Pole, by American standards he was considered a German because he had been born in that country. It is not impossible that he might have been considered for admission on a nonquota basis. The consul, after all, had asked him about his professional qualifications, which indicated that Golomb was seeking entrance to the United States to pursue an academic career.

Golomb was cleared to leave by October 15, a month and a half before he was scheduled to be kicked out of Yugoslavia. His visa to the United States was valid, like all immigrant visas, for only four months. Golomb therefore had little time to spare. In addition to arranging passage through Switzerland and France and getting reservations on a boat from Le Havre to New York, he had to provide for his younger brother, who had come to live with him, and for his marriage to Dagmar. She would not be allowed to go with him when he left, but once Michael was in the United States, he intended to arrange her admission under the nonquota category of wife of a U.S. resident.

GOLOMB: What we first found out was that there was no civil marriage in Yugoslavia. Croatia allowed only two possibilities: marriage in a Catholic church or in a synagogue. Although we found both prospects distasteful, we chose the synagogue. So I went to Dr. Makso Pscherhof, the president of the Zagreb Jewish Congregation, whom I considered a friend, and alerted him to our intentions. He said he would speak with the rabbi, who would perform the ceremony. When I saw Pscherhof a few days later, he was visibly embarrassed. He told me that the rabbi had refused to perform a mixed marriage, Dagmar being a baptized Roman Catholic. He agreed to do so only if Dagmar were to convert to Judaism, a process that would take two years. The rabbi said that during the current period of danger for the Jewish people no Jewish soul must be lost.

Thus by default the only other avenue open to us was to get married in a Catholic church. We went to the diocese chancellery to announce our intention, but were told that Catholics also do not perform mixed marriages. However, the priest told us that we could try to obtain a special dispensation from the Vatican. Fortunately a brother-in-law of one of Dagmar's aunts was the bishop of Zagreb, and he wrote to the pope [then Pius XI] asking for permission and stressing the urgency of the situation. We "miraculously" received the dispensation in time for us to get married, just two weeks before I was scheduled to depart. The ceremony took place in the dingy vestry of St. Peter's Cathedral, not the church itself. The priest officiated with visible displeasure. On our marriage certificate is the number of the Vatican's special dispensation.

Golomb left Zagreb on March 3, 1939. The Comité d'assistance aux émigrants Juifs (Committee to aid Jewish emigration) purchased a ticket for him on the *Île de France.*

GOLOMB: I will always cherish the wonderful people who befriended me in Yugoslavia, and I will never forget the beauty of the country. I liked living in Zagreb and would not have minded settling there. The city had a fine opera, theater, a concert hall, and some good museums. There were excellent restaurants serving Viennese as well as Balkan cuisine. The local wines were quite good. I particularly liked the outdoor cafés, where you could drink your coffee and eat a dish of delicious ice cream and read European newspapers provided by the management. I liked sitting there and watching the *corso,* that Mediterranean custom in which masses of people of all ages stroll up and down window shopping, conversing, ogling, flirting, and kissing.

However, on balance, I must admit that the years I spent in Yugoslavia were the darkest period of my life. It was a time when I was at my creative peak and should have been successful in building a respectable professional career. Instead, I was being threatened with expulsion time after time, and I had to depend on the support of others for even the bare necessities of subsistence. Nor can I forget the harassment and the indignities that the Yugoslav state authorities made me suffer. My case was not unique. Yugoslavia did not grant asylum to a single Jewish refugee from Germany.[13] Many of its citizens, especially in the western provinces, were plainly sympathetic toward either Nazi Germany or fascist Italy. Croatia, under the rule of the quisling Ante Paveliă, actually became a willing satellite of Nazi Germany and carried out its own bloody massacres of Jews, Gypsies, Serbs, and other minorities.

Yugoslavia declared neutrality when war began in September 1939. The previous month, Croatia had been granted home rule, but the passion for complete independence had not diminished. Germany and Italy continued to be regarded as potential liberators. Thus Yugoslavia was as divided as ever as Hitler drew the country increasingly within the German economic and political orbit. In March 1941, the Germans invaded Greece. The following month, a group of Serbian nationalists seized power in Belgrade and tried to restore Yugoslavia's sovereignty. The Germans immediately sent in troops, and on April 17, Yugoslavia formally capitulated.

The Nazis partitioned the country. They recognized a "separate" independent state in Croatia, under Ante Paveliå, that lost no time in embarking on a crusade of ethnic and religious purification. Croatia was purged of its more than two million Serbs. The Jews were also marked for elimination. Most were put at the disposal of the Nazis, who sent them to the death camps. Only those Jews who had one Christian parent, were partners in a mixed marriage, or managed to flee were saved.

While you lived in Zagreb, what news did get about the family you had left behind in Munich?

GOLOMB: Life became progressively worse for my parents. They essentially lived on welfare from charity organizations of the local Jewish community. My younger sister had a job as an au pair for a wealthy Jewish family, so she could contribute. But finally in 1938 my parents and a younger brother were summarily deported to Poland. With the help of my sister we did manage to smuggle my nine-year-old brother to Yugoslavia. My sister had married a physician from Afghanistan and had an Afghan passport, which gave her some freedom to maneuver. She got my brother across the border by paying some Yugoslav woman to bring him over as her son.

Were your parents simply trucked to the border and pushed over?

GOLOMB: Right, on very short notice. And the Poles couldn't refuse to take them, because they were Polish citizens.

In their determination to create a *Judenrein* Reich, the Nazis decided to expel the 50,000 to 60,000 Jews of Polish nationality, many of whom, like the Golombs, had arrived before the First World War and had raised children who knew no other country than Germany. Immediately following the Munich Agreement, signed September 30, 1938, Berlin broached the subject to Warsaw. The Poles were not receptive and reacted by declaring that all Poles living outside the country were stateless unless they could obtain special authentication of their passports. This decree was to take effect on October 29, 1938.

On October 28, the day before the Polish decree would go into effect, the German police began rounding up Polish Jews. They roused them from their beds, picked them up off the streets, and arrested them in their places of congregation. Then they were hustled on trucks and trains and sent to the Polish frontier, near Posen.

The Poles, faced with the sudden arrival of almost 15,000 Jews on their frontier, refused them admission. Some Jews were allowed to go back home, but most were stranded. They could not enter Poland; they could not return to Germany. And more Jews continued to arrive. One batch of 10,000 Jews was simply herded across the border and abandoned in an open field.

The Poles finally gave way and began housing this mass of people in military camps, stables, vacant buildings—whatever was available. The Nazis continued their policy of forced deportation until most of Germany's Polish residents were gone. The Poles no longer gave Hitler any trouble. He bought them off by giving them a slice of Czechoslovakia—the district of Teschen, which had been awarded to the Czechs at the Paris Peace Conference in 1919. With this, the Poles became Hitler's accomplice.

The deportations also had important consequences for German Jews. The first bunch of forced deportations had contained the parents of Herschel Grynszpan, a stateless refugee living in Paris. Bent on revenge, the son went to the German legation at the Hôtel Beauharnais on November 7 and demanded to see the ambassador. He saw instead the embassy's third secretary, Ernst vom Rath, whom he shot dead. No sooner had propaganda minister Josef Goebbels in Berlin heard of the assassination than he ordered party and SA leaders throughout Germany to carry out an organized pogrom. The action had the approval of Hitler, who, when news came to him of vom Rath's death, had quipped that the "SA should be allowed to have a fling."[14]

Operation Kristallnacht began in the late hours of November 9 and lasted throughout the following day. Synagogues were burned and dynamited, Jewish businesses were plundered, and people were savagely attacked. In Berlin, mobs of demonstrators were let loose on the Jewish quarters to smash, loot, and maim at will. The city's seven large synagogues were torched while the police watched. Scenes of similar conflagration were repeated in Leipzig, Stuttgart, Freiburg, Heidelberg, Karlsruhe, and Frankfurt—in fact, in most of Germany's major cities that had not already experienced the destruction of their synagogues.[15]

Hitler left the details of the pogrom to his subordinates, especially to Goebbels and SS chief Heinrich Himmler, both of whom used it to seize control of Jewish policy. In the end, Himmler came out on top. Kristallnacht dramatized the danger, earlier experienced in the Boycott, of resorting to mob action to carry out policy. Therefore Himmler was able to convince Hitler that the "Jewish Question" needed to be handled in a systematic, controlled manner, and that the only agency capable of ensuring this was the SS.

Himmler rounded up some 20,000 Jewish men between the ages of sixteen and eighty and put them in concentration camps, primarily Dachau, Buchenwald, and Sachsenhausen, where he held them for ransom. As an additional insult, the entire Jewish community was fined one billion marks for having provoked the German people. Perhaps as many as 2,500 men, women, and children died as a result of the action, including several hundred who perished in detention. The other prisoners were ultimately released in batches, but not before turning over money or property to the state. After Kristallnacht, even the most optimistic *Deutschjuden* no longer needed to be convinced of the mortal danger of staying in Germany.

GOLOMB: My parents ended up in Lodz and were eventually put into the ghetto that the Germans created there. Before the war I got some letters from my father telling me about his fears for his family and the fate of the Jewish community there, but I never found out what eventually happened to my parents or other members of my family: my grandparents, my uncles, aunts, cousins—those close members of my family I had grown up with. They all perished, one way or another, probably before the end of 1942.

Shortly after the conquest of Poland in September 1939, the Germans created the first urban Jewish ghetto in Lodz, seventy-five miles southwest of Warsaw. By May 1940, this restricted area had been walled off from the rest of the city and soon became crammed with 160,000 Jews. Any Jew caught outside its confines could be shot on sight. Its cramped quarters, lack of food, and absence of sanitation and medical supplies led to a high death rate. During the first half of 1941, 5,000 people perished. But worse was to follow.

In 1942, 55,000 people from Lodz were transported to Chelmno, a secret killing center thirty-five miles to the northwest. Chelmno had no barracks or places of detention, and prisoners were exterminated the same day they arrived in gas vans. The corpses were then cremated. Those in the Lodz ghetto who managed to survive the selections continued working in its factories until they died of hunger and disease. In August 1944, 60,000 were finished off in the gas chambers at Auschwitz.

GOLOMB: When I crossed into Switzerland, a border guard examined my passport and my transit visa, and he began asking me all sorts of questions about my life and my parents. He wanted to find out if I might get off the train. He must not have believed me when I told him I was going to the United States because he stayed with me until we reached the French border. That's how it was in Switzerland.

Were there similar harassments in France?

GOLOMB: No. While I was in Paris I met a relative of my wife, who was a rather famous biologist at the Sorbonne. He showed me around. It was a very satisfying experience. I was on the threshold of a new life. I knew that there was going to be a war, although not on the scale it in fact became; and I knew that the only way the Nazis would be overthrown was if they were to lose. I didn't know what I was going to do in the United States. I didn't know if I could find a position. But I felt liberated from my misery in Yugoslavia and Europe, and I was optimistic.

You did not feel that your family was in danger of death?

GOLOMB: I did not suspect that their lives would be threatened; I felt that they certainly would become more and more economically deprived. I thought that eventually I would get established in my new homeland and that I could bring my wife and my younger brother over and possibly others of my relatives, especially my parents.

The Way the Wind Was Blowing: Walter Hirsch

"I had always wanted to go to America, it was my dream. I had read Karl May and I wanted to be a cowboy."

A Smooth Departure

In the election of March 5, 1933, the National Socialists captured about 30 percent of the popular vote in Württemberg. The result, although one of the lowest percentages in Germany, was impressive considering that four years before, the Nazi Party had only managed to get 1.9 percent. Storm Troopers now owned the streets. They shouted such chants as: "Blood must flow / Let's smash it up / Let's smash it up / That god-damned Jewish Republic."

WALTER HIRSCH: Stuttgart had quite a bit of Nazi agitation, but nothing like they had in Berlin. We had our book burnings. And I saw signs: "Don't buy from Jews." This left me with a sense of disgust that persecution of the Jews was starting over again.

You mean starting over in the historical sense, but certainly not in a personal sense.

HIRSCH: No, not in a personal sense. Not yet.

What about antisemitism in your school?

HIRSCH: On the whole the kids behaved pretty decently. I had been a member of the Wandervögel, who were not Jewish. But then when I saw which way the wind was blowing, I decided the Wandervögel wouldn't like Jews, so I joined the Ha-Shomer ha-Za'ir, which was trying to recruit young people to go to Palestine. I had not planned to go to Palestine, but I felt more at home with them than I did with the Wandervögel. That is where I got most of my Jewish education.

Did you feel good about that?

HIRSCH: I felt very much at home with them and had a sense of identity and identification, yes.

As the antisemitic tide was rising, did you sense increasing anxiety at home?

HIRSCH: No, because we could see the way out. We already had many members of the family living in the United States. My grandfather had gone there and became an American citizen in 1865. He had come back, but other members of the family had stayed. And my father had spent time in the United States and spoke English. His decision that it was no good to stay in Germany was reinforced by our American relatives telling him not to wait to come on over. I had always wanted to go to America, it was my dream. I had read Karl May[16] and I wanted to be a cowboy. Going there would be pretty much of a lark, and now I could see that I was going to get my wish.

Were you the only ones of your family that left at that early time?

HIRSCH: All my family except my father's cousin, Otto Hirsch, the head of the Reichsvertretung der Deutschen Juden, left.[17] He could have done so, but he decided to stay behind and wind up business for all the others first. So he didn't make it and his wife didn't make it. His father, though, got out.

T he Hirsches' family connections in America were immensely useful in helping them obtain the necessary visas. But also, Stuttgart had an understanding American consul in the person of Leon Dominion. At a time when Green Hackworth, the legal advisor to the State Department, was arguing that the mere fact that a Jew was being persecuted by the Nazis did not make him a desirable immigrant, Dominion cabled on August 17, 1933: "It is interesting to note that the Jewish applicants are uniformly of the better class, [including] many young professional men and sons of wealthy families"[18]—a dramatic contrast in attitude with his own State Department, whose advisors suspected that the German authorities were deliberately laundering the criminal records of potential Jewish immigrants.

Did coming to America constitute an enormous rupture?

HIRSCH: No, no, quite the contrary.

No Heimweh? *A sense that something had been taken from you?*

HIRSCH: No, it all went very smoothly.

What had being German meant for you?

HIRSCH: Well, I don't think I spent much time thinking about this when I was still living there. I didn't think about it until after I left.

You felt no sense of loss when you left Germany, no feeling you were giving something up?

HIRSCH: No, no.

Because of your association with the Zionist youth group, would it be fair to say that your Jewish identity was strengthened?

HIRSCH: Yes.

When you came to America, you felt, not religiously, but culturally more Jewish than before?

HIRSCH: That's right.

The Hirsches arrived in the United States on the Hamburg-Amerika Line in December 1933. They came at a time when the Nazi authorities still allowed Jews to take out a moderate amount of their wealth. However, this generosity changed rapidly. At the beginning of the Nazi regime Jews could leave with 25,000 marks (about $10,000) per person, but by October 1934 this had been reduced to a mere 10 marks per person. Thus many Jews who could not somehow circumvent the law or could not gain sponsorship found it impossible to avoid exclusion under the "public charge" restriction of American immigration law.

The Difficulties of Leaving: Solomon Gartenhaus

"It would be like a parent telling a child that he had to change jobs."

A Train to Amsterdam

Stung by the criticism that American consuls were not carrying out the visa work in a fair and impartial manner and that the consuls were operating as if it were their duty to keep the number of immigrants to a minimum, the U.S. State Department issued new instructions (January 12, 1937) making "probability" rather than "possibility" the standard by which a determination of acceptability under the public charge clause be made. The change increased the total of German immigrants in 1937 to 11,536, or 4,894 more than during the previous year—a more than 40 percent rise. The new liberalization policy helped families like the Gartenhauses, but the number of individual visas issued for 1937 still fell shy of the overall permissible German quota by 14,464 visas.

SOL GARTENHAUS: One day as I was walking through the middle of the Königsberg district I saw signs in a department store window which said "Juden sind verboten Eintritt (Jews not permitted to enter)." That put me on such guard that later, when I was on an errand downtown and a policeman stopped me, I simply froze. I was just a little kid, you know, skipping happily along. And all he said was, "You shouldn't jump like that. You're liable to fall down and hurt yourself." But he had scared the daylights out of me. So I knew! I had been warned to be very careful.

And sometime in 1935 my father got a telephone call around 3:00 o'clock in the morning. The caller told him that somebody at the police station warned him that my father should "get out of town quickly." So my father hastily dressed and disappeared. An hour or so later, there was a heavy knock on the door, and some Brown Shirts said they were looking for my father. My mother told them that he was away on a business trip, and that was the end of that.

It turned out that a half a dozen other Jewish shopkeepers and small businessmen were arrested that night and taken off to jail. They were beaten up, but after two days or so, they were let go. It was fortunate that my father had been friendly with the people in the community, with non-Jews as well as Jews, and someone on the police force warned him to get away. Such consideration was rather remarkable considering the period in which we were living.

Were there any indications in school that your lives were changing?

GARTENHAUS: In school, things seemed normal. Politics of the day were not discussed.

Did you notice any change in the way your family now acted socially?

GARTENHAUS: My parents interacted mainly with the Jewish community. But I didn't sense they interacted differently with the Gentiles in the building where we lived. Once, a couple of Brown Shirts came to my father's clothing store, bought two suits, and then refused to pay. So my father went to the police and complained. These two guys were taken in; they had to pay and apologize. This also happened in 1935.

In this situation your father didn't seem to maintain a low profile.

GARTENHAUS: I think Dad was afraid that if he allowed this to happen, people would come in and just take his merchandise, and there was no way then that we could survive.

Was there any increased hostility toward you among the children you played with on the street?

GARTENHAUS: I was kind of tolerated, but no longer part of the group.

Did this bother you?

GARTENHAUS: A little bit, but you know, I had been prepared for this by my parents. As I said, I had been inculcated with the idea that there's *rischus* (malice) out there, and I was aware that Jews were different because of it.

For somebody your age it became a sort of a normal thing, the "change" was not perceived as being specifically Nazi? It was, in other words, what you expected?

GARTENHAUS: Yes. Since the age of four, I had been told to watch my step. Another thing: we were kosher, and you couldn't get kosher meat in Germany at this time. Luckily, there was a guy from Holland, a business associate of my father, who would come periodically and smuggle kosher meat to us. Otherwise we would not have had any.

When did getting out of Germany become serious business?

GARTENHAUS: We had relatives in the United States. My mother was one of seven children, and all her siblings had already immigrated to the United States. Two of my uncles, who went in the 1920s, had become wealthy businessmen in Washington, D.C., and brought the rest of the family over, all except for my mother and father. My father's business was good, even in 1935, and he had little desire to suddenly leave and abandon all he had built up. Leaving, to cross the ocean in a boat to start a new life, was not a trivial task. Not something to be taken lightly.

What my uncle Willie did, thank God, was send his wife, Irma, to Germany in 1935 to talk my parents into leaving. And luckily she succeeded.

Then your American relatives were more apprehensive about what was happening in Germany than your own parents?

GARTENHAUS: I think so. They sensed that things were becoming bad in Germany and in Europe in general. And my aunt convinced my father to leave.

Michael Rossmann and his mother.

Michael Rossmann playing outside
the apartment building where he
lived with his mother and maternal
grandparents.

Michael Golomb's residency permits to live in Zagreb
in 1938. Note the frequent renewals.

Did your mother have any opinions of her own on this subject?

GARTENHAUS: In our Orthodox home my mother was required to be subservient to her husband in all things or, at least, pretend.

And did she pretend?

GARTENHAUS: I don't know. I have no idea how the decisions were arrived at.

You weren't very close to your father?

GARTENHAUS: No. My main interaction was his teaching me how to read Hebrew.

How did he tell you and the other children that you were leaving Germany?

GARTENHAUS: He just told us that we were going to try to go to America.

When did you leave?

GARTENHAUS: In May 1937. From the time of my aunt Irma's visit in 1935, it took two years to get all the papers processed. Getting to the United States was not easy. You had to have an affidavit from someone who would guarantee your support. And we had to start collecting our documents and make all sorts of trips to Stuttgart, the nearest American consulate.

Did your father sell his business?

GARTENHAUS: I do not think he ever sold the business; he just gave it up. My parents never went in for getting compensation after the war. They didn't want to have anything to do with that.

Government bureaucrats had to approve the "sale" of each Jewish business to a non-Jewish buyer, such permission being given only if the business was to be sold for a fraction of its worth. Until November, such "Ayranizations" were deemed voluntary because they were supposedly made between equal partners. Jews could always refuse to sell, but time was hardly on their side.

Another fate of Jewish enterprises was simple liquidation, especially for those small businesses, like the Gartenhaus clothing store. However, before he went into exile, Sol's father sold off most of the store's merchandise—at a discount—and he managed to smuggle this money, plus other savings, out of the country.

He did this by giving a Dutch business associate, the same man who brought the Gartenhaus family kosher food, the cash equivalent of ten thousand American dollars (probably at least ten times that sum in today's values), telling him to hold on to it until the family arrived in the Netherlands on its way to the United States. Emigrants, as noted, could take abroad no more than 10 marks each—a sixty mark total in the Gartenhaus family, a sum duly noted by the Nazi authorities in the mother's passport (stamped, dated, signed on May 10, 1937, the day before the family left for Holland). Had the father's violation of the Nazi currency restrictions been discovered, he certainly would have been arrested and the rest of his family placed in jeopardy. When the Gartenhauses came through Holland, the money was waiting for them and became the principal source of their support when they arrived in the United States on board the *Statendam*.[19]

The dislocation sounds painless as far as you kids were concerned. When your parents told you that you were going to go to America, what was the reaction?

GARTENHAUS: If you look at in contemporary terms, it would be like a parent telling a child that he had to change jobs and now the family was going to live in Cleveland.

Did you still feel German in any meaningful sense? Would the term "das Vaterland" mean anything?

GARTENHAUS: It wasn't an emotional thing. I knew I was a German, but probably less than what it means for an eight-year-old kid to be an American. Unless there is a lot of propaganda about patriotism, it doesn't mean very much. The major concerns of someone that age are with his parents, his relatives, and his friends.

You didn't feel that you were being torn from your Heimat?

GARTENHAUS: Of course not. But I had a hint of such feelings forty years later when I returned to Kassel and wandered around the city, remembering things. So there must have been some emotional tie that I was unaware of at the time.

How about your parents?

GARTENHAUS: They wanted nothing to do with Germany. Neither did my brothers and sisters.

Did your parents prepare you for living in a different culture? Did you realize that you'd have to learn another language?

GARTENHAUS: I didn't consider that. I had heard that in the United States the streets were paved in gold. That's the first thing I looked for, and it wasn't true. I don't know where I got that notion.

We packed two enormous wooden boxes. I can't imagine how big they were, but bigger than I was tall, and large enough to hold some of our possessions. I had gotten an Erector set for my sixth birthday, and I carefully put it in one of those boxes. And when we came to the United States I discovered that someone had broken in and the Erector set was missing. That was crushing for me.

Anyway, we finished packing, and somebody took the boxes away. We left on the train for Amsterdam on May 11, 1937.

The Gartenhauses came to the United States under the Polish quota. Of the 6,524 allowable, only 1,212 Polish visas were issued that year. They crossed the Dutch border at Enschede, the entrance stamp specifying that they were allowed to enter the country only for transit purposes. The family, including the four children and the father, traveled on the mother's visa (issued in Frankfurt on August 10, 1934, renewed April 10, 1936). The Polish consulate general in Frankfurt had put a special stamp on the passport attesting to the fact that Przeworsk had been established as Jacob Gartenhaus's place of birth. The American consulate at Stuttgart added the six immigration identification cards permitting entry into the United States. These stamps would become their certificates of permanent residence.

GARTENHAUS: At that time, a lot of people were trying to get out. I went around to visit all my Jewish friends and several gave me a bar of chocolate. I had the sense they were envious of our being able to leave.

In 1933, 2,300 Jews lived in Kassel, comprising a mere 1.31 percent of the population. Since all the records of emigration and deportation were destroyed, it is impossible to tell how many of these managed to escape. During Kristallnacht (November 9, 1938) both the main and the Orthodox synagogues of Kassel were burned.

Not until 1965 was there to be another such structure, built with municipal aid for a community of about one hundred. In 1946 only about two hundred Jews lived in Kassel, most of these displaced persons.

Did your father later talk much about these events?

GARTENHAUS: He never talked about most things in his life. I'm sure he realized what a lucky escape we had, even though he ascribed it to the will of God.

The Nazi Flag in Wrong Colors: Fritz Cohen

"This feeling that you were no longer worthy of the village was an interesting phenomenon because after a while you knew you were not wanted there and you began to think of yourself as not belonging."

No More Sunday Walks

Ronnenberg had no Gymnasium, so those wanting a high-school education had to go elsewhere. Cohen's father sent Fritz to the Humboltschule, located in one of Hannover's industrial suburbs, the same school he himself had attended. It took Fritz about an hour to make the trip—half an hour by train, half an hour on foot from the station. The other boys from Ronnenberg who made the same trip refused to talk to him or sit near him. Other than one older student, whom he never met, Cohen was the only Jewish kid in the school.

The first few months after he started school were relatively peaceful, despite the fact that most of the other boys in his class were members of the Hitler Youth and occasionally appeared in class in their uniforms. However, some of the more enthusiastic members of the group, eager to put Nazi racial beliefs into practice, soon singled out Fritz as "the Jew" and called him names. This abuse soon escalated into physical mistreatment. The homeroom teacher was a member of the SS and sometimes wore his uniform to class.

FRITZ COHEN: Suddenly in Ronnenberg the thing to do was to become a Storm Trooper, and a local group was organized. A few of these men had already been Storm Troopers in Hannover, but now dozens joined their ranks. They assembled very close to our house in a large open area in front of the *Gasthaus*. The younger groups, the Hitler Jugend and Pimpfe, the girls' organizations, had demonstrations there as well. We could see them from our doorstep, numerically small gatherings at first but becoming larger. Across the street from our house was also a box displaying *Der Stürmer* [the virulently antisemitic newspaper of Jules Streicher]. I don't know that we suspected that any of this would lead to the end of our existence in Ronnenberg.

What happened to you during the Boycott?

COHEN: We closed the store and rolled down the wooden blinds. I remember that the leaders of the Jewish community in Hannover sent messages advising Jews to stay in their houses and close their shutters.

Were there any antisemitic signs in windows?

COHEN: No signs, the Storm Troopers walked up and down outside our store to prevent anyone from coming in. They must have come from out of town, because I recognized none of them.

Was your father's business the only Jewish business in town?

COHEN: No, a couple of our cousins had butcher shops, and their shops were also closed on that day. The Boycott was an event that was very disturbing to us, although we were not then threatened physically. This was still a period where all this was very new. The one thing that immediately set me and my cousins apart was that we could not join the Hitler Youth. Also, my older cousins who were of draft age found out that they would not be allowed to join the army.

What about the reaction of your parents and your other relatives?

COHEN: There was more anxiety than panic. They tried to reassure one another that this government couldn't possibly last.

Some of our non-Jewish friends even told us that the French and British would step in and put a halt to this, that we really had nothing to worry about, since we were respected citizens of the town. But as time progressed and developments became more antisemitically hostile, these notions became increasingly unconvincing, and you heard them less and less. We then identified certain local people who were becoming fanatical Nazis and who might report anything that we did to the authorities.

I was even excluded from some of the conversations that my father had with his cousins in our house because they feared that I might repeat them to others. People talked about those who just emigrated to Brazil, or some other place either in South or North America. And our family members started looking around for a place to which they also could go.

How did the atmosphere change between you and your school friends?

COHEN: In school nothing changed that drastically, other than some of my contemporaries were now members of the Hitler Youth, wore uniforms, and marched on weekends. I was affected by this sense of exclusion.

These children in their uniforms were, of course, being indoctrinated into antisemitism. How did they express this toward you?

COHEN: It did not become a personal matter until after the Nürnberg Laws. Then we could no longer employ maids who were not Jewish in our household. We got around that by hiring someone who was Austrian. I don't recall the details, but she had been in the household of one of our cousins and then came over to our house. In the business, though, we still managed to employ non-Jewish people.

Even women?

COHEN: Even women. We had a young lady from a nearby town who came on her bicycle every morning, and she was able to work in our store. Ultimately, of course, she had to leave. But that was not until about 1938.

Aside from that, did the business continue along the same lines as before?

COHEN: There was a loss of customers because people were discouraged from buying in our store. Another store opened up, smaller than ours, but owned and operated by a Nazi. It offered the same goods as our store, and my parents suspected that the Nazi Party had financed it.

When did things begin to get really nasty?

COHEN: For me, it was in May 1935, when I was sent to the school in Hannover. Herr Härtl, my homeroom teacher, had been in the German army in the First World War. He had been taken as a prisoner to England — that's where he learned English — and had been a member of a dueling fraternity. He had these *Schmisse,* scars, on his face. All very Prussian. He joined the SS because that was the thoroughly and properly authoritarian thing to do. We called it *stramm —* strict, military. He would come into the classroom and the first thing always was "Heil Hitler."

Incidentally, this "Heil Hitler" was said with varying degrees of enthusiasm depending on the teacher. You could always detect when a classroom teacher came and said this from the bottom of his heart. But we had a German composition teacher who was less than enthusiastic. He would come in and give a pro forma "Heil Hitler." You could tell he was neither a member of the party, nor did he care to be.

When the teachers saluted, did the class salute back?

COHEN: Of course, we always got up and also said, "Heil Hitler." In every classroom, in every change of the day, the first time the teacher would come into the classroom, the greeting was "Heil Hitler," and we responded, "Heil Hitler." If you had the same teacher twice, you wouldn't do it again. But always the first time.

Did Härtl take it out on you in class?

COHEN: Actually no, he did not tolerate any harassment in class. He knew about it, but he didn't tolerate it in class. I visited him after the war, and his wife explained to me that when it came time to serve, he refused to become a concentration camp guard. So he was given a job as an escort for supply columns that went to Russia. But since he was a member of a "criminal organization," he was tried as a war criminal, and he spent time in jail. What I found interesting was that he was not forced to become a camp guard. You became one only if you wanted to. He didn't advance his career, but he was not punished.

There were other teachers in that school who were also party members. The young teacher who taught art was a fanatic SS man. Art was a subject that I was miserable at, and I committed the unpardonable sin of coloring a Nazi flag brown instead of red. Terrible. And the art teacher thoroughly berated me for it. I had done the unforgivable.

Knowing the intense feeling of young people to belong, did you have any desire to be part of this Nazi movement?

COHEN: Well, I suspect that very early, that is, in 1933, I would have joined if I could have. I really didn't understand to what extent the Nazi ideology excluded me on racial grounds. This I understood later, but in the beginning if I could have, I quite honestly would have.

When did you sense that the "honeymoon period" was over?

COHEN: I noticed that at summer camp. The school had a facility in the woods outside Hannover, and we were sent there for a week's vacation. Only a good deal of time was spent in indoctrination of ultranationalist Nazi ideology. We did a lot of marching and mock fighting with people wearing armbands to distinguish between different groups. It had military overtones intended to make us more receptive later on to what would be expected of a young man.

Did any racist ideology creep into this instruction?

COHEN: Not in the lectures and discussions, but I detected that several of my classmates who were enthusiastic Nazis were avoiding me and were telling others to do the same. This was accomplished through body language, through looks, by saying things behind my back; some of these remarks were told to me by a person who was then still a friend and was very offended. Later on, though, he became one of them. Continuing to associate with me was no longer profitable or useful.

What was the nature of the verbal harassment?

COHEN: The verbal harassments were taken from the text of songs that were sung by the Hitler Youth and Storm Troopers. An epithet would usually be prefaced by "you" followed with a slur. They were not terribly inventive, simple name-calling easily put together. The official propaganda depicted the Jews as an element foreign to the German *Volk*. It compared them to a virus that threatened the German people with disease, an alien body that must be excised.

Not German and not human?

COHEN: "Not human" was the critical point. Not only were we held not to share the same traditions, the same interests, the same values, but also we were vermin who didn't have the right to live.

That already in 1935?

COHEN: Oh, yes. Oh, yes, oh, yes.

Was this being taught in the classroom?

COHEN: No, not in school. But the coursework created the intellectual foundations for that sort of slander nonetheless. For example, one of the focal points in our history course was the "Jewish menace." Our maps showed the centers of Jewish population from Roman until contemporary times with captions always pointing out the spread of the Jewish contagion.

The Nazis promoted this in the popular culture through its declarations, its publication of *Der Stürmer,* the Nürnberg Laws, the songs, and popular entertainment, all showing the Jews to be subhuman.

When did the verbal harassment become physical?

COHEN: It occurred during class breaks, and especially at noon, when we had our lunch—everybody brought his own lunch and ate it out in the courtyard. Some bullies would then feel perfectly free and at ease to assault me physically. Not in a major way, but, you know, tripping and punching. I dreaded the lunch period.

Nobody came to your help?

COHEN: In all fairness, not everybody had the same degree of acceptance. There were some young fellows whom I considered decent people who were by no means interested in making life miserable for me, and they never participated in any attacks against me. One fellow, one of the very few, would even tell the others to lay off. This boy was very popular with the other students, an excellent athlete, a first-class student, well-built, very strong, already a ladies' man, definitely not an outsider, an amateur boxer. Everyone in a sense idolized him and wanted to be like him. But rarely did any others ever say, "Now enough; leave the guy alone."

I looked that person up after the war. In 1952, we were in Germany, and I visited Hannover. I remembered his name and that his parents had a butcher shop, so it was not very difficult to find him. We went to that place, and when I saw the lady behind the counter, I knew she was his mother, and I asked her if this was the Schoen family. She asked me why, and when I said I'm looking for Friedl Schoen, she looked at me as though she'd seen a ghost. She asked me to come to the back of the shop and then asked me if I knew him. I told her, and she explained to me that he had vanished, that he had been taken prisoner in Russia, and they had never seen him again.

Did you ever complain about the abuse?

COHEN: I did at home, and my father, who usually was not particularly sympathetic to much of anything that I felt, took it seriously enough that he went to see the rector of our school during my second year. My father relayed what I had said, and the rector, his name was Wolf, came to visit the class. I was called out, and he told me in a very warm sympathetic voice to wait in his office. I remember he used the diminutive "Mein jungkin." And he read the riot act to the other students. He was a man who could afford to do that. He was a World War I veteran, had lost a leg in the war, and was a personification of Prussianism, absolutely correct in every way. No one was going to question his patriotism or his qualifications. He did not for a single moment sympathize with what was happening to me. It was calm for a few days, only a few days, and slowly things started up again.

Did such a stressful situation affect your grades?

COHEN: They were okay to begin with, but then they tailed off drastically. I simply wasn't able to concentrate. Except for that one brief truce because of the rector, never a day passed without some harassment. It was really torture. When a question was asked in class, I didn't feel I could or should answer. I totally and completely shrank away from all participation.

Did you feel more protected in Ronnenberg than you did in Hannover?

COHEN: We did not move about as freely as we used to. It became more and more unpleasant to go here and there. This feeling that you were no longer worthy of the village was an interesting phenomenon, because after a while you knew you were not wanted there, and you began to think of yourself as not belonging. Such thoughts were enough to discourage you from just taking a walk in the village, or taking the Sunday afternoon walk to a stretch of woods outside the village where you had coffee in a restaurant.

The Sunday afternoon walk is a tradition with the Germans, but after 1935, we didn't do it anymore. It was obvious that some of our neighbors had decided that we really were undesirables. Other people, who were more bystanders than accomplices, probably never agreed with that, but they did not feel that it was advantageous to show any kind of cordiality toward us. It had come that far.

And it was embarrassing for them to see you and for you to see them because you had known them, so you stayed away?

COHEN: People fit into that anti-Jewish mind-set, whether they wanted to or not. My father, for example, avoided going to the inn, which was only across the street. There was a large hall in back run by the *Turnverein,* but my father was no longer allowed to be a member. And my mother, who used to participate in an organization that did philanthropic work, also lost her membership. Somebody in the organization probably said, "I'm sorry, but we cannot allow you to come anymore."

My parents belonged to a group that had tickets to the opera in Hannover, and that stopped too. It was also difficult and unpleasant to go out to eat in Hannover; in the village there weren't any incidents, but in Hannover it became difficult because many of the restaurants started carrying signs, "Jews not allowed." All those things. We became more and more isolated.

Once, when I was sitting with my father in Cafe Kräpcke waiting for my mother, I suddenly noticed a young boy and his mother a table or two away. He was pointing a finger at us, and I could hear him say "Juden? sind das Juden?" And she answered, "Yes, they're Jews." The Cafe Kräpcke is probably Hannover's best-known, most popular café, and it's still there incidentally, right near the train station.

Were you by then wearing Stars of David?

COHEN: No, but somehow or other, they identified us. That was a terrible moment, more so for my father than for me. That is readily understandable. That was the last time he went there. I went to a Rotary meeting last May at the Cafe Kräpcke, and it was the first time I'd been there since that incident.

Could you use the pharmacies in your town? Because that prohibition also became part of the Nürnberg Laws.

COHEN: Oh, yes. Living in that small town made us part of the scene. We were not Johnny-come-latelies. And despite the fact that the pharmacist was, I believe, an enthusiastic Nazi—I remember that quite well—we were able to get prescriptions filled.

And were you able to use "Aryan" doctors?

COHEN: We already were going to a Jewish doctor, a neighbor. And in case of special needs, there was a physician in Hannover.

You never had an occasion to use a hospital?

COHEN: My grandmother did. It was a Jewish hospital in Hannover. She went there when she had some surgery.

Did you feel your personal security was endangered?

COHEN: We tried not to get into a situation where we would violate a law or need the protection of the law. I remember there was one incident:

We had a very large garden around two sides of our house, it was really quite a large yard, and ordinarily a maid and my grandma worked the garden, planted, weeded, and so forth. I remember we had planted peas, and the birds liked the seeds, and they would try to pick them out of the ground. My grandmother told the maid to get some materials in the attic that could be used to cover the ground to keep the birds at bay. Well, what the maid had done was to tear up an old flag, the black, white, and red imperial flag, to cover the seeds.

Walter Hirsch

Michael Golomb with his
fiancée, Dagmar, in Zagreb,
February 19, 1939.

The Gartenhaus family
store in Kassel.

As it happened, on the second floor of the next house over lived a family named Schwartz. The husband, an insurance broker who worked in Hannover, was an enthusiastic Nazi, and he could see the flag from the window overlooking our garden. He therefore called the police, denouncing us for desecrating the flag.

The local policeman, a nice old gentleman who had been a customer at my father's store, came over on his bicycle to talk with my father. He explained the complaint and told him to please remove the flag right away. He assured him he would make no official report. That was an advantage of living in a small town and having been an honored and honorable citizen. It was a very dicey situation and could have easily caused an arrest or heaven knows what. But the slow change of attitude on the part of those who were our neighbors was devastating.

I think there were two kinds of Holocausts: the physical one and the emotional and psychological one. The psychological devastation was terrible. It was one of the most wretched periods of my life, and I think I've lived with it ever since.

An Address in Zanesville

After suffering for two years at the hands of his fellow students in the Gymnasium in Hannover, Cohen was sent to a private school in Florence, Italy, run by German Jews. A cousin for whom school life had also become impossible attended the same institution. While Fritz was there, his parents made plans to leave Germany, following family members who had already emigrated. Two young sons from one of the other families had set the pattern by going to South America.

Late in 1936, Fritz's mother searched for sponsors in other countries, particularly in the United States. She had found the name of Siegelbaum in an old family Bible. Nobody knew how the name had got there or whether the people mentioned were even blood relatives, but the name had an address in Zanesville, Ohio. She therefore wrote a letter of inquiry addressed to the Zanesville city hall.

Instead of throwing the letter in the trash, a municipal official answered, telling her that a Siegelbaum family had indeed once lived in Zanesville, but it had since moved to Sedelia, Missouri. So Fritz's mother wrote to the Sedelia city hall, and again she got an answer with a similar message: the Siegelbaum family had once lived there but had moved, this time to Kansas City, Kansas. There was a third letter of inquiry, and again a reply. This time it contained an address. She wrote to the people at this address, telling them that she thought they were related. They answered; there was further correspondence.

In the end the Siegelbaums agreed to sign an affidavit, stating they were willing to guarantee the refugees' needs until they were able to support themselves. With such a document the Cohens could now apply for a visa at the American consulate in Hamburg.

Until they had received this letter from Germany, the Siegelbaums had no idea of the Cohens' existence. But to them proof of a blood relationship did not matter. The two Siegelbaum sisters who were willing to sign the important affidavit simply wanted to help people in need.

COHEN: One day in June 1938, I received a letter from my father that I should come home because we had to get physical examinations to go to the United States. He also told me not to let the border police take my passport. That's the first time I heard about plans to leave Germany.

Shortly after I came home, we went to Bremen for our physicals and were given the visas. My grandmother could not go, she had had a fall and broken a hip, so, being physically handicapped she could not get a visa and had to stay behind. My aunt, her daughter, stayed with her. They ultimately went to a *Judenhaus* (Jewish hostel) in Ahlen that eventually became a Gestapo holding station for deportation to a concentration camp.

Had your father's dry goods business already been liquidated?

COHEN: Not yet. But it was as good as dead. The Nazis arranged for a buyer and the buyer paid the proceeds to the state.

The Nazi drive to eliminate Jewish participation in the German economy with the liquidation of all Jewish-owned enterprises or their "voluntary" sale to Aryans created a huge buyer's market. German banks specialized in such transactions and made a fortune in commissions. During the first five years, Aryanization of small family businesses was accomplished without much direct government intervention. However, the longer a Jewish owner waited, the more disadvantageous it became.

In April 1938, the economics ministry required that all property sales receive official approval, something that was not given unless the price was at least one-fourth less than the current market value — already artificially low due to the overabundance of sellers. In July 1938, real estate took a further tumble in price when the state decreed that all Jewish business activity cease by the end of the year. After that all Jewish commercial enterprises still in existence or unsold would be confiscated without compensation. The Nazi government subsequently applied the law to all real estate and land, plus stocks, bonds, and other securities.

Thus confiscation helped speed your departure?

COHEN: Yes. You could not take a thing with you except clothes and some personal items. While we were packing, an official from the emigration office came to our house, sat in the room where the trunks were, watched every piece that was put into it, and then sealed it.

Did he check the clothes to see if there was any jewelry in the pockets?

COHEN: He was a nice gentleman; he never asked to see anything. I don't think the trunks were opened once they were sealed. The suitcases we took with us — one for each of us — were of course opened at the border station and examined. We were allowed to take with us the grand total of thirty marks. But all the transportation had been paid for ahead of time. In addition, my mother already managed to get two or three Leica cameras, a pair of field glasses, and some money to our relatives in Holland.

We crossed the border into the Netherlands and met our relatives in Rotterdam. I recall that my father told them that as soon as he had a job in the United States, he would sign an affidavit for them. Well, my uncle thought this was totally unnecessary, because as long as Queen Wilhelmina was alive, nothing would ever happen to them. They were absolutely convinced that they would be safe.

We exchanged letters with them before the start of the war, but after 1940 we never heard from them again. They totally disappeared. We know it wasn't only the Germans who were responsible. There were segments of the Dutch population who were only too eager help the Nazis find the Jews and send them on their way. It's not a very nice chapter in the history of the Netherlands, but it happened.

The Cohens left Rotterdam for Paris, where they stayed for a few days before taking a train to Le Havre to board the *President Theodore Roosevelt*.[20] The trip to New York took ten days.

COHEN: For me, boarding that old tub was a relief from all the tensions and pressures. There was an adjustment for me that would come when I arrived in this country. I wish I had some insight into what my parents felt. They never let me know.

On the ship there were a lot of new things, activities, kids my own age to talk to. By and large it was very pleasant. We arrived in New York, on Friday, August 13 [1938], a hot summer day. And we all wore clothes that you wear in Europe in the summertime, which are awfully warm, far too heavy for the climate over here. So there was a lot of discomfort, a lot of sweating, a lot of waiting on the dock to have your trunks inspected, going through customs, et cetera. Then we had to go to some sort of office near the docks and pick up our railway tickets from New York to Kansas City.

We left immediately, spending a very uncomfortable night on the train, and arrived in Kansas City the next day in late afternoon. One of our two "cousins" who signed the paper was waiting at the station, and she picked us out immediately by looking at our clothes. I remember her saying, "I'm so glad that you're here." It didn't matter whether or not we were related. She had a Chevrolet, which I thought was huge, bigger than the German automobiles, and we drove to where she and her half sister and the latter's husband lived in Kansas City, Kansas.

Their house was nice but simple and not large, with three bedrooms. We lived there about a month. I slept downstairs in the living room on a cot. It wasn't all that easy—suddenly three people coming into the house added to the cost of a household. But the people were very pleasant, and the important thing was that we were in America and we were safe.

The Coldest Winter in a Hundred Years: Joseph Haberer

"My parents saw which way the wind was blowing, and they decided very quickly to get me out of Germany into a better situation."

The Kindertransport

On November 11, 1938, the day after the Kristallnacht, Haberer came to school and found everybody pointing their fingers at him. He was then told to leave. Many Jewish children had already dropped out of the public school system, even before being officially kicked out. Some, like Fritz Cohen, continued their educations abroad, while others enrolled in newly created Jewish schools, many of which were staffed with teachers who had been previously discharged. Jewish Councils helped establish these schools and facilitate their staffing.

Ironically, many sons and daughters of assimilated Jews, before attending these special schools, had had little exposure to the tenets of Judaism. Many who had previously celebrated Christian holidays, putting up Christmas trees and hunting Easter eggs, now began lighting Hanukkah candles and learning about Purim.

Your whole way of life collapsed when you were thrown out of school. But maybe being picked on was the lesser of the two evils? At least when you're being picked on, you're the center of attention. Do you think that's too perverse a way of putting it?

JOSEPH HABERER: No, because if you're being punished, that means you amount to something, whereas if you're not being punished, then you're nothing. When my mother would punish me, it would sometimes seem as if I wanted to be punished. Because that was the way I would get recognition. She would spank me, and I'd think, well, at least she must care something about me. Now I was out of school and alone. In Villingen there were no other Jewish children, and therefore there was no Jewish school. It was not practical to send me to another Jewish community.

Either my parents would have had to move to a town with a larger Jewish population where there were Jewish schools, or they would have had to send me to a Jewish boarding school. Neither alternative was feasible because of our impoverishment. Besides, my parents had already decided that there was no future for Jews in Germany.

My parents had seen which way the wind was blowing, and they resolved to get me out of Germany as soon as possible and into a better situation. My father apparently had connections with the Jewish Council, and within less than two weeks he was able to arrange for me to be sent to England.

Until 1938, German and Austrian citizens could enter Great Britain without a visa, providing they could support themselves and were not looking for work. When Hitler came to power, various Jewish community organizations helped meet this "requirement of maintenance." The British had seldom attached limitations on how long exiles could stay in their country. However, the threat of a mass exodus of refugees from Nazi Germany changed that. The government tightened controls, making entry into Britain more difficult. The immigrant now had to prove acceptability by presenting his or her case to a passport control officer attached to an embassy or consulate. Long stays were discouraged. Britain was willing to serve only as a way station until permanent residence could be found elsewhere.[21]

Immediately after Kristallnacht, the British Council for German Jewry petitioned the Tory government to allow Jewish refugee children under eighteen years of age into the country without their parents. They would receive schooling and eventually be resettled in another country. The Council pledged that Jewish organizations would underwrite the expense so as to not put a drain on the public treasury. Viscount Herbert Samuel, the Council's spokesman, urged that British consulates in Germany be assigned extra personnel to expedite the applications.

The British government moved with surprising speed. In less than two weeks, the House of Commons passed a bill granting Jewish refugee children temporary asylum, and the Home Office began streamlining its procedures. It lifted passport and visa requirements, substituting instead a single-form application. Thus the first *Kindertransport* was born.

In Germany, the Central Committee of German Jews for Relief and Rehabilitation (Zentralauschuss der Deutschen Juden für Hilfe und Aufbau) pushed various local Jewish Councils to take advantage of the new British legislation. On December 1, 1938, the first contingent of two hundred Jewish children left Berlin, and they arrived in Harwich, England, two days later.

More evacuations followed and continued until September 1939, right up to the outbreak of the war. In nine months of operation the *Kindertransport* brought over 10,000 Jewish boys and girls between the ages of five and seventeen to England. Most of these came from Germany. On the day they left, many of these children, like Joseph Haberer, saw their parents for the last time.[22]

HABERER: My father took me on the train to the boat at Hamburg. On the way he tried to explain why they were sending me away. It was a big moment, a very emotional moment for him. But it didn't come across that way because he had always been so reticent and withdrawn. I'm not sitting in judgment. He was not glum without reason. But even before the Hitler thing, the Seckles family and Haberer family were very repressed people. And that repression had its repercussions in making me question what was wrong with myself. It made me ask,

"Why were these all these things happening to me? Was it because my parents didn't love me enough?"

Did you feel that when your father announced to you that you were leaving that he was trying to get rid of you?

HABERER: Perhaps. Although because I was no longer going to school, I could believe that they were sending me away so I could get an education. I knew something extraordinary was taking place and that my father was very concerned. At a conscious level I doubt that I thought my parents wanted to get rid of me, but who knows how the unconscious interpreted these events?

Your parents certainly felt that the situation in Germany was dangerous enough to send their only child out of the country. How much of this fear did they communicate to you?

HABERER: I think my father was trying to explain this to me, but I was not in very good shape because everything was very traumatic. All the harassment, being kicked out of school, all these changes. Everything was buzzing, and I didn't know what was happening.

Did you think that maybe you deserved to be picked on? That maybe the Jews really were bad? Maybe the Jews really were inferior?

HABERER: Probably this went on, at least, on a subconscious level.

If your parents saw which way the wind was blowing, why didn't they start making preparations to leave themselves?

HABERER: They did. They were working on getting an affidavit. But they weren't able to assemble the necessary documentation. It seems that some of their records were lost during the burning and looting that was going on during Kristallnacht. It wasn't as though they wanted to stay in Germany. But, like so many others, they couldn't obtain an affidavit.

The *Kindertransport* had been assembled with much haste and confusion. British groups interested in refugee children formed the Movement for the Care of Children from Germany, which provided a central organization for a hundred or so scattered local committees that were finding places for the refugees to stay. The movement also agreed to provide the children with financial support until they reached maturity. Since government money was scarce, private donations were crucial.

Stanley Baldwin launched his Lord Baldwin Fund for Refugees. The Home Office gave the scheme its blessing but admonished the former prime minister to avoid making his solicitations for money seem like an attack on the Nazi regime. Much support also came from individual citizens; many were willing to pledge £50 in sponsorship. In addition, countless volunteers helped at various stages, beginning with the initial processing when the boats landed and the transfer of the refugees to hostels or foster homes began.

HABERER: I left Germany in early December 1938—the coldest winter in a hundred years. The boat had hundreds of children, and it was chaos. After we landed, I was sent to Lowestoft, on the southeast coast of England, where we were processed, given a medical exam, and fed. Some people came with us from Germany [chaperones of the Jewish Refugee Committee], but there were not enough of them to take care of all these children, most of whom spoke no English.

They put me in one of those wooden shacks that you have on the seashore where people change and dress, and for a couple of nights I slept there by myself. I was terrified, not knowing what was going on, asking myself, "Why am I here?" The people looking out for us apparently had no psychological understanding of the situation.

They gave me a hot water bottle, but it was so cold that the hot water bottle became a block of ice. Consequently I caught a bladder infection, and they sent me to a hospital where the nurses didn't speak German, and I didn't speak English. Nobody visited me. So I was by myself.

History Taught as Propaganda: Michael Rossmann

"It was a daily struggle coming to school and also going home. I always tried to hide on my way home because there were kids who would lie in wait and beat me up."

Hiding on the Way Home

Despite being a Quaker, despite her strong identification with Germany and German culture, Rossmann's mother was nonetheless considered a Jew and a threat, and in 1935 the Nazis forced the *Frankfurter Zeitung* to fire her. It's unclear why it took so long, since the Boycott of April 1, 1933, had signaled the expulsion of the *Rassejuden* from the press, the theater, and the motion picture industry, and special legislation of September 22, 1933, made employment in these industries dependent on joining specific professional organizations, or chambers, which prohibited Jewish membership.

What did your mother do after she lost her job?

MICHAEL ROSSMANN: She opened a crafts studio and gave lessons to Jewish children.

When did you start school?

ROSSMANN: I started in 1936, shortly after Easter. I was five years old. I first attended a Jewish school, but after my first year I was transferred to a *Volksschule,* a public school. And this immediately caused me a great deal of trouble.

Rossmann switched from a Jewish school to a German public school at a time when most Jewish children were doing just the opposite. Because his mother was Jewish and his father was Aryan, the Nazis considered him a *Mischling,* a "non-Aryan," that is, one not of "pure German blood," but neither a "full-blood Jew."

The Nazis had a bit of trouble sorting out such distinctions and putting them into legislation. The racial decree of April 11, 1933, had defined non-Aryans as persons who had one Jewish parent or grandparent and who belonged to the Jewish religious community. But this law was found to lack precision.

For example, it made no distinction between "full Jews"—that is, those with four Jewish grandparents—and "quarter Jews," those with only one Jewish grandparent. Nazi racial experts had a problem determining at what point the Aryan genes predominated and at what point the Jewish genes prevailed. Some maintained that Teutonic genes took charge only when the ratio was three to one, thus making all quarter Jews German, an approach the Nazi Party favored. But others disagreed, and their views influenced those who drafted the Reich Citizenship Law of November 14, 1935.

This law, finalized during the Nazi Party Congress at Nürnberg, divided non-Aryans into Jews and *Mischlinge*. It said that a Jew was anyone who had at least three Jewish grandparents or who had two Jewish grandparents and either practiced the Jewish religion or was married to a Jew. It said that the *Mischling*, or person of mixed blood, was someone who had two Jewish grandparents and did not practice the Jewish religion or someone who was married to a Jew. In subsequent legislation the categories of "*Mischling* of the First Degree" and "*Mischling* of the Second Degree" were added. A *Mischling* of the First Degree was one who fit the 1935 Nürnberg definition; a *Mischling* of the Second Degree was anyone who had one Jewish grandparent.

Life for a *Mischling* of either category often meant repression and humiliation. They were discharged from the civil service, they could not join the Nazi Party, they could not become officers in the armed forces, and they could not marry Germans without permission. However, such denigration was still preferable to being classified a full Jew. The Nazis targeted the full Jews for their greatest fury. But the *Mischlinge* were also scorned, since these people were still tainted with Jewish blood.

Children of mixed marriages, like Michael Rossmann, whose parents had severed ties with the Jewish religion, were obviously better off than those who had not. Rossmann's continuance in a Jewish school would have been considered ipso facto adherence to the Jewish religion and have resulted in his classification as a full Jew. Sending him to a public school strengthened his Christian identity (albeit not that strongly in a nontraditional sect like the Quakers) and helped to confirm him as a *Mischling*. A formal challenge of this might have led to a hearing in a racial court. Evidence against him might have included the fact that he was still living in a "Jewish household," both his grandmother and mother—despite her conversion to Quakerism—being considered full Jews.

However, from the way he was treated at the *Volksschule*, the distinction between Jew and *Mischling* hardly seemed to matter. Rossmann clearly became a victim of the regime's *Judenpolitik*. Any people who were deemed to carry the Jewish contagion were considered racial enemies worthy of dehumanization and isolation from the *Volksgemeinschaft*, or to use a contemporary German metaphor, eliminated like poisoned mushrooms in a forest.

ROSSMANN: From the time I entered the *Volksschule,* my life became terrible. I was considered "the Jewish boy," and other students would call me names, and shout, "Jude, Jude, Jude!" I was chased all the time, people howling behind me. It was a daily struggle coming to school and also going home. I always tried to hide on my way home because there were kids who would lie in wait and beat me up.

Did this harassment happen just outside of class?

ROSSMANN: In class too. I was rather good at mathematics, but my mathematics teacher, a man named Schenk, made it a practice of terrorizing me. He'd stride into class, a big class of forty to fifty students, and greet us with "Heil Hitler," and, of course, we all had to answer in the same way. (I knew that was the wrong thing to do, but I had to do it like all the rest.) And then he would call on people to answer questions. When it came my turn, he would badger me with questions to make me nervous. I would make mistakes, and then he'd shout, "You, Jewish boy, come up here."

Once when I went before the class, the teacher took out a long ruler, which he used for drawing on the blackboard, and he hit me across the face with it. The ruler broke, and the whole class laughed.

They were taking away your self-worth, weren't they? Kind of what the Americans did to the blacks. Ultimately people would internalize this treatment and begin to think that maybe they were inferior.

ROSSMANN: I don't think I saw myself as inferior, but I began to perform badly at school, making careless mistakes. I still have that problem. I can easily make mistakes.

What you went through for those two years was horribly traumatic.

ROSSMANN: Nothing compared to what people went through in the concentration camps.

You can always compare yourself to those who had it worse, but you don't have to be up against a firing squad to have traumatic experiences. In your case, it would seem, it took a terrible psychic toll.

ROSSMANN: I think it did.

What were you taught in social studies or literature classes?

ROSSMANN: We learned a lot of Teutonic mythology, about the German gods—Wotan and Donner and Siegfried. The invasion of Austria [in March 1938] was, of course, justified as lawful and right. I knew that the history I was taught was propaganda. But I have a difficult time recalling the details because I had such a hard time learning with all that harassment.

I was fortunate, after a while, in being able to change into the class of a teacher who lived a block away from our apartment, and he took pity on me and had me walk with him to school. But on the way home I could not always rely on him. He had other things to do, and his schedule was not always the same as mine. I had to be careful going home.

On one occasion, I ran to get away. But when I came to my apartment building and buzzed to get in, nobody was home. I pushed every buzzer in the building and finally somebody from another apartment let me in just in time. Once, though, I was not so lucky and got hot tar poured down my back. Another time I was tied up.

Did you tell your mother about what was happening to you?

ROSSMANN: I never told her much about it.

Then by not complaining you were trying to protect your mother?

ROSSMANN: Tried to, yes. My mother had a very good friend from the *Frankfurter Zeitung,* and he had two daughters who attended the same school as I. One of them was in the same class with Herr Schenk. Once when I was visiting this friend with my mother, he told her that this daughter had told him that "one of the Jewish boys" was hit with a ruler. I blushed very strongly. I thought nothing more had to be said. But my mother didn't appear to react.

There was never any protest to the school?

ROSSMANN: My mother could not possibly have protested.

How did you feel about being tagged as a Jew, even though "officially" you were not?

ROSSMANN: I felt that if that's the way my parents were, then "Okay, I'm Jewish." But religion didn't come into this. We were not religious. And my mother was, as I said, a Quaker.

Were you aware of Kristallnacht [November 9, 1938]?

ROSSMANN: Not directly. My mother and grandmother told me about the synagogues being burned, how many of their friends had their businesses smashed and looted, about the anti-Jewish signs on the storefronts.

On the night of November 9–10, Frankfurt's four major synagogues were all torched. In addition, SA units attacked and looted Jewish businesses, community halls, and dwellings. The vandals were joined by other street ruffians. But the greatest thieves were the German insurance companies, which were threatened with heavy losses because of the destruction of Jewish property and connived with the Nazi leaders to cheat their policyholders out of what was owed.

Kristallnacht also saw the arrest of hundreds of Frankfurt's Jewish men, who were then sent to concentration camps, notably Dachau and Buchenwald. The Nazis then merged the members of the Orthodox and the Reform Communities into a single organization: the Jüdische Gemeinde. Following Kristallnacht, Jews were expelled from German schools. The decree, strictly speaking, did not apply to *Mischlinge,* but those who stayed were made to suffer.

ROSSMANN: We were visited by the Gestapo. The agents seemed to be looking for some papers pertaining to my grandfather's numismatic business. After his death, it had been moved to Switzerland, and its remaining files taken into the garden and burned. So the Gestapo agents found nothing. They ransacked the place and stole many things.

Shortly after Kristallnacht, my mother sent me to a school in Holland.

In 1938, the Nazis pushed Aryanization into high gear. A decree of April 25 ordered the registration of all Jewish assets and property, both in and outside the country. This included all agricultural property, urban real estate, business capital, personal wealth—i.e., money held in bank notes, insurance policies, unpaid debts, securities, and valuable art, stamps, and coins—anything which exceeded a combined value of 5,000 marks. The official registration of assets form was a highly detailed multipage document. This legislation was followed by a series of decrees resulting in the almost total elimination of Jewish participation in the German economy, except as consumers.

The November pogrom highlighted the determination to enforce this policy and to confiscate as much of the Jewish assets as possible. Some of the most outrageous examples of brutalization, extortion, and confiscation now took place. The looting of the Rossmann apartment shows that Gestapo agents thought it was now their turn to grab what they could of Jewish private assets.

The numismatic business would have, in any case, been confiscated. The interior ministry paved the way for the destruction of Jewish economic activity in industry and in wholesale and retail trade by requiring the registration of all Jewish commercial activity. Jews were also prohibited from engaging in any trade outside their official town or residence. Still left on the agenda was the "Aryanization" of Jewish homes and apartments, especially in urban areas. The ultimate goal was the resettlement and ghettoizing of those who had not fled.

ROSSMANN: I didn't have many friends. I had one very good non-Jewish friend. We were always together. But toward the end, I couldn't go and see him anymore because his mother was just afraid. Not that she disliked me, but, you know, she also had to think about her own safety.

After Christmas in 1938, Rossmann's mother sent him to Holland to continue his education. Most of the kids in the school he attended were from German Jewish families. The languages of instruction were Dutch, German, and English.

An Education Clearing Scheme allowed German Jewish parents to deposit tuition and maintenance money with the Berlin-based Palestine Trusteeship Corporation to support their children's study outside Germany. The Nazi authorities wanted to stimulate Jewish emigration and at the same time maintain control over the money involved. In 1937, the economy ministry used Paltrau as a source of foreign exchange by allowing foreign organizations and individuals to contribute to the fund—a possibility that existed until 1941.

ROSSMANN: I was very, very happy to go. But I wasn't very good at the school because I felt alone without my family and home. I didn't seem able to learn and was regarded as somewhat slow. They were very nice, but they put me in a sort of remedial class. I think they thought I was retarded.

You were there for the whole spring term?

ROSSMANN: Until the summer of 1939, when I returned to Germany.

When you returned the preparations for leaving Germany had already been completed?

ROSSMANN: My grandmother had already emigrated to England.[23] And before she left, she told my mother that it was time for the rest of us to "get out."

Why didn't your mother leave with her?

ROSSMANN: She was very fond of Germany. It must have been a terrible time for her. She wanted to stay, but her brother and my grandmother and other members of the family persuaded her to leave. But she wanted to stay long enough to attend the annual meeting of the German Society of Friends.

Why do you think your grandmother was more aware of the danger than your mother?

ROSSMANN: My grandmother used to have constant arguments with a friend of hers who lived in Hamburg. My grandmother would say, "You've got to get out. It's not going to be safe here." And the friend replied, "No, I'm safe here because my late husband was a judge. Nobody will do anything to me." My grandmother was still in a way very Jewish in her thought. On the other hand, my mother was more cosmopolitan and assimilated and perhaps was hoping the Nazi repression would blow over.

Before we left, we buried our knives and forks and other silver in the garden of one of my mother's non-Jewish friends. As you know, we couldn't take anything out of Germany. We got it all back after the war and now use it for parties and special occasions.

We left for England in July, traveling through the Netherlands: The Hague, Heok van Holland. It was a rather enjoyable experience. We crossed the channel at night; my mother and I had a little cabin, and I went to sleep and woke up when the boat docked at Harwich. We took the train to London, and my grandmother was there to meet us when we got off at Liverpool Street Station. It was very nice to see my grandmother.

I thought my stay in England would be short. I fully expected to go back to that school in Holland to begin the fall term, and I made absolutely no effort to learn English. I didn't need to. I was completely surrounded by my German-speaking family.

That summer we all went on a vacation to the beach near Worthing [a popular sea resort in West Sussex]. It was to be a last reunion before I would return to Holland for the fall term. I don't know what my mother's thinking was. I guess because the Dutch schooling had been already paid for, I was supposed to learn English in Holland in order to get an Oxford school certificate. But then I had to stay in England, where we lived in vastly reduced circumstances, dependent on the charity of my grandmother's brother-in-law.

Rossmann was to report back to the Dutch school on September 3. But on Friday, September 1, at 4:45 in the morning, Wehrmacht *Panzer* units rolled across the Polish frontier. All those kids who remained in that school Rossmann attended in Holland had little chance to survive.

Notes

1. See Rogers Brubaker, *Citizenship and Nationhood in France and Germany* (Cambridge, Mass.: Harvard University Press, 1992), 123.
2. In very few cases some Jews did amazingly survive. One of these was the famous scholar Victor Klemperer, who remained in Dresden, one of the only 198 Jews still there at the beginning of 1945. Even as the war drew to an end, the Nazis worked hard to dispatch the few remaining Jews still alive in Germany. Ordered to report for deportation, Klemperer took advantage of the confusion resulting from the Allied firebombing of the city to flee to southern Bavaria and the safety of the American army. Klemperer's unique view of life in Nazi Germany is recounted in his *I Will Bear Witness: A Diary of the Nazi Years, 1933–1941* (New York: Random House, 1999).
3. These were the top ten countries worldwide.
4. Enumerated by Section 3 of Immigration Act of February 5, 1917.
5. Documents were judged "unavailable" if they could not be obtained without risk of serious inconvenience (aside from normal delay and expense in obtaining it) "involving personal injury, embarrassment, or financial loss either to the immigrant or to a member of his family, as might occur in the case of a immigrant who is a political or religious refugee." Statement of the Immigration Laws and Practices of the United States of America Governing the Reception of Immigrants, in *The Holocaust: Selected Documents,* 5:236.
6. There were 1,919 visas issued in 1933, 4,393 in 1934, 5,201 in 1935, 6,346 in

1936, 10,895 in 1937, 17,199 in 1938, and 33,515 in 1939. The last two years include the quotas for Austria.

7. The idea that led to the solution of problems he had originally formulated came to him on New Year's Eve in 1932. The next day he wrote it down, and when school opened in the new year, he conferred with Professor Hammerstein, who encouraged him to elaborate on these thoughts. That was the last time Golomb saw his advisor until he presented him with a finished copy of the thesis the following April.

8. At the beginning of 1933, the prominent mathematician Alexander Ostrowsky at the University of Basel had asked him to come to Switzerland to finish his dissertation and become his assistant. Golomb turned him down, so confident he was of his prospects in Germany. In retrospect, Golomb called this "possibly the dumbest thing I had done in my life."

9. The assonance obviously disappears in translation.

10. These collectives, which first appeared in 1909, were intentionally small, so that their members could constitute a sort of extended family. The units concentrated exclusively on farming. By contrast, the kibbutzim were large, self-sufficient villages combining both agriculture and industry. Today, the distinction between the two has virtually disappeared, with the term "kibbutz" freely applied to both.

11. Histadrut, General Federation of Jewish Labor, was the largest organization of its type in Palestine, but it was more than a trade union movement. It combined under its large umbrella educational and cultural services, business and factory ownership, workers' cooperatives, and various personnel services, like underwriting insurance policies.

12. The reply came at the end of the year, written by Lady Russell and sent from Chicago. She said that his letter had moved them very much and they would be glad to help as much as they could, but they were unable to get Golomb a visa or a work permit for Great Britain. However, they did give him the names of some people in the United States who might help him should he manage to get there. Because of the Russells, Golomb was introduced to an American Quaker organization and to another refugee from Nazi Germany, Professor Hermann Weyl at Princeton University. Both contacts proved to be of immense help.

13. The judgment is too harsh. According to the 1935 census, Yugoslavia had a native population of 70,000 Jews. The Karageorgevich government and the Orthodox Church were generally tolerant, and prior to the war, there was no organized antisemitic political faction. In the 1930s, Yugoslavia accepted about 7,000 Jewish refugees, although it did not give them permission to remain in the country per-

manently. Those that could not move elsewhere were practically all exterminated during the Nazi conquest, with the exception of those living in the Italian zone of occupation (Dalmatia and Montenegro) and in the areas reclaimed by Hungary. After the collapse of the Mussolini regime in 1943 and the installation of a Nazi puppet government in Hungary the following year, the lives of these Jews were again at risk.

14. Rita Thalmann and Emmanuel Feinermann, *Crystal Night* (New York: Holocaust Library, 1974), 58.

15. On June 9, 1938, the Great Synagogue of Munich had gone up in flames in an arson personally ordered by Hitler. This vandalism was followed with the destruction of synagogues in Nürnburg and Dortmund, the arrest of Jews all over Germany, and the looting of Jewish businesses throughout the country.

16. Before the First World War, Karl May (1842–1912) was the most popular writer of juvenile adventure fiction in Germany. Even afterwards, his popularity was immense. Writing in the first person to bolster the illusion of authenticity, May churned out a series of novels about the American Far West in the 1880s and 90s, which earned him a fortune and an indelible place in the hearts of German boys. He also wrote tales set in the Near East and South America. A definitive edition of his collected works fills thirty-three volumes.

17. Dr. Otto Hirsch was the president of the Reichsvertretung der Deutschen Juden (Reich Representation of Jews in Germany), headquartered in Berlin. He perished at Mauthausen.

18. Quoted in Arthur D. Morse, *While Six Million Died: A Chronicle of American Apathy* (New York: Random House, 1967), 137–38. For more on immigration policy, see William S. Bernard, ed., *American Immigration Policy—A Reappraisal* (New York: Harper Brothers, 1950); and *Whom We Shall Welcome? Report of the President's Commission on Immigration and Naturalization* (Washington, D.C.: U.S. Government Printing Office, 1953).

19. This three-stacker (29,51 tons, 740 feet long by 86 feet wide) was the flagship and pride of the Holland-America Line. It remained in service a scant eleven years. In 1940, hit by crossfire when the German blitzkrieg moved into Rotterdam, it burned for five days into a blackened hulk.

20. The 13,869-ton ship of the United States Lines entered into service in 1922. One-funnel, 516 feet long by 72 feet wide, it cruised at a respectable eighteen knots. It became a troopship during the Second World War and was scrapped in 1948.

21. Most of the Germans who came to Britain between 1933 and 1939 did, in fact, go elsewhere. In 1938, for example, 79,652 Germans immigrants arrived; that same

year 72,358 left. In the first six months of the following year 90,677 landed; 47,092 embarked. The increasing number of those who stayed undoubtedly reflects the increasing difficulty of the Jews to find other places of refuge.

22. A similar save-the-children scheme had caught fire in the United States, and led to the Wagner-Rogers Bill, authorizing the admission of 20,000 German refugee children. The legislation was introduced in Congress in early 1939. It died in committee.

23. During 1938 and 1939, some 40,000 German Jews immigrated to England, out of a total of 118,000 emigrations.

3
A European War Becomes a World War

itler's determination to destroy the European balance of power
and create a Greater German Reich made World War II inevitable. Yet during the 1930s foreign leaders did not find him a person with whom it was impossible to do business. They did not see him as the screaming madman of popular vision, but rather as mature and sensible. Indeed, his ability to create a scene appeared more a deliberate ploy to intimidate and control than an indication of mental imbalance. Moreover, his commitment to peace seemed genuine. Shortly after he came to power in 1933, Hitler claimed he wanted "to guide the rivalries of the peoples of Europe once more to those spheres in which they had given to humanity in the noblest of mutual rivalries those supreme gifts to civilization, of culture, of art which today enrich and beautify the picture of the world."[1]

It was a frequent theme. While it did not exactly fit the Führer's later actions, especially in the way he treated subject peoples, it did not mean to many that he was a man of unlimited objectives. British Prime Minister Neville Chamberlain, at any rate, assumed that Hitler's goals were definable, and that his ambitions could be satisfied without going to war. Since Great Britain had never promised to guarantee the inviolability of the Eastern Peace Treaties, the sacrifice of Czechoslovakia at the Munich Conference in September 1938 was a small price to pay for "peace in our time." Besides, who could take seriously Hitler's intent, expressed in *Mein Kampf,* to construct a vast empire with the Aryans as its master race? Surely, it was thought, this was only the boasting of a vote-getting politician. Statesmen of such literal-mindedness came along rarely.

Appeasement was not necessarily bad policy. It had worked well during the 1920s, when adjustments were being made to accommodate the increasing strength of Germany, inevitably recovering from the Great War. But times had changed, and Chamberlain had not changed with them. The appeasement he practiced at Munich was not a policy of strength dictated by a victorious power but a policy of weakness determined by the demands of an aggressor. Chamberlain was sure he could avoid a European conflict, but Hitler was mobilizing his country for the struggle ahead. While the war clouds gathered in European skies, those Jews who had left Germany for the safety of exile could only rejoice at their good fortune but dread the fate of their family and friends left behind. Many, though, were too young to understand these events and were too busy coming to terms with their new lives.

Roosevelt the Angel: Solomon Gartenhaus

"These crazy Americans, what are they doing showing off their dead lions?"

A Vast Secular Dimension

The Gartenhaus family lived first for two months with relatives in the Bronx. Then they moved to Philadelphia, where Sol attended an American school. It came as a bit of a shock to him when he discovered that his fellow classmates did not speak German. Put into the third grade, he gradually acclimated.

SOL GARTENHAUS: I learned English without consciously sitting down to study vocabulary and grammar. I simply interacted with kids on the street and at the playground and gradually picked it up. Sometimes I would get caught up. I remember once, when we went to the zoo in the Bronx, and I saw these arrows pointing out directions to the animals. One of them said: "To the Lions." I could make out the word "lions," but the "to the" looked to me like "tote," which in German means "dead." I thought, "These crazy Americans, what are they doing showing off their dead lions?"

But in school the kids helped out—for example, once when I didn't know the words for addition and subtraction. After six months, though, I had little difficulty communicating.

Your transition from Germany to America was not difficult or traumatic?

GARTENHAUS: Not that I can recall. An eight-year-old adjusts easily to a new environment.

Did you experience any antisemitism?

GARTENHAUS: I was never treated differently because I was Jewish. We settled in South Philadelphia, which then was a kind of mixture: some Irish, some Polish, and some Jews. In the summer we would play baseball and sit around and sing songs. We were all in the same boat, and there was a mutual respect for each other's culture. Some of my best friends were Italian, not Jewish. If I was unpopular during World War II, it was because I was German. I remember there was a group I used to play ball with who used to call me "schmaltz" because of my German origins. That is a derogatory term meaning "chicken fat."

Jews or non-Jews?

GARTENHAUS: Both. They were all were very anti-German.

What language did you speak at home?

GARTENHAUS: We still spoke German. My parents didn't learn English until many years later. They continued speaking German. I think, though, in the United States my parents became less German and more Yiddish. All the people they associated with in the United States, especially those from the synagogue, were all Eastern European people like themselves.

My father would sit down with some friends after prayers to drink whiskey and eat coffee cake, and they would regale each other with stories. I would listen to these guys for hours, and they would never run out of stories. You know, when we talk, we usually talk about ourselves or about people we know. But these men were not like that. They never told personal stories. They told Sholem Alechem–type stories. I don't know where they got them. I don't think that they were true stories, but they told each one as if it had actually happened.

Did your father go back into business?

GARTENHAUS: No. He thought about it, but being Orthodox and in the United States, he felt he couldn't make ends meet with a business closed on Saturday. And he refused to work on Saturday, so he started his economic life all over again. He became a cantor and a ritual slaughterer. He had to learn how to do that. And I remember that while he was apprenticing he used to come home with his hands all bloody. He and my mother remained Orthodox all their lives.

Did they give any signals as to what they wanted you to become?

GARTENHAUS: They wanted me to become a rabbi. A week after we arrived in Philadelphia, my father enrolled me and my younger brother in the Yeshiva summer school. We attended classes two hours a day, four days a week. We continued to attend even when we started the public school. We went after our regular classes, four days a week, from four o'clock to seven o'clock. I did that until I was fourteen. Then I quit. The trick I used was to get a job in a grocery store. I gave the money I earned to my parents and told them to hold it for me until I got older. But I think they used it to help support the family.

What turned you away from the Yeshiva?

GARTENHAUS: Ultra-orthodoxy just didn't move me. When I stopped going to Hebrew school, I essentially dropped out. I didn't go to synagogue anymore, I didn't do the religious things anymore.

You stopped eating kosher?

GARTENHAUS: Essentially, except when I ate at home. During my senior year, our high-school class (half Italian and half Jewish) went for a field trip to Washington, D.C. We were staying in this big hotel, and when I came down from my room to the dining room one day, I noticed all my Italians classmates sitting around the tables acting funny. And then it came to me: the waiter had just served me a plate of ham. And that's the first time I had ever eaten pork!

And you went ahead and ate it?

GARTENHAUS: I had to, with all these guys waiting for me to falter. But I was afraid that when I ate the first mouthful something dreadful would happen.

And when the lightening didn't strike you, you sort of said, "Oh, well."

GARTENHAUS: I guess.

Did your parents give you much grief?

GARTENHAUS: They weren't happy with it, but what could they do? Outside the confines of Orthodoxy there were other enticements. The United States was such a spirited place. It had a vast secular dimension. You were not put into a single mold. I used to go to the library, which was two or three blocks from our house, and read all kinds of things.

Did you see this as a sort of a rebellion against your Orthodox parents?

GARTENHAUS: I don't think so. It was just something that gave me pleasure. That's why we do most things, you know. And I was a big library buff. I used to bring library books into school and read them at my desk. One of my teachers dubbed me "the bookworm," but she didn't mean it in a negative way. Comic books were also big in those days. But my parents wouldn't allow them in the house. So we had to sneak them in and read them secretly. I read the whole *schmier*. That was the time when Superman comics and Batman comics were created. And then there were *Classic Comics*. I read *A Tale of Two Cities* in pictures before I read the book.

And the high school I went to had some really excellent teachers. Had it not been for the Depression they probably would have made top-level college professors. My plane geometry teacher recognized my talent in math and would have me go to the blackboard and work out difficult problems for the rest of the class. Under the tutelage of teachers like him, I learned more things than I learned from all the reading I used to do, and in the process I became more American. I also had friends who had similar talents, and several of them also went on to get Ph.D.s.

You were going to school in south Philadelphia during the time of the Second World War. What did you understand about what was going on back in Europe?

GARTENHAUS: I was glad that my father had the good sense to get us out of Germany. But until the attack on Pearl Harbor, I was afraid the Nazis would come to the United States. I was happy when the United States declared war on

Germany, because at last there was somebody fighting on our side. My mother always used to say to me, "God sent a devil," which was Hitler, "and he also sent the angel to rescue us," and that was Roosevelt.

What did they teach you about the war in school?

GARTENHAUS: Nothing much that I can recall. We were encouraged to buy "savings stamps" to help the war effort, and I grew a "victory garden" in the backyard.

Did your parents follow the war?

GARTENHAUS: My father used to listen to the radio all during the war. There was a Yiddish station in Philadelphia that had a news commentator named Nathan Fleischer. Every night my father would listen to him give the war news, but the station was so full of static that my father practically had to stick his head in the speaker to hear what was going on.

An Offer of Employment: Michael Golomb

"Even though I was not yet a citizen, I felt accepted. I didn't have to constantly produce my papers."

Looking for Work

Michael Golomb arrived in New York with fifty dollars. He was met at dockside by the cousins who had given him the affidavit to come to the United States. They had rented a room for him in the attic of a house in the Bronx occupied by a tailor who had emigrated from Poland with his family and worked part-time in the garment district. The landlord had a grown-up daughter, who was unemployed and complained all the time about the immigrants who came and took the jobs of the Americans. Golomb paid $1.50 per week for the room.

MICHAEL GOLOMB: You wouldn't believe what kind of room that was. There was just enough space for a bed and a chair, and the first night I felt itching all over. When I turned on the light—an overhead bulb with a string attached—the bed sheet was covered with bedbugs. I'd never seen that before, and I called the landlady. It was about 1:00 A.M., but she came up in her bathrobe to see what was the matter. When she found out, she said, "So what's your problem? It's just bedbugs." But they were nice people, and the next morning they sprayed to try to get rid of the vermin.

All in all, it was a pretty miserable life there in the Bronx. The only money I lived on was the seven dollars I got each Tuesday from a Jewish relief agency in Manhattan. Most of the time I spent looking for a job. I followed some leads, signed up with an employment agency for teachers. I would have accepted a position teaching in a high school or some private academy.

I went for advice to Professor Richard Courant, a well-known mathematician who had to resign his professorship at the University of Göttingen and was now teaching at New York University. He was one of the very few internationally known, mostly Jewish scientists who after being kicked out of the Nazi Reich had obtained a satisfactory position in this country. Courant asked me about my background, about what I had published, and so forth; and then he said, "There was another young mathematician who came to see me a few days ago, and now he's doing well. He has a job in a dairy store." After that I felt as bad as I had ever felt in my life. I had come from the hell of Yugoslavia, expecting at least a modest career in this country, and it looked as remote now as ever before.

This was the summer of 1939 — an especially hot and humid summer — and I lived there in this furnace-like attic room. I felt worse than I felt during the whole time in Yugoslavia. Courant had a brilliant professional career throughout his life, but his greatest ambition was in promoting his own career, and he exploited many young mathematicians.

A fter several months without success, Golomb contacted Professor Hermann Weyl, whose name Bertrand Russell had given him, and other mathematicians at the Princeton Institute of Advanced Studies. Weyl answered Golomb's letter with an invitation for him to attend one of the weekly colloquia. Weyl then recommended Golomb to an engineering professor at Cornell, who employed young refugee mathematicians as his personal assistants with funds from a Westinghouse research fellowship. The job paid $1,200 for a full, not academic, year and started in September.

Golomb was overjoyed. As soon as he had signed the contract, he went to the immigration office in New York to arrange a visa for his wife. He figured that with his recent offer of employment he was now in a position to support her, but he still needed the help of the

Quakers to arrange the appropriate affidavits. Thus Dagmar was able to make immediate preparations to join her husband in the United States.

The Society of Friends proved helpful in other ways. During the summer of 1939, Golomb attended a retreat they had sponsored for refugee scholars to help them become acquainted with American politics, history, and culture. The retreat was held on a big estate at Nyack-on-the-Hudson, the property of a wealthy Quaker widow, but the émigré intellectuals had to do all their own housekeeping. Shortly after the end of this camp, Golomb moved to Ithaca. A few days later his wife arrived from Europe.

Dagmar Golomb's departure had not occurred without incident. She had booked a ticket on the famous ocean liner *Le Normandie,* scheduled to leave on September 3, 1939, from Le Havre to New York, but when she arrived at the French port, she learned that the crossing had been cancelled. The ship's French owners had ordered her to remain in New York indefinitely.[2] The day she was to have sailed was the day Great Britain and France declared war on Germany. Although the actual fighting was still confined to the east, the Atlantic had automatically become a war zone, with all Allied shipping prey to German U-boats. Thus, civilian shipping was restricted, and Dagmar was assigned a rather low travel priority. Since all personal communication between France and the United States was interrupted, she could only communicate with her husband via her sister in Zagreb. And she asked Michael to wire her money for a ticket on another ship, if one could be found. The next time he heard from her was when she had arrived in New York. She had fortunately been able to book passage on another French-line ship, actually a cargo ship. The passage took thirteen days, the ship zigzagging to avoid submarines.

GOLOMB: The Cornell professor I was to work for had a background in electrical engineering, with some, but not very much, knowledge of mathematics. But he was quite a manipulator. Before I came, he had already had two other German immigrant mathematicians in that position, and when I left after three years, I was followed by another German mathematician, who kept it a year or two longer. All these people stayed only until they could find other positions. And every one left with the feeling that they had been exploited.

Hanna Gartenhaus's Polish passport; the five children are listed on the lower left-hand page.

Joseph Haberer (second from left), August 23, 1942, after being sent to England through the *Kindertransport*.

When I arrived, I was made to sign a letter of resignation with an open date. The professor would fill that in at some later time if he wanted to. All my predecessors had been required to do the same, the letters being kept as a constant threat to enforce unquestioned submission to the professor's wishes.

But at this point in your life something was better than nothing?

GOLOMB: Of course. Right from the beginning he used me to help him write a book he was doing on circuit analysis. I wrote several chapters, and these appeared, with the rest of the work, under his name.

No attribution for Golomb?

GOLOMB: He didn't want anybody to find out where the mathematical work was coming from. But fortunately, after one year, I also became a part-time instructor in the mathematics department. I had to get the permission of my boss in the electrical engineering department to accept the job. This was my first teaching position and a great advance.

Did you feel any sort of anti-Jewish, antisemitic prejudices at Cornell? Any stereotypical thinking?

GOLOMB: Cornell, at that time, did not have many Jewish professors. The mathematics department had only one Jewish professor, one full-time Jewish instructor, and myself, who was part-time. In engineering, they had only one Jewish professor. One of the non-Jewish professors who served on the admissions committee told me that he was instructed to go through the applications and cross out the candidates who had Jewish names. Until after the Second World War, as far as I know, there was only a handful of Jewish engineers in the whole country.

I think restrictions on Jewish enrollment were the norm at most places, including, of course, Purdue.

GOLOMB: Cornell was more liberal than most. For example, it had an interdenominational chapel on campus, and I was surprised that on some Sundays a rabbi would be officiating.

While you were there, did you have any connection with the local Jewish community?

GOLOMB: Well, from time to time I gave money for their various causes, but I certainly didn't go to synagogue.

Were people curious about your experiences as a refugee?

GOLOMB: Not really. They seemed more interested in those of my wife, who was a native of what many Americans considered an exotic country. Dagmar sometimes gave talks about what she had gone through. All in all we felt we were treated well. We made some very good friends.

Does making friends in America mean the same to you as when you say "making friends" in Germany or Yugoslavia?

GOLOMB: When I was in Germany, I was an adolescent. In this country, it was entirely different, both in Ithaca and then when we came here to Purdue. I made friends early. Good friends. I was a family man. Even though I was not yet a citizen, I felt accepted. I didn't have to constantly produce my papers. I never even had to prove that I had a degree. My English wasn't perfect yet, but I was treated like everybody else. In Europe, this was unthinkable. Even outstanding mathematicians couldn't get university positions if they were not citizens. Thus, a German mathematician couldn't get a position at a French university unless he became naturalized French, and vice versa.

An Appreciated Member of the Department

Golomb came to West Lafayette in September 1942, a time when the mathematics department was still pretty small. He grew with the department, so to speak.

How did you hear about Purdue?

GOLOMB: The chairman of the math department, William Ayres, offered me a position as an assistant professor. Ayres had been mandated by President Edward Elliott to transform what had been essentially a service department for engineering and science students into a research department. When Ayres took over, there were quite a few members of the department who didn't have Ph.D.s.

As part of the interview process, I had to talk to the dean of the School of Science, a man named Howard Enders, a professor of biology. When I arrived in his office, his first question was, "Are you Jewish?" I said, "Yes, I am." And he replied, "Are you aware that Jews are not liked in this part of the country because we consider them clannish?" Well, of course, I couldn't answer back. Then he went on: "I see that Professor Ayres proposes a salary of $1,800 dollars. I consider that much too high. I think that when a young member comes in, he should be treated like an apprentice, and we should first try him out before we pay him a salary like that." Fortunately Professor Ayres was of a different mind. Among the ten new people he hired, there were at least three Jews.

We had been somewhat concerned and didn't know what to expect when we arrived here, West Lafayette being a small Midwestern town. We were cautioned that we might not find many congenial people here. Also we were told that we would be expected to immediately join a church. That part was true. A week or so after we arrived, neighbors came by and asked us to join their church.

Did anybody come and ask you to join the synagogue?

GOLOMB: There were very few Jews at the university then; what Jews there were in Lafayette proper were mostly business people with whom we had no contact.

In a sense, you and your Jewish colleagues were breaking through the antisemitic barrier?

GOLOMB: There was one Jew in the physics department, Karl Lark-Horowitz, but I believe he went to the Lutheran church.

And also the dean of engineering, Andrey Potter, was Jewish. He also didn't want his Jewishness known.

GOLOMB: I knew of Potter, and I suspected that he was Jewish, but he hid it, and there was no way of telling.

Did you find the atmosphere here at Purdue fairly congenial for scholarly output?

GOLOMB: Very much so in my department. Among all those young people who were hired by Ayres, many of them became well-established mathematicians later on. And we all became close friends. But it seemed as if we had two departments: this young group against the old-timers. I'm sure they resented our presence a lot.

Were you given a free hand to develop your own courses?

GOLOMB: I wouldn't say that. First of all, we taught somewhere between fifteen hours and sixteen hours a week, a load that later on became unthinkable. But then it was necessary, because there wasn't enough staff to teach all the students. All the professors taught analytic geometry and trigonometry and first-year calculus—these courses made up most of our schedule. Then we were asked to teach an advanced course. Professor Ayres said, "Well, you have a European education, which gave you a wider choice of subjects than you could get over here. So I suppose you can teach applied mathematics." I was therefore given a course in theoretical mechanics, which was outside my research interest, but I got into it. At that time, I was happy to do whatever I was asked to do. And I really felt for the first time that I had arrived. I mean, I was doing what I had wished for a career. Of course, teaching took a lot of time and didn't allow too much time for research, but that was the same for all the young people who came here.

Why was there such a shortage of math instructors at Purdue?

GOLOMB: Because there was not enough money in the departmental budget to hire more.

You stated that when you were in Yugoslavia, you felt that you were in sort of a deep freeze because, having to struggle for bare subsistence, you couldn't develop your mathematics career by exploring the ideas of your thesis. Did you feel that Purdue provided the opportunity?

GOLOMB: I didn't feel any obstacles, except that I did not have enough time. But in 1942, I was already thirty-three years old, and, as I told you before, that's really beyond the peak of productivity for mathematicians.

But not in your case?

GOLOMB: No, but what I had started developing with my thesis was no longer an active field of research in mathematics, because others had worked on it and had exhausted its line of inquiry. New fields had since developed, making it necessary for me to change the interests of my earlier years.

In what way did the participation of the United States in the war influence the direction of mathematics?

GOLOMB: After Pearl Harbor, the enrollments at Purdue decreased because many of the young people were, of course, in the armed forces. At the same time work for the government was opening up, especially for scientists. Many of my colleagues at Purdue became engaged in government work.

In my case, I accepted a position with the Franklin Institute in Philadelphia, which had a contract with the navy to develop gun and bomb sights for war planes. The work was really more for an engineer than a mathematician, but I was eager to do what I could to help defeat the Nazis.

At that time, engineers in this country had a very narrow education, and they often were working on one particular machine and were not trained to develop products entirely new to them. Mathematicians were more flexible, even though they had no special preparation. We used analog computers—digital computers hadn't been invented yet—to help in the targeting of machine guns and the launching of rockets and bombs.

After half a year, I became chief of the analysis section at the Franklin Institute. I was there until the end of the war, when I returned to Purdue. They clearly wanted me back, and I was happy to return. Probably I could have found a position at a more advanced university, but I enjoyed being a big fish in a small pond. Besides, I felt like a much-appreciated member of the department, and my wife and I were quite happy in the community.

Antisemitism was no problem?

GOLOMB: Not really, but I think I should mention an experience I had in Philadelphia. During the war, accommodations were in short supply, and I spent several weeks looking for a place to live. I signed up with a real-estate agency, and they would take me around. Finally, I found a very nice apartment in Germantown that I wanted to rent. The real-estate agent said he would tell the owner, but when I called him back, he said, "The owner won't rent to you." I asked, "Why?" He said, "Because you are Jewish." This attitude was not uncommon at that time. Ads would carry the word "Restricted," which meant no blacks and no Jews.

Nowadays, such discrimination is illegal. But even then things were changing. During the war Jews found employment in government service, which had never had them before. And after the war, many universities started hiring Jews.

Do you think this was a conscious effort, or was it just because it no longer became an issue?

GOLOMB: I don't think this was a conscious effort, nothing like affirmative action. There was a shortage of well-trained people, and Jews were in the market.

Necessity was more important than a conscious decision on tolerance?

GOLOMB: Exactly. Antisemitism, when it did surface, didn't surprise me. I knew it was very common. We had to live with it. I didn't find the antisemitism in Germany before the time of Hitler much different from what I had experienced in the United States.

An English Public School Education: Michael Rossmann

"Part of the Quaker teaching is to be a pacifist, not to fight, and I can tell you many anecdotes which the Quakers tell to extol the pacifist approach in difficult situations. I could agree that was the right way, but I don't think approaching Hitler this way was likely to succeed."

Regaining Equilibrium

Michael Rossmann and his mother arrived in Britain with few financial resources. They were fortunate in having relatives in Britain willing to guarantee that they would not become a burden to the public treasury. Since Jewish emigrants were legally allowed to take out of Germany only ten marks each if they were traveling to a country whose borders were not contiguous with Germany, like Britain or the United States, Rossmann and his mother had twenty marks tops, or roughly eight dollars. Of course, their railway and boat passages had been prepaid in Reichsmarks.

As they were settling in, the British government was implementing its crisis emergency plans. It established special ministries for shipping, information, economic warfare, and food. Under a program of civilian defense adopted in 1935, the British began constructing air-raid warning systems and bomb shelters. The country was divided into several evacuation zones for the transfer of people, mostly juveniles from large urban areas. The government also ordered the distribution of gas masks, imposed blackouts in large cities, closed movie theaters, and began to ration foodstuffs. The progress was slow, as the Chamberlain government felt the best attitude toward the war was one of restraint.

The prime minister favored imposing a blockade on Germany, hoping that this would bring about the collapse of the German homefront. The Royal Air Force flew some "truth" missions, in which planes dumped millions of propaganda leaflets on German cities to convince the people they could not win the war. Until April 1940, British military operations were confined to keeping the German U-boats and commerce raiders at bay. The reluctance to begin land operations stemmed from a lack of preparation and a fear of repeating the bloodletting of the First World War. Had it not been for the blackouts and the mass evacuation of children, mainly from the London area, domestic daily life seemed pretty much like that of peacetime.

MICHAEL ROSSMANN: My mother and grandmother got this little flat in North Finchley [about ten miles northwest of downtown London], and that's where I lived until the war started and the evacuations of the children began.

The first evacuations began on September 1, 1939. During the first month, 827,000 unaccompanied children and 524,000 mothers with preschoolers left the country's larger cities. However, after six months, when expected German air attacks failed to materialize, about 80 percent of those evacuated returned home. A second wave of evacuations began with the start of the Blitz in September 1940, and then a third wave in 1944 with the V-weapons attack. In all, the British government moved about 4 million adults and children out of the big cities during the course of the war, with another 2 million leaving privately. Many, though, moved back and forth, depending on their perception of the danger. British parents also sent their children out of harm's way to the United States and Canada.

ROSSMANN: My mother took me to live in a small village in Hartfordshire in a home with people who were friends of my uncle. That's where I started school; many of my classmates were kids who had been evacuated from London's East End. I couldn't speak any English, and all the kids sort of crowded around me and kind of poked me. It was all a bit frightening. I thought my mind was normal. But it was a painful time. I felt isolated and I didn't have anyone I could talk to at that school. But my teacher gave me a book of arithmetic, which is, after all, international, and he had me sit there and do sums while the other kids did something else. I thought it was fun, because I knew I could do the assignments. But actually I did the part of calculating money all wrong. English money operated on calculations of twelve and twenty, not decimals. It took me about two weeks to figure that out.

But somehow I started to learn English quite quickly. I don't know how that happened. I could soon understand the other kids. And then my mother and I returned to North Finchley, maybe in October, and I entered this private school—I think my uncle Henry must have arranged it—and that was fantastic, because we had small classes. And the teacher was caring.

She started me on things like geometry and taught me a lot of English, and by Christmas I was reading! I was actually enjoying reading books in English. The first English book I ever read was a *Doctor Doolittle*. I was fascinated. I went to the public library and got more and more of his books. And after a while I started reading other books. There was Robert Louis Stevenson's *Treasure Island,* and [Baroness Emmuska Orczy's] *The Scarlet Pimpernel.* I started to read Dickens. *Oliver Twist* and *A Tale of Two Cities,* by which I was overtaken with sadness. I couldn't stop reading books. By January 1940, I must have been speaking English okay. So it didn't take me that long. However, until then, my life was very difficult. After I learned English, I transferred to Finchley High School.

> *By then you must have felt that changing schools was normal, that this is what you do when you're growing up.*

ROSSMANN: I thought that was exactly the case. But as long as it was a decent school, it was all right.

> *Did you feel at this point that you were safe?*

ROSSMANN: Well, you see, soon after that the real war started. And every night the place was being bombed. Houses were falling down all around us.

> *You were there during the Blitz?*

ROSSMANN: At the beginning of the Blitz. I was desperately nervous. They had air-raid shelters, but we stayed in our apartment. There was an antiaircraft battery just outside our place, and in the morning the place was littered with shrapnel, which we boys actually liked to collect. There was a public swimming pool on some high ground, and from there you could see the whole horizon. And at night you could see the fires burning in East London.

The Battle of Britain reached its climax in August 1940 as the Luftwaffe shifted to a tactic of destroying Britain's major cities, in addition to smashing air defenses, communication networks, and armaments factories. London became a major target in both daytime and nighttime raids. As the Blitz continued and the likelihood of destroying the Royal Air Force receded, breaking the morale of the British people through terror became the foremost goal.

In the opening phase of the Blitz, which lasted until November 1940, London was bombed every night save one, the heaviest attack taking place on October 15. Helped by bright moonlight, four hundred German bombers hit the capital in successive waves from half past eight in the evening until half past four the next morning. The British met the attack with antiaircraft fire and fighter planes but managed to destroy only one Heinkel 111.

Was North Finchley bombed?

ROSSMANN: Oh, yes! Buildings were destroyed everywhere.

And you still stayed?

ROSSMANN: Toward the end of the year, I was evacuated again to a place in Hartfordshire, where I attended a different school, and nobody spoke any German there. I lived with a family called Rose. The wife was very sympathetic, but the husband was not. He worked in the War Office and took the train to London every day. He must have felt uncomfortable having a German boy living in his house. I think he actually wanted to be kind, but he couldn't be.

Every night the air-raid sirens would go off around eight o'clock, and the all clear wasn't sounded until the next morning. But one night to everyone's surprise there were no sirens, no air raid. And shortly after that I returned to London and Finchley High School.

Since mid-November 1940, the Luftwaffe increasingly attacked industrial inland targets, such as Coventry, Nottingham, Birmingham, and Newcastle, as well as hitting various port cities: Southampton, Liverpool, Swansea, Bristol, Hull, Cardiff, and especially Plymouth. All England and southern Wales in effect became a battle zone. This phase of the Blitz ended in May 1941, when the German air fleets were withdrawn to participate in the forthcoming invasion of the Soviet Union.

Until then your life had been one of tremendous dislocation. At what point did you feel a certain stability?

ROSSMANN: Not until my mother got me a scholarship to go to Saffron Walden Finishing School, a Quaker boarding school in Essex, where I would remain for the next six years.[3] I was homesick and not very happy there at first, but after a while I got to love the place, and it was there I regained my equilibrium. I started to enjoy life. I made lots of friends, some of whom I'm still in contact with today. Only about 50 percent of the people going to these schools at that time were from Quaker families; the others were from non-Quaker families.

How did you relate to your fellow classmates? After all, you had experiences that most of them could not share.

ROSSMANN: They knew I was not English by birth. But they didn't know about my experiences. Normally I didn't, and I still don't, tell these things to people.

You weren't singled out then as some sort of rare bird?

ROSSMANN: I felt accepted. We were not supposed to go out at night. But sometimes we did anyway. And sometimes we got caught. On one of those occasions, a mistress referred to me as "the German boy." And that really bugged me. I didn't want to be thought of as "the German boy."

I was not very keen on sports. Cricket, football, didn't impress me. I was more interested in my radio sets, and I was a woodworker. I liked to go for walks and explore, and I loved geography.

How did your studies there help shape your future?

ROSSMANN: There were nine Quaker boarding schools in Britain, all good schools. For instance, my math teacher, Arnold Brerton, confirmed my love of math and the way I think about it.

My grades in English and in English literature were never very good. I was pretty good at science and math, but not linguistics. And this now strikes me as funny, because when I look at my students and postdocs, I think their English is terrible. Learning Latin was quite a help in understanding grammar and construction and word origin.

In all your school experiences in England, did you ever get any nasty behavior from other students because you were Jewish?

ROSSMANN: Oh, no. No. No. None whatsoever.

Had any of your Jewish relatives remained in Germany?

ROSSMANN: None remained that I know of. Much of our family now lived in London. Mostly aunts and uncles. One of my great-uncles had a son who joined the British army and was in the war. He changed his name from Oppenheimer to Orpen, making it sound less Jewish should he ever have been captured by the

Germans. Some members of the family eventually emigrated to Canada or to the United States. My cousin Ralph, whose bar mitzvah I went to, ended up marrying the daughter of an Anglican bishop. They had a church wedding in a very nice cathedral.

As far as you know there is no longer any German side to your mother's family? I mean, none of these people who left ever returned?

ROSSMANN: That's right.

Those who wanted to get out got out?

ROSSMANN: And I think that's because we were moderately wealthy.

Between 1933 and 1939, 15,355 of Frankfurt's 26,158 Jews left for various destinations. In all some 52,000 German Jewish refugees found safety in Great Britain. After the invasion of the Soviet Union in 1941, the Nazis rounded up most of those who remained and "resettled" them in the East: Minsk, Riga, and Theresienstadt — all way stations for the extermination camps. Only 600 Jews and *Mischlinge* remained in Frankfurt toward war's end.

Did socializing with the members of your mother's family involve participating in their religious ceremonies?

ROSSMANN: Hardly at all. Many were already assimilated or were well on the way. They considered themselves primarily Germans.

However, the Nazi racial laws determined that only certain ethnic groups could be part of the fatherland. For you, as a small child, not being considered German must have been terribly traumatic, and for your mother it must have been devastating.

ROSSMANN: Much more devastating for my mother than for me.

Because she identified much more strongly with her Deutschtum, *which she liked, than with her* Judentum, *which she didn't. Something not uncommon among some German Jews. It often led to a certain amount of self-hatred.*

ROSSMANN: I recently saw a production of *The Diary of Anne Frank* that illustrates that point. There's this dentist who joins the Franks in their hiding place, and he makes a comment that he's Dutch, and why is he suddenly being identified as a Jew?

What were you learning about the war other than what was happening during the Blitz?

ROSSMANN: I knew about the many Jewish refugees arriving in Britain. Many of these were interned in a big camp on the Isle of Man. At the time, it was difficult to understand why these people should be confined. Maybe the British feared that there might be some sham refugees who might actually be spies. But how could they be? I think it was a lack of understanding. Obviously internment on the Isle of Man was not like Dachau. They had entertainment and seminars, and they were released fairly quickly. But some of our friends feared they might be sent to Canada.

How were you keeping up with the progress of the war?

ROSSMANN: My mother got a job drawing maps for the *Zeitung,* a newspaper operated by the ministry of information for German refugees that reported the daily progress of the war. I was following the action very closely. I knew all the towns in Russia along the battlefront. I read the newspaper. Our class in boarding school subscribed to the *News Chronicle,* and on Sundays we went into Saffron Walden to attend the Friends meeting, and I would always stop at a certain shop and buy *The Observer.*

Were you cheering the Allies on?

ROSSMANN: Oh, yeah.

What about the bombings of Frankfurt? How did that affect you?

ROSSMANN: It didn't affect me too much, but it did my mother and grandmother. The destruction of the old town, which my mother loved. The scenes that she drew for the *Frankfurter Zeitung* were of places that were now gone. But I was happy the Allies were winning.

Was there a feeling that the Germans were getting what they deserved?

ROSSMANN: No. That would have been un-Quakerly. But I don't think I ever entertained the concept that the Allies might not win. Only much later did I realize how close Britain came to invasion. I don't think that it crossed my mind at the time.

You still had your family. And in London there were a lot of German Jews, a community. Were people beginning to realize that terrible things were happening to Jews in Europe?

ROSSMANN: I think we knew it even before we found out in the news commentaries. Even before coming to England. I knew that life was not safe in Germany. That Jews were being tortured and killed in concentration camps.

True, but still that is certainly not the Final Solution.

ROSSMANN: That's right, but after the war, when the concentration camps were being liberated and reports were appearing in the newspaper—my grandmother tried to stop me from reading the newspapers, but I read them anyway—the horrors did not come as a surprise.

So you suspected the worst?

ROSSMANN: Not suspected, I knew. I didn't think of anything else. I didn't know the details or the numbers, but my experience in Germany made me believe that Hitler was out there to remove the Jews by one means or another.[4]

After the war, a lot of our English friends would ask if we would return to Germany. I can't explain now why it's such a strange thought. I suppose it was a logical thought to those English, but at the time it didn't seem that way. To us such a prospect seemed totally impossible. Even now, when I go to Germany, I kind of feel uneasy. Not that I'm afraid of being harassed, but I just don't feel very comfortable.

Growth of a Jewish Identity: Joseph Haberer

> **"I hung on to books like a lifeboat, trying to refashion myself by reading and living in another, more hopeful world."**

An Orthodox Religious Environment

When Haberer was at Lowestoft, one of the children came down with the measles. This led to everybody being quarantined, and Haberer remained there several weeks in total isolation.

JOSEPH HABERER: The nurses were nice, but we couldn't communicate. It was like being in school in Germany, separated from the other kids so as not to give them a disease. When I was finally discharged, I was in a terrible state. I walked around in a daze.

And then I shut down and sank into some sort of black hole. I had an almost total loss of memory, which lasted about two and a half years. I had apparently lost a sense of self, causing a repression of my memories of that time. I just lived from day to day, trying to function. I'm not sure how much English I learned. My impression is that I continued to speak mostly German until I reached bar-mitzvah age, three years later. People may have thought I was retarded.

There were generally two options for the children of the transports: either to be sent to a foster home, not necessarily Jewish, or to be sent to a hostel. Haberer was sent to a hostel—actually, a series of hostels.

From Lowestoft, he went to Welwyn Garden City on the outskirts of London in Hertfordshire. Then from Welwyn Garden, he went to Nottingham in the eastern midlands, and from Nottingham to Northampton, where he stayed for about four years. The hostel was on an estate that the British government had requisitioned. There was a four-story manor house, which was surrounded by huge grounds with a lake, woods, and sweeping lawns.

The man in charge was Isador Marx, who had once directed a Jewish orphanage in Frankfurt am Main and personally led many Jewish children to England, including his two children. He was in England when the war broke out; his wife had remained behind to care for the children still in the Frankfurt orphanage. She perished.[5]

HABERER: The estate in Northampton was very beautiful, at least it was when we first got there. But within six months the place was trashed. A shambles.

The Jewish children in that home were not all refugees. About one-third of the seventy or eighty children had been evacuated during the bombing of London and later on would return to their parents. Most of the others were like me, those whose parents would perish in the Holocaust. I remember no culture conflict or cliquishness between the refugee children and the English children. Most of the refugee children excelled.

I attended a vocational high school, the Paddington Technical Institute, which had been moved from London to Northampton during the Blitz. I was a very poor student, probably placing near the bottom of the class, certainly among that of the refugee children.

I very quickly caught up with them in learning the English language, however. I began to read voraciously, all sorts—fiction and nonfiction. Everything I could get my hands on. I read books by Freud and Adler, especially

Adler, who wrote a book about the inferiority complex. That resonated with me. I read *Robinson Crusoe* and other children's literature classics. To get out of the terrible psychological situation I was in, I would go to the do-it-yourself books, like Dale Carnegie's *How to Win Friends and Influence People*. I probably read three books a week. More than anything else, reading was probably what saved me.

We had no counselors to whom one could go and say, "Look, I'm depressed, can you help me?" You had to try to figure it out yourself, which I did very quickly. I was practically failing in that school system, but I was a reader. I hung on to books like a lifeboat, trying to refashion myself by reading and living in another, more hopeful world.

I also listened to the BBC. I loved its classical music. I loved the plays. I loved the discussions. Many of the kids listened to the jazz and the popular music, but I was very much in tune with high culture. And I did a lot of walking in the English countryside. I would lie under the sun and look up into the sky and make myself more cheerful.

While Haberer was trying to adjust to his new surroundings in Northampton, the Nazis began eliminating the remaining Jewish presence from western Germany. In October 1940, four months after the armistice with France, they seized the remaining property and possessions of more than 15,000 Jews in Baden, the Saar, and the Palatinate and deported them to concentration camps in the French Pyrenees, the largest of these being the Camp de Gurs, a former reception center for Spanish Loyalist refugees following the collapse of the Second Republic in early 1939. Haberer's parents were sent there.

Before the war Haberer used to receive letters from them. Even afterwards, thanks to the Red Cross, some messages got through. It was also possible to send money and even packages with foodstuffs via the Red Cross. This help from American relatives kept life in the camp from becoming completely gruesome. But the sense of abandonment and loss was overwhelming. Joe's parents had taken his foster brother, Eric, with them, and when Eric became sick, they managed to get him medical attention outside the camp. He was subsequently hidden by French nuns and survived the war. Thus the parents were able to save both of their children.

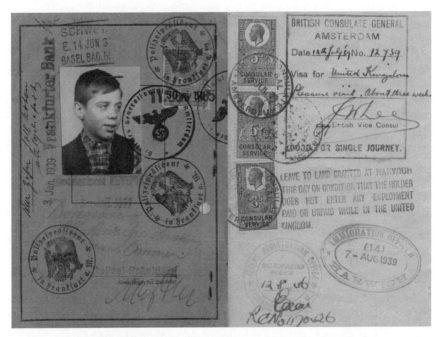

Michael Rossmann's 1939 visa to enter the United Kingdom specified
a pleasure visit of about three weeks. Germany's invasion of Poland,
and subsequent war with England, extended his stay until 1956.

Fritz Cohen in Florence, Italy, 1938,
where he attended a private school
run by German Jews.

Conditions in the Camp de Gurs gradually deteriorated. Food supplies and sanitary and living conditions were woefully inadequate, and during the first winter 800 succumbed. The dead, including Joe's father, were more than replaced by new arrivals, which by 1941 pushed the population of the camp beyond 15,000, a number that included 7,222 Jews from Germany and 3,000 from Belgium.

Following the Wannsee Conference, which in January 1942 formalized the Final Solution, Adolf Eichmann sent Hauptsturmführer Theodor Dannecker to the camp to prepare the transfer of the inmates to the death camps. Dannecker was his chief Jewish-affairs troubleshooter in Paris. He completed his task with efficiency. By the summer of 1943, only 1,200 Jews were left at Gurs. The camp today is difficult to find; few guidebooks mention its existence. Its cemetery contains the graves of 1,500 people, probably one of those being that of Joe's father, Bertold Haberer.

HABERER: Mr. Marx was well-intentioned, but very ineffectual and severely lacking in understanding of how to mobilize the energies or respond to the idealism of young people. He did a very good job providing for their material well-being, he was a good man and reasonably well-educated, one of the pillars of the community of Orthodox Judaism, but he represented an inadequate, ineffectual presence in understanding the psychological needs of these children. He cared a lot about making them go to the synagogue, something we had to do two times a day. There was a service in the morning and two combined services in the late afternoon and evening. Altogether we probably spent about forty-five minutes a day during the week and two hours on Saturday in the *schul* (prayer room) at the hostel.

He was not unlike a fair number of Germans whose authority did not come from the force of personality but from the operation of position. While that may have worked in Germany, where there existed a fairly autocratic family structure, it didn't work well in England.

Things got particularly bad after the war when the English children went back to their parents and we received a group of about thirty-five children who were direct survivors of the Holocaust. They ranged in age from seven to probably sixteen and were part of a group of one thousand orphan boys who had roamed around Europe after the collapse of the Third Reich, creating all kinds of problems. Somebody got them together and kind of calmed them down and sent them to England. The ultimate purpose was to take these children to Palestine.

I talked to them at great length to find out what their stories were. Two or three of them, for example, were survivors of the Warsaw ghetto and had escaped through the sewers. Others had seen people thrown into ovens. They had seen and experienced the worst. From them, at the age of sixteen, I got a picture of what hell was like. They all had stories about their hair-raising experiences, but after all they had been through, they generated the powers of human goodness and still wanted to lead a better life. That amazed me the most.

But when Mr. Marx tried to force them to conform to Orthodox Jewish norms, go to synagogue, wear yarmulkes, they refused. They were not going to be coerced into being religious. These children needed a warm, loving person who would bring them to Orthodoxy in a loving way, not order them to come and pray. After what they had been through, they wanted somebody who understood them, who empathized with them, who could mentor them, not somebody saying, "You're going to have to pray in the morning," and get angry if they didn't do it. They didn't want to be forced into religiosity after what they'd been through.

Marx pushed them to the point where they felt they had to rebel in order to maintain their own integrity. All hell broke lose. It was civil war. These kids could've murdered this guy. They were a lot tougher than he was, and he didn't understand that. Marx got into his German mode and blamed the rebellion on the *Ostjuden,* the Polacks.

Didn't you also have problems with that authoritarian approach?

HABERER: I played along. I was ambivalent. On the one hand, I liked the Orthodox way of life. Its religious aspects. The rituals. The total way of life. The commitment. But what bothered me was the mindless adherence to certain minutiae that seemed to be lacking great import. For example, Mr. Marx would insist that everybody wear their skullcap. There's nothing wrong with wearing a yarmulke, but I didn't think God Almighty was going to get terribly upset if I didn't wear one.

I really didn't relish the idea of being out on my own because of all the difficulties I had experienced: what I had to contend with in Germany as a Jew, my father being brutally dismissed and our family put in a dire situation, the trauma of coming to England and not speaking for three years, not remembering anything about myself. I had never been on my own before, and I was enormously fearful that if I were really on my own, I would not be able to find work, and I would go under. This sense of inferiority and insecurity went way beyond what one would expect of most people going into a new situation. Intellectually

I might say it provided me with a new opportunity, but my emotions told me of danger. The fear of rejection was so painful that I wanted to avoid any situation where I might be rejected.

On the other hand, the fact that I came as far as I have now is really quite marvelous. Who would have thought when I was sixteen that I would finally become a professor of political science? That in itself is kind of a testimony to something. Don't ask me what it is testimony to, but it is testimony to something.

> *Is that why we're friends—because you instinctively felt that I was an individual that wouldn't reject you?*

HABERER: That's undoubtedly the case, because if I had sensed that you would reject me, I would've said, "Screw you, buddy." (Laughter)

> *In Germany you were rejected because you were a Jew. At a certain level you found security at the institution run by Marx, notwithstanding your general feeling of depression. But now you had to face a change. Is part of the apprehension you had in some way linked to the fact that you had to go out into the big, non-Jewish community?*

HABERER: There was something of the fear of the *goyim*, because Orthodox Judaism has the task to ensure Jewish religious survival by trying to minimize the assimilation into a dominant goyish culture. But that wasn't much of a problem in that home, because we didn't interact very much with non-Jewish people. I don't think the element was that I was a Jew in a hostile Gentile world. In Germany there was obvious hostility, and I couldn't understand why they were picking on me.

I was a Jew, so what? My family was not Orthodox. My father did not come from a religious family. My Jewish, or religious, identity came about much more in the English home, where I learned about Judaism and experienced it in a very positive way. In the hostel, I was in a strong Orthodox religious environment in the tradition of Samuel Raphael Hirsch, whose basic tenet was that modern enlightenment and modern culture and the Torah, in the traditional sense, were compatible. You could do both. You could be a cultured modern person, and you could also be Orthodox. I think personally that does require a certain division. You have a certain blockage, so you kind of pretend that's true.

For four years I was immersed in that Jewish tradition. I learned the service backward and forward. I could still do it now. I learned how to say the prayers of thanks after meals, the *benschen*, which lasts about five minutes. I could say that by heart. So it was a very thorough, intense, complete Jewish life, which appealed to me in many ways. I got great satisfaction out of actually leading the service. Mastering this intricate religious service gave me a feeling of accomplishment. You don't have to believe it literally, but it can still become an important part of you. It moves you. Since I was one of the more obedient children in that hostel, I was also trying in some way to please Mr. Marx.

I also liked the English, I liked the English mentality. I liked the country, I liked the people, I liked the history. I don't remember experiencing any antisemitism in England. It never seemed to be a problem. I didn't particularly like the class system, and I realized there had been some antisemitism there, but I had never experienced it. My apprehension was not that they were going to throw stones, but at not being able to cope.

Experience of Becoming American: Fritz Cohen

> "I had to see the Germans defeated, and for that I would have been willing to do anything, do whatever I was called on to do."

Object of Attention

Fritz Cohen was enrolled in Northeast High School in Kansas City, Missouri. Whereas in Germany he had been the main target of abuse, here he became the main object of friendly curiosity. Everybody wanted to get to know him and find out about him. Considering what he had been through, the transition was not easy. The ostracism of the past had deprived him of the ability to grow socially, and it took a while before he could react to this attention without alarm and irritation.

FRITZ COHEN: I was very immature, very immature in dealing with that situation, but that was my first real experience as a fully and completely free person, and I naively felt that being the center of such attention was intrusive. However, being in school with kids my own age, I adjusted very quickly.

What about your father?

COHEN: It was much more difficult for him. He found work in a tie factory in downtown Kansas City, Missouri, working in the stockroom. For a guy used to having his own business, used to having things his own way, it was difficult, but there was no choice. I forget what his wages were, but they were not very much. He made enough to support us, however, and we lived according to our needs, which weren't very much.

After six months in Kansas City, the Cohens moved to St. Joseph, Missouri, where the father worked for a wholesale candy company, again in the stockroom. While there, he met some businessmen who convinced him he should look for a place to start his own store. He therefore surveyed the local area and discovered from an advertisement placed in the weekly newspaper that financing was available for opening a local dry goods store in Reinbeck, Iowa.

After a visit, the parents decided that this would be the place to begin, and they signed the appropriate contracts. The move to Reinbeck was made on August 31, 1939, the day before Germany invaded Poland.

Since coming to the United States in August 1938, you had changed schools three times within a year. Wasn't that painful?

COHEN: After all the moving we had done, settling in this town of Reinbeck didn't seem all that traumatic.

Did your father's store succeed?

COHEN: It did well—probably largely due to my mother's ability to interact with the local people. She had a nice way about her. She was friendly, generous, outgoing, and a very strong person. But I think my father did his darnedest to sustain the notion that he was the boss of the family.

What happened to your Jewish identity?

COHEN: I felt Jewish for the wrong reasons. I felt Jewish because I didn't belong to a church. But since we had very little contact with a Jewish community, my Jewish upbringing was a leftover from Germany, where I had learned the negative aspects of being a Jew. I lacked the positive side of Judaism. I must say I didn't evaluate it that way until much, much later, when my Judaism became a matter of self-education. Fortunately my children didn't have to grow up like that.

What was the attitude of the people in Reinbeck toward these German Jews who came to their community?

COHEN: We were well-received. Reinbeck is an old German community, and we were thought to be fellow Germans, so to speak. I never heard a single word that could be construed as anti-Jewish, either to my face, or to us, and not even thirdhand. Never, never.

Did these people know why you had come there?

COHEN: Yes, they knew, but I think they preferred not to talk about it. The people there were very insular, and I have a notion that they may have blocked out all the unpleasant aspects of German culture. They might even have been impressed with the rebirth of German strength and respect in the world. After all, these people were not all that well-educated, and their response was sort of visceral. But the people in Reinbeck were very nice and very supportive. I must say, I have a very warm spot in my heart for Reinbeck. Both my parents are buried there.

You finished high school there?

COHEN: Yes, I graduated in 1940, and then I helped in my parents' store until I left for the service. We were very conscious of what was going on with the war in Europe. We'd listen to the radio every evening, and we were very concerned that the war was going badly.

By the time Cohen graduated from high school, the Nazis had overrun western Poland; they were masters of Denmark, Norway, Belgium, and the Netherlands; and they had just defeated France. Shortly after the conclusion of the armistice negotiations at Réthondes, which officially ended French resistance, Winston Churchill declared that His Majesty's government would carry on the war to a successful conclusion come what may. However, in June 1940, such optimism as that displayed by the British prime minister was rare.

COHEN: I suspected that ultimately the United States would get involved in it. I'm not sure that my fellow citizens in Reinbeck felt the same way. I think that many of them were not very pro-British and were sympathetic toward Wendell Wilkie, who promised to keep the United States out of the war.

Assignment to Italy

When the Japanese attacked Pearl Harbor on December 7, 1941, Congress retaliated by declaring war on Japan, but on Japan alone, not on Germany and Italy. It was the European dictators who declared war on the United States first. Hitler joyfully showed his chiefs of staff the telegram with the news about the Japanese attack and on December 11 declared war on the United States. Italy almost immediately followed suit.

According to the military alliance that Germany and Italy had with Japan (signed on September 27, 1940), the signatories pledged to assist each other with all political, military, and economic means if any would become involved in a war with a power not currently involved in the European war or the Sino-Japanese conflict—i.e., with the United States.

Hitler's action, though, seems the height of folly. At a time when he was fully engaged against the Russians and the British, tackling another adversary was reckless; all the more so, since neither he nor Mussolini had done any strategic planning for such a confrontation; they even considered it unnecessary because Hitler calculated that the European war would be over before American participation could make a difference.

He thought he could force the United States to waste its resources in a two-theater war, completely underestimating the American capacity for the rapid mobilization of its overwhelming resources. He further believed the United States was demoralized and economically weak, perhaps on the verge of social upheaval.

Did the neutralist attitude of the Reinbeck community change when the United States officially got into the war in December 1941?

COHEN: All sympathy with Germany vanished overnight and was nowhere to be found. We were not yet citizens and had to register as enemy aliens. I had to turn in my .22 caliber hunting rifle, and we could not travel beyond a certain radius without permission. I found it humiliating, because certainly no one was more interested in seeing the Allied cause win than I.

When the United States declared war on Germany, all contact with my grandmother in Hannover ceased. We didn't know that she had died in Theresienstadt until after 1945, when a niece of my grandmother who was also deported sent my father news of her death.

Fritz Cohen wanted to join the armed forces, but had difficulties because of his classification as an enemy alien. However, after demonstrating his determination to the local draft board, he was interviewed by someone from the FBI who wanted to find out if Cohen's reasons for volunteering were valid. In December 1942 he received orders directing him to Camp Dodge in Des Moines for his physical, and he reported for duty shortly after New Year's Day 1943.

Cohen did his basic training in Miami Beach. (The army had requisitioned the hotels along Ocean Drive and put four GIs to a room in bunk beds.) From Miami Beach, he was sent to Venice, Florida, for further training. While there, in the fall of 1943, he became a U.S. citizen, the oath of allegiance given in the courthouse at nearby Tampa. Prior to administering the oath, the judge went around and asked everyone why they wanted to be citizens. When he got to Cohen, he said, "Well, it's obvious why you want to be," and moved on to the next person. In December the whole unit was moved from Venice to Newport News, Virginia, for final processing before being sent to Naples, Italy.

COHEN: Shortly before going overseas, I had a furlough; and when I returned to Reinbeck, I was made to feel as though I was now special, in a class by myself. I was at last an American. I went to the county seat to reclaim my .22 rifle, which they gave back to me immediately.

At the time I came home, I didn't know that my mother was terminally ill. They kept that from me. She had radiation treatments, but they were only partly successful. They made up some story about having had some temporary illness in order not to worry me now that I was now ready to go overseas, but I knew differently.

Shortly before we left, somebody from Army Intelligence interviewed me and asked me if there was any information I could give him that might be of military interest. I explained to him that located on the railroad line between Hannover and Ronnenberg was a large ammunition factory, which had at one time made blasting caps for the mines, that its roof had been camouflaged green, as though grass were growing there. They took this all down, but I found out after the war that they never found it. They got the railway stations, but the factory never missed a day of production.

W ithout being told where they were going, the soldiers boarded Liberty ships at Hampton Roads, Virginia. There were about eighty to ninety ships in the convoy, and the entire trip took about thirty days.

COHEN: I had no idea what to expect. On the one hand, I looked forward to it; on the other, I was concerned about what I might be getting into. But I wanted to do what I could to help bring this war to an end. I had to see the Germans defeated, and for that I would have been willing to do anything, do whatever I was called on to do.

What was your task?

COHEN: I was assigned to the 484th Bombardment Group (B-24s) in Foggia, Italy.

F oggia, on the Adriatic side, near the spur of the Italian boot, had fallen to the British Eighth Army on September 27, 1943, following the landings three weeks earlier at Reggio di Calabria in the Strait of Messina. The American and British landings at Salerno began on September 9, shortly after the announcement of the Italian surrender, and the Allies were almost driven back into the sea. It took a week for the position to be consolidated.

The Germans withdrew to a new position north of Naples, allowing the enemy's Salerno and the Calabrian pincers to join forces. On October 1, when the first Allied force entered Naples, the whole southern tip of the peninsula was under Anglo-American control. However, a spirited German defense from positions north of Naples, the so-called Gustav Line, turned the Italian campaign into a war of attrition.

But the Allies now possessed southern Italy's finest airport facilities, including the base at Foggia, and in Operation Strangle began interdicting the German lines of communication. Not until May 1944 was the Gustav Line breached and the road open to Rome. However, by then the Italian theater was a sideshow for the impending cross-channel invasion of France.

The Italian air war intensified as British and American bombers struck targets in the Balkans, up the Italian peninsula, and into southern Germany, some flights going even as far as Warsaw.

COHEN: I was in an Air Corps unit whose mission was salvage and recovery. We had a large truck with a crane and a very long flatbed, which could transport a whole fuselage, the wings, and the four engines of a B-24. There were about twenty or twenty-five of us—welders, mechanics, ordnance experts—people who could bring back the salvageable parts of bombers that had crashed inside our lines. But I often regret that I didn't have the opportunity to put my knowledge of German or Italian to better use.

How could you have done that?

COHEN: I think maybe I did not project the kind of enterprising personality that they may have been looking for. It occurs to me that probably I should have insisted.

What sense of identity was then reinforced? Your Jewish sense of identity seemed to be on hold.

COHEN: More than anything, that experience contributed to becoming American.

By June 1944, there no longer seemed any doubt about the eventual outcome of the war. The Soviet army had pushed beyond the Dnieper River, liberating Kiev. It had broken the siege of Leningrad in the north and cleaned the Germans out of the Crimea in the south. It now able to strike at will along the whole battle line.

Cohen was discharged at the end of September 1945. He returned to Reinbeck, where his mother had been buried. He had not yet decided on what he was going to do.

Return to Germany: Walter Hirsch

"I was really eager to go to Europe. I did not feel that I was going to have any trouble fighting my former countrymen."

Low-Level Stuff

When he had arrived in the United States, Walter Hirsch spoke no English. The prevailing educational philosophy, which succeeded with countless other non-Anglophone immigrants, also proved successful in his: he was put in classes where only English was spoken and was forced to pick it up. He did it so rapidly that he was able to maintain his class level in school.

The family first lived in Boston with Walter's uncle Siegfried, who had come to the United States as a young man. It then moved to Jackson Heights, New York, within commuting distance of New York City, where his father worked in a Wall Street brokerage house. Walter graduated from Flushing High School in 1937. That same year, shortly after his eighteenth birthday, he became a U.S. citizen. Then he began attending Queens College. Some of his high-school teachers thought he was college material, and his parents went along with it. He was the first one in his family who went to college.

He majored in sociology, possibly because of its relation to his life experience. He became president of the student council and graduated in 1941 in the institution's first graduating class. He then went to the University of Connecticut, where he had received a fellowship and an assistantship, but shortly afterwards, the Japanese attacked Pearl Harbor, and in April 1942, he was drafted.

Did you feel Americanized by then?

WALTER HIRSCH: I would say 90 percent.

What were your feelings in regard to fighting Germany?

HIRSCH: I was really eager to go to Europe. I did not feel that I was going to have any trouble fighting my former countrymen.

You felt that you were helping to right wrongs that had been committed to you and other people?

HIRSCH: I think that feeling was there.

Was this "personal element" also present with those you were serving with?

HIRSCH: I would say that most of them went along with it, but there was no great surge of patriotism.

When did you arrive in Europe?

HIRSCH: October 1944. We landed in England, spent about four weeks there, and then went across the channel to Le Havre. We crossed on Thanksgiving Day. The navy gave us a great turkey dinner. We ended up in a place near Paris and then went out to the front, which was somewhere in the Ardennes [that hilly, wooded region in northern France and eastern Belgium, well-known to the Germans from their successful offensive against France in May 1940].

The Battle of the Bulge, in which Hirsch would participate, was the largest land battle the American forces fought in Europe during World War II. By attacking a weakly held sector of the Allied front, Hitler hoped to split the British and American armies and push on to the capture of Antwerp. Hitler's commander-in-chief, Field Marshal Gerd von Rundstedt, thought the plan nonsensical, as did the tactical field commander Fieldmarshal Walter Model. But Hitler dismissed their reservations and committed thirty divisions, or roughly a quarter of a million men, to the operation.

The attack began on December 16, 1944, just before dawn, searchlights playing off the low cloud cover to illuminate the way of the first units. Among these soldiers was a handful of English-speaking soldiers of the 150 SS-Brigade who were disguised in American uniforms and driving captured American vehicles. Their job was to infiltrate the U.S. positions and sow maximum confusion among the defending troops by changing road signs and giving false directions. This idea was Hitler's and it was carried out by one of his most admired daredevil commanders, Otto Skorzeny. The presence of these bogus Americans did not change the course of the battle, but they did manage to stir up a considerable amount of initial suspicion and apprehension among the Americans. U.S. General Omar Bradley had to prove who he was on three occasions by answering questions that only Americans supposedly would get correctly. He was asked the capital of Illinois; the name of the position between center and tackle on a line of scrimmage; and the husband of Betty Grable. Fortunately he passed, although he had to argue his way out when he answered Springfield as the capital of Illinois instead of Chicago, his interrogator's choice.

During the battle Hirsch served an intelligence unit attached to the 203rd Regiment. Being a native speaker of German, his job was the interrogation of enemy prisoners, in itself not hazardous, but the presence of those American imposters heightened his sense of danger, especially since he knew nothing about American football, let alone bandleader Harry James, the husband of Betty Grable, and did not speak like a native-born American.

HIRSCH: You never knew who was who. So it was a danger that if you had a German accent and an American uniform and Americans caught you, you might get shot right there. And that happened to a couple of my colleagues.

Shot?

HIRSCH: Yeah. So I was very careful at the time. And if the Germans caught you and they found out you were Jewish, it might also be your neck.[6]

How would they find that out?

HIRSCH: If you were wearing your ID tag, you had an "H" standing for Hebrew. Therefore, I usually took it off. At certain times when it looked like I might be captured, I hid it somewhere.

The work of interrogation sounds like it was terribly romantic, but you asked questions like, "How many machine guns are over that hill?" The guy might or might not tell you, or maybe he didn't know. But you'd try to pinpoint as much information as you could.

Once I interrogated a cook, and I asked him, "How many people do you have in your company?" And the cook said, "I can tell you that exactly, because I made 107 wursts in my pot last night, and that's how many people are in my company." That's the kind of information you got, all pretty low-level, but if people put it all together, you could get a perfect picture.

Did you act alone or as a team?

HIRSCH: There was a team of three, and the number of native speakers varied. But in my case I was the only native speaker. One of the others spoke Russian. So once in a while we might get a German who wouldn't talk, and we'd bring in the Russian speaker and say, "If you don't want to talk to us, here is Lieutenant Raskolnikov, you can talk to him. If you can't talk to the Americans, then talk to the Russians." Usually that worked.[7]

The German momentum in the Ardennes continued for ten days and succeeded in pushing a gigantic salient into Allied lines. However, when first apprised of the attack, American commander Eisenhower immediately ordered the American forces to the north and south of the bulge to counterattack. Weakened by their losses suffered from these blows, stalled by heavy snows, with their supply lines interdicted by Allied air power, the Germans steadily retreated. On January 4, Hitler virtually gave up when he ordered the 6th SS Panzer Division, the spearhead of the Ardennes defense, to the eastern front.

How long did you remain in that sector?

HIRSCH: Until March, until the Remagen bridge was captured intact and we used it to cross the Rhine. I was in the first infantry unit to go over.

An armored patrol of the First U.S. Army captured the Ludendorff bridge at Remagen, near Bonn, on March 7, 1945, before the Germans could complete its destruction. This feat was of great military value, for within the first twenty-four hours more than eight thousand troops and a large quantity of tanks and self-propelled guns managed to make it over. During the next ten days, five divisions followed. The Germans tried frantically to destroy the structure, even launching V-2 rockets in their first tactical use of this weapon.

On March 17, the badly weakened structure collapsed. But by then American engineers had bridged the Rhine with pontoons and had assembled sufficient strength on the far side of the river to begin the final offensive of the war. At the same time, the Soviets had crossed the Oder in the east and were threatening Berlin from the south and the north. Hitler ordered the city be defended to the "last man and the last shot."

HIRSCH: I then went to Kassel, where I was assigned the job of looking for German war criminals.

How did you know whom to interrogate?

HIRSCH: It was a pretty haphazard operation. We didn't have any lists or names. Somebody might not like what was going on, they were not necessarily anti-Nazis, but they didn't like strangers in their village. So they might tell us that somebody was hiding out who used to be a *Gauleiter,* and we'd go out and get him and put him in the clink. Xenophobia was probably a greater motivation than anything else.

How did you handle the fact that these Germans were part of a system responsible for your exile?

HIRSCH: Yes, well, I tried to be pretty objective so that I could get the information that was required. But at the same time, if I felt that the subject was not cooperating, I might get angry, disgusted. I tried to be a nice guy, unless there was a good reason not for being a nice guy.

When you were disgusted, how did your behavior change?

HIRSCH: I might threaten him with being put away for the rest of his life. But there was no real probability of that happening.

Did you let them know that you were Jewish? Did they know?

HIRSCH: I did not announce it, and they might know it or not.

What information did you get about the Final Solution? There were concentration camps in West Germany like Bergen-Belsen and Buchenwald. They weren't extermination camps per se, but many people died in them. Did you hear anything about them?

HIRSCH: I heard what everybody else soon heard.

Their Just Deserts

With the Allied armies closing in from east and west, the Nazis tried destroying evidence of the death camps. At the same time, they continued their murder of the Jews. The last gassing at Auschwitz took place on November 28, 1944, and the crematoria were razed. Those Jews still alive were marched or sent in railway wagons to concentration and labor camps within Germany. Many, reportedly a quarter of a million people, perished from starvation, disease, or execution en route. Other camps were similarly dismantled and evacuated.

The SS maintained the strictest secrecy about the Final Solution. But even before the proof became palpable with the liberation of the camps, details about the mass murder had filtered out of Germany. Jewish refugee groups had learned of the gas chambers at Auschwitz and had informed the British and American authorities in the spring of 1944, hoping that the two countries would mount an air attack against the camp's infrastructure and technical installations. However, their pleas went unanswered. Only at the end of the war did the grim details of the genocide become generally known.

On 4 April U.S. troops discovered in a work camp near the village of Ohrdruf the emaciated corpses, still in striped uniforms, of four thousand Jews and Polish and Russian prisoners of war. Many had been shot just before the Americans arrived. Supreme Commander Dwight Eisenhower came to the camp and was so shocked by what he saw that he ordered pictures taken and sent to the British and American governments. Churchill circulated the photos to members of his cabinet. On April 15, British troops entered Bergen-Belsen, a labor camp that had recently served as a reception area for prisoners evacuated from the other camps in the path of the Allied armies. Of the 70,000, mostly Jewish inmates it had received, 30,000 had perished, mostly from starvation. Of these, 10,000 corpses were as yet unburied, gathered around in heaps or tossed into open pits.

The British, fearing the spread of disease from all these rotting bodies, cleared the camp with bulldozers. The operation was filmed and the newsreels widely distributed. Many people got their first visual proof of Nazi tyranny from viewing these in movie houses. The Americans took special pains to make the Germans aware of the suffering they had caused. One example of their approach to denazification was to bus the citizens of Munich out to Dachau to view, and in some cases to clean up, the rotting corpses. They also showed films of Nazi atrocities to German elementary and secondary school children and to entire populations in some towns.

HIRSCH: We saw some of the remnants of the concentration camp victims being put into places where they might recuperate.

Did you go into any of the camps?

HIRSCH: No, I didn't.

Being in military intelligence, then, was no guarantee that you found out such things?

HIRSCH: That was not the kind of information that came to us. Most of what I found out came when I returned to the United States.

Did what you found out when you were still in Europe change the way you did your job?

HIRSCH: It hardened my view toward Germany, even for years to come.

Did it increase your determination to root out the Nazi officials?

HIRSCH: "Root out" is too strong a term, but it did make me more determined to contain their power and give them their just deserts.

You had power to remove them from office?

HIRSCH: I had the power to send them to a military tribunal. But after they had been taken there, we had no more power. We didn't even know what the judgment was.

How many of those you interrogated did you think worthy of being sent on?

HIRSCH: Oh, probably one out of three.

How did you determine this?

HIRSCH: Intuitively.

How intuitively?

HIRSCH: I had no real method of doing it. You had to figure out whether they would lie to save their own skin. For example, if they couldn't look you in the eye when you were talking to them.

What kind of questions did you ask?

HIRSCH: Very simple questions, like "Where were you on such and such a day?" and "What were you doing when such and such a thing happened?" Most of the time they were not doing anything. They were just doing their duty, sitting in their office.

How did you determine whether someone might have been doing something more than just shuffling papers?

HIRSCH: You had to have more information, and most of the time it wasn't there. We rarely interrogated people who had much real power. We dealt with pretty low-level functionaries.

Did you have any lists of party members?

HIRSCH: We had no names, no lists, nothing to go by. Later on those came out, but not at the beginning.

Did you take advantage of that?

HIRSCH: By then I was gone.

You were still in Germany when the atomic bomb was dropped on Hiroshima and Nagasaki. What was your reaction to that?

HIRSCH: It was essentially *c'est la guerre*. But I do remember thinking "thank God, now I won't have to go to the Pacific."

How much destruction did you see of German cities?

HIRSCH: I didn't tour around very much, but there was considerable damage to Bremen, the port from which I left.

Did you feel the Germans got what they deserved?

HIRSCH: Yeah, precisely.

You never got back to Stuttgart?

HIRSCH: I did, and I looked for one of my former teachers, but he was still a prisoner of war, a French prisoner of war. Years later when I returned, I again looked him up, and in fact he came here. He was one of the first German teachers who were allowed out of the country and into the United States. He came right to this house and stayed with us for a while.

Stuttgart was pretty much flattened, at least the center of the town. Did you see if your old house was still standing?

HIRSCH: It was, and I felt very nostalgic.

How about visiting the neighbors?

HIRSCH: I didn't look up any neighbors, and I didn't look up my friends, either.

But you did not have the attitude of, say, Albert Einstein, who was so nauseated by what the Germans had done that he didn't want to write or talk to any of them.

HIRSCH: I still ask myself if the people, the older generation in Germany, could have done more than they did at the time to fight the Nazis.

You find yourself asking "What would I have done if I hadn't been Jewish?" And because of such willingness to empathize with ordinary Germans, you could not become so judgmental?

HIRSCH: I think you could say that.

But you also were angry?

HIRSCH: I was angry, yes.

How did that anger express itself?

HIRSCH: The question is: To whom should this anger be expressed? I had no-body in Germany I wanted to attack point-blank. Just recently I got a commem-orative volume about the school I went to. Everybody, including myself, made some sort of contribution. That's nice to have.

But you never resumed any real connection with any of these former friends. Was there any reason for that?

HIRSCH: I would say that times had changed.

Were you uncomfortable about making contact?

HIRSCH: Yes.

Hirsch returned from Europe in October 1945 and was dis-charged from the army shortly after. His younger brother had also served in the European sector. Both of them had reached the rank of staff sergeant. They had a reunion in Paris on V-E Day.

Notes

1. *Speeches of Adolf Hitler,* ed. Norman H. Baynes (London: Oxford University Press, 1942), 2:1098.
2. Other ocean liners also sought safe haven. The *Europa* stayed in Bremerhaven; the *Île de France* stayed in New York. The *De Grasse,* which was eastbound, turned around in midocean and headed for Halifax. The westbound *Queen Mary* increased its speed to get to New York. The *Athenia* bravely sailed from Glasgow, only to be sunk off the coast of Ireland by *U-boat 30* on the day war was declared.
3. Located forty miles northeast of London, Saffron Walden is one of the most charming villages in East Anglia and is known for its fine medieval and Georgian houses. The surrounding countryside is mainly low rolling chalk hills.
4. From September 1 until May 8, 1945, the Nazis murdered 160,000 German Jews, not counting 65,000 Jews from Austria, then part of the Reich.

5. Isador Marx's story vis-à-vis the *Kindertransport* is told in *Vor den Nazis gerettet: Eine Hilfsaktion für Frankfurter Kinder 1939–40* (Frankfurt: Jüdisches Museum, 1995).

6. Probably more than Hirsch realized, if it were discovered he was not only Jewish but also a former German citizen. This latter category of prisoner could be summarily shot. Of course, unless the prisoner in question were to have told his interrogators about this past association, they would probably never have found out.

7. "The Convention Relative to the Treatment of Prisoners of War," signed at Geneva on July 27, 1929, specified: "Every prisoner of war is required to declare, if he is interrogated on the subject, his true names and rank, or his regimental number. . . . No pressure shall be exercised on prisoners to obtain information regarding the situation in their armed forces or their country. Prisoners who refuse to reply may not be threatened, insulted, or exposed to unpleasantness or disadvantages of any kind whatsoever." *The Laws of Armed Conflicts: A Collection of Conventions, Resolutions and Other Documents,* ed. Dietrich Schindler and Jiri Toman (Geneva: Henri Dunant Institute, 1981), 274.

4
Reestablishing Roots

A Sense of Isolation: Michael Golomb

"The economic power and . . . political power of the ruling class is so strong that the state has to counteract and play a leading role in standing up for the interests of the common man."

The Protection of Well-Being

Michael Golomb favorably compared the postwar mathematical creativity of the United States with that in leading European countries. He believed this situation was due in no small part to the large number of mathematicians who had left Europe and settled here, not only from Germany but also from France, Italy, the Netherlands, and the Scandinavian countries. This trend toward excellence had begun earlier, in the 1930s, when universities like Princeton and Harvard had built up prominent math departments, but in most other institutions of higher learning this was more the exception than the rule.

MICHAEL GOLOMB: After the war, even if I had the choice, there was no reason for me to leave the United States to further my career in mathematics.

*In coming to West Lafayette, which was then a sort of a cultural back-
water, didn't you miss the intellectual stimulation of a big city?*

GOLOMB: In some ways I did. Sometimes we would go to Chicago to an opera
or a concert. When we were in Philadelphia, we had the Philharmonic and
good theaters. But when I returned here, I had started a family, and we felt it was
better to bring up children in a small community rather than in a big city.

You became a U.S. citizen, I assume.

GOLOMB: After five and a half years.

*When you were living in Germany and later Yugoslavia, you had a very
strong identification with what could be called radical or socialistic
causes. What were your politics here?*

GOLOMB: When I came here, [Franklin D.] Roosevelt was still president. And I
told myself that the New Deal policies he was pursuing were far superior to what
was going on in European countries—like in Scandinavia and in Holland—and
I became a Roosevelt Democrat. I hoped the New Deal would lead to a more progressive society. After all, the war brought socialized production and a somewhat
egalitarian society. But as long as the fighting continued, much of our effort was
directed to the defeat of fascism. After 1945, though, I thought the person who
best exemplified the policies I wanted the country to pursue was Henry Wallace.
I became quite active in his campaign for the presidency.

*Those were the days of the beginning of the Cold War, the House of Rep-
resentatives' Un-American Activities Committee and the Truman Loyalty
Oath business. What were your concerns at that time?*

GOLOMB: I was quite disillusioned in those days. I strongly hoped that after the
war ended, we would have an international community, and that the United
States and the Soviet Union, which had been wartime allies, would work together. Instead, we seemed to be going in opposite directions.

How did the resultant anticommunist hysteria manifest itself at Purdue?

GOLOMB: To give an example: after we returned from Philadelphia, we lived in
a faculty housing development out by the golf course. They had about twenty-
five National Homes units there, and all the mailboxes were lined up next to
each other at the entrance to the drive. Shortly after we moved in, I got a call
from the head of the mathematics department telling me that I should go to see

the president of the university, who at that time was Frederick Hovde. I went to see him, and Hovde told me that a neighbor of mine found a letter in his mailbox that had been meant for me, a letter that had come from the Association of Atomic Scientists. You know, the organization to which Bertrand Russell and Albert Einstein, among others, belonged. (It still exists.) The letter had been addressed to my Philadelphia address and was forwarded to me in West Lafayette, but it supposedly had ended up in the wrong mailbox.

"Well," President Hovde said, "this Association of Atomic Scientists is suspected of being a somewhat subversive organization; what is your association with it?" I told him that I didn't have any association, that I had attended one or two of their meetings, that I shared their opposition to developing the atomic weapons, but, I said, "I am not a member or anything. I simply was on their mailing list." The letter, by the way, was not a personal communication; it was just an announcement of a meeting. President Hovde said, "I understand, there's nothing wrong with that, but it's best to clear this up. See the local agent of the FBI and tell them about this." So I went to the agent of the FBI, and I told him the same things that I had told President Hovde, that I had nothing to do with the organization.

I never believed that the letter had got into another mailbox by mistake. It was clear that in such an atmosphere you had to be very careful. I subsequently cancelled my subscription to the *New Republic,* because it was considered a subversive magazine. You could only get the copy at the Purdue University library by written request.

What are your personal ideas of the "good society" and about the proper role of government in such a society?

GOLOMB: I feel that the economic power, and with it, the political power of the ruling class, is so strong that the state has to counteract and play a leading role in standing up for the interests of the common man. There's no other way. How can people pursue their interests and opportunities if the state doesn't protect them and promote their well-being?

But beyond that, would you say that the basic philosophy of what you would call socialism or Marxism is still valid?

GOLOMB: I recognize that many of those positions and ideals were compromised in practice, but I still believe in the development of a just and more cooperative society. It will no longer come during my lifetime but possibly in the lifetime of my grandchildren. Nowadays, I consider myself a socially conscious humanist; indeed I am a member of the American Humanist Association, although not very active.

How do you vote?

GOLOMB: We have voted the Democratic ticket. There was no other choice.

Do you feel you're voting for the lesser of two evils?

GOLOMB: That's exactly it.

You've been back to Germany?

GOLOMB: Visiting.

What did you seek out? Did you talk with former friends? Search out your roots?

GOLOMB: No, there's nobody in Germany that I have any connection with. When I go to Germany, I do not feel any hostility, but I don't see that the present Germany is a continuation of the Germany I accepted as my homeland—the Germany in the 1920s and the early 1930s before the Nazi regime. In the early years just after the Second World War, I often played with the idea that I might want to spend a length of time in East Germany, possibly retire there.

What attracted you to this idea?

GOLOMB: I once thought that East Germany was developing a progressive socialist society.

You've gone through many changes of place and home, you've been uprooted from the country of your birth, you had a transitional period in Yugoslavia, you came to the United States and have remained here ever since. Do you feel that West Lafayette is now your home, as opposed to a mere place to live? What are your feelings of belonging?

GOLOMB: I certainly owe very much to this country. Essentially, it saved my life, certainly helped me to develop a career, to develop a family, and generally treated me as a human being, not a member of this or that group. I am always conscious of this. But mentally and philosophically, I feel rather isolated from American life.

A bit like being a displaced person?

GOLOMB: Yes, but I ask, where would I not be? I have to be realistic about it, and I have to accept what there is. It helps very much that we have good friends and wonderful family relations here. There's one brother and one sister and their families and our own family—our children and grandchildren. They know that this is our country. And when I retired, we decided to stay in West Lafayette. It's hard for me to give up the roots, the connections that I have at Purdue, that I have here with colleagues and friends.

There is a tradition among Jews in which they tell their children what their most important values were in terms of the way they lived their lives. What might you include in such a summarization?

GOLOMB: I wish that a young person dear to me would have the determination to realize his/her talents and develop them to the fullest; to have the motivation and the strength to develop a life of creative excellence; to develop the power of conviction, skepticism, intelligence, and reason; to develop the highest moral concern for the needs of human beings; to work for justice and peace in the world; and, finally, to find happiness in music, literature, science, and the arts. Despite all the violence, brutality, wickedness, and inhumanity that have plagued the human race throughout the ages, I have always gained comfort from contemplating what goodness the human mind has wrought.

If the Spark Disappears: Walter Hirsch

"I expect people to be benign until their own interests are jeopardized. At that point they may no longer be benign or benevolent."

A Good Jewish Value

When he returned to civilian life, Walter Hirsch resumed graduate studies at Columbia University, married Lotte Landmann, a Holocaust survivor from Mannheim (one of the few in her family to escape), and started a family. The newlyweds lived on the educational subsidies of the GI Bill and on Walter's salary as a temporary lecturer at Queens College, his alma mater. When the job at Queens ended, he became a graduate assistant at the University of Connecticut at Storrs. When his first son was born, he rejected the idea of returning to New York City and began looking around for a permanent position. Even though he did not even have a master's degree, Purdue University hired him as an assistant professor in 1947. Hirsch had never heard of Purdue before going there. "They must have been pretty hard up at the time for professors," he commented.

Hirsch finished his graduate work at Northwestern University, because Evanston, Illinois, was relatively close to West Lafayette, and received his Ph.D. in sociology in 1957. Incidentally, his brother earned a doctorate from the University of Kansas in psychology, later becoming senior psychologist at the Menninger Foundation. No members of the Hirsch family had gone to college before Walter and Ernest had. The atmosphere at home had not even been particularly intellectual. Hirsch knew he did not want to follow his father into business, viewing his choice of the academic profession as one arrived at "only by default." The selection of a specialty, however, did have specific origins.

During his early teens he had become attracted to Marxism, resulting in part from his association with the Ha-Shomer ha-Za'ir. He took from the ideology its positive utopian message, seeing in psychology the whole notion of human engineering, a way to focus on the question of "the degree to which human society can be run along rational lines."

Additionally Hirsch became impressed with Franklin Roosevelt's New Deal. He had come here during its heyday, seeing in it the possibilities of the positive power and influence of government in helping to alleviate human misery, end exploitation, and modify the harmful effects of class differences. Hirsch's attraction for a society run along scientific principles, he conceded, was always a more intellectual and romantic fascination than a call to arms. Marxism, or communism, as practiced in the Soviet Union, hardly satisfied his desire for a humanitarian social democracy. Arthur Koestler's compelling denunciation of Stalinism in *Darkness at Noon* also helped to disabuse him of the worth of communism.

WALTER HIRSCH: In my classes, I tried to make my students aware of the difference between reality and ideology, and the role that ideology plays in human life, not necessarily the debunking of ideology per se, but the recognition of its goals. Of course, the particular course I was teaching determined how this would be handled.

Can you give us any specific examples?

HIRSCH: One would be the question of whether the Nazis really had any idea of what they were doing when they persecuted the Jews. Did the Nazi antisemitism result in anything that benefited the Germans or was it simply a way in which their aggression found an outlet? In other words, were the Nazis sincere in their attempts to benefit the German nation or were they simply using the Jews as a scapegoat?

What conclusions did you want drawn?

HIRSCH: That some of them were quite sincere, but they didn't know what the hell they were doing. Unfortunately, most Germans thought the Nazis were a positive force.

What courses did you develop when you came to Purdue?

HIRSCH: I developed one in social psychology, which was a continuation of the undergraduate work I had done at Queens, and a course in social movements, which reflected my whole life up to then. And finally a course in sociology of science, which at that time was a new thing.

You said the course in social movements "reflected my life up to then." What does that mean?

HIRSCH: My exposure to National Socialism determined the fact that I came to this country in the first place. Another was the communal movements, such as the kibbutzim and of course others like Amana and New Harmony. They helped determine the kind of movements I was teaching about. Another social psychological interest was reflected in the first paper I ever wrote: it was on assimilation, which is not surprising.

What was the gist of the paper?

HIRSCH: It was a conceptual piece, a theoretical piece trying to determine who assimilates to what, to discover the important elements in assimilation, to determine if the social environment is the requirement or the agent. I tried to tease out these elements with a theoretical spin.

You have been part of what would probably be called "liberal causes."
Amnesty International, for example. The American Civil Liberties
Union. What determined your involvement?

HIRSCH: I thought of myself as a persecuted individual, and I wanted to help others who were in a similar situation. And occasionally I was in trouble as a result. When McCarthyism flourished, the Indiana State Teachers Association invited me to give a talk on McCarthy at its annual meeting in Indianapolis. So I did, and the next day the *Indianapolis Star* had a big headline: "Purdue Professor Opposes McCarthy," and implied that I was a communist. So the next day, I got a telephone call from the president of the university, Fred Hovde, and he asked me if I had a copy of my paper available. I gave him one, but the *Star's* remarks concerned the discussion after the paper, of which I didn't have any copies. I told Hovde that, and he said, "Okay, we'll take care of it." And I never heard from him afterwards. I was also chairman of the board of the ACLU, but I did not do anything outstanding in that respect.

Didn't you get involved in the controversial Skokie business?[1]

HIRSCH: I felt a little queasy about that issue, and I decided not to push it. I didn't feel very well about the official position. Lotte, my wife, disagreed strongly with the ACLU on that issue.

What would your decision have been in regards to the march?

HIRSCH: I don't know, frankly.

It's a difficult decision.

HIRSCH: Very difficult.

Particularly for somebody like yourself.

HIRSCH: Yes, yes.

You're glad somebody else made the decision?

HIRSCH: Exactly.

Did you ever feel that you were in an exposed situation where you might have suffered some bad consequences?

HIRSCH: No, I never was afraid that I would be harmed for being a member of some organization.

You admitted that you didn't think of yourself in the terms of being "Jewish or non-Jewish," yet you became involved in certain Jewish activities. How was your Jewish identity awakened when you came to Purdue?

HIRSCH: When we got here, we had very little contact with the so-called Jewish community. There was a Hillel, there were two Jewish congregations, but we did not want to affiliate with either congregation, so we belonged to a group of so called nonaffiliates, an organized group of Jewish nonaffiliates. But the time came for our oldest boy to become bar mitzvahed. We discussed the problem with the rabbi of the Hillel Foundation, and he was bar mitzvahed there. But when our second boy's time came, we joined Temple Israel, and we have remained members ever since and thereby became "integrated," if that's the word, into the Jewish community. I also felt myself more Jewish because of the trips we took to Israel. I began going there since the time of my first sabbatical.

Do you identify with it in terms of its religious Jewishness, or because Jews live there?

HIRSCH: I would say pretty much the latter.

Does the religious part move you?

HIRSCH: I cannot help but be positively affected by this aspect of Israel. It's part of history, part of the people with whom I identify more than any other people, including the American people. But it's hard to say if I consider myself more a Jew or more an American.

What was the influence of your wife in reshaping your concept of Judaism?

HIRSCH: Lotte was always a more fervent Jew than I was. Her family belonged to a very conservative temple in Mannheim, and she was exposed to more Jewish learning and more Jewish traditions than I was. She believes in the basic tenets of the faith.

Thus had you married somebody who was not as conservative, you might have retained more of your assimilated past?

HIRSCH: I would say my wife's effect on me in that respect was greater than my cultural background or my experiences of the war. So a certain amount of assimilationist tendencies are no longer as evident as they used to be.

Is there anything about going to temple that moves you? Is there anything in the liturgy that matters?

HIRSCH: I think it depends pretty much on the specific situation; the music, but I can't put my hand on it exactly; it depends on the mood I'm in, rather than the specifics.

Have you ever had a kind of religious experience?

HIRSCH: No, I can't say that I have had. By and large I consider myself a secularist.

By secularist you mean an agnostic?

HIRSCH: Pretty much of an agnostic, not atheist, but agnostic, yeah.

When you think of assimilation, do you think it would matter if 99.9 percent of the Jews in the United States were to intermarry and lose their Jewishness?

HIRSCH: I can't say that it does. One of my sons has intermarried, and I can't decry the fact that he did, because he married a wonderful woman. Others who marry within the faith do not necessarily marry better people. So if the spark disappears, that is the way history works. If there is a lack of divine mission, so be it.

But your whole life has been a reaffirmation of certain humanitarian values, which most religions share. Certainly the disappearance of these basics would be of major concern. We can talk about secular humanism, but secular humanism "ain't bad," if it affirms certain fundamental values. What values do you think would transcend religious experience, maybe even emanate from it, but nonetheless are the values that really matter?

HIRSCH: The basic ones: do unto others as you would like them to do unto you, help the downtrodden, may truth prevail.

What are your general expectations about people? Not what you'd ideally like them to be, but what you can realistically expect them to be?

HIRSCH: I expect people to be benign until their own interests are jeopardized. At that point they may no longer be benign or benevolent.

You then wouldn't be surprised if people act badly?

HIRSCH: I would not be surprised. I would be chagrined, but not surprised.

Was there a time when you didn't have that sort of attitude? You know, thinking you should prepare for the worst, and hope for the best.

HIRSCH: If there was, I couldn't really construct it.

Certainly before Hitler came to power, your life in Stuttgart seemed secure enough. Your family was not being pushed around; you were part of the German community. Certainly there was more optimism at that time, wasn't there?

HIRSCH: Yes, there was.

At what point did you become more skeptical?

HIRSCH: In growing up people become more realistic. But the Second World

War destroyed some people's illusions. There was a time when people thought war could be avoided. At one time I was a pacifist, but no longer after the Second World War.

What do you think gave you your greatest sense of accomplishment?

HIRSCH: The fact that I picked or was picked by my wife for a strong marriage and that we were able to raise a great family—a good Jewish value.

A Strong Sense of Continuity: Fritz Cohen

"I am especially comfortable with [Thomas] Mann's antipathy toward any kind of ideology and his notion that things are not always what they appear to be. Mann believes that the polarity existing in all things enjoins us from becoming ideologues."

Reaffirmation of Humanism

Fritz Cohen's family did not have particularly strong academic traditions, although his father had graduated from a Gymnasium, giving him the rough equivalent of two years at an American university. In Germany the elder Cohen wanted his son to become a dentist. Now he would have liked nothing better than his son to succeed him in the dry goods store business in Reinbeck. But Fritz had no desire to follow a career lacking intellectual stimulation. The father consequently sold the store, and in November 1945 Fritz enrolled in the nearby teacher's college in Cedar Falls (now the University of Northern Iowa). He followed a general course of study, which he did not find sufficiently challenging. Therefore, in the summer of 1947, he transferred to the University of Iowa.

The registration was held in the field house. Tables had been set up there with an advisor from each of the various departments. Cohen stopped at the German table and talked to the head of the department, who urged him to take a course in German literature, and one course led to another.

He was not absolutely certain that majoring in German was his best choice, but it seemed congenial to his ideas of becoming educated. He received his B.A. in December 1948 and immediately went to graduate school.[2] Fritz finished his master's in August 1950, taught two years at the Alabama State College for Women, studied a year at Heidelberg University in Germany, and in 1953 returned to the University of Iowa for his Ph.D., specializing in German literature.

Some people with your experience might conclude that they never wanted to hear German spoken again.

FRITZ COHEN: That really didn't occur to me. That is not to say that some areas of German literature did not make me uncomfortable, areas to which I could relate only in an adversarial way. For example, certain romantic and neo-romantic authors of the nineteenth century were unpleasant: those precursors and exponents of the *Blut und Boden* movement, who saw German culture as the natural outgrowth of some organic whole, encompassing a common tradition and a common religion. Such writers were fascinated with sustaining certain monolithic moral values, but the underlying current was rejection of all those who didn't fit into a certain mold. This would certainly eliminate many who considered themselves German, including me. Even many famous writers who tried their damnedest to be German could never really be accepted.

Was graduate school the first time you came in contact with these writers?

COHEN: Yes, but I must say that my professors generally avoided people like Gustav Freitag, who represented some of the worst aspects of antisemitism.

Your main interest was literature rather than linguistics?

COHEN: The literature and the context in which it was produced. That is, the historical context and the political thinking. For example, I read all of Alfred Rosenberg's *Der Mythus des 20 Jahrhunderts.* It was a terrible book, but I wanted to get an insight into what drove the Nazis: their muddled thinking, the vagueness, use of terminology, and lack of definition that was such an important component of their psyche.[3]

What periods of German literature or writers did you consider more congenial?

COHEN: From the late nineteenth and twentieth centuries, I could name Arthur Schnitzler, Hermann Hesse, and particularly Thomas Mann. I am especially comfortable with Mann's antipathy toward any kind of ideology and his notion that things are not always what they appear to be. Mann believes that the polarity existing in all things enjoins us from becoming ideologues. The same is true of Hesse.

However, I chose the seventeenth century as an area of research, because I found that period less partisan than the age of the Reformation and Counter-Reformation, which immediately preceded it, and less nationalistic than those that followed. In the seventeenth century, German literature went back to the sophistication of the Renaissance, thereby rejoining a European humanistic tradition in form, intellectual content, and moral philosophy.

Who were its important precursors?

COHEN: An obvious source of inspiration was Petrarch, as well as the lesser-known Lorenzo Scupoli, an Italian monk who gave his book the fierce title of *Combattimento spirituale* (Spiritual Combat). Scupoli called on the individual to undergo a daily spiritual review, to measure life against certain standards, and never be satisfied with the feeling that one can ever rest on his laurels. I might also mention an important work I found in midcareer: *On Constancy,* by the Belgian monk Lipsius.

I felt comfortable with the period of the seventeenth century because I didn't encounter anything that made me feel self-conscious, anything that I felt would be unacceptable to me intellectually and in every other way. I found something that was truly cosmopolitan.

Did it reinforce a positive sense of German identity?

COHEN: Yes, insofar as seventeenth-century German writers were concerned with existential questions. They reacted to a world that was in flux and subject to forces beyond their control by searching for stability in a sort of neo-Stoic philosophy.

What writers in particular?

COHEN: Authors like Paul Fleming and Andreas Gryphius, both of whom got their educations in the humanistic Gymnasiums of their day. Many such authors very often took advanced degrees in Dutch universities, particularly the one at Leiden, which was extremely liberal by European standards.

How did you transmit the values of such people to your students?

COHEN: I tried to emphasize the existential quest and show them how reading such important writers would give them the opportunity to examine themselves and the confidence to stay from ideologies and always keep an open mind. I tried to show that looking at things only one way can lead to fanaticism.

You said that much of the German literature that came later was concerned with a relationship to land and blood?

COHEN: That kind of romanticism you're talking about can be very dangerous.

Can this apply to [Wolfgang] Goethe and [Friedrich] Schiller?

COHEN: In Goethe there is the best and the worst. Although his poetry is beautiful, it often lacks a great deal of warmth. He creates magnificent creatures who are often devoid of sympathy and empathy.

But Goethe was fairly cosmopolitan?

COHEN: No question—he's a towering figure in German literature and immensely significant. I don't think that in reading him you would ever be affected with rampant nationalism, but still some of his writings have to be taken with a huge grain of salt.

Schiller reminds us to be decent. His sense of what is moral and ethical is highly defined, and he would never lead us along the wrong path. Whatever nationalism you find in Schiller, it is not the exclusive nationalism that other German poets and the Nazis found so attractive.

Yet for all his humanity, doesn't Schiller serve as a basis for later extremism?

COHEN: That would be a corruption of Schiller, because he was one of the first poets who was outraged by the immorality of the nobility and their exploitation of plain decent common people.

So his nationalism to you is not exploitative?

COHEN: It is not. Schiller's philosophy is one of liberation; he calls upon his contemporaries to search for the best.

You said that you studied in Heidelberg in 1952. How did you feel going back, one might say, to the land of the murderers?

COHEN: I didn't know Heidelberg, it was not my home, but still I had the notion that I would encounter a great many people who had been enthusiastic Nazis and would hide it. And this did not make me feel particularly comfortable.

Did you find yourself looking at people from an age point of view and automatically wondering?

COHEN: Yes, you wondered. But having made the investment of time and money and so on, I stuck it out. With hindsight I probably would not have gone at that time.

But you have been back several times since.

COHEN: In May 1996, I attended a reunion of those from my grade school who had been born in 1922. There were about fifteen or twenty. I remember one who had been a close friend but had become a very enthusiastic Hitler Youth and whose attitude toward me changed into one of real hostility. I saw him last May and several times before. We don't talk about those Nazi times. I think he knows very well that he betrayed me, and that I would never trust him again. Still, he tried to ingratiate himself with me.

How about the rest of the group?

COHEN: I had one who had remained a good friend throughout—he wasn't there this time, because he had died—but he had remained a loyal friend. After I came back from that school in Florence, Italy, he came to visit me just before we left. He was the only one who came to seek me out, and we exchanged experiences, and he told me he thought that I was doing the right thing, that we were doing the right thing in leaving Germany, because there was absolutely nothing in Germany anymore for us. He went on to serve in the war in Russia, and he lost both legs there. We resumed our friendship in the 1950s, and this continued until he died a few years ago. He was a loyal friend, and I'm still friends with his widow.

On the other hand, there was a guy in our class who became a Nazi with all of his heart and is still considered to be such. He didn't come to our reunion. I think he knew very well that I would have a difficult time shaking hands with him. As a matter of fact I wouldn't have shaken his hand. There are certain things you don't forget and don't forgive. And he has never made an attempt to say, "Well, we were stupid and I realize that now."

Now, your other "friend," the one who tried to ingratiate himself with you, did he say he was stupid or anything like that?

COHEN: Well, he did say something like that a number of years ago, something to the effect that we were young and impressionable and so forth. But that he became personally hostile to me I hold against him. That I hold against him.

How did such hostility from former friends affect your perception of yourself?

COHEN: I had to make a real effort to convince myself that I was really worth something. And it made me cautious in making new acquaintances. I tend to listen and observe for a while before I show cordiality and warmth. It took me a long time, after getting to the United States, to believe that I was a normal human being. I had to get to know who I was. So I needed constant validation from others.

Did seeing how easily friendships had been betrayed make you feel that all friendships could be betrayed?

COHEN: It must have, because I made no really good friends until I joined the armed forces and, after the war, when I started college.

Did you ever have people ask you how you could study German?

COHEN: Even my cousins, who are German and live in this country. They decided that German was not a language they wanted to speak among themselves anymore. And I can't argue with them on this. However, I feel differently. I will not repudiate what I value about German culture because of what was done to me.

Can you talk freely about your experiences with others?

COHEN: There is reluctance on my part because what I have to relate is so out of context with the average person's experience that I often think there's really no point in talking about it.

Have you shared any of your experiences with your children?

COHEN: Yes, but this came over a period of time. I never sat them down and talked about it.

Have they become more interested as they get older?

COHEN: Yes, as a matter of fact, they have been hounding me to write a kind of narrative; and I've started, but there are too many things that you have to do.

What did you find out about the rest of your family?

COHEN: I found out that on July 23, 1942, my grandmother had been taken from the Jewish hostel and deported to Theresienstadt [outside Prague], where she died shortly after arriving. In December 1941 she had seen her daughter, my father's sister, sent to Majdanek [near Lublin, Poland], where she also perished. My great-aunt—my grandmother's sister—and her husband also didn't make it. The great-aunt suffered the same fate as my grandmother; her husband was simply worked to death before he could be deported. They had him on a construction project, this man who had run a store and who never lifted anything heavier than a box of stockings in his life.

A few survived, though. My father's first cousin married an Italian and moved to Genoa, where she converted to Catholicism. Both her sons became officers in the Italian army without any problems. In 1938, this cousin's sister fled to Brussels, where she married a lumber dealer. But she kept in touch with her mother (my great-aunt) and my grandmother back in Hannover. This correspondence, about fifty or sixty postcards, has come into my possession quite recently, and it's quite interesting. Here was this lady in Belgium corresponding with her Jewish mother in Germany, and her mother, Etta "Sara" Abramson, was sending cards back to her, addressed to "mein liebes Kind" (my dear child) and signed "deine Mutter" (your mother). Since these postcards were obviously read by German control officers, they might have reported the existence of a Jewish lady who was married to a Belgian in Brussels: "You should probably pay her a visit, like the other German Jews." But nothing of the sort was done.

I always found that kind of intriguing, because it shows that there were Germans who were not zealous. Or, let's put it this way: if these people had been zealots, they no doubt could have won praise from their superiors.

There's one card in particular that I have read over and over. My grandmother is writing to her niece that they're going to be sent to Theresienstadt. See, they knew where they were going, and of course, it was a terrifying thought.

Despite all that you have been through, you still have very positive feelings toward some aspects of German culture and literature, and toward certain of your past experiences. There's even a strong German affinity in your personality?

COHEN: I could never deny it, nor would I want to deny that there is. I realize that there were people who wanted to weed me out, who wanted to tell me I don't belong, but they had no right to do that.

Have you felt yourself to be culturally German-Jewish or more Jewish-German?

COHEN: It's very difficult to define such questions of religious and cultural identity. But I have a notion that cultivating a Jewish identity was a slow, general kind of metamorphosis, a gradual transition; it was not something that happened suddenly.

I probably would give my wife primary responsibility for helping me with this process. When we came to Lafayette, it was important that we joined the temple as soon as possible. I believe that joining shaped my sense of community and contributed to my religious education as well as that of my children. And in a sense I learned through them.

Were you an agnostic?

COHEN: Not anymore.

So for you there is a religious Judaism?

COHEN: I think so.

What does it mean to you religiously when you go to the synagogue or the Reform temple?

COHEN: What's important to me is the strong sense of continuity. Unfortunately, the Reform service lacks emotional content. On the other hand, I cannot identify with the Orthodox service, which is so remote and different.

Let me ask you the basic question whose answer no doubt has troubled you, as it has others: If there is a God, how could the Holocaust have happened?

COHEN: I can only reply that its occurrence does not in any way amount to a renunciation of the presence of God in history. We are limited in our ability to comprehend God's presence. And by recognizing that lack of comprehension, I can live with the idea of God. I don't think God decreed certain people to be abominations. He has given all of us free will.

Have you experienced antisemitism or Jewish stereotyping in this community?

COHEN: There's very little external evidence of the kind of active anti-Judaism to which you are referring. Real evidence of animosity comes primarily from the Arab community, the Islamic community, and from the black community on campus. Other than that, anti-Judaism has been confined to the offhand expression made by someone who is not particularly well-educated.

There is a tendency among fundamentalist Christians to support Israel vigorously. But I'm suspicious of their agenda, because you discover that they want to preserve Israel in order to convert the Jews to Christianity and to create a New Jerusalem. It's something like Martin Luther's attitude of preserving the Jewish people in the expectation that they will ultimately "listen to reason." Now, obviously Jews are in no position to reject friends—they don't have that many—but I'm always fearful that if Jews, confronted with that agenda, refuse to convert, all this sympathy or this empathy could easily revert to hostility and violent antisemitism.

But what you get from Luther is the idea that once the "listen to reason" process takes place, antisemitism will stop.

COHEN: With conversion it ceases to exist.

Do you feel that with these evangelicals you're referring to, antisemitism will stop once the Jews become Christians?

COHEN: That would be an interesting discussion and maybe very revealing. I've never had a discussion like that. Certainly with the kind of antisemitism expressed in Nazi Germany conversion didn't mean a thing.

Do you think antisemitism is an integral part of Christianity?

COHEN: I'm more and more inclined to believe so. Stigmatization of the Jews became almost an article of faith. Although the modern phenomenon of antisemitism also has racial, economic, sociological, and political facets, I think its vital source can be found in the belief that the Jews betrayed Christ for money and then crucified him because they saw him as a threat to their establishment.

Do you think it has anything to do with the phenomenon, present in most religions, that keeping the faith necessitates having a strong enemy?

COHEN: The Jew as Satan was particularly pronounced in the late Middle Ages and at the time of the Reformation and became part of popular culture. Popular culture does not introduce people to new ideas, but reinforces and elaborates beliefs already held. All you need to do is walk up to a German cathedral and see statues showing the Apostles standing on the shoulders of the Hebrew prophets — the church triumphant defeating the synagogue — to show present-day antisemitism's links to the past. The visual is always more effective than what is heard or read.

Did you feel that your Christian friends, those you had gone to school with in Germany, were being influenced by that sort of popular-culture antisemitism?

COHEN: There was religious instruction in our grade school, and it was often painful for me even as a child to hear about the Jews and the story of the Passion.

On an emotional level, do you ever feel that at some future point, antisemitism in the United States might get really nasty?

COHEN: I'm inclined to believe that won't happen as long as our country remains prosperous, but there's no assurance that this could not change.

The German Jews felt pretty secure.

COHEN: German Jews were more German than the Germans. I know that from my own family.

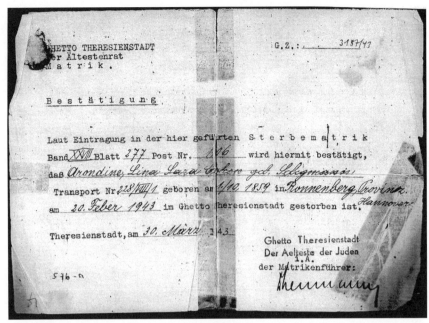

GHETTO THERESIENSTADT
Der Ältestenrat
Matrik.

G.Z.: 3187/43

Bestätigung

Laut Eintragung in der hier geführten Sterbematrik
Band XXVIII Blatt 277 Post Nr. 106 wird hiermit bestätigt,
daß Arondine, Lina Sara Erber gb. Seligmann,
Transport Nr 228/VIII/1 geboren am 4/10 1859 in Ronnenberg, Provinz.
am 20. Feber 1943 im Ghetto Theresienstadt gestorben ist. Hannover.

Theresienstadt, am 30. März 1943

Ghetto Theresienstadt
Der Aelteste der Juden
i.A.
der Matrikenführer:

The death certificate of Fritz Cohen's grandmother; she is listed on
page 277, volume 28, of Theresienstadt's registry of deaths.

Fritz Cohen at the time of his U.S.
military service.

Joseph Haberer in Oakland, 1947

What would be your reaction if, let's say, in a hundred years because of intermarriage and increased assimilation, most Jews would just melt into the general population and disappear?

COHEN: Well, for one thing, I certainly cannot look in a crystal ball and say that this would happen. But if it did, I think it would be a great loss. Being a Jew commits one to social justice, to extol the dignity of a human being, no matter what his socioeconomic status. It obliges one to recognize that there is a justice that is higher than the secular kind of justice, which is always susceptible to change and alteration.

But Judaism is also a whole series of theological imperatives, like a belief in a personal God. Because of the Holocaust have some people rejected the whole notion of the importance of God?

COHEN: I think that's fallacious. God was not responsible for the murder of the Jews. That was caused by two-legged individuals who took leave of their conscience.

Insofar as these human values have become the fundamental values of all ethical societies, does that mean a loss of identity for those who have originated them?

COHEN: No, I don't think so.

It would in a certain sense, wouldn't it? I mean insofar as something particular to one group now becomes mainstream?

COHEN: Yes, if identity means separateness for the sake of separateness. But I would never accept that.

I think the Orthodox might argue that separateness is a means toward a greater goal.

COHEN: That's interesting, but I do not believe that such separateness is essential for the survival of Judaism. And if ritual is the only guarantee of survival, then I think it's very shallow. I don't think that's where it's at. Not at all. I don't attach particular significance to someone who insists that in order to be Jewish you have to walk to synagogue on Saturday mornings, that one must not use public transportation. I don't know what that has to do with Judaism. The survival of Judaism depends on a certain degree of adaptation to the culture in which you decide to live. A weakness of Orthodox Judaism is its emphasis upon the Talmud as a primary book of instruction, which I find intellectually not particularly relevant. Interesting, perhaps, but not relevant.

Do you consider yourself a Zionist?

COHEN: If Zionism means that ultimately I should return to the land of my ancestors, I would have to say, quite honestly, no. But I do believe it's important to preserve Israel, which does tend to reinforce our sense of legitimacy, and I'm willing to support it emotionally, intellectually, and sometimes even financially.

Do you have a sense of a Jewish peoplehood?

COHEN: Yes, but membership is not automatic. It's something that has to be affirmed and renewed continuously. It's not a political entity, whereby if you pay taxes and do all the right things, then you have membership in it. It's an intellectual, an emotional, and a moral commitment. Otherwise, I think it loses its viability and then becomes simply a matter of saying, "Yeah. I'm Jewish."

You don't feel that you are in exile in America?

COHEN: I don't feel I'm in exile at all. I'm not in a Diaspora.

But do you ever feel that you're not fully at home? You had your roots in Europe and now you're a displaced person?

COHEN: I think any feelings like that that I might have are totally secondary to my sense of obligation to this country, which saved my life. That is an absolute. It's an absolute. There's nothing that can take precedence over that. And if there were ever in this country an agenda that made me a second-class citizen or insisted that I shouldn't be here, it's their mistake. It's not my fault.

Earlier you said that faith should be tempered with reason.

COHEN: Yes.

Being decent is reasonable then?

COHEN: It's reasonable, right, it's reasonable.

As Much Social As Religious: Solomon Gartenhaus

"Every German I met, I asked myself their age to determine how old they were during the Nazi period."

An Abhorrence of Violence

Immediately following his graduation from high school in 1947, Sol Gartenhaus began attending the University of Pennsylvania.

His parents did not have the financial resources to give him much support, but because he had graduated in the top of his high-school class, he was awarded a Board of Education scholarship, which guaranteed the payment of full tuition for education within the state. He continued to live at home and met pocket money expenses primarily with odd jobs. Thus he managed to pay his way through. Gartenhaus attended the university until 1951, when he graduated with a B.A. He first intended to major in mathematics, but during his junior year in college he changed that to physics. At that time, with the encouragement of his professors, he decided to go to graduate school to study to become a university professor. He earned his M.A. and Ph.D. in physics at the University of Illinois, from 1951 to 1955.

Did your background help shape your desire to teach at a university?

SOL GARTENHAUS: I thought that if we had stayed in Germany, I would never have gone to college. There were few such opportunities for those who came from my milieu. I probably would have become a businessman. Becoming a professor had a certain prestige that making money didn't.

Gartenhaus taught for three years at Stanford University before coming to Purdue in 1958.[4]

You certainly have a Jewish identity. But did you drop your religious identity—you know, belief in the five books of Moses, belief in the Torah?

GARTENHAUS: Essentially. But whenever I have found myself in a life-threatening situation, I found myself repeating those prayers that I used to learn as a kid.

Did your wife grow up in a similar kind of Orthodox home?

GARTENHAUS: She came from a non-Eastern German Jewish family that was a family of property owners. She never learned to read Hebrew.

Traditional Judaism doesn't particularly move you?

GARTENHAUS: Only to a limited extent.

Do you have seders?

GARTENHAUS: Yes.

But you say the Haggadah?

GARTENHAUS: We usually have about twenty people over, and we go through the Haggadah in about an hour. We go around the table and each person reads a paragraph or two in English, and I read some of the Hebrew. Then when we're done, we eat and have a good time.

What does it mean to be a Jew?

GARTENHAUS: I'm glad I'm a Jew. But I don't feel I have to believe and practice all of the Orthodox traditions. I don't believe that I'm going to heaven or hell when I die, for example. As I became more educated scientifically, I realized that those who were involved in writing the Talmud had no scientific knowledge beyond what was generally known at the time. When the Talmud was completed around the fourth or fifth century A.D., people still believed that the earth was flat and that the sun revolved around the earth. And they put these beliefs into the Talmud.

Nevertheless, today Orthodox scholars and rabbis still take those writings literally. They have difficulty acknowledging that scientific discoveries have changed our perception of the universe. Many rabbis today still paint what is written in the Talmud as the absolute truth, perhaps because they worry that if you question one thing you will next question other things. Rabbis that I have talked with have been intolerant of serious scientific discussion because they felt that it is their job to take away any doubts about Orthodox truth. So I just stopped talking.

However, you said that when you were in some crisis, you tended to say some prayers. Why do you do that?

GARTENHAUS: I don't know. It just it calms me.

Something like Pascal's bet: that even if you doubt, it's wise to believe, because if you guess wrong, you might really be in trouble?

GARTENHAUS: Something like that. You might need it. (Laughs)

But if there is not God, you . . .

GARTENHAUS: . . . haven't lost a thing.

But you have been active in the local synagogue, the traditional synagogue, as has your wife. You have even been president of the congregation. Why do you do that?

GARTENHAUS: That's as much social as religious. Some of our best friends are members of the synagogue. Also, I'm one of the few people in town who can speak Yiddish. So once a year I emcee the Yiddish evening that is run to raise money for Hadassah.

What kind of Jewish identity did you want your children to have?

GARTENHAUS: I never really thought about it. I didn't teach my kids how to read Hebrew as my father had to me. When my oldest son turned ten years old, we joined the synagogue, and he learned how to read Hebrew, and read the material for his bar mitzvah. And then my younger son did the same. But they both quit studying Hebrew after their bar mitzvah. Both my sons married non-Jewish girls.

Does that bother you?

GARTENHAUS: No. My younger brother, who is an Orthodox rabbi, refused to come to the weddings or even talk to us because my sons didn't marry Jewish girls.

Is your brother like a stranger?

GARTENHAUS: To some extent. Years ago, we once visited him on a Saturday afternoon, and at the end of the visit, as we were leaving, he said, "Please don't visit me again on Saturday if you have to drive." He knew we had to drive there, but he waited until we were leaving to remind me that driving was forbidden on the Sabbath. It was courteous, but unsettling.

Did you ever visit him again?

GARTENHAUS: We did once many years later, and there was a problem. They wanted us to stay for dinner on Friday evening, and this meant that we would have to stay overnight, because we couldn't drive on Shabbat. So I thought that we would get a room in a hotel within walking distance to avoid sleeping in their house. They said, "Fine." So his wife went to the phone book and looked up a hotel close to where they lived, and I gave the hotel a call. "Have you got any rooms?" I asked. "Oh, yeah," he said. And I replied, "How much are they?" And the guy answered, "Thirty dollars an hour!" That was Brooklyn! (Laughter)

You allowed that your children don't have a strong Jewish identity, at least at this point? How about your grandsons? Do you think they will have a bar mitzvah?

GARTENHAUS: I'm curious myself. I was down in Dallas a few years ago, and I brought presents. Somebody remarked, "Oh! You got a new present for Christmas." And one of my grandsons piped up and said, "No, it's a Hanukkah present." He's ten, his mother is Catholic, and they're going to come to some decision about that soon. Whatever they decide is fine with me.

How do you feel about Israel?

GARTENHAUS: I feel very pro-Israel.

What about your German side?

GARTENHAUS: Maybe it's wrong, but today I feel more neutral about Germany. I speak the language, and I'm familiar with the culture and have some good friends over there. About twenty years ago, I went to Germany as director of the Purdue Study Abroad program, to Hamburg University. My brothers and sisters became angry with me for doing it. My brother wrote me a vituperative letter. But now some of my brothers and sisters talk about going themselves.

At any rate, when I returned to Germany, I felt kind of funny because I could imagine myself walking along the streets in 1939 and being afraid of being picked up. And I wondered whether the next guy I met was going to arrest me. Every German I met, I asked myself their age to determine how old they were during the Nazi period.

I met this historian at the University of Hamburg, who called me up out of the blue. We went to lunch together. He told me he had lived through the Nazi era and went to a Napola, that's where they raised the blue-eyed, blond-haired Germans to be future leaders.[5] The guy had been only about eleven or twelve years old at the end of the war. But because he was forced to go to that school by his father, who was a minister, he had many guilt feelings, and he unloaded them on me.

Oftentimes the second generation feels terribly guilty for what their parents have done.

GARTENHAUS: That's what I thought, but I don't know why he picked on me. I saw him a couple of times after that, but we lacked a community of interest.

You seem to identify with a reborn Germany and wish it well despite your having had a narrow escape from the Nazis.

GARTENHAUS: No, I don't think so. If anything, as I said, I feel neutral about it.

Some people, when they came to the United States under similar circumstances, never felt quite at home, they always felt like displaced people. They could not go back to the old country, but they were not fully rooted in the new country. Do you feel that way?

GARTENHAUS: To some extent. But this country has made it possible for me to survive. Without the United States opening up its borders to me and my family, we would all have been dead. Some of our colleagues have no hesitation in criticizing the American government, but generally I feel uncomfortable doing that.

A lot of people criticize because they want to make things better.

GARTENHAUS: That's true, but what I'm talking about is the constant putting down that took place during the Vietnam War, when there was a lot of anti-American feeling. I disagreed with American involvement, but I never felt down on the United States.

What values did you try to teach your children?

GARTENHAUS: I wanted them to have strong moral and academic values. I wanted them to read and stay away from TV, but I didn't succeed. I had more luck when I encouraged them to participate in sports. They both participated in sports very extensively.

What kind of human values?

GARTENHAUS: Well, strong family ties; an abhorrence of violence.

Do you talk with them about your experiences? The sorts of things that we talked about today?

GARTENHAUS: No!

Have they asked about what happened to you?

GARTENHAUS: No! But once my oldest grandson was given a school assignment to write a paper on what life was like for a member of his family when that person was nine years old, his age at the time. So, I told him about my life in coming here from Germany. In it I talked about many things, including the Erector set theft that crushed me.

Considering the fate of others, you were very lucky.

GARTENHAUS: You bet!

The experience doesn't seem to have traumatized you terribly much. I don't sense a great feeling of loss.

GARTENHAUS: I don't feel it left much emotional damage. I was much too young to realize what was going on until much later.

For many American Jews, and Jews elsewhere, the Holocaust has become enormously important; even for people who didn't experience it personally, it often is a scarring event.

GARTENHAUS: We were lucky, thanks to Aunt Irma, to get out before the terrible things began to happen. By contrast, my wife's family had the opposite experience. Their escape from Germany was most traumatic, and not surprisingly, my wife is emotionally very involved with the Holocaust. Johanna serves on committees, gives talks at the local schools, and other sorts of things. And I think it's because she experienced Kristallnacht. She saw her Jewish neighbor's house burned down. In 1939, when she was six years old, just before the outbreak of the war, she was smuggled across the border into Holland, knowing that it would mean death if she were caught. I didn't have any experiences like that. Leaving Germany for me, as I said, was as if my father were changing jobs and we were moving to another city.

It was only years later that I realized that I would have been dead, that the whole family would have been gassed had we not left. But at the time, I was worried about other things.

I remember we were all getting on the train to leave Germany. My father had to go run an errand, and I was afraid the train would leave without him. I yanked up the window in the train and kept looking and looking. When at last I saw him coming, I screamed at him.

Whether you were aware of it or not, your parents did a rather remarkable job in protecting you against the trauma. Maybe it was their nature not to share such things with their children?

GARTENHAUS: I think you are right. There were certain words you could never say, words like "death" or "cancer." There was someone in our family who had TB, a disease from which you then usually died. Whenever they used the word, they lowered their voices. In our family unpleasantness was talked about in whispers.

Had they been more open, you might have been more fearful?

GARTENHAUS: Perhaps. It also might have had something to do with the fact that my parents thought themselves more Jewish than German. I have heard that exile was often more painful for those Jews who felt themselves more German than Jewish.

Also it was easier on you that most of your family got out. That you were not a sole survivor.

GARTENHAUS: In my immediate family, only my paternal grandmother didn't make it. Before we left, my father set her up in a place of her own in a small town near Kassel. But in 1942, she was picked up and, with the rest of the Kassel Jews, sent to a concentration camp, and to her death.

Also in Germany my best friend was a guy named Siegi Adler. One winter, we were walking across the Fulda River when it was frozen over. The ice broke; I fell into the river and would have drowned had he not pulled me out. I remember afterwards sitting by the stove, warming my frozen wet clothes without realizing that he had saved my life!

Did he get out?

GARTENHAUS: He didn't make it. He was supposed to go to Australia, but he never got there. Nobody in Kassel, as far as I know, survived if they stayed.

A More Rational Than Mystic Approach: Michael Rossmann

"I don't think [my children or their children] will ever have this feeling of being outsiders in terms of race or religion or speech in any way, and that makes me very happy."

My Heimat *Is Science*

Rossmann graduated from secondary school in 1948 at the top of his class; he intended to go to the university and major in science. But the Friends School at Saffron Walden had not catered to such academic needs, giving him only superficial preparation in physics, chemistry, and mathematics. He knew he was not getting the best instruction, but saw the long-run benefit in having to teach himself. Not being spoon-fed was a good experience.

He began his higher education at the Polytechnic Institute, an external college of the University of London, graduating three years later with a degree in physics and mathematics. Eventually, he became a Ph.D. student at the University of Glasgow, and at the same time taught as an instructor at the local Royal Technical College (now the University of Strathclyde). After three years, he received his doctoral degree (in 1956).

Were you a British citizen by then?

MICHAEL ROSSMANN: Yes. My mother became a British citizen in 1945, when I was still a minor, and I got my citizenship through her.

Were you identifying with your new country?

ROSSMANN: In England, I always felt not English. I had an accent. Most people who came to England at my age would have lost it, but I didn't. Accents in England do count. I was always identified as not being English. But my education was English. I was a teenager in England, and that was very meaningful. I had left home and was no longer part of the German refugee community.

I wanted to stay in England. But after I got my Ph.D., I wanted postdoctorate experience in the United States. Many of the graduates from the university had gone to the United States for postdoctoral studies. By then I had married Audrey, and although we never discussed coming to the United States, when one of the professors from the University of Minnesota, someone who had been a visiting professor at Oxford, offered me an assistantship, we decided to accept and stay there for two years. After that, we would return, and I would get a position in some British university.

At the point when we were ready to leave America and come back to England, we found that we could easily have stayed. It was a fine university, and Minnesota had all these lakes and beautiful blue skies. But then I got a senior postdoc with the Medical Research Council Unit for Molecular Biology in the Cavandish Laboratory of Cambridge University.

R ossmann worked for the Medical Research Council. He also had a tutoring position, which involved giving tutorials and monitoring the progress of undergraduates of Peterhouse (College).[6] The cost of living in Cambridge was very high, which the presence of American military personnel living in the area exacerbated. But with an inheritance from his mother's and grandmother's estates, he was able to buy a small house for about two thousand pounds. His contract was initially for three years and was extended once.

ROSSMANN: Cambridge was very, very exciting. This was where molecular biology had started. I was literally next door to people like Francis Crick, the discoverer of the double helix. We would meet for coffee time at 11:00 in the morning. I wrote a whole paper based on coffee time conversations with Francis.

I wanted to stay there. At Cambridge I was able to develop a technology that is now used in biological sciences all over the world. But when my second contract was not renewed after six years, I had to look around for another job. I was sad to leave.

After he had returned from his postdoctoral experience in Minnesota, he never considered that he would return to the United States. He considered himself a British resident. However, it was apparent Oxford and Cambridge "old boys" were preferred for permanent employment.

You felt like you had been treated as an outsider?

ROSSMANN: Those with the wrong accent are not so easily accepted in Cambridge. It doesn't matter so much in America, because so many people are foreign.[7]

Did you feel that things were unfair in many ways?

ROSSMANN: I would never use the word "unfair." I felt envious of those who had a chance of going to the best universities. I had not attended "The Good University." I subsequently found out, when I was a tutor at Cambridge, that the students there weren't all that stupendous and gifted. A lot of them had ability, but they were hardly outstanding.

When you encountered this contretemps at Cambridge, did it seem logical for you to consider coming to the United States, or to find a position in, say, Europe?

ROSSMANN: I received six separate good offers to come to America, and I chose Purdue because I was offered more personal support in terms of what I wanted to do.

Today we've got a structural biology subgroup in the department with thirteen faculty members. That represents one of the largest, if not the largest, such division in any American university. I think this continuing support came because we did good science, but also because when I persevered, I usually got what I wanted.

Coming from Cambridge, England, to the American Midwest at times must have seemed like a lonely battle.

ROSSMANN: The first five years, especially. I had come from a place, which, for my science, was the center of the universe, and there was nothing here. Purdue lacked the stimulation that I had at Cambridge. Here I had to teach people to achieve the level that I felt was acceptable.

Also coming here we encountered racial prejudice. My first assistant was a black woman from Gary. At that time, in 1964, there were maybe only a dozen or so African-Americans at Purdue. When she first came to Purdue, this graduate assistant had to live in what was called the "black ghetto" across town by Market Square. Considering my own experience with racial prejudice, none of this made any sense, and as a result I became very involved in the local civil rights movement. I was active on campus with various black groups. We actually tried to get the university to establish a Black Cultural Center, but were turned down flat. Later on it was established.

When did you become a citizen?

ROSSMANN: We waited approximately ten years, and that was because of the Vietnam War, which didn't exactly agree with our pacifist principles.

Considering that you were torn from your homeland and had undergone many dislocations since, did you feel at home here?

ROSSMANN: If you had asked me where my home was, where I would want to retire, I would say Lafayette, Indiana.

You don't feel now like a displaced person? As if this were not your Heimat?

ROSSMANN: No. I was not born in Lafayette, but I've lived here most of my adult life — longer than in any other place. In a way my *Heimat* is science. The international community of scientists means a lot to me. I have friends all over the world, and if I were to ever retire, I wouldn't mind being, say, the corresponding secretary of the National Academy of Sciences.

But I would be reluctant to leave this particular house, where our family grew up. We want to be sure that anyone of our family can always feel that they can come back to this home, to their roots, if you like.

Did you ever entertain thoughts of going back to England?

ROSSMANN: Living in England now doesn't make sense. It seems a concept almost as strange as the one of returning to Germany after the war. We're settled here.

Any kind of questions about "who am I really?"

ROSSMANN: Not in a very conscious way.

AUDREY ROSSMANN: He doesn't know who he is. And he doesn't want to know, either.

ROSSMANN: I still think of myself as Jewish in ancestry, whether or not I am a practicing Jew or Christian.

Could you expand on these various identities?

ROSSMANN: In terms of religion, my mother thought that being Jewish was a matter of private concern, like being a Protestant or a Catholic in the United States. She considered herself a Jew from a genetic point of view. And that's how I feel about myself. Of course Jewishness also includes religion, but there are all kinds of Jewish religions: Orthodox and non-Orthodox, all with their own differences.

> *There have been many studies of the experiences of Jewish children, not all of them refugees, who went to a culture, a non-Jewish culture, one different from theirs, and that left an enormous imprint on them with negative psychological consequences, affecting them for the rest of their lives.*

ROSSMANN: I was aware that I came from a partly Jewish background, but in Britain I considered myself primarily a Quaker.

Your mother, I take it, tried to persuade you to become a Quaker?

ROSSMANN: It was very obvious. In England, she was an active member of the Quaker meeting and would take me to Sunday school there. I always had the feeling, and it was certainly true for me, that my mother was primarily interested in the philanthropic aspect of Quakerism, in the concept of creating an ideal community.

Other than genetics, what did being Jewish mean to your mother?

ROSSMANN: One could almost say that certain aspects of my mother were antisemitic. She had hair color and blue eyes like mine. I think she was quite happy to not look Jewish. My grandmother, on the other hand, looked very Jewish, but she was quite negative and prejudiced about the Jews who came from the east, from Poland.

> *German Jews were very sensitive to the bad impression these eastern people would create and they wanted to get them out of Germany very quickly. That feeling was very common.*

ROSSMANN: Yeah, she would tell me all the time that they behaved differently from Germans.

How much have you told your children about your life story?

ROSSMANN: Our three children are all different. Alice, the middle one, asks us much more than the other two and seems to have a genuine understanding of what I had lived through. Once when we were together in Stockholm, my wife suggested that we go see *Schindler's List.* And Alice said, "Oh no, Mom, that won't be very good for Dad, it will hurt him." So we didn't go.

My guess would be that you would not particularly want to tell your story to them, unless they asked you?

ROSSMANN: I think that's right. Only Alice so far.

How important is religion to your life?

ROSSMANN: I would say that my approach to life has always been more rational than mystical.

Never have had any Damascus Road experience?

ROSSMANN: No. But one of the aspects of Quakerism in which I believe is the concept of God in everyone. This I translate to mean that there is good in every person, and you should strive to bring that out.

So there's a natural religion?

ROSSMANN: Yes.

Earlier you mentioned The Diary of Anne Frank. *Do you agree with her conclusion that somehow all people are good at heart?*

ROSSMANN: That's certainly a Quaker point of view. In the thirties some English Quakers went to talk to Adolf Hitler; they believed that there was something good, something of God, in everybody. But, of course, their attempts to persuade Hitler to be more humane didn't succeed. But that's the sort of attitude Anne Frank has in her diary.

How do you feel about that? If your mother had stayed in Germany, it would have been unfortunate. To put it mildly.

ROSSMANN: It would have cost her her life. But I find this very difficult to answer. Part of the Quaker teaching is to be pacifist, not to fight, and I can tell you many anecdotes that the Quakers tell to extol the pacifist approach in difficult situations. I would agree that this was the right way, but I don't think approaching Hitler this way was likely to succeed.

Was this pacifism something that kept you from complaining to your mother about the harassment that you had received?

ROSSMANN: I don't think so. I just couldn't tell my mother that this was happening. I can't fully explain it.

Anything to do with a religious conviction? A faith in God?

ROSSMANN: When I was at Saffron Walden Friends School, I went around asking very seriously, "Is there a God and what does God mean?" For a long time I made myself a nuisance, disturbing my teachers because of my questions. But that is my nature. I tend to question everything. Nothing is ever simple to me. I think I would have done that under any circumstances.

Ever feel any personal association with the figure of Jesus?

ROSSMANN: Christ never played a significant part in my thinking. I was never sure my interpretations of the New Testament were correct, but I continued to take it in the sense of being kind to people, working to bringing out their best.

The Sermon on the Mount?

ROSSMANN: Yes, maybe that's my mother's influence. I am much like my mother in character. Very similar in many ways. My mother indoctrinated me with the basic humanitarian values of Quakerism. I appreciate these very much and always have.

What about the lessons learned from your experience?

ROSSMANN: Well, you know, I don't think things entirely die out with your generation. Values and attitudes get passed down.

The Bible says the sins of the father are passed on to the seventh generation. What if your children were to come and ask you to tell them about your personal values, what would you say?

ROSSMANN: I suspect they probably wouldn't ask quite as searching questions as you do. But I would tell them to try and discover the good qualities of individuals.

What do you feel is the role of government in creating a good society?

ROSSMANN: Oh, my.

Well, you've been a victim of government-created ideal society.

ROSSMANN: There probably is no such thing as a perfect government, "perfect" cannot be because society is, after all, made up of different people, and different people have different ideas. So government in a sense can be only a lowest common denominator.

Certainly you believe in more than that. You certainly believe in a strong role for the government in education, and that's not the lowest common denominator, because you would then only be educating "the masses," whoever they might be. Education is also for the elite. You can have universal suffrage, but laws are not made or passed by "everybody."

ROSSMANN: True. In England, the laws on compulsory education were indeed passed at a time when there wasn't universal suffrage. The more educated part of the population forced these laws on a part of society that did not have any say in the matter. Improvements do not always come about because of democracy.

How do you feel about the responsibility of government in this respect today?

ROSSMANN: It should work for good. For example, I applaud strong government action in the area of civil rights. It is unacceptable to discriminate against anybody on the basis of race or religion in job applications, housing, and so on. And my children and their children are free from that. I don't think they will ever have this feeling of being outsiders in terms of race or religion or speech in any way, and that makes me very happy.

Assuming they will someday read these words, what else would you like them to know?

ROSSMANN: I haven't exactly thought about it. That's a very difficult thing, I don't know if I can answer that, what advice I would pass on to my children, to my grandchildren. I don't know. I might say let's go and get the tapes of these conversations. They will probably tell more about my history now than anything else.

Some Transcendental Way: Joseph Haberer

> **"Throughout my life, I have always been amazed at the enormous capacity of people to recuperate from great injury, and the enormous potential that people have to realize their better self, their ability to live full rich lives in decent relationships with others."**

Daffodils Going On for Miles

After his graduation from the Paddington Technical Institute at the age of sixteen, Haberer considered emigrating to Palestine. In the hostel he had been a member of a religious Zionist movement inspired by Rabbi Bnai Akiba. He liked its socialist and idealistic spirit and the boost it gave to his Jewish identity. But on a very deep level he understood that it would be extremely difficult for him to adapt to the life of a kibbutz and lose himself in a collective whole. On the other hand, fitting into the highly structured class system of England was not going to be easy, despite his preference for the English mentality. Even if he had not done so poorly at the Paddington Technical Institute, refugees like him were hardly considered fit material for Oxford or Cambridge.

Haberer wanted a smaller, more nurturing environment; he wanted to get away from institutions and the huge business of an extended family. So when an aunt living in California got in touch with him and asked him if he wanted to come to the United States, he accepted immediately.

JOSEPH HABERER: I had read a lot about America. I got an idealized picture from the *National Geographic*. It was all a very wonderful, beautiful country. I saw an article about California, and there was a picture of an enormous patch of daffodils going on for miles and I said, "My God, I like daffodils."

I was also attracted to America as a place where you were not frozen into a position by the time you were fourteen, as you were in England. America was a land of real opportunity, whereas in England the ethos of aristocracy still ruled. I probably would have come here in any case, but I also realized that there was that part, which I liked very much. Not the idea that the streets were paved of gold, but that there was democracy and apparently a place for the small guy.

Haberer left Southampton for New York in November 1946. Distant relatives met him at the boat when he arrived. He stayed with them for several weeks in Manhattan and then was put on a train for the trip across the country to Oakland, California, where his uncle and aunt lived. He was still Orthodox and ate nothing but kosher food. He ate only the food his relatives had given him. He also had very little money and was very frugal. The trip took about five days.

HABERER: I arrived in November, and I immediately went to Oakland High School. I got put in the twelfth grade. I knew about the American school system from John Dewey, a big contrast from the one in England. It was really a very good experience. As soon as I got there, the teachers had me talk about my experiences in Europe to the other students.

You didn't resent being an object of curiosity?

HABERER: No. I was a very serious person. Much more serious than my age indicated. And talking about my experiences apparently made quite an impression. It was a good experience, it made me feel important.

You didn't encounter any antisemitism in high school?

HABERER: Rarely overtly, but I experienced some stereotypical thinking about Jews.

They are only interested in money and they are pushy? That kind of crap?

HABERER: But personally I've never seen this as a problem. I'm not saying there are not serious cases of hatred around; there obviously are in this country, but that is hardly mainstream.

What were your expectations in that regard?

HABERER: I didn't expect antisemitism. Strange as it may seem, I never worried about it. That this was the America I had imagined was revealed when I received my high-school diploma. I was amazed. This was the America where anybody could advance. It didn't matter that I hadn't passed the college entrance exams in England. They didn't care that I wasn't a great student over there. I was judged capable now, and they gave me a diploma.

But even before I graduated, the question came up about what I would do afterwards. I discussed my future with my high-school counselors and said I wanted to become a teacher. I wanted to make a difference, to have an impact, to do something worthwhile. I wanted to justify my existence. And my solution was to continue my education.

My initial goal was not to become a scholar, but simply to become a high-school teacher. In England, I had seen *Good-bye Mr. Chips,* and from that movie I got a notion of the marvelous opportunity to help and change and mold human lives through education and teaching. I wanted to be somebody who would be dealing with young people and who would be able to help their development and inspire them and have an impact on their lives.

aberer attended San Francisco State University, taking courses in history, sociology, philosophy, and English. The more he studied, the more he liked it, and despite having a half-time job, got mostly A's. He found practice teaching daunting, but he forced himself to do it and eventually emerged with his secondary-school teaching certificate.

You entered college at about the same age as did the other students at San Francisco State, but your background certainly was different from theirs, one hardly typical of an American student. Did you have an opportunity to share any of your experiences with them?

HABERER: I had no friends at San Francisco State with whom I could talk about my experiences. The conversation among the undergraduates was mainly about certain common problems concerning the school. The friends that I did have tended to come from Europe. There was one, for example, whom I met through the synagogue. His parents had survived the Nazis by going to Spain. And we got fairly close.

In America, people were so friendly, but it was a sort of social lubricant so that people could get along. Americans have so much mobility, people moving all the time, not wanting to invest in relationships too much, because that doesn't pay. So there wasn't very much community. There wasn't much cohesion. Everyone was going about their own business, and business was the business of America.

Now, there are always exceptions to this, but this was a picture that I got very quickly. And I think, I still think, that's true. It was always a great disappointment to me because everybody is hell-bent on their career. That's the part of America I don't particularly like. I also know throughout my life I have always felt a sort of distance with most Americans, including colleagues. With Europeans, I don't feel that.

Part of that may be due to me, part of my personality, I don't know. I don't see myself as rejecting people or not wanting to get close to them, but who knows? Some of the reason, though, is American culture.

Michael Golomb's visas to travel through France and Switzerland in 1939.

Michael Rossmann in England when he was an instructor at the Royal Technical College.

Walter Hirsch in his U.S. Army uniform.

So what interested me is what brings people together and what divides them. And those were some of the intellectual problems that I focused on in my studies.

What did you do after you graduated from San Francisco State?

HABERER: After I got my general secondary-school credential in 1951, I got an offer for a job in a rural community in northern California. I sent my books up there, but then when I got up there, I felt I couldn't do it, and I returned to Oakland. I did not feel ready for teaching. I tried other jobs, and I then I decided to go to New York to "find myself."

Social Work

In the three months before he left for the East, Haberer worked in a cannery—seven days a week, twelve hours a day—in order to save enough money to support himself while he would look for work. However, the day after arriving in New York City, he accepted a clerical position with WQXR, the New York Times Radio station. It was a dead-end job and not very demanding. He earned the minimum wage, 95 cents an hour for a 40-hour week, running the station's addressograph machine for the monthly program guide. He stayed at this work for two years until the station's management decided to do away with the publication and he had to look for work elsewhere.

He found a more challenging position with the New York City Welfare Department. Hired as a social worker for the branch office in Harlem, he was in charge of monitoring 110 cases, which dealt with anything from aid to dependent children to assistance for the elderly to home relief. His clients were black, white, Jewish, non-Jewish, old, and young. Haberer tried to make sure that these people received the benefits to which they were entitled. He also had to ascertain whether any factors arose that affected continued eligibility.

HABERER: I saw around me a lot of chaos: case workers having nervous breakdowns, clients very upset they weren't getting the money, food, or clothes they were supposed to get. I figured out you needed to go into the homes of these people with no chip on your shoulder, without an attitude that these people on public assistance must be somehow defective or morally tainted. I told myself, "It's not my job to sit in judgment on these individuals. If they are entitled to public assistance, by God, they're going to get it." And I tried to give it to them as quickly as possible. I would always ask them, "What is it that you need for your children? Do you need clothes? What do you need? Give me a list. What do you need for this, that, and the other?"

And as soon as I had interviewed them, I would go to my office, dictate the case and immediately process the form to ensure they got their money within a week. I also would try to do something if they had problems with their housing. If there was a health problem, I would then call in the public nurse. And if there were absentee husbands who weren't paying, I would hunt down the delinquents. I was very good at that. I became a very good detective.

In my judgment, those on public assistance were trying to manage as best they could under very trying circumstances, and I respected a lot of them. So they were all serviced, and when they came into the office, I would see them as quickly as possible. Why should they wait while I go and diddle around? My job was not to discourage them from getting welfare; my job was to see that if they were entitled to it, they got it quickly. Soon my caseload was the only one in the whole bloody joint that had no serious problems.

The other thing is that I don't like to see injustice. I've always had empathy for the underdog, for people who are despised. I don't mean the psychopaths, I mean the people in society who get the dirty end of the stick, the people we use as scapegoats, the people who get trod on, the people who are the victims of our arrangements that create a lot of social injustice. I'm not holding myself as a great moral person, but that's just the way I feel. I think the well off and the affluent can take pretty good care of themselves, and they have battalions of people to protect them, but the poor and the weak and the defenseless don't have that. I knew what it was like to be despised, especially in Germany and in England, when I was thought to be mentally backward.

At what point did you decide you wanted to go to graduate school?

HABERER: I already was getting my master's degree at Columbia in history. I was going to classes in the afternoon. It took me about two years or so to complete, and after I got that, I told myself that I ought to venture forth, take the jump, and go on for my Ph.D.

I applied for admission at the University of California at Berkeley. This was very risky for me psychologically, because I was secure at this welfare agency. But I realized that I was in a rut, and that I had to go, even if it was painful, even if I failed. When I got accepted at the University of California, I severed my connections in New York and moved to Berkeley.

I decided to major in political science because, although history was very interesting, I didn't quite see what the connection was between, let's say, being a professor of history in ancient Egyptian history and the modern condition. I desired everything to have a direct bearing on people's lives. Political philosophy and political theory interested me because I was concerned about certain fundamental issues in the social order. I wanted to connect the theory of social justice to its practice.

Back to Academe

Haberer went to Berkeley in 1957, a time when American campuses were said to be "Hotbeds of Rest." The Cold War was still in full swing, but both of the superpowers had learned to pull their punches, and mutually assured destruction appeared remote despite a continued arms race. Such complacency on the part of the Americans seemed misguided when the Soviets (on October 4, 1957) put an artificial satellite (*Sputnik*) in orbit around the earth. This act, coupled with a Soviet launch of a 4,500-mile intercontinental ballistic missile, sparked American fears that all their cities were now vulnerable to attack. Politicians now demanded that something be done about this "missile gap."

Haberer found his fellow students disturbingly complacent about such international storm clouds. He was interested in world politics and wanted to discover ways to bring about peaceful change to lessen tension and promote harmony among nations. The gray-flannel-suit mentality of his fellow political science graduate students turned him off. He felt that they were only interested in getting good grades.

Haberer suspended his studies for the doctorate to work in the San Francisco welfare department. The break was prompted more by educational burnout than financial necessity. At Berkeley he was under considerable psychological pressure: he felt inadequate compared to the other students, had a problem with one of the professors, and was anxious about the responsibilities of a proffered teaching assistantship. So he ran away. Of course, in the end it didn't work, because problems in the final analysis have to be met head-on to be resolved.

The return to social work was a case of déjà vu, only the bureaucrats in the Bay area seemed even more arrogant than those in the Big Apple. While he was working there, the agency's directors hired a Minnesota research firm to measure the "pathological level" of people on welfare. This $100,000 pseudoscientific study touted the efficiency and accountability of the welfare agency by producing evidence of its dedication to depriving people of the support to which they were entitled.

Haberer returned to Berkeley in 1961. One of the reasons he gave for this decision was the urging of his first wife, Beverly, who "didn't want to be married to an inconsequential social worker." His reapplication brought with it a teaching assistantship. Within two years he became the head teaching assistant of the American government course. He helped organize the course and supervise the performance of twenty-five other TAs.

Haberer chose political theory as his main field, the subject of his thesis being the relationship between the political community and the scientific community. Specifically, he wanted to study how the interests of the state directed the nature of scientific research.

HABERER: When I did the sections on the National Socialist period, I tried not to sit in judgment beforehand. As a matter of fact, I was trying to discover cases that would challenge the obvious conclusion to which I was driven. I didn't want to find out that there was no real opposition on the part of the scientific community to Hitler. But I discovered that all these eminent German scientists had no real integrity, they played along, they all sold out. I took no pleasure in this conclusion. When later I was working on a study about Einstein and the other German physicists, I was told that I couldn't sit in judgment because I was not there. Well, I could sit in judgment because I was there. The man who challenged me didn't know that. I wasn't trying to sit in judgment actually; I was trying to find out what happened.

The top German scientists in physics, the ones Einstein had been associated with, were not Nazis. They were often conservatives and didn't like National Socialism one bit, but they went along. Perhaps there were some cases where somebody really spoke out and maybe did something. But the attitudes of many of those great physicists were highly ambivalent. After all, Hitler was very successful, and he had brought Germany back into the limelight.

Until the war, many Germans did not see much that was negative about the Nazis.

HABERER: The Nazis brought prosperity, national pride, and all those things that make your blood tingle and send a German's soul into ecstasy. But I think I'd want to be careful about sitting too much in judgment, because most people are not terribly courageous. Sometimes they surprise you when they are courageous. In fact, sometimes the people from whom you least expect it are the ones who show the most courage. But I wouldn't put people on trial simply because they were bystanders, because I don't know how I would've reacted. How do I know that I wouldn't have been one of the perpetrators? I'm not saying that there are no moral rules that ought to be applied. I'm simply saying I don't want to rush to judgment. And I think we have to understand that life was difficult and that there were many excruciating choices that people had to make. But that doesn't mean that when we look at the Germans, we have no right to judge because we have our own sins. I don't think that's relevant. I think we ought to look at the American things that are unjust or reprehensible, and we ought to look at those things that are unjust or reprehensible in Germany. We don't have to make them equivalent.

A Sense of What Is Fair

The year following the receipt of his doctor's degree, Haberer taught as an instructor at Berkeley. The political science faculty treated him with indifference—a not unusual attitude toward newly minted Ph.D.s hired as cheap labor to handle the department's basic courses. Nobody wanted to invest the emotional energy in someone who would soon leave to go elsewhere. Still, the lack of warmth from those people, who made a pretense of belonging to a community of scholars, was difficult to accept. The search for any community—religious, social, intellectual—was something that Haberer pursued throughout his life.

In 1966, Haberer went to Rutgers University in New Brunswick, New Jersey, where he stayed until 1971, teaching courses in political philosophy, and science and politics. While at Rutgers he published his book, which led to his being offered a position at Purdue as the director of a program in science and technology and public policy in the political science department.

One of Haberer's first acts at Purdue was to found a national newsletter, called *Science, Technology and Public Policy.* But the support for the program he was hired to establish proved elusive. A new head of the department decided to put his academic resources elsewhere and unilaterally abolished the science and technology program. A year later, at the request of his colleague Bob Melson [also interviewed in this book], he began *Shofar,* a newsletter to complement the recently established Jewish studies program.

When did you become aware of the basic horror of the Holocaust, and how did this affect your beliefs and the way you've lived your life?

HABERER: I became aware of the basic dimensions of the tragedy quite early. Even before the end of the war, I had a pretty good sense of some of the horror of what had happened. It was very clear from what I was reading that there had been a mass killing of Jews. People were asking where all the Jews were going, and reports were talking about large-scale executions.

The American and British governments had put their priority on ending the war and not on what was happening to the Jews. Not that they wanted Jews exterminated, but this was not something they wanted to deal with. I think it is a scandal that such a moral wrong was done, but I can understand some of it, and I don't want to be too harsh in judging it.

I knew terrible things were happening, although I didn't know what specifically. But as soon as the war was over, the news about the death camps became public. The stories came out, the pictures came out. And in that English hostel we had children who had been right in the center of it, in the vortex of the horror. They were in the death camps; they saw people, children, being led to their deaths. So I had no illusions about what had happened. I got more stories when I came to the United States. I also read a lot about it as more and more details were becoming known. It became clear that close to six million Jews had been murdered and exterminated by the National Socialist policy.

I became a bit obsessed with the subject, but I discovered that the American Jews didn't particularly want to hear about the details. It was not a taboo subject, but it was not something that took hold of the imagination of American Jews or of Americans in general. There was a real desire to shield oneself from as much of this as one could, until finally fifteen years later Holocaust studies sort of took off.

In Israel it had been the same way. Israel wanted to get on with the business of building a state, and they weren't terribly interested in the Holocaust until the 1960s, when it played an important role in solidifying Israeli national consciousness. To drive the message home that never again will Jews be led to the slaughter, and to drive home the point that we have to look out for ourselves even though the whole world is against us.

But at some point, I had to decide what my position was going to be, how I was going to react. My parents had been killed by it. Not directly in my father's case, but that didn't make it easier. My mother was directly murdered and lots of other members of the family, to say nothing of millions more.

But I decided very consciously not to shout and scream and spend the rest of my life being a victim. I decided never to make the Holocaust a personal mantra to justify certain things about myself. I always took the attitude that I was ultimately responsible for my life. I couldn't go through life feeling sorry for myself because I was the victim, and use this as an excuse to cover up my inadequacies. I could have said my distant and emotionally cold parents were at fault or the Germans were at fault. From the time I was thirteen, I could have become the great victim. I clearly did not want to do that. I realized that not all Germans were Nazis and not all Germans were concentration camp guards, and if I became intentionally bitter toward the Germans, it would only damage me and I would have no future. Maybe this explains why, unlike some people, I never had a visceral hatred of the Germans.

I don't want to minimize for a moment what happened, but I also want to understand and through understanding to transform the experience in a positive way. That's very pretentious, but that was the way I wanted to deal with it. I tried to understand it in its larger dimension and react constructively, not necessarily positively, but constructively.

Maybe because of these experiences I have developed a very strong sense of what is fair, what is just, what is right. I get very upset when I see people being mistreated or misjudged. I am always concerned with the larger issue of justice, social justice, not just for Jews, and not just for Americans, but also for people all over.

I have a pretty good understanding of the evil human beings are capable of, so I never shook my fist into heaven and said, "God was responsible for the murder of Jews." I never had that kind of a simple view of God. So I wasn't going to reject God, or the notion of God, because God didn't create one of His great miracles and save the Jews from Auschwitz.

We've heard a lot about the animosity between the German Jews and the Eastern Jews.

HABERER: I know it's a terrible thing and I experienced it in my family, especially when I came to America. My uncle and aunt and others in the family who were German Jews had these really reprehensible stereotypical negative condescending attitudes toward the East European Jews: "they're not like us," "they are culturally inferior," and "we don't want our kind marrying their kind." My aunt always lectured me about dating the right kind of Jewish girl, one who had to come from a good, preferably German, middle-class family. "A Polish Jew is very *unappetitlich* (unappetizing), you know." I don't think it was racism, it was just a typical attitude found in many cultures toward the outsider. There was a whole variety of Polish Jews who came to Germany: some were brilliant, some were refined, some very modern, but the German attitude toward them was totally stereotypical. No matter what you were, you were still a Polack.

On the one hand, you feel a certain sympathy toward the Polish Jewish brethren who are being beaten and persecuted, but you still look down on them. You could idealize Eastern European traditional beliefs, but you didn't want your daughter to marry an *Ostjude*. They smelled, or looked primitive, and you wanted to get rid of them as quickly as possible.

Can you ascribe these prejudices to things other than cultural differences?

HABERER: In a bourgeois society you really can never be sure what your class situation is going to be, whether you're going to go up or down. Therefore you become very fearful that if you marry the wrong person, you're going to drop in class, drop in position. Therefore you do everything to protect your class status. The second thing is that the outsider poses a threat to our image because the outsider might do things that might be blamed on us.

On the other hand, the Torah enjoins us to help those less fortunate than ourselves. This very ambivalent attitude of German Jews toward Polish Jews caused deep-seated resentment, which continues to this day. I would always argue with my uncle and aunt about this and say that we should judge people by who they are and not by our stereotypes.

There's a lot of stereotyping on both sides, isn't there?

HABERER: Sure, of course there is. There was a lot of *Schadenfreude* (pleasure over someone's misfortune) among American Jews of East European extraction when their fellow German Jews were having a hard time in Germany. "Well, you're getting it in the neck now; you can know what it was like when we were having a hard time." There were even cases where East European American Jews refused to get affidavits for German Jews.

There was also an enormous fear that Jewish sons and daughters would intermarry with Gentiles. This is no longer the big thing except among the Orthodox.

Over 50 percent of the Jewish people now intermarry. But fifty years ago inter-marriage was a *schand,* a disgrace, and people would go into official mourning if their child did so. They would literally put ashes on their head and be in mourning for seven days as though the child had died. All this was part of an effort to main-tain solidarity within the group.

> *What if somebody were to ask you how you would feel if there were no more Jews and no more Judaism? Let's say it would disappear voluntar-ily, say, through intermarriage. What would your reaction be?*

HABERER: That it would be a bad thing. I am connected enough with the Jewish tradition that I would feel enormously saddened if the Jews as a people and a historical experience were to disappear. I happen to have an immense intellec-tual and emotional resonance with the fundamental notions of Judaism, the be-liefs vis-à-vis God, vis-à-vis the Torah, and vis-à-vis the nation of Israel.

> *A lot of Jews don't believe in the religion but certainly believe in the tra-ditions. They still consider themselves Jewish.*

HABERER: I happen to feel good about being Jewish, but the kind of Jewishness that you now have, except really among very few, is not the kind of religious faith that will get you very far in the long run. People need to make the religious experience a vital part of their life; otherwise it's just a convenience, a bit of an insurance policy.

Here in the Lafayette community, I think that for 90 to 95 percent of the Jews the God experience, whatever that may be, is very limited. I don't think most of them, when they read their prayer book, know what those prayers say or care what they mean. Their Judaism is a kind of tribal connection.

> *Also a sort of* Gemeinschaft?

HABERER: Yeah, but you seek a *Gemeinschaft,* and most Jews in our community don't go to the synagogue more than twice a year. Going is not an important experience in their life. Twice a year, what does that mean? And how often are their children going to go?

> *If you say that nine-tenths of the Jews here are not strong in their faith, that they have no true religious commitment, can't you postulate the end of the Jewish community—except, that is, for a very small group of people?*

HABERER: That's exactly how it stands. Because if you accept my premise that with assimilation and acculturation the traditional synagogue is probably a sinking ship, then it stands to reason that it won't be around much longer. Add to this the increasing rate of intermarriage and the prospect that the second generation will typically be less observant than their Jewish parents, and it becomes a real problem.

Being Jewish must be made a much more central part of your life, and this translates, as in all religions, into something mystical. To have this experience, either of the heart or of the psyche, you have to work at it. It's like becoming a good pianist or a great painter. You have to go and do it until something happens. The rabbis understood that being religious is not waiting for God to speak to you, but doing certain things that will enable you to connect to that force, to that reality, which transcends mere human existence. You have to prepare yourself for it in some way. That's what religion is about.

My problem was that the world into which I was moving was profoundly secular, not religious, and I was interested in that secular culture. I feel my loss of religion, and still do, but I can't fake it. I can't say, "I'm religious, yet I don't feel it."

There's a philosophy that I came across in my late teens or early twenties: the philosophy of "as if." That is, should one act "as if" something were true, it would be possible to follow certain tenets. In my religious experience I have not had a direct contact with a transcendent God, no voice talking to me. But I found that experiencing the Shabbat or going to prayer has a very positive effect, but not because God has spoken to me and says, "Joseph, do this and do that." I'm not quite sure what prayer means, because I've never been very comfortable with prayer.

I haven't had that mystical experience, possibly because I haven't been sufficiently involved or committed. I suppose if you would push me hard enough, I might even say that possibly I'm agnostic, but it doesn't make sense to me that the whole universe is meaningless. I think it more likely than not that there may very well be something there. Lots of people have had mystical experiences. Others might dismiss this as psychosis or believe that there are always rational explanations for things that don't fit into a rational model. But who is to say that the rational mode of human experience is the only true model of experience? I don't believe that it is. I believe the mystic or the religious impulse or the intuitive spirit carries as much weight in some areas as does rationalism.

Do you think that this mystical experience is an essential part of being a Jew?

HABERER: Yes, I think that's what we call faith. If you could prove everything by some scientific experiment, it wouldn't be faith.

Then what would you feel if this mystical experience were to disappear?
If it's already gone in 90 percent of the Jews in the Lafayette community,
could you say that 90 percent have lost their Jewishness?

HABERER: You should have gone to a rabbinical school, but I'll give it an answer. Just because 90 percent of the population are vitamin-starved, just because they haven't eaten the right diet, doesn't mean that to eat the right diet wouldn't be good for them. Those 90 percent of the people are spiritually impoverished in ways they don't even understand. The general culture (the consumer culture, the rational culture) in which they operate has deadened their religious spirit, and those people don't know what they're missing.

Until that 90 percent take their religious vitamins, then the Jewish community is just sort of hanging on?

HABERER: Yes, but this is nothing new. The question you ask about the majority is nothing new — look at the Hebrew Scriptures and the experience of the Exodus, for example. The Hebrews have gone out of Egypt, having gone through a whole set of miracles from God. Then when Moses goes up Mt. Sinai and doesn't come down for a while, they get hysterical and start worshiping a golden calf. Of course, God gets very angry and wipes out about 90 percent of them. God isn't always a kindly old man. Out of the ten tribes of Judah, eight disappeared into history, no one knows where.

You recognize certain theological difficulties in reconciling the belief of a chosen people and a commanding God with the Holocaust?

HABERER: True, but the Jewish tradition has always had a way out by saying that ultimately we cannot understand certain things about human existence. The presence of evil, for example.

A bit of a cop-out, don't you think?

HABERER: No doubt, but the ultimate mystery of human existence, or the ultimate nature of God, is something about which Jews don't think too much. Since you're not even supposed to pronounce the name of God, how would you know what God is really like? All we can know is a presence or a reality — call it what you will — which manifests itself in some transcendental way in history. Perhaps you can feel it or believe it or act upon it or not act upon it.

Consequently I think of Judaism as a way of life. And I believe that faith is the will to act upon something as if it were true. There is no proof that it's true, but you act upon it as if it were. Therefore, I can believe that there is an ultimate purpose and meaning to existence. So I am prepared to gamble on the proposition that there is a God. I may not have experienced God, I may not have had any visions, I may not have entered any mystical experiences, as some people have, but if the chips are down, I think it makes sense to act in a religious paradigm. Not just to believe but to act. I probably am, at some point, agnostic, but

I think the ultimate essence of the religious conception is that life has meaning and purpose. I think that all people need an answer to the question of meaning and purpose and relationship to the cosmos, because if human beings act in a world that they think is meaningless and absurd, they go crazy.

Then you say that faith is a psychological necessity?

HABERER: No, I don't say that. My wife, Rose, would say that religion is sort of a structural necessity for people to live by. No, I don't say that, because that is a very neat little compartmentalization for social scientists.

Okay, a sociological necessity.

HABERER: I think it is a deeply embedded part of human beings, and I'm prepared to believe that it relates to some larger reality in the universe. Throughout my life, I have always been amazed at the enormous capacity of people to recuperate from great injury, and the enormous potential that people have to realize their better self, their ability to live full rich lives in decent relationships with others. In that sense I'm sort of utopian, but you have to create the social conditions for this to happen. It doesn't happen in a vacuum. By the way, one of the greatest disappointments of academic life was not finding that kind of community feeling. I really thought there would be more of it, but it didn't happen that way. The problem for society, therefore, is how to build that vibrant human community.

Notes

1. The village of Skokie, located just north of Chicago, is home to a large Jewish community, many of whom were Holocaust survivors. In 1977, a Chicago-based section of the National Socialist Party of America proclaimed its intention to hold a white-power (clearly antisemitic) demonstration on May 1 in front of the Skokie village hall. Under protest from various Jewish groups, the Skokie Board of Trustees obtained an injunction against the manifestation. The neo-Nazis counterattacked by pushing for reversal in the federal courts, which in June vacated the injunction on the grounds that it violated the First Amendment of the U.S. Constitution. The court held that only physical interference with other legitimate activities could justify any injunction and emphasized that political speech could not be amended, no matter how unpopular. The American Civil Liberties Union had joined the NSPA suit and provided it with legal assistance—a move that cost the organization dearly. About 30,000, or 15 percent, of its listed members resigned, a loss in monetary terms of $500,000 a year. Although the announced demonstration never took

place, because the neo-Nazis feared they might be putting themselves at physical risk, the Skokie affair raised lasting, fundamental questions about the permissible expression of free speech, especially if such an expression was hateful and emotionally destructive. See Donald Alexander Downs, *Nazis in Skokie: Freedom, Community, and the First Amendment* (Notre Dame, Ind.: Notre Dame Press, 1985).

2. During this time he met his future wife, Leonore, in Kansas City, and in December 1950 they were married. They would have three children: Suzanne, born in 1951; Elizabeth, in 1956; and Jonathan, in 1966.

3. *The Myth of the Twentieth Century*, published in 1930, was considered a fundamental part of Nazi literature. Rosenberg argues that the German people had an obligation to subdue Europe's lesser races and crush liberalism, thereby affirming Nordic leadership. Born in Russian Estonia in 1893, Rosenberg came to Munich after World War I, joined Hitler's fledgling party, and became the editor of the Nazi newspaper, the *Völkischer Beobachter* (People's Observer). Regarded as sort of a Nazi Party philosopher, but not one of its best-organized functionaries, Rosenberg was put in charge of the party's foreign affairs department. In 1941, he became the minister for eastern occupied territories and was sufficiently involved in the atrocities committed there that he was placed in the dock at Nürnberg as a major war criminal. He was hanged in 1946.

4. Gartenhaus married Johanna Laura Weiss in August 1953. Their son Michael was born in 1955, Kevin in 1958.

5. The *Nazionalpolitische Erziehungsanstalten* (national political educational establishments), or Napolas for short, were a Nazi attempt to continue the Prussian cadet academy tradition for the production of a future military and governmental elite. Napola education emphasized the development of sporting and mechanical skills. A candidate had to have been a member of the Hitler Youth and have the sponsorship of the Nazi Party, in addition to possessing the right physical qualifications. In 1936, the SS assumed direction of the program, eventually establishing forty such schools throughout the Reich.

6. Founded in 1284, Peterhouse was the oldest and one of Cambridge's smallest colleges. The poet Thomas Gray was once one of its fellows. Located on Trumpington Street, it is visited by tourists primarily for its William Morris tiles, which decorate the great hall's Tudor fireplace.

7. "That's not the case in the United States," Rossmann explains. "Five or six years after I came to this country, I was on an NEH panel. The two dozen of us had to assign research money, in effect, determining national biological policy. Fully half of us were people like me who had come from Europe, many from Germany. That would never have happened in Britain."

Part Two
Austria

5
Imperial Twilight

At 11 A.M. on July 28, 1914, Austria-Hungary declared war on Serbia. Following the assassination of Archduke Francis Ferdinand one month earlier, the government of the Dual Monarchy had begun drafting a harsh ultimatum, whose anticipated rejection would provide a pretext for a bold move in Eastern Europe. With the unconditional support of Germany, the Austro-Hungarians were eager to eliminate Serbia as a power factor in the Balkans. The conflict did not stay localized, however, and by August 4 it involved most of the great powers of Europe. This war, deemed so necessary for the political regeneration of the Dual Monarchy, led, after four years of fighting, to the empire's collapse and dissolution.

Austria became a republic, reduced in size to a scant 33,000 square miles of almost exclusively German-speaking areas. It was the weakest state to stagger out of the wreckage of the Dual Monarchy; and its new government faced the ominous task of building a new national unity, restructuring a viable economy, and protecting the people from civil war and starvation. This task was not going to be easy.

A sharp rise in unemployment and increasing economic instability marked the early years of the Austrian Republic. Cut off from most of the resources of the former empire, the new country's industrial plant could produce only a fraction of its previous output. Unemployment payments and the general costs of recovery caused government expenses to skyrocket. The state tried to meet its obligations by devaluing its money, thereby worsening an already dangerous inflation. Trade unions demanded constant salary readjustments to keep wages in step with prices. In August 1922, with the Krone worth less than 2 percent of the money's prewar gold value, the government appealed to the Allied Powers for a loan of $70 million. The request was referred to the League of Nations, which promised to sponsor the necessary loans, provided a special high commissioner be appointed to direct Austrian finances and carry out a program of economic reform. Not until 1926 was the period of foreign stewardship ended. The temporary loss of sovereignty, though, compounded the country's prevailing political confusion and division, isolation, and national weakness.

Reduced Circumstances: Anna Mandler Frost Akeley

"We had rococo, Maria Theresa–style furniture, inlaid with marquetry, and the chairs were covered in embroidered silk cloth."

An Elegant District and a Well-Dressed Wife

Paul Mandler married well. His wife, Emma Löw-Beer, had a dowry that included a large apartment house in Vienna's historic First District on the Salztorgasse,[1] a large chunk of Nordbahn Gesellschaft (North Railroad Company), stocks, and various other liquid assets. Ten years younger than her husband, she had been born in Brünn (Brno) in 1869, into a family of Moravian "textile barons," whose factories were scattered across the Austro-Hungarian Empire's northern crown lands. She spoke German, French, Czech, and English fluently and could read and make herself understood in Italian and Spanish. She was an accomplished pianist. One of her early classmates was Arnold Schönberg.

The cultural richness of Vienna proved irresistible to the Löw-Beers, as it did to many of these wealthy Jews from the Bohemian and Moravian territories, and they tried to spend as much time there as possible. This strong German-Austrian cultural identity usually came at the expense of their Jewish identity and the maintenance of traditional religious beliefs. The Löw-Beers, for example, contributed to various Jewish causes and charities, but did not go to synagogue or keep kosher.

Emma married Paul Mandler in 1892. Mandler's background was less impressive than his wife's. Although born in Vienna, he had not come from an old or rich Viennese family. (Most of the city's Jews had arrived only after 1848, when the residence prohibitions had been dropped.) His background was lower middle class, his father being a tradesman, but he was determined to succeed, and he invested his wife's dowry wisely, becoming a partner in a company that manufactured men's underwear and hosiery. Within a decade, this company became one of the largest concerns of its kind, with a contract to supply socks to the entire Austrian army.

The Mandlers had three children: Auguste, born in 1894; Kurt, born in 1901; and Anna, born in 1904. The Mandlers ran their lives and raised their children in the grand bourgeois style befitting the circles in which they traveled. Their household had a staff of five: a cook, a chauffeur, a first-floor maid, a second-floor maid, and a French governess. They also owned a villa at Altaussee, a small resort village about forty miles southeast of Salzburg.

ANNA AKELEY: An Austrian Jewish businessman had to be very careful that he lived in an elegant district, that his wife was very well dressed, that his children went to first-rate schools, and that his wife had the correct jewelry on every day. She would wear pearls before 5 P.M. and diamonds after 5 P.M. — those were the rules, because if people saw a Jew that didn't dress his wife well or allow her to dress well and the children were not sent to very good, high-class schools, he could not get a loan from a bank or from more wealthy Jews. You never went to a Jewish moneylender, because only the lowest classes went to moneylenders.

Those Jews who wanted to fit in and who wanted to make it had to behave like genuine Austrians?

AKELEY: That's right. It was absolutely necessary to behave the same way. The children of the wealthy were usually born at home, and I, my sister, and my brother were all born at home. The doctor and the midwife both came to the house. In my case, the midwife did most of the work while the doctor sat in a nice chair and smoked cigars and drank coffee and had to be served. But he got about ten times more pay. My mother never breast-fed her children. A lady did not do that. I had a wet nurse who came from Olmütz (Olomouc), a town known for its supply of wet nurses. Mine got beer every night, because that produces more milk. I don't know if she also breast fed her own child.

We occupied two of the eight apartments in that building, and at Christmas time we would all assemble in the grand salon of our quarters. In this large room with high ceilings there stood an enormous Christmas tree that my mother had decorated. It was very beautiful. Our presents were underneath. The servants got envelopes containing money. They lined up, and my mother played "Silent Night, Holy Night" on the piano, and the servants sang. Then the envelopes were passed out. The servants took them and came up to us and we shook hands and said, "Happy Christmas." Only after that were we allowed to get our own presents.

Did you celebrate Hanukkah?

AKELEY: No, never. Nobody went to synagogue. But we had to be very careful that the five servants, who were all Catholics, could go to High Mass at St. Stephen's Cathedral on Sunday at 11:00. That meant that Sunday dinner was late. We also had fish on Friday.

Did you ever have a seder at home?

AKELEY: My father told me that sometimes they used to celebrate that in his home, but I had never seen one before I came to this country, when I was invited by one of my friends. My mother insisted that we know what Passover means, and she told us the story. And we were not allowed to go to school on Yom Kippur. My father insisted that my brother become bar mitzvah. My father gave a large amount of money to B'nai B'rith, an organization he once served as president. He was also involved with a scheme to finance Jewish emigration.

I found this out by eavesdropping on one of my father's meetings. I must have been eight years old. I saw men come into the big entrance hall, and I ran around into another room so I could hear what they would say. I recognized some of them from having come to our house before. I'm not quite sure how many there were, perhaps ten. And they sat around that very long dining room table. And they were talking about helping the Jews get to Palestine. Something that Theodor Herzl advocated. My father and some others said that Palestine was too small and what they should do was buy land in Canada. And I heard them talk of millions and millions of Kronen. I remember my father saying,

The Mandler family,
July 1914. Anna Mandler
Akeley is seated on the left.

The Mandler family home on the Vegagasse, where Anna Akeley grew up
in a privileged environment.

"This place is nearly as large as Austria. And there the Jews can be settled. One can grow enough wheat in Canada to feed the whole world and earn much money." And there were others who disagreed, "The Jews don't belong in Canada. It has a horrible climate. They belong in Israel." So there were those two sides. And they fought. And I remember that the vote was about six to four in favor of Palestine. And my father hit his hand on the table and said, "It's hopeless with Palestine, it is too small."

I didn't understand what they were talking about because I thought, "Why should the Jews go away anyhow? Why should they go to a place called Palestine or Canada if they can stay in Vienna?" It didn't make sense to me. I asked my mother, and she explained to me what Jerusalem meant to the Jews. She was very careful to explain the whole thing to me without saying that the Jews were persecuted, because I asked, "Why do they want to go away? It's so nice in the Alps. We can go skiing and you said that in Palestine you can't go skiing." I mean, that was the answer of a little girl.

Did you parents have a good marriage?

AKELEY: I think it was quite a good marriage. My father admired my mother's elegance; she was very well educated, and he liked to learn things from her. She used to read Balzac and Voltaire, and Goethe and Schiller and Grillparzer—the whole caboodle. And one afternoon a month, she had a *jour,* an open house for other ladies who came for tea. Every woman had a thing like that, a *jour,* a special day, her special day. We had rococo, Maria Theresa–style furniture, inlaid with marquetry, and the chairs were covered in embroidered silk cloth: there was even embroidered silk on the walls. And here came the women with those corsets. I was naturally not invited, but I did a lot of spying.

What activities did you have outside the home?

AKELEY: Once a year just before World War I we went to an audience of the Emperor [Francis Joseph]. In 1912, my father got the title of *Kaiserlicher Rat,* which gave him the right to be received at court.

> In order to get this title, something he had wanted his whole life, Paul Mandler had to agree to be baptized a Christian. He never considered that he was not a Jew, however, and continued to support Jewish causes. He arranged that a rabbi give special lessons to his son for a successful bar mitzvah. Conversion for Paul was not a

religious question. It was a formality, a business transaction, a necessity for reception at court, a stepping-stone to honor as Herr Kaiserlicher Rat (The Honorable Advisor to the Emperor). Only people
like the already titled Rothschilds could be received at court and
still remain Jews. Paul Mandler, his wife, and his daughter Anna
were baptized. But Anna never considered herself a Christian, nor
was she Jewish in matters of religion. She would grow up believing
that religion was prompted by a fear of the unknown, and that there
was no life after death. In the dynamic assimilationist world of
upper-class Viennese Jewry, questions of religion, tradition, and identity were, like salami, sliced thickly or thinly according to individual
taste. In the Mandler family, religion was for the servants.

Were you included when your parents were received by the emperor?

AKELEY: I did it twice. My mother—who hated it, by the way—said that I
should see it at least once to see how ridiculous it was. My father had to bow
until he saw the hand of the emperor. My mother had to go way down in a
curtsy, keeping her back very straight. It was difficult, considering the tight corsets. Next to the emperor stood an officer who held out his hand to get the ladies up. Naturally, for me and my sister, going down and up was easy. I knew I
wasn't supposed to laugh, but it seemed hilarious. I saw it twice because I
begged to go the second time.

I also curtsied to my parents. I didn't say "good morning" or "good evening"
when I would leave them; I would have to make a little curtsy and say, "I kiss
your hand." In our house we were treated very nicely, but not with loving em-
braces. My mother sometimes made us put our hands behind our backs when we
kissed her because she did not want us to get her clothes dirty, and my father was
suffering from tuberculosis, so he only kissed us on the back of our necks. But
here comes the story that I like best:

One Sunday morning my father said to me, "Come on, you little monkey.
I'll take you in the car to a park where there is a concert." There were always
concerts on Sunday. Vienna had two big parks—the Stadtpark (city park) and
the Volksgarten (the people's garden). At the Stadtpark they played classical
music: Paganini, Beethoven, Mozart, Haydn, Schumann. But not Brahms,
Brahms was considered too modern. At the Volksgarten they played musicals,
operetta-type music with the popular songs. My father would have loved to go
to the concert where they played musicals, but he said we shouldn't be seen
there. And I said, "But Papa, why can't we go?" And he replied, "You will not

understand. We have to go to the one where they play classical music." He never explained why. But one Sunday, he said to me, "I don't want you to be dressed up in your Sunday things, and I'm just going to go without a hat." And we went to the Volksgarten. He sang along with the orchestra and was so happy there.

Did your mother look down on your father because of his social background?

AKELEY: Probably.

Why, then, did she marry him?

AKELEY: Because she was twenty-two and at that time an old maid was a terrible thing to be.

But certainly there were other eligible bachelors. She did have a lot of assets.

AKELEY: Probably there were others. But he was quite attractive, and she was not religious. And it had to be a Jew. A non-Jew was out of the question.

A World Transformed

Despite the declaration of war in 1914, Paul Mandler still contemplated a promising future for his children. He wanted his oldest daughter, Auguste, to marry an aristocrat, perhaps a baron, or at least somebody with a "von." Such a match could easily be arranged; many nobles had more impressive names than family fortunes. To make sure his son Kurt would be a success, he employed the services of a *Hofmeister,* a special tutor to teach the young man courtly grace. His youngest daughter, Anna, had a French governess, spoke the language fluently by the age of four, received special instruction in swimming, fencing (with Italian foils), gymnastics, and skiing. She went to a Protestant finishing school, where the girls wore special uniforms with little white aprons and little black ties. Mandler expected all of his children to excel in school. Once when Anna brought home a C in geography, she was threatened with having a special tutor. The prospect was so humiliating, considering that other students might find out, that Anna soon improved her grade.

AKELEY: I was ten years old when the war began, and naturally, I had no understanding of what such an undertaking involved. I do remember, though, during the war we moved to the suburbs to a rather elegant villa in the Nineteenth

Döbling (Cottage District) on the Vegagasse. (We lived there until the Nazis forced us out in 1938.) The property had its own garden. We left our city house because my parents wanted to get away from the thousands of Polish Jews who had fled to Vienna when the Russians invaded Galicia in 1916. Many of these were very poor Jews who settled in the Second District, which was just across the Danube canal from where we lived. My parents decided that we could not live there anymore next to those messy and dirty Polish Jews with their *payos* [the side curls and hair locks typical of Orthodox Hasidic Jews from Eastern Europe]. We still owned the old house in the First District but rented it out.

I was taken out of that private girls' school and enrolled in a public Gymnasium, the Schwartzwaldschule named after the director. I don't think it exists any more, although I believe there is another school that now bears the same name. When you registered your child into that school, you had to bring your income tax return, and you paid tuition according to how much you earned, so the wealthy helped subsidize those who were poorer. It was a very good school. Most of the teachers had doctor's degrees. Oscar Kokoschka, the painter, was our instructor in art. (I went to a three-month summer camp. Rudolf Serkin was one of the campers and he used to play the grand piano in the evenings and tell me not to bother him. "Go away, fat Anni," he'd say.)

The first day I came to that Schwartzwaldschule, I wore the uniform from my old private school—you know, navy skirt, navy blouse, a little white apron, red silk stockings and high button shoes—and they howled with laughter and called me a "robber baron," after those nobles who used to storm down from their mountain castles and rob the merchants. And I came home in tears and I said, "I will not stay in that school. Everybody makes fun of me." And my mother was very nice, and said, "What do the other kids wear?" Well, I said, "They have skirts and blouses on of different colors, but nobody dresses in a navy uniform." So my mother had some new clothes made for me, and when I went back to school the next day, nobody cared. I was not funny anymore.

That must have been a great comedown, going to a school that was more democratic?

AKELEY: It was a new world. One of my friends was Franzi Dreyer; she was a carpenter's daughter and sat next to me in class. And once I invited her over to my house for tea. We sat in the living room and were served by the maid. Then she invited me over to her house. It was out in the Seventeenth District, the working-class quarter, and she lived on the fourth floor of a drab apartment building without an elevator. The first room we went in was the kitchen, and the kitchen had no running water. And then she brought me into a larger room with two beds. In one corner was a palm tree and two or three chairs. And she said, "This is my parents' bedroom and also our living room." Naturally, I didn't show how astonished I was, but it was the first time that I had seen anything like that.

In school there was a new way of teaching. We had a girls-only class called "human reproduction." Our teacher was a wonderful woman, Doctor Teleki, and she told us that most mammals reproduce in the same way and showed us slides of the anatomy of men and women and explained what happens. When she was finished, she asked if there were any questions. Most of the girls in the class seemed to already know about that, but I said, "I would like to make a statement. My parents would never have done a thing like that." And that brought me down again, the howls of laughter. And Dr. Teleki said, "I do not permit any laughing here. If someone doesn't know something, she has to learn it and not be laughed at." And then she said to me, "I'm not going to take the time now. I will wait in the main office, and after class you come to me."

When I did, she said, "You know, the nice part of it is that these people love each other. And therefore something which you seem not to be able to accept becomes something very nice. It is one of the most intimate things." I asked, "Does one have to be married?" and she said, "No, but it is better if you are married."

This is 1917 and you're thirteen. Sex education for thirteen-year-olds at that time is very progressive. Even today in parts of the United States it would be considered controversial. Such liberalism is something you usually don't associate with Austro-Hungarian society, which was supposed to be so very prim and proper and restrained in such matters.

What about your other studies? What were you learning about the war, for example?

AKELEY: Herr Rommel, our history professor, did not want to discuss the war. He said that we did not know enough about the situation in the monarchy to discuss it, and therefore the war was not going to be discussed in his class.

What was this school teaching you about citizenship?

AKELEY: That the state and government protects you and offers you all kinds of opportunities, and therefore it was your duty to repay what the government, the state, or the city offers you by giving the state and the government your loyalty.

What did this school teach you about social classes?

AKELEY: Nothing.

How about religious tolerance and ethnic differences?

AKELEY: The Catholic religion was, of course, the state religion, but by law everybody got religious instruction. A Jesuit taught the Catholics, a Calvinist or Lutheran minister the Protestants, and a rabbi taught us. We had Rabbi Fuchs. He was very funny, and I got a bad grade.

Did you learn about other religions?

AKELEY: We did not speak in the Jewish class about other religions. It was not done. After the war, when the Social Democrats took over, religious instruction was dropped completely.

What impact did this religious education have upon you?

AKELEY: I don't remember much. But when I went to the university, I wanted to major in comparative philosophy of religion.

To what extent was the school trying to create an Austro-Hungarian identity that would transcend the empire's different peoples?

AKELEY: There was an attempt to make everybody speak German.

Did the school try to teach that everybody was equal, or that some were more equal than others?

AKELEY: That some are more equal than others.

Were you ever made to feel that you were less than a citizen because you came from a Jewish family?

AKELEY: In school they punished you heavily if they saw any discrimination. Right away you were not admitted to any of the school's social events.

But outside school there were certain organizations that would not admit Jews. My father would have paid anything to get into the Jockey Club. It was a most elegant club. But he never could make it. Then there was the Alpenverein [Alpine Society]. It did fantastic things, like constructing trails through the mountains, grading them according to the degree of difficulty, and erecting a network of sleeping lodges. You could not be a member of the Alpenverein if you were Jewish. That exclusion continued even after the war. Officially they could not refuse you, but they could make it impossible for you.

Was there discrimination among the Jews themselves?

AKELEY: The Jews who had lived in Vienna for several generations were very antagonistic toward those hundreds of thousands of very poor, very uneducated Jews who had fled from Austrian Poland to Vienna in 1916. They treated them as social outcasts.

> *Would you say that there was more of a difference, perceived or otherwise, between the Viennese-born Jews and the Polish Jews than between the Viennese Jews and the Austrian Catholics?*

AKELEY: The difference was unbelievable. The customs of the Eastern Jews were completely different. The Viennese Jews were not accustomed to seeing the way they dressed and found them extremely dirty. In Vienna in the summer it goes sometimes up to eighty degrees Fahrenheit, and despite the heat, the men wore those long black coats with black hats and *payos*. They, of course, sweated terribly, and there were no antiperspirants at that time. In the treatment of the Polish Jews I experienced discrimination for the first time, but it was more a question of social class than race. The old Jewish families in Vienna felt threatened because the Polish Jews ruined the relationship between the Jews and the Viennese.

For the young Adolf Hitler, living in Vienna from 1907 to 1913, racial considerations, of course, came first. The future Führer was especially jarred by the cultural differences between the westernized Viennese bourgeoisie and the kind of Jews of whom Akeley speaks. Hitler came to regard Vienna as "the embodiment of racial desecration." He wrote of his revulsion of the city's conglomeration of races, especially the proliferation of its Jews.

> *With the exception of the Alpenverein and the fact that your father couldn't get into the Jockey Club, was the atmosphere in which the old Viennese Jewish families operated fairly protected from antisemitism?*

AKELEY: At least openly. I was not aware of antisemitism before my parents warned me about it. They told me that Gentiles here of the same social level sometimes did not associate with Jews. I knew a little bit already, because in school I went out socially with a mixed group and was not invited to some events, like St. Nicholas Day, where there were no Jews. And the older I got, the more sensitive I became. We were very careful not to have people of only one religion at our home when we entertained. Sometimes, though, when my sister entertained her friends, it happened that many more Jews were invited. Sometimes not. It depended. But it was considered very low-class to invite people of only one religion. One had to show that religion was irrelevant in social life. But one of those Gentile guys we knew once asked me, "Anni, am I the honor *goy?*" The honor *goy* was the one who was there so the whole thing would not be only Jewish.

Did any of your Jewish friends marry non-Jews?

AKELEY: A lot. There was intermarriage already in my older sister's time, although not among the blue-collar classes.

In what religion would the children be raised?

AKELEY: Well, I cannot tell you too much about my generation because of Hitler. But among my sister's contemporaries, the children all became Christian. Many of these families, though, celebrated both Easter and Passover, and for Christmas got Hanukkah and Christmas presents.

So the kind of society you were in then was assimilating?

AKELEY: The Viennese had an old expression that garlic and incense go very well together.

How did you feel about the war? Were you a patriot? Did you want the Germans and the Austrians to win?

AKELEY: I just wanted one thing—I wanted it to end. I couldn't stand seeing blind soldiers being led around on the streets. When I went to school, I had to take the streetcar to the First District. And when wounded soldiers got on, people would give them their seats. I felt so horrible, and a kind of desperation overtook me. When the Russians advanced into Austrian Poland, people feared that they would come all the way to Vienna.

During the opening months of the war the Russian army had captured most of Galicia; an Austro-German counteroffensive in the spring of the following year, however, had recaptured most of this lost territory and pushed the enemy armies back into their own country. In June 1916, however, General Alexei Brusilov avenged the previous year's losses by launching a massive attack into Poland and Galicia along a 200-mile front, from the Pripet marshes to Bukovina. By the first week of August, the Russians had captured Stanislau in Eastern Galicia, touching off popular hysteria that they might soon reach Vienna. Although exaggerated, such fear did not seem unreasonable then. General Max Hoffmann, who was directing the German forces in Galicia, complained about the worth of his allies: the armchair Austrian staff officers and their polyglot soldiery speaking twenty-three languages, no nationality being able to understand the other.

AKELEY: My mother said, "The Russians will burn our house and they will burn us," and she couldn't sleep and walked around half the night. She went to a psychiatrist, who said she had "agitated depression," an affliction that her mother and brother had also suffered from. Both of them had committed suicide.

The situation was made worse by the lack of heat and food. The last winter of the war our rooms were about fifty degrees Fahrenheit. We sat around a little iron stove to keep warm. And because there were no vegetables, I suffered from scurvy. My teeth became loose. And the doctor told us to gather all the grass and leaves in our garden, chop them up, put salt and vinegar on them, and eat them uncooked three times a day. "If your stomach gets upset, take some antacids." After three weeks of that I actually got better. There was only one trouble: we had a large dog: and he could no longer have free run of the yard! We also got some food from some farmers in the country. Perhaps eggs or maybe a chicken, which my mother always shared with the servants. There was also some corn, not the hybrid corn we have in Indiana. We had to boil that corn about an hour before we could eat it. We also ate the cobs. We put them through a meat grinder, mixed them with yeast, salt, and water and made this into a horrible-tasting bread. We naturally had no coffee or tea. There was a substitute, *Ersatz* was the word for it.

It seems your lifestyle then would depress anybody who was accustomed, as you were, to a life of privilege.

AKELEY: My mother got well after a few months, but she had fits of depression throughout the rest of her life. Because of that, she died in the Holocaust instead of coming here.

Did any members of your family serve in the Austrian armed forces?

AKELEY: Yes, I had two cousins by the name of Deutsch and one cousin named Kuffler who served. And my sister was a nurse. As soon as the war broke out, she went to the hospital and volunteered. She took a course and within six months passed the exam. She eventually became head nurse of one of the big Vienna hospitals. She naturally did not take the money from her nursing.

My father did not live to see the end of the war. Cancer of the tongue compounded the tuberculosis from which he had suffered all his life. Just before he died in January 1918, he was in great agony and made such noise that I prayed that it would stop. I couldn't stand listening to my father in such pain. He got massive doses of narcotics, but they were not enough. He left most of his assets to my mother.

An End to Patriotism

After a series of preparatory strikes in August and early September 1918, Allied Generalissimo Ferdinand Foch ordered an all-out offensive that methodically forced the German army back toward the Rhine. Meanwhile the Austro-Hungarian Monarchy was breaking apart in great pieces. Even since the beginning of the year, when a series of strikes swept the empire, the Habsburg regime had to rely almost exclusively on the military to maintain order. As the inevitability of German defeat became clear, the hope of keeping the empire together faded. In a last desperate attempt to save his dynasty, Emperor Charles, who had succeeded his uncle Francis Joseph two years before, advocated changing the Dual Monarchy into a federated monarchy. His manifesto, dated October 16, 1918, informed the empire's main national groups that they could exercise home rule through their own local assemblies. The promise came too late to have much effect. But Charles could not bring himself to abdicate. His family had been sovereigns since the thirteenth century. Shortly after midday on November 11, he signed a proclamation "removing himself from all affairs of state" and for the next five months lived on his estates northeast of Vienna before he finally fled to Switzerland.

AKELEY: In the two years following the end of the war, the Krone lost about 80 percent of its value. In 1920, it was officially devalued and replaced with the Schilling at a rate of 10,000 to one. When that happened, my mother came to me and said, "We are not poor, but we are no longer well-to-do. We can only have one servant now. You will have to do your own things, take care of your clothes." We moved to the second floor of our house and rented out the whole downstairs. That's how we were able to stay there.

The postwar inflation, in many ways, wiped you out.

AKELEY: Almost completely. It was a complete comedown. And I asked, "Can't I go skiing anymore?" And she just looked at me and laughed. You know, I was so innocent about money. Money was always there. But I was able to continue at the Gymnasium and get my *Matura,* passing with "unanimous consent."[2]

I began studies at the university in comparative philosophy of religion. My mother agreed to pay for my studies if I also studied something that would earn me a living, because there was no money for a dowry. So I decided on something that had to do with my skiing.

When the ski trains came back on Sunday evening, at the station was an X-ray machine and a doctor who would see whether those injured on the slopes had any broken bones. I had once torn two tendons in my leg, and he was able to tell that I should be sent home rather than to a hospital. I was so impressed that I wanted to study that.

Were many women getting a higher education at that time?

AKELEY: The medical school of the University of Vienna had many women. There were already quite a few women physicians.

Isn't that rather unusual?

AKELEY: Not for Vienna, which had the best medical school in Europe.

You obviously were expected to get good grades and go to the university. But did your parents want you to be educated for the sake of education or to be educated for the sake of having a profession and getting a job?

AKELEY: As long as my father lived and we were so well-to-do, the idea of a career came into nobody's head. Earning money came after my father had died, and we became what my mother called "poor," which wasn't exactly true.

You were eighteen in 1922. Was that the year you went to the university?

AKELEY: I had graduated from the Gymnasium in June and entered the university in September. I also attended the Roentgen Institute of Vienna.

My classes at the university lasted until three o'clock in the afternoon. I took Semitic languages, a course entitled "What Is Philosophy?" and a course about Christianity and Judaism. At 5 o'clock every day I went to the Roentgen Institute, where I studied physics; I had a course in statistics and one in differential equations. I was loaded with work.

My classes ended at 9 o'clock, and then I had to take the streetcar out to where we lived there in the suburbs. Sometimes I would not go directly home, but stop first at a coffeehouse, and I might get home by 11. I studied in the morning between classes.

Akeley did not take a straight path to her degree. After a year she broke off her academic studies to work at the Norbertus Verlag, a publishing house, where she typed, took shorthand (an aptitude she taught herself), and was a translator of French. When she returned to her studies, it was only to those at the Roentgen Institute. Her research and full-time coursework so monopolized her time that she abandoned her study of comparative religion at the university. In 1925, she graduated from the Roentgen Institute with the equivalent of a master's degree.[3] She returned to the Norbertus Verlag, rising to the rank of editor-in-chief. She stayed in that job until 1938, when the Nazis confiscated the firm because the owner was Jewish, and Akeley would be enlisted to participate in the process of liquidation.

Akeley had not been particularly interested in politics until 1933, when the Reichstag in Berlin was burned. Whether the Nazis set it on fire is still subject to controversy, but what is certain is that Hitler used the arson as an excuse to consolidate his power by having the Decree for the Protection of the People and the State passed. The resulting suspension of civil liberties was followed by the notorious Enabling Law, which gave Hitler the power to legislate on his own authority and carry out the nazification of German institutions and society. Nazi destruction of German democracy and the subsequent racial laws encouraged the consolidation of dictatorial government and an increase of antisemitism throughout Central Europe.

AKELEY: I became more and more interested in what was happening in Germany. Until 1933 I had little time for politics. I did my work, went skiing, and discussed with my friends how Marlene Dietrich looked in *The Blue Angel* or what Max Reinhardt[4] was producing in the theater. We also discussed Freud, and I even learned the difference between Freud, Jung, and Adler.

After Hitler came to power, those of us who were Jewish became very concerned and worried. We were no longer lighthearted kids—or, more precisely—young people in a world of kids. People would now ask, "What will you do when Hitler comes?" One might answer, "I will go to America," or "I will go to Africa," or "I will go to Australia." I remember people saying, "That is the end of us, because if they can do that in Germany, which has 65 million people, they can do it to Austria, with only six and a half million people." We never met in coffeehouses anymore, but at each other's homes as antisemitism grew by leaps and bounds.

I remember one incident quite clearly. I belonged to a mountaineering group. And in the autumn of 1933 we went to Styria to walk on one of the small glaciers. We would climb for about five hours to get there and stay overnight in one of the Alpenverein huts. When we got to the hut, my heart sank. On the door was a sign which said: "Juden sind nicht erwünscht hier" (Jews are not welcomed here). Our group had both Jews and Gentiles. The Jews were shocked; the Gentiles embarrassed. At that moment a sort of desperation overtook me. I knew about antisemitism, I had even seen some of it at the university when Gentiles didn't want Jews to eat at their tables in the student cafeteria, but the sign came as a complete surprise. We didn't stay in that hut but went over the glacier to another place that didn't belong to the Alpenverein. During the night I started to feel very funny, and when I took my pulse it was 160. I thought I was going to die. Anyhow, next day, we went back down.

I saw a doctor; he gave me bromides, and I was better after two days. From that moment on I looked everywhere, I listened to what people said. I never had been suspicious before, but from that moment on, I paid attention. I never went up any mountain where the Alpenverein had huts.

But you knew before that the Alpenverein did not want Jews to use their huts.

AKELEY: But they wouldn't have it written, you see. My parents had warned me that I might encounter antisemitism where I least expected it.

You were determined not to allow yourself to be put in this position again, right?

AKELEY: Correct, and I was terribly hurt.

Did you sense that the Austrian Catholic Church was antisemitic?

AKELEY: Never officially. I remember that one church paper came out and said that the Jews were the killers of Christ, but the Vatican corrected the newspaper, saying that the Romans killed Christ.

Your friends seemed to fear that the advent of Hitler to power and the end of Austrian democracy were going to result in a German attack on Austria.

AKELEY: Absolutely.

Did you consider yourself an Austrian patriot?

AKELEY: No longer, when I was being discriminated against.

This was more than legal discrimination, it was particular organizations simply saying: "Jews not wanted." And that was difficult because most Austrian Jews considered themselves Austrians, didn't they?

AKELEY: Very much. It was our home. I was very proud to be fourth-generation Viennese.

Your loyalty was to Vienna rather than to the state?

AKELEY: But we also had the Alps. Although they had no social connection, they were lovely. The loveliness of Austria is unbelievable. You could walk up into the Alps and find a village next to the glacier. Here there is nothing like that.

You have a loyalty, an attachment to the beauty of the country.

AKELEY: Definitely, I had a great attachment.

To you it's a Heimat?

AKELEY: Not anymore.

But then?

AKELEY: Oh, absolutely. You know, I had a *Heimat* and my *Heimat* was Österreich. But I always used to proudly claim that I was a Wienerin, a Viennese. But after they kicked me out, I never said that anymore.

Even before, though, you didn't feel any sense of nationalism?

AKELEY: I had no sense of nationalism. Nationalism wasn't particularly stressed, even in Habsburg times. In our history classes we always learned that the Austrians lost wars. There was a famous saying that "We Austrians marry instead of fight." In fact, the empire got most of its lands by marrying instead of fighting, because they were not good fighters.

But you had roots, you felt you had roots.

AKELEY: Absolutely, my roots were Austrian.

You said that many of your friends felt that Austria's days were numbered. Did many of them leave?

AKELEY: Not many.

Didn't they fear that there was going to be an Anschluss?

AKELEY: Yes, but they thought they could live with it. It would be very disagree-able, a great inconvenience, but they could put up with the restrictions. They were too much attached to the *Heimatland*. And where would you go? To get to the United States you had to have a sponsor. Even those who had relatives in America hung on. They asked their relatives if they could count on them if a time came.

Did you or anyone in your circle come in contact with the Zionist movement?

AKELEY: We knew about it, of course, and we thought that if the Jews thought they came from Palestine and wanted to go, it would be a very good thing. But for us it had no attraction. We had good jobs and were making enough money to enjoy life. We were told that only date trees, camels, and nomadic Arabs lived there. The Polish Jews were more willing to go to Palestine than the old Vi-ennese Jews, who wanted to stay where they were.

An Outlet for Misery: Henry Feuer

"I was alarmed at the tremendous class differences, the poor people, the unemployment. I felt that all this mis-ery had to find an outlet, and that's the reason that people wanted to join Germany."

The Flight from Galicia

The Russian offensive into central Galicia, which began on August 18, 1914, two weeks after the start of World War I, caught the Austrians off guard. Conrad von Hötzendorf, chief of the Dual Monarchy's General Staff, had expected the attack farther north, near the Warsaw-bulge sector. However, the Austrians put up a spirited defense, especially around Komarov. But in doing so, they exposed their southern flank to encirclement and had to withdraw, leaving Galicia open to Russian occupation. The citizens panicked.

Many Jews, knowing the Russian appetite for pogroms, took to the roads in flight.[5] When units of the Russian 8th Army entered Stanislau on August 25, many had left, including the Feuer family, which had fled to Vienna. They thus abandoned the family dried fruit and fur business, arriving only with the clothes they wore and the horsedrawn carriage that made their flight possible. Henry's parents, Jakob and Julia, now faced the prospect of rebuilding their lives practically from scratch.

The Feuers came with a strong German-Austrian background. They spoke German at home and had been strong supporters of the Dual Monarchy. Vienna, to them, was a progressive and civilized city, relatively free from the excesses of antisemitism often present in more backward areas of the empire. Henry grew up here, receiving what was surely one of the best formal educations of the age.

FEUER: In addition to German my parents spoke Polish, Ukrainian, and Yiddish. I understood Yiddish, but I never spoke it. I didn't like the sound. I thought it was bad German.

Did your parents belong to a synagogue?

FEUER: We went to a temple on the high holidays, but not on a regular basis. They even worked on Saturday. However, my grandparents were highly Orthodox. They observed the laws very, very strictly. They did not travel during the Sabbath or even turn on the lights.

Did you have a seder?

FEUER: Oh, yes. And I would say that as long as my grandparents lived, we observed things very strictly. We had separate dishes for the dairy products and for the meat.

Was there mandatory religious education in the schools?

FEUER: In Gymnasium, we had religion as one of the subjects. When it was time for the religious class, the Catholics, Protestants, and Jews were all separated. I also had a private tutor, who came to our home and taught me Hebrew. I was very interested in learning it. I used to sing in the choir in the temple when I was eight or nine. I didn't give such participation much thought. It was a natural phase of my life, and religious observance did not seem forced on me. But as I grew up I became more independent.

To what extent did these libertarian and egalitarian values that you had developed come from a religious dimension?

FEUER: I don't think any did. I never integrated my religious lessons into that aspect of my life. I used to ask my grandfather why he would not work the electric lights on the Sabbath. I mean, this is just a switch, it's not like making a fire. I think my skepticism started this way. And then we had some differences because I started participating in sports, like skiing. My grandfather disapproved of it; he was afraid that I would get injured. His generation did almost no physical exercise, let alone any sports.

Orthodoxy then became an impediment to leading what you would consider a normal life?

FEUER: It was impossible to get kosher food if you went skiing in the mountains.

You believed in a personal God?

FEUER: Not really. When I was young, I did. But as I got older, I didn't. The change started when I entered the Gymnasium. Religion was hardly discussed there, except when we were separated and had formal instruction. I don't remember any of my non-Jewish colleagues who were especially religious, either.

So you were growing up in an increasing secular society.

FEUER: That's right.

Did you have a bar mitzvah?

FEUER: Oh yes, sure. I vividly remember reading from the Torah directly.

I assume with this liberalization came more assimilation into the greater community? Where did this begin?

FEUER: Well, my father, despite having arrived in Vienna practically broke, became a very successful businessman with a big enterprise. He had many non-Jewish friends, despite his strong sense of Jewish identity. And he empathized with the Zionism of Theodor Herzl, but he was primarily a businessman. He did not participate in politics very much.

Well, Herzl argued that antisemitism was such an endemic thing in European culture that there was no future for Jews there. Is that what your father believed?

FEUER: No, he never planned to leave. Had it not been for the Nazi takeover of Austria, he would have stayed in Vienna. In fact, he went back after World War II. For me, Zionism was a wonderful outlet. When I was ten or eleven, I joined the left-wing Ha-Shomir ha-Za'ir, and I stayed with the group until I went to the university. I might have gone to Palestine if I had thought that I could help there. Many young Jews from Poland came through Vienna on their way to

After being released
from prison in July 1938,
Henry Feuer hastened to
obtain a passport. It was
marked with a "J" for *Jude*
and was issued by the
"German Empire."

Number 9 Fischerstiege in Vienna, where the Feuer family once lived.
Henry Feuer stands in the doorway in this photo, taken in March 1992.

Palestine. They worked on farms close to the city to gain experience, because they were not farmers and didn't know what it meant to work the soil. We used to visit with them. But when I entered the university, I joined the Socialist Student Movement.

Politics of the Outside World

The Austrian Social Democrats were Marxist and their goals were revolutionary, but they devoted their energy to the establishment of a democratic constitutional government, rather than to government control of the means of production. Their party chief, Karl Renner, was a moderate and a pragmatist who avoided enacting radical programs, because he feared they might contribute to the distress of the proletariat. Even Otto Bauer, chief of the party's radical wing, favored gradualism. Political strength was particularly evident in Vienna, wnere the party controlled two-thirds of the seats on the city council. In parliament, it held about 50 percent of the seats. Its influence was strong in the free trade unions and in a broad array of party organizations, which provided a variety of educational and social services.

It ran the *Kinderfreunde* (children's friends), which were elementary schools with libraries and special day-care centers. The *Kinderfreunde* also sponsored the Red Falcon youth movement for boys and girls between the ages of ten and fourteen. For the adults there were theater groups, choral clubs, a stamp collector's guild, an Esperanto league, a mushroom growers' interest group, an anti-Catholic Federation of Freethinkers, the Association for Biblical Socialism, the Union of Religious Socialists, and the Flame Crematory Society. There was also a full complement of student political groups and, as protection against class enemies, the Republikanischer Schutzbund (Republican Defense Alliance).

You came from a very entrepreneurial background. Your father was a businessman; one might even claim he was a sort of capitalist. How do you explain your obvious social conscience?

FEUER: I was affected by the class differences and the high rate of unemployment that existed in Vienna. Those were some of the reasons the Nazis managed to gain such a foothold there. The existence of social injustice directed me toward socialism. But I never discussed my beliefs with my father because of the way he had been raised and educated.

But he knew that you were in the socialist movement?

FEUER: Of course he knew. I had this quandary: I didn't have to pinch pennies, but I knew people and colleagues who didn't have enough money to buy books.

Did you think of yourself as an Austrian, the way Germans think of themselves as German belonging to a Heimat *or homeland?*

FEUER: I never had that feeling. In fact, I had no intention of staying in Austria, because there were very few prospects in my field.

Among the Jewish community, did you feel any sense of discrimination because you had not been born in Vienna?

FEUER: I had no difficulty fitting in. I had many friends of different Jewish backgrounds, and I never felt that I was discriminated against. Among the grownups it was different. Many of the "Western Jews" didn't like the "Eastern Jews," but that animosity did not carry over in school at all.

How about your father?

FEUER: I'm sure that by being a newcomer he was resented by people who had grown up in Vienna and were well-established.

What about the attitude of the Gentiles? One of Austria's main political parties, the Christian Social Party, was openly antisemitic. And Vienna was the city in which Hitler developed his hatred toward the Jews. To what extent were you aware of these anti-Jewish currents? Not only in Austria, but in Germany as well?

FEUER: We were certainly aware of it, but it didn't directly affect our lives very much, at least not when I was in the Gymnasium.

Did your father worry about this?

FEUER: He worried about it, but he was more optimistic than realistic, that was the interesting thing.

He talked about it at home?

FEUER: All the time. I told him what would happen. I told him to cut down on his business and to try to resettle someplace else. I also had a lot of arguments with my father about Mussolini. He did a lot of fruit business in Italy, and he liked Mussolini because, he said, Mussolini had brought order—the trains now ran on time. When he made such remarks, I told him that such things were not very important.[6]

But my father's business hadn't suffered. In fact, he enlarged it, moving to bigger quarters and expanding the dealings he had with the Department of Commerce. Since he managed to export more goods than he imported, he had special privileges. So he thought that the Christian Social government would protect him because it was a government of law and order.

Why do you think that you were a pessimist on this issue, whereas he was an optimist?

FEUER: My father didn't like to think about what was going to happen in the near future, because he didn't want to admit that he would have to leave again and start from the beginning. It's human nature. Everything was more or less given to me. He had to fight for it. I didn't have that much involved. I didn't have to give up a big business. He had a very big enterprise and was well-known all over town. He had a lot of people working with him.

I was alarmed at the tremendous class differences, the poor people, the unemployment. I felt that all this misery had to find an outlet, and that's the reason that people wanted to join Germany. This was especially true in the Tyrol, where most of the business came from German tourists, who flooded the whole area in the summer.

A tremendous division existed between "Red Vienna" and the Catholic rest of the country. The Christian Social Party professed a belief in democracy but had no tolerance for any other point of view than its own increasingly theological one. The Roman Catholic bishops, in their pastoral letter of December 1925, had threatened the Social Democrats with a quotation from Matthew 18:8: "Whoever destroys the faith of one of the little ones and blights his eternal salvation deserves that a millstone be hanged around his neck and that he be drowned in the depth of the sea."

The Right also had its share of paramilitary organizations, the most important of which was the Heimwehr (Home Guard), which was originally formed to maintain the security of border areas and had developed into a force in domestic politics. Heimwehr units acted, often with official sanction, against worker demonstrations and as strikebreakers. Some of its leaders were even involved in a scheme to create a separate Roman Catholic state under a Wittelsbach king, whose realm would include western Austria and southern Germany.

The Christian Social Party became increasingly attracted to authoritarian government, especially as it seemed the best way of crushing the power of its archrival, the Social Democratic Party. In 1933, Chancellor Engelbert Dollfuss stepped up the attack. He obtained power to rule by decree from President Wilhelm Miklas and proceeded to curtail freedom of the press and forbid political parades and assemblies. In 1934 he made his Fatherland Front Austria's only political party. The socialists protested with a general strike. Dollfuss proclaimed martial law and in February ordered government forces to shell the great blocks of workers' apartments in Vienna's Ottakring, Döbling, and Floridsdorf districts. The burial of Austrian democracy followed quickly. Although Dollfuss was also a strong opponent of National Socialism, crushing the Social Democrats further weakened the country's independence, opening the door wider to Adolf Hitler.

FEUER: The politics of the outside world became more apparent when I went to the university. First, there were many strikes, and you never knew, when you went in the morning to the laboratory and you came out in the evening, whether there would be any streetcars. Then, as the Nationalist Party became stronger, there were fights on the street between students and workers. There were fights in the university. Often the university was completely shut down, and you needed a special permit to go in. Laboratories were very often closed because of fear of sabotage. I had to work extremely fast to finish my studies. I don't think that was really good for my education, because I could not go into certain subjects as thoroughly as I wanted to. When I got closer to the Ph.D. degree, I got my own key to the laboratory, but I never knew whether I would be allowed to finish my thesis. I remember that a fight broke out during a lecture at the Faculty of Medicine, and some of the Nazis students threw Jewish women students out of the window, killing some of them. I'm sure there were many Nazis among my colleagues in the laboratory, but there were never any incidents.

Why are you sure many were Nazis?

FEUER: They admitted it in discussions. We had a lot of political discussions, and you could tell who they were.

How did that affect you personally?

FEUER: Well, I was a socialist. I had to avoid certain places. I couldn't go to the university on a Saturday when they paraded around in uniform. Then there were small incidents. When I walked in the area of the university, somebody might bump into me on purpose.

Were many remarks made?

FEUER: Oh yes, yes. And of course, we returned the remarks. I didn't fear walking in the street, but I stayed away from areas where they were concentrated, where they were more boisterous and wanted to show each other that they were really tough nationalists. But if you lived there then, it didn't seem that oppressive. I wanted to finish my studies as fast as possible and then leave Austria.

When did you know this for sure?

FEUER: In 1933, when Hitler became the chancellor of Germany. Then there was no doubt in my mind.

You knew that the Anschluss *was inevitable?*

FEUER: To me it was obvious. Many of my friends thought so as well.

Feuer graduated from the University of Vienna in 1936 with a Ph.D. in chemistry. Even had there been no Nazi threat, he knew a career in his specialty would be difficult in Austria, a country with few opportunities for employment in chemicals. Austrian universities usually turned out more Ph.D.s than the economy could absorb. Many of those working for advanced degrees knew they would have to seek jobs abroad. Feuer thought of coming to the United States. However, immediately following the receipt of his degree, he began working in his father's enterprise. The work in commodities was interesting, but he never considered making it a career. He felt his father needed him and that he owed him thanks for the support he had been given. For two years he worked in the family business while the Germans intensified their pressure on Austria.

Notes

1. The Mandler house was one block from the Rudolfsplatz, site of the famous Metropole Hotel, which from 1938 to 1945 was headquarters of the Vienna Gestapo. The Metropole building was destroyed in 1945 and replaced by a memorial to the victims of Nazi tyranny.
2. The three grades were: "excellent," "unanimous consent," and "majority consent."
3. Anna Mandler married Felix Frost in September 1925. He had been her childhood sweetheart and played in the first-violin section of the Vienna Philharmonic, then led by Wilhelm Furtwängler. The couple lived together for only a brief time but hesitated getting a formal divorce, since the only grounds were adultery or abuse. Because neither wanted to accuse the other of an untruth, they stayed married until 1933, the first year of no-fault divorce.
4. Reinhardt was one of the most important Jewish stage directors of modern time. His daring and provocative staging of Oscar Wilde's *Salomé* influenced Richard Strauss to write his opera of the same name.
5. This, despite the fact that at least a quarter of a million Jews were serving in the Russian army. Considering the large numbers of Jews who were similarly fighting in the Austro-Hungarian armies, this meant that World War I was a conflict in which Jew often fought against Jew.
6. Mussolini was also acceptable to many politically conservative Jews because fascism seemed fairly free of antisemitism. Only in the late thirties, under the influence of National Socialism, did Mussolini have passed a series of racial laws that began compartmentalizing the Jews, excluding them from the nation's active life.

6

The *Anschluss*

Hermann Göring was an irrepressible show-off. On June 10, 1934, the number-two Nazi played host to some members of the foreign diplomatic corps at his recently completed baronial estate of Karinhall, located an hour's drive north of Berlin. Karinhall was built with state money, and Göring had been involved closely with all aspects of its planning, even down to the design of the door handles at the main lodge. Göring, acting in his capacity of Chief Huntsman of the Realm (*Reichsjägermeister*), greeted the visitors at the entrance to the property, his ample figure costumed in a nifty flying suit and a large horn-handled deer knife stuck in his black leather belt.

Göring began the personal tour with a visit to a bison enclosure to watch a breeding demonstration, which fizzled when the male bison appeared not to be in the mood. There were trips to other places of interest, one being the edge of a vast marsh, where Göring delivered a lecture on the splendors of bird life. Afterwards he raced ahead of his guests to his lodge for a quick change of clothes, appearing, when they next saw him, in a green leather jerkin, white flannel coat, duck-cloth trousers, and tennis shoes. The sightseeing continued with a room-by-room inspection of the lodge, the high-light being the great hall, with its huge oak tree growing up through the roof like in a set from a Wagnerian opera. Dinner was served outside on the stone terrace, followed by a stroll to the mausoleum of Göring's late wife, after whom the estate was named. The tomb's vault had walls six feet thick, Göring boasted.

British ambassador Sir Eric Phipps was appalled at Göring's pompous bragging: "He showed us his toys, like a big, fat, spoiled child: his primeval woods, his bison and birds, his shooting-box and lake and bathing beach, his blond 'private' secretary [Emmy Sonnemann, Göring's companion, later his wife], his [late] wife's mausoleum and swans and sarsen stones, all mere toys to satisfy his varying moods, and all, or nearly all, as he was careful to explain, Germanic. [And I thought] there were other toys, less innocent, though winged, and these might some day be launched in their murderous mission in the same childlike spirit and with the same child-like glee."[1]

Not all of Phipps's countrymen looked on the new National Socialist overlords with such trepidation. During the 1920s, Great Britain had tried to maintain the European balance of power through cooperation with Germany, and when Hitler became chancellor, it saw no reason to change the policy. British leaders anticipated that the Nazi regime would become more moderate as it became more secure. They did not find it alarming that Hitler should advocate revising the Paris Peace Settlement, nor were they surprised that Germany might seek other territorial adjustments. They were even sympathetic with Hitler's claim that the principle of self-determination established at the Paris Peace Conference gave the German peoples the right to live together in a Greater Germany.

Hitler scoffed at the idea of just getting back the territory Germany had lost in the First World War. The goal was too modest and hardly worth the necessary bloodshed. He had aims more grandiose. The Führer was an easterner. What he had in mind was German expansion into the vast open spaces of Russia and all the lands in between. But this *Drang nach Osten* (urge to move eastward) would not be "the breath-taking sensation of a new Alexander's conquest." It was to build a vast empire for the survival and growth of the Aryan race. The "sword need only give soil" for "the industrious work of the German plow."[2] Hitler's declaration of *Lebensraum* (living space) was hardly traditional German foreign policy, and there were few statesmen in the European democracies who took him at his word.

One of the exceptions was Sir Robert Vansittart, the permanent undersecretary of the British Foreign Office, who, even before Hitler had come to power, predicted that Germany would change the status quo in Europe by annexing Austria and revising its current frontiers with Poland. Vansittart feared that the British had lost their capacity for self-preservation and would do little to prevent this aggression from taking place.

Hitler believed that the union of his Austrian homeland with Germany was "a life work" to be furthered with every means possible.[3] As soon as he became chancellor, he began a policy of harassment and intimidation. He encouraged the Austrian Nazis, a section of the German Party, to demonstrate against their government; he imposed a thousand-mark tax on all Germans visiting Austria in an effort to weaken the Austrian economy; and he began denouncing the Austrian government for frustrating the desire of its people to be incorporated into a greater German Reich.

On June 19, 1933, Austrian Chancellor Engelbert Dollfuss ordered the Austrian Nazi Party dissolved. In retaliation, the Germans formed the Austrian Legion, training its soldiers with units of the SS and the SA in encampments near the Bavarian-Austrian frontier. The force soon numbered 6,000 men. Hitler then approved a plan to kidnap Dollfuss and his entire cabinet, thereby creating an instant power vacuum that would bring a National Socialist government to power. The government would petition Germany for incorporation into the Reich.

The attempted takeover took place on July 25, 1934, when members of the Austrian Legion entered the courtyard of the chancellery in Vienna, overpowered the guards, and broke into the building. Most of the ministers had been warned and had fled, but the Nazis captured Chancellor Engelbert Dollfuss, wounding him in the process. Meanwhile units of the Austrian army surrounded the building. Shot in the neck, Dollfuss slowly bled to death while the Nazis negotiated safe passage to Germany.

During these events Hitler was attending a performance of *Das Rheingold* in Bayreuth, and the news was flashed to him in his box at the Festival Hall. Adjutants rushed back and forth from a telephone in a nearby anteroom to get the latest developments. The news was not good, and Hitler became so excited that his nostrils flared out until "they stretched almost to his ears."[4] But afterwards, he tried to remove any suspicion that he had anything to do with the coup by appearing in town for a post-opera snack. He and his entourage sat in a local restaurant "eating liver dumplings."[5] The Führer "denounced the rashness and stupidity" of the Austrian Nazi Party for having involved him in such an appalling situation.

The attempt to seize power in Vienna was his first great blunder. But it had no effect on his position in Germany, and international reaction was fairly mild. Nevertheless, Hitler felt humiliated and vowed to succeed the next time, determined not to leave the planning in the hands of amateurs.

Yet, for all the conceit about his firmness of will, Hitler was a procrastinator. He filled his days with trivia until decisions on important matters could no longer be delayed; then he would burst into a flurry of activity and "spend a few days of intensive work giving shape to his solutions [only to relapse] again into his idleness."[6] The Führer was afraid that he would die before his life's work was accomplished. He constantly complained of pains and insomnia. His personal physician, Theodore Morell, diagnosed his complaints as "complete exhaustion of the intestinal flora [due to] the overburdening of his nervous system" and treated him with capsules of bacteria from Bulgarian peasants and injections from animal testicles. Morell was never able to cure his patient's morbidity. "I always counted on having time to realize my plan," Hitler lamented. "I must carry them out myself. None of my successors will have the force to. I must carry out my aims as long as I can hold up, for my health is growing worse all the time."[7] But Hitler's method of work made the formulation of schedules and timetables difficult.

In a memorandum of August 1936, Hitler specified that the army had to be operational and the economy fit for war within four years. "The final solution lies in extending the space of our people and/or the sources of its raw materials and food stuffs." He made no attempt to be more specific, adding vaguely, "It is the task of the political leadership one day to solve this problem."[8] One evening in 1936, at his Obersalzburg retreat, as he sat looking out a window at the gathering dusk, he told his court architect, Albert Speer, that there were two possibilities: "To win through with all plans, or to fail. If I win, I shall be one of the greatest men in history. If I fail, I shall be condemned, despised and damned."[9]

On July 11, 1936, Germany had forced Austria to recognize that it was part of the "German cultural orbit" and should now conduct "its foreign policy in the light of the peaceful endeavors of the German government's foreign policy." This policy, which the Nazis called *Gleichschaltung* (coordination), gradually led to the complete union, or *Anschluss,* with Germany. Austrian Chancellor Kurt von Schuschnigg, who had succeeded Dollfuss, feebly tried to play for time while trying to shore up his political position at home by cracking down on the operations of the local Nazi Party and casting about for foreign support.

But none of the Western powers were willing to guarantee the country's independence; and Mussolini, who had seemed a protector in 1934, was now so bogged down in his adventures in Ethiopia and Spain that he no longer had the desire or the power to stand by Austria's side. Furthermore, many of the Austrian people were anti-Italian and pro-German and frankly welcomed an *Anschluss* with its larger neighbor.

On November 5, 1937, in the formal surroundings of the Reich Chancellery, Hitler told the head of the foreign office and his military chiefs that "it was his unalterable resolve to solve Germany's problem of space no later than 1943 to 1945. He explained that within six to eight years, German power would have reached its peak. Afterwards "our relative strength would decrease in relation to the rearmament which would by then have been carried out by the rest of the world." The first objective "must be to overthrow Czechoslovakia and Austria simultaneously in order to remove the threat to our flank in any possible operation against the West." Hitler believed that Britain and France "had already tacitly written off the Czechs and were reconciled to the fact that this question would be cleared up in due course by Germany." He spoke for more than four hours and with characteristic melodrama enjoined his audience to regard his exposition "in the event of his death, as his last will and testament."[10] No one at the meeting doubted that Hitler meant what he said. The chancellery meeting did not reveal any new departures in

National Socialist policy. Pan-Germanism and *Lebensraum* were still priorities. There was no blueprint, but Hitler had considerably narrowed his immediate objectives. But Austria's fate would be decided before that of Czechoslovakia.

Early the following year, Hitler decided to complete the economic integration of Austria with Germany, a loss of sovereignty that would inevitably lead to a complete takeover of the country. On February 12, 1938, Hitler met with Schuschnigg at the Berghof, the German leader's retreat in the Bavarian Alps. Hitler demanded that Austria prepare itself for complete economic integration with Germany. The Führer had a justifiably low opinion of the Austrian sense of national identity, for the question of *Anschluss* was one of the most tangled and fractional issues in Austria's history. Developing out of the Pan-German movements of the nineteenth century, it transcended religion, political affiliation, geography, and social class. The Social Democrats, for example, were of two minds: some favored union because of the potential benefits of association with a strong socialist movement; others feared such ties would lead to a decline in their independence. Many Austrians who supported *Anschluss* immediately after the World War would develop second thoughts with the rise of Adolf Hitler, but others saw the Nazi leader as the means for Austrian revival and greatness.

Hitler ordered Schuschnigg to legalize the Austrian Nazi Party and appoint Austrian Nazi Artur von Seyss-Inquart as minister of the interior, a post giving him control of the national police. He also required that an amnesty be granted to those Nazi Party members in jail and threatened to invade the country in three days if these terms were not accepted.

Schuschnigg returned home and began carrying out the demands, but he then tried a desperate gamble. On March 9, he announced that he would let the Austrian people decide their own fate by voting whether or not they favored an independent Austria. Schuschnigg had no assurance that this would be successful, and even many members of his own party favored union with Germany. Hitler, however, was furious and warned Schuschnigg that unless the referendum was immediately canceled, Germany would intervene. Hitler further demanded that Seyss-Inquart be appointed chancellor in Schuschnigg's place. At the same time Hitler ordered the German army to prepare to invade Austria.

At daybreak on March 12, Wehrmacht troops, accompanied by the Gestapo and agents of the SS Security Service, invaded Austria. It was the largest operation of the German army since World War I, but somewhat ill-organized. The invasion followed a plan improvised from one originally intended to prevent a Habsburg restoration. Logistics were so poor that the motorized columns advancing on Vienna were instructed to refuel at Austrian filling stations. Many of the tanks and trucks had repair problems en route.

The afternoon of day one, Hitler arrived in Linz, the village of his youth, and from there headed to Vienna. His reception in the Austrian capital was so jubilant and spontaneous that he changed his original plan to administer Austria as a separate satellite state and now decided on direct incorporation. On March 13 a proclamation from Berlin announced the "reunification" of the Ostmark with the German Reich.

Through Italy to France: Henry Feuer

"Many of the Viennese participated in the behavior against Jews, but you didn't know whether they did this because they really believed in Nazism or whether they were afraid they might suffer if they didn't participate."

A Jew Was a Jew No Matter What

The Nazi invasion prompted a frenzied display of popular anti-semitism. Austrian mobs shouting "Death to the Jews" and "Jews get out" invaded the Leopoldstadt Jewish district. They forced people from their homes, making them scrub the sidewalks; they broke into and looted Jewish-owned shops; they beat up individuals and stole their personal jewelry and other valuables; they demanded money. The new Nazi bosses were more systematic. They ordered wholesale arrests and began immediate application of the Nürnberg Laws. This action meant loss of citizenship and employment, confiscation of property, arrest and deportation, and forced emigration.

The number of Austrian citizens who were considered Jews had been declining since the end of the First World War. In the decade between 1923 and 1934, the number had dropped from 201,513 to 191,458 and continued to decline. About 90 percent of these Austrian Jews lived in Vienna. During the six-month period following Nazi annexation of the country, about 2,000 Jews became Roman Catholics. But these conversions did not change official Jewish status. The Nürnberg Laws considered a person Jewish if he or she had at least three Jewish grandparents, notwithstanding present religion. This classification also included those who had changed religion, even before the Nazi occupation, adding as many as 5,000 people to those defined as Jews, thereby raising the overall number of Austrian Jews to 195,000. Overnight these people had lost their country, soon their communities, and finally their lives, if they remained. Mass arrests of opponents of the regime and of Jews began even before the formal authority to do so had been granted. Within a year a concentration camp built in Mauthausen, near Linz in Upper Austria, was ready for business.

HENRY FEUER: I knew the Germans would come twenty-four hours before their actual invasion because I overheard some telephone conversations. Due to a faulty connection in my office, I heard about the arrival of German troops. I told my father, "The German troops are going to come in tomorrow." I knew that they would come to my parents' apartment immediately. So I asked my parents to stay with me, but that didn't do much good. They went first to his apartment in the First District, and then came to my apartment—it was about fifteen or twenty minutes away by car—and they just came in and arrested my father and me. They searched the apartment—I had a lot of books, many of them were socialistic—but I don't think they took anything. They wore Nazi uniforms.

These were Austrian Nazis?

FEUER: Yes. Some of them were even university students.

When did your arrest occur?

FEUER: The evening of March 13, the day after the invasion. They pinpointed people. I wonder whether they would have come to get me if my father had stayed in his apartment. Because they must have found out that he was with me. Or they might have come to get me too. I don't know.

That your father was on the first list of roundups testifies to his importance. Whom else did they arrest that you knew?

FEUER: Other individuals who were in the same type of business. Friends of my father. All Jewish, of course.

What happened after your arrest?

FEUER: We were taken into a house, and they gathered us in a room. More people were constantly added. There were chairs, and we all had to sit there. I mean, that's how it went. They took me down to the street, gave me a broom, and ordered me to clean the sidewalk. If I didn't work fast enough, they pushed me with the butts of their rifles. We didn't get anything to eat for twenty-four hours. I don't know how long we were there, perhaps two days, and then we were shipped to a school in the Twentieth District, where we were kept in the gymnastics room. We slept on the floor. It was chilly and unpleasant, but at least we got food, and there were no more excesses of the type I described before. I stayed there for about two or three weeks, and then I was transferred to the *Landesgericht* prison, where the people were crammed together in cells, some of them students, some elderly people. We had to work, clean the corridors, and things like this, but we were just treated like political prisoners. *Schutzkraft* (special protection), they called it.

Did you have prison garb?

FEUER: No, but there were many interrogations from the Gestapo. They dragged me back and forth from the prison to their headquarters on the Morzin Platz.

What did they ask you in these grillings?

FEUER: All kinds of things about socialism, and whether I ever had sexual intercourse with non-Jewish girls.

They asked you to reveal names of other people?

FEUER: No. They didn't need me to give them the names. They had all the lists, which they probably got directly from Socialist Party headquarters.

Were these Gestapo people abusive?

FEUER: They didn't hit me, but they were verbally very abusive, and not very clever in their interrogation. I didn't know where these people came from, but I think they were Austrian.

How would you define your Austrian identity during this period?

FEUER: I didn't feel much attachment to the Austrian individuals after I saw how they behaved.

You told us that when you were growing up you didn't feel much anti-semitism, but after the Anschluss *it really became obvious.*

FEUER: Well, it all came out. I knew it would. I can only talk about the Viennese. I was a member of the Socialist Party, and before the so-called *Anschluss* the members behaved very well. There were antisemitic remarks, especially among the blue-collar workers, but many had no work, so you could understand how they could fall for the propaganda that the Jews have all the money. It's the old story. They hoped that their lot would be improved.

An opportunistic type of antisemitism?

FEUER: Yes, I think so. True for many, many of them.

That must have come as a big surprise and disillusionment?

FEUER: Yes, of course. If someone talks to me now about socialism and socialist parties, I don't even listen. People don't really know what they're talking about. I mean the idea is wonderful, but the people who pretend to be socialists don't always behave accordingly. Vienna was socialist after World War I. There were all these socialist mayors and all those organizations. But the socialists apparently didn't practice what they preached.

Do you think this had something to do with the Austrian national character?

FEUER: It's very difficult to define what an Austrian is, because there was a tremendous influx from the east, even before World War I. I mean, this was the capital of a big empire, people came and stayed, others left. Some of the best composers and writers were not born in Vienna. So I don't know who you would consider to be Austrian. That's very difficult to determine.

Do you think this antisemitic outrage that came about was directed against certain kinds of Jews? What about those Jews, unlike your family, who were not as well-established?

FEUER: It didn't make any difference. A Jew was a Jew no matter what. Many of the Viennese participated in the behavior against Jews, but you didn't know whether they did this because they really believed in Nazism or whether they were afraid they might suffer if they didn't participate.

How long were you in custody?

FEUER: From March to the end of July [1938]. And then I was released and told I should leave the country as soon as possible, otherwise I would be arrested again.

During the time you were incarcerated, did you get any news about your father?

FEUER: Later on. He was released a little earlier than I.

What happened to his business in the meantime?

FEUER: That was taken over. The Nazis installed one of my father's non-Jewish business representatives as commissioner. And I got a letter from him while I was in prison that said that I was no longer an employee of the company.[11]

He is the one, then, who benefited from this?

FEUER: I'm sure he benefited, but he wasn't a cruel man, and he knew the business very well. It never occurred to me that he was a member of the Nazi Party. One of his partners was Jewish. And to his credit, he treated my father very well. I mean as far as giving him money until my father left Austria.

But your father no longer owned the business?

FEUER: Nothing. He also owned a villa outside of Vienna, and that was taken away from him. He owned a car and that was taken away. He was, in fact, just about penniless, and so was I, except that my dismissal date from the company was September 30. So I got paid for two more months after my release from prison. People could still sell personal property. In fact, many Germans came to Vienna to buy household goods and other things, like works of art from the Jews. I sold some of my belongings to a German officer—at very reduced prices, naturally.

What did you do after your release from prison in July?

FEUER: I had to get a passport. I had to get papers proving that I could not serve in the army. I had to prove that I did not owe any taxes. I had to get permission to send things, like books and personal effects, out of the country. All this took a tremendous amount of time. There were long lines of people.

Did you get much help from the non-Jewish people after your release?

FEUER: Many of our business associates were very sympathetic to us after the *Anschluss,* but there was very little they could do for me.

Did you come across people who showed you how they felt about this?

FEUER: Yes. I'll give you an example. In sending your things out of the country, you had to conform to a procedure whereby somebody from the police would watch you pack. Only then could the trunk be officially sealed. I remember that the person supervising me paid no attention to what I was doing, and from his remarks I understood that I could have put in anything I wanted. So there were some who felt that way, although I don't know the percentage.

Did you have any negative experiences with people who you thought were your friends?

FEUER: I had two close non-Jewish friends. We used to go climbing a lot together, but I never saw either of them after the *Anschluss.* I don't know what happened to them. Whether they were arrested or were part of the Nazi movement, in addition to being socialist, I don't know.

Did you share experiences with your father after your release?

FEUER: We didn't talk very much about it. It was a very unhappy time. We were much too occupied with settling our things and getting out of the country. Perhaps also we were not that type of people. I never talked about these things until now, and very few people know about them. Even my wife sometimes tells me, "You never told me about this." It becomes unreal. One of the reasons I don't try to talk about it is because you cannot understand it if you were not there. There is nothing to which it can be compared. People can listen and say, "that is terrible" or "this is very nice," but they can't feel the same way.

But with your father you could.

FEUER: Yes, but we were not that close.

And perhaps there was a feeling in such a bourgeois family like yours not to show your emotions too much?

FEUER: I was a member of the Socialist Party (laughing).

What about your mother?

FEUER: She coped very well, considering. They left her alone; she was never attacked or anything like that.

Was she actively involved in this process of trying to find ways to leave Austria?

FEUER: No, I don't think so. She would not have had the knowledge of what to do. She was a housewife and didn't have many friends. Her outlet was the family.

The family really lacked an extensive support group and was forced back on its own resources?

FEUER: Yes, yes. We didn't get any support from the outside.

What kind of support was the Jewish community giving?

FEUER: None, to any of us.

Possibly the people who were in charge of the Jewish community there thought that your father and you would be able to manage yourselves and they helped others more defenseless than you?

FEUER: Well, the only thing they could have helped with would have been to get us visas, probably to go to Israel. Many of these people were in a very precarious situation themselves, many of them were arrested.

When did you finally leave?

FEUER: At the end of October, October 29, to be exact. My father left later. In December, I believe. He went to Israel. To Tel Aviv. He got a visa; how he got it I don't know. I never asked him.

Where did you go?

FEUER: I didn't have any place to go. Everything was closed; every frontier was closed for Jews. You see, the passport I finally got was a German passport — Austria didn't exist anymore — it had a "J" stamped on it, which says that you are Jewish. I took a terrific risk and just bought a first-class ticket and took a train to Italy. I bribed the porter, and during the night we went across the frontier. I heard voices outside my compartment when the passport control came through, but they never opened the door or anything. I think the bribery did its work.

An Enemy Alien

Feuer first went to the port city of Trieste, where he had an uncle who worked with his father, supervising the import of Italian merchandise that was shipped to Vienna. The uncle, a long-term resident, had married an Italian woman,[12] but was unable to get his nephew a residency permit. Feuer decided he might have better luck in Palermo, where his father had business associates, one of whom was a member of the Fascist Party. Feuer's sister also lived there. (She had fled to Sicily earlier with her husband and young son. Eventually they would go to Israel.) Despite these connections, his request for residency in Palermo was also refused. The authorities feared repercussions from the Germans, insofar as Palermo was a port of call for German tourists on vacation in the *Kraft durch Freude* (Strength through Joy) program of the Nazi Labor Front.

Feuer arrived in Italy during the first flurry of anti-Jewish legislation. As Mussolini had moved closer to a German alliance during the late 1930s, he and his regime became officially more antisemitic. In July 1938 the Charter of Race was published in which Ethopians, Arabs, and Jews were listed as inferior races. The first antisemitic law, enacted on August 8, ordered that all Jews be struck off the diplomatic list. More comprehensive legislation produced in November excluded Jews from the armed forces, from the civil service, and from the Fascist Party. Jews were forbidden to own businesses that employed more than 100 employees, own real estate worth more than 20,000 lire, or have agricultural property worth more than 5,000 lire. Additional measures followed,[13] culminating in the law of November 17, 1938, which nullified naturalization obtained after January 1, 1919, and decreed that all foreign Jews were to leave Italy by March 12, 1939. Although the total package was severe, implementation was remarkably lax, and Italian Jews, unlike their German counterparts, did not rush wholesale to leave the country. The Italian people were not known for their racism. They had willingly accepted Jews in the highest positions of state from the prime ministry on down; Italian Jews were among the most highly assimilated in Europe. The Catholic Church was more religiously than racially antisemitic.[14]

Henry Feuer, despite his rebuff in Palermo, did not feel any immediate threat to his security. The business associate of his father's agreed to help him transfer to Rome, where his chances of obtaining a visa might be better.

FEUER: Rome in those days was a delightful place, in spite of my situation. You see, I knew Italian quite well. So I went to the Questura (interior ministry) and applied for a permit to stay in Rome. They had me fill out a form and told me to come back in two weeks. In the meantime, my passport, which was good for only three months, expired; so I called the German embassy, and they told me to bring it in and they would grant an extension. They did. It was a different world there. I went back to the Questura after two weeks, and they had no answer—it was Christmas time—and they told me not to worry. But I didn't wait for an answer and left for France.

I n order to obtain permission to enter France, Feuer obtained a visa allowing him to go to Cuba. This was arranged through a Jewish organization that helped refugees like himself.

One of the many organizations attempting to facilitate the emigration of Jews from Europe was the Intergovernmental Committee, established at the conference that opened on July 6, 1938, at Evian-les-Bains in France to help German and Austrian refugees. This conference was called at the insistence of President Franklin Roosevelt because he feared the United States would be inundated with Jewish refugees and wanted to establish a system whereby thirty-one other countries would each agree to accept a quota of 17,000 each. The Americans considered that their immigration policy toward refugees was already among the most generous in the world, and they saw no reason to liberalize it beyond already established quotas, which they promised would now be filled in full. Other countries also showed little desire to go beyond the policies they had already put in force or those established by the Intergovernmental Committee. Therefore the Evian conference stands out as an exercise in false hopes and broken promises.

To convince the French to grant him a laissez-passer, on December 15, 1938, he bought a one-way steamer ticket from the Compagnie Générale Transatlantique on one of its passenger ships leaving from Bordeaux to Santiago, Cuba. However, Feuer had no intention of actually using the ticket. Once he got to France, he intended to obtain permission to come to the United States. He entered France at Menton on December 21.

This *Heimatschein,* issued in 1930, confirms Anna Mandler Frost's rights as a citizen and resident of Vienna.

Anna Akeley in 1924.

Henry Feuer's passport.

At that time, France had about 200,000 refugees, 40,000 of which were Jews. The problem had recently become more acute because of the anti-Jewish frenzy of *Kristallnacht*, which followed the assassination several days before of a German diplomat in Paris. The French did not feel they could absorb any more refugees.

The French government optimistically envisaged German cooperation in solving the refugee problem. But when Nazi foreign minister Joachim von Ribbentrop came to Paris on December 6–7, he insisted that no mention of the "Jewish problem" be made in the French press. He was willing only to sign a general Franco-German agreement affirming mutual peaceful relations and recognizing the inviolability of existing frontiers. The Germans interpreted this to mean that the French had acquiesced in the expansion of Nazi influence in Eastern Europe.

FEUER: I had no difficulty at the French frontier. The border guard looked at my transit visa and my passport with its big "J" and swastika emblem and said, "Très bien. This is the first time I have seen one of these." I then got back on the train and was off to Paris. Shortly after I got there, I contacted a man I knew by reputation, a Professor Tiffeneau, who was dean of the faculty at the Sorbonne. I asked him for permission to work in his laboratory. He assigned me to one of his assistants, and I started working. I was treated very well. There were a lot of people doing research there who were not French; many, in fact, had come from Russia. It was very interesting research and quite successful. In fact I have a publication from it. But I found that it was impossible to get a *permis de séjour* (residency permit). So I talked to the man I worked with, because he was very close to Tiffeneau. I asked him whether Tiffeneau could intervene somehow. Although Tiffeneau hardly knew me, he pulled some strings and made it possible for me to stay in France. But I had to leave Paris.

Sending the Jews to the provinces to get them out of Paris was part of a deliberate French policy called "decongestion," which had been set in place the previous October. Other measures against refugees were enacted, including an increased surveillance for illegal entry at the frontiers and close monitoring of those aliens who had already arrived. On November 12, 1938, a decree was passed that

stripped French nationality from those who had already been naturalized but who were judged to be "unworthy of the title of French
citizen." Although Jews were not targeted specifically, many French
feared that an increasing Jewish presence, especially from those
Orthodox, unassimilated exiles from Eastern Europe, would have a
deleterious effect on French civilization and society.

At the time, France was receiving proportionally more refugees
than any other country, and despite the new regulations, many
French people felt that their country was still one that should welcome the politically oppressed. Other countries, including the United
States, more severely regulated the influx of refugees than France did.

FEUER: The authorities told me that I could go to Nantes, which is by the Atlantic Ocean, close to Saint-Nazaire. When I arrived there in March 1939, I
went to the city hall to obtain my *carte d'identité* (identity card) and the papers allowing me to work.

Feuer found work at the Melun Pharmaceutical Company, filling
drug orders for shipment to various pharmacies in the region.
He applied for a visa at the local U.S. consulate but was given no
indication how long it might take. The Americans considered him
a citizen of Poland. Stanislau, where he had been born as a subject
of the Austrian Emperor Francis Joseph, had been in that part of
the Austro-Hungarian Empire that had been awarded to Poland in
1919 and the Polish quota was filled. By contrast, his younger
brother Karl, who was born in Vienna and considered Austrian,
got an American visa immediately. Feuer also needed an affidavit,
and he didn't know anybody in the United States who could
vouch for him.

FEUER: The police in Nantes were very nice. That was a relief. Until now nobody had done anything against me personally, but you never knew. The police
frequently stopped people in Paris on the streets and asked for identification. In
Nantes, I made enough money to live comfortably. And my coworkers sort of
took me in. They knew I was an Austrian refugee and I was in their hands.
When they went out to celebrate in a bistro, they always invited me. It was a
very nice relationship. And I met some other French people. We used to meet in
coffee houses, have drinks together, and discuss politics. By then I was fluent in

French. When I was in Paris I took courses at the Alliance française,[15] and I was even able to solve crossword puzzles.

What were you doing to promote your "escape" from the continent?

FEUER: There was a Jewish organization in Nantes, run by French Jews, and they managed to find me a sponsor, somebody with the same name as mine who lived in Brooklyn. He might have been a distant cousin of my father.

How long after you had a sponsor did you get an affidavit?

FEUER: It took about three months. But that still didn't mean that I had a visa. That would not come until May 1940.

But on September 3, 1939, the French and the British declared war against Germany. How did that affect you?

FEUER: Shortly before the outbreak of war, the French interned me as an enemy alien. I, of course, had a German passport. I was incarcerated with many other people in an abandoned factory somewhere in the suburbs of Nantes. Some of my fellow detainees had come from Vienna. One man, named Wasicky, had been the head of the pharmacognosy department at the University of Vienna. I knew him quite well. He had written books; I had attended some of his lectures. I had not known that he was Jewish.

We all slept on straw, and it wasn't very hygienic. I wasn't there long before a French dignitary came to interview everybody. I told him that I was a pharmacist, and he immediately signed a paper releasing me so I could go back to the pharmaceutical company. But I was only back on the job a short time when the owner of the company fired me because I was "German." He didn't want to risk dissention among his workers. The owner's son, with whom I got along very well, was also a pharmacist. The son said that he was sorry I was fired and didn't approve of it, but that he couldn't do anything. It wasn't really that bad. I had saved some money.

I spent many hours of my free time at the harbor. The Loire River is very wide at Nantes and lot of ships came in there, even several American warships. You could visit the ships, and that was my first encounter with Americans. I don't think that the German or the French navy would have allowed such visits. The Americans were very relaxed while we walked around the decks of this gunship. I noticed that there were two or three sailors peeling potatoes at the stern of the ship singing very happily, not showing signs of being disciplined very much.

I felt that the people in Nantes were generally very friendly. I never had any altercation or any problem. And, of course, life was much cheaper there than in Paris. I could get my main noontime dinner of six courses very cheaply. Wine was included.

According to the 1920 military convention signed with Poland, France agreed to attack Germany in force fifteen days after mobilization for war. The offensive never materialized. As the French army sat behind its Maginot Line fortifications, the Germans handily defeated the Poles in three weeks (with a slight assist from Soviet Russia). France's desire to save lives came from a deep-seated fear of repeating the bloodbath battles of the First World War.

The period of relative inactivity following the collapse of Poland, known as the *drôle de guerre,* or phony war, ended on May 10, 1940, when the Wehrmacht invaded the Low Countries and northern France. The collapse of Dutch and Belgian resistance was achieved in the first forty-eight hours of the assault as the Germans moved unexpectedly through the Ardennes to reach the Meuse River, which they crossed on May 13. Now began the implementation of the "sickle stroke" strategy, which took the German army all the way to the English Channel within six days, trapping the British and the French northern armies in a huge pocket.

The British troops retreated to Dunkirk, where they were evacuated; the French were left to their fate. Fighting alone, their soldiers were no match for the invaders. On June 14, the Germans entered an undefended Paris. By June 20, units of the Wehrmacht had reached Lyons, Vichy, Tours, Angers, and Nantes. Also on June 20 a French delegation traveled to Rethondes near Compiègne to meet a German delegation to discuss an armistice.

FEUER: Shortly after the war began in the west, I was arrested again and taken this time to La Rochelle, on the Atlantic Ocean [112 miles north of Bordeaux.] We were put to work with axes and spades clearing a landing strip for airplanes. I was sort of an auxiliary soldier, a *prestataire.* We also helped move beds and other furniture into a hospital. Our movement was restricted; we could only circulate with a French soldier present. But we were treated and housed pretty well.

These *groupements de travailleurs étrangers* (foreign labor battalions) later on became a means to intern all immigrants who were judged "superfluous in the national economy." While Feuer served, they acted as a draft labor force to do work which might have been done by soldiers.

Was this hard labor?

FEUER: It wasn't easy. But I didn't feel exploited, because France had helped me and was now fighting the Nazis.

How many were in that camp?

FEUER: I think about fifty, mostly refugees. We were from different backgrounds. Times were so uncertain that we mostly talked about the progress of the war.

Were you depressed?

FEUER: No, no, no. I never suffered from depression.

What sustained you?

FEUER: That's difficult to say. I had no idea that the war was going so badly. But I was not very optimistic about whether France could survive, or about whether I would survive. I was not depressed, however.

Did religious faith keep you going?

FEUER: No, no, certainly not.

And your experience gave you second thoughts about socialism?

FEUER: About the people, not about the ideology—a big difference as far as I was concerned.

How long were you in this particular labor battalion?

FEUER: Until the Germans entered Paris [on June 14, 1940]. I returned to Nantes to get some of my things. I knew it would be very dangerous to stay there, because it was close to St. Nazaire, an important naval base, which I assumed the Germans would take over. So I felt I had to leave while the Germans were still organizing in Paris. And some of us thought that the only sensible thing to do was to flee toward the Spanish frontier.

There was a well-to-do family of Russian Jewish refugees, and they told me exactly when they were going to leave, but since they had no space in their car, I and another young man, a Polish Jew, hopped a ride on the open extended grill of the rear-end luggage carrier. This was all right with them; they knew it was a life-or-death situation.

It was really dangerous. They drove pretty fast, and the roads were not very good, and it would have been easy to fall off. During the trip, we saw the exodus of the French coming from Paris—the cars and carts with horses and people walking. An incredible sight.

Before the path of the German attack, millions of French took to the roads, taking as much of their personal belongings with them as possible, some loading mattresses on the tops of their cars and carts. Two million fled from the Paris region alone. All headed south or toward the coast or anywhere the war was not, clogging the roads, sleeping in the fields, and draining the services of the communities in their path.

FEUER: Our destination was Luchon, a spa and ski resort, more or less in the center of the Pyrenees on the French side. The journey was over three hundred miles away and took us two days, with a one-night stopover.

So you had a narrow escape?

FEUER: Well, I might have walked or obtained a ride from someone else. I don't know, but, yes, it was a lucky thing.[16] Luchon had many refugees, especially from Belgium. A significant number, but not all, were Jewish. And the French there took care of us. They gave us meals and put us up in one of the numerous hotels. I stayed in one of the smaller ones. I don't remember whether I had to pay for my room or not. All the money I had brought out of Austria was gone. I only had the little I had received from working in that camp at La Rochelle.

After the Franco-German armistice [signed June 22, 1940], the authorities announced that people should go back to their previous places of residence. I did not consider myself part of that refugee group. But I went to the mayor's office anyway to find out if the order applied to me. My French was pretty good, and because of the way I spoke they first thought that I was from Paris. When they found out who I was, the secretary said, "No, you stay put. Don't pay any attention to the announcements." And that's what I did. I don't know what happened to the people who left. If they were Jews, they were probably detained in concentration camps and shipped to Poland.

Marshal Henri Philippe Pétain, hero of the 1916 battle of Verdun, became head of the French State on July 11, 1940, after the National Assembly of the Third Republic in the Grand Casino at Vichy endorsed a committee report, which gave him "plenary governmental powers" with the force of law. Pétain's regime, based on the principles of "work, family, country," led to the establishment of a new corporative order emphasizing authority and conformity, with repression of all dissent and increasing suppression of the pernicious influence of the Jews.

The new regime made a concerted effort to get those four million French, Belgian, Dutch, Luxembourgian and other refugees who had fled the German advance to return to their homes. A law of October 4, 1940, directed prefects to either intern foreign Jewish refugees in special camps or exile them to remote villages. But in the confused early days of the Vichy regime, compliance depended on the zeal or willingness of those responsible for the law's enforcement. Later on, more and more foreign Jews were rounded up and held in camps. The conditions in some of these were so bad that a group of German World War I veterans in detention in the unoccupied zone actually appealed to the German foreign office to save them from their inhumane conditions.

You were fortunate in going to the mayor's office rather than the gendarmerie.

FEUER: Well, I had done the same thing in Nantes. I went to the mayor's office to obtain my identity card, not the police.

You were wise to avoid the national authorities.

FEUER: I was lucky.

Your antennae were finely attuned to survival especially since the Vichy regime had little sympathy toward refugees or Jews.

FEUER: You mean the government?

Yes.

FEUER: Yes, that's true. But the people in Luchon treated me very well. To them I was a Frenchman. I even got a pass to the local mineral springs establishment. I went to the director and told him I was a pharmacist, handed him my documents, and asked if I could get a reduced price to take a bath. He said, "I give you a pass and you can come and go whenever you want." I still have it [dated June 24, 1940]. That was an indication of the attitude of people there.

Of course, there was no work. But I like mountains very much, and that town was in the midst of the Pyrenees, very close to the Spanish border. So whenever I had time and the weather was all right, I used to go hiking and climbing, mostly by myself, because the others I knew didn't care for it. I got to know the region very well. If the Germans would have taken over Vichy France, I knew I could walk to Spain. I knew exactly how to do it. In fact, many times I had already done so. Once I met some Spanish soldiers and they gave me wine and I gave them some chocolate. When winter came, I got a pair of skis and did quite a lot of skiing.

You didn't have a job. Were you getting any help from the Jewish community there?

FEUER: No, I just had my savings. In my hotel we were three in a room, with no hot water. The proprietor and his wife were very nice. He was named Rios, a Frenchman of Basque descent. They had two sons in the army. They allowed us to cook in their kitchen, and we became very good friends. We did some chores for them. I used to stand in line to get milk. And quite often I helped him collect potatoes from the vegetable plot behind his house. I walked behind his plough and picked them up.

In your efforts to leave Europe, did you encounter a considerable amount of kindness?

FEUER: Definitely. Another thing—I had left everything in Nantes. And I wrote to the owner of the place where I had stayed, and she sent me everything. I don't believe anybody who tells me that French people are not good. I found out that when you were friendly and you communicated this, there was no trouble whatsoever.

There also must have been some tolerance on the part of the local authorities?

FEUER: I had to go to Marseilles several times to report to the prefecture there and to arrange an immigration visa to enter the United States, but I never had any trouble getting permission to go there or was given a hard time while I was there.

Once, though, I was sitting with a friend in a park and a young man came up to us and asked for our papers. He was obviously German, Gestapo. And I asked him, "Why do you want our papers? What right do you have?" Well, I showed them to him, and then I went to the police and complained.

They didn't listen. They said, "We don't know anything about it," you know, *je m'en fous* (delicately translated: Who cares?). As long as they didn't have to do anything.

Je-m'en-foutism also seemed to be a prevailing attitude of many French concerning Vichy's antisemitic legislation. On October 3, 1940, the Pétain government adopted a *Statut des juifs* (Jewish Statute), which demoted Jews to inferiors and annulled the rights of all Jews living on French soil—citizens, legal residents, and foreigners. Jews were henceforth excluded from civil service cadres, from the officer and noncommissioned ranks of the armed forces, from the teaching profession, and from the press, radio, theater, and cinema. The Nazi overlords had not yet insisted such laws be passed. They were currently more concerned with mobilizing French economic resources in the fight against Great Britain. However, those directing the Vichy government saw the denigration of the Jews as a necessary component of their national revolution to cleanse France of the corruption of the past and the pernicious elements of the present. The legislation hardly represented the will of the French people, who were never asked for approval. At the very least, most French seemed indifferent and concentrated on getting their lives back together following the debacle of 1940. Without such a devastating defeat, in which three-fifths of the country was directly under German occupation, such legislation, given the libertarian tradition of France, would have been inconceivable.

FEUER: Once, when I heard that Pétain was going to visit Marseilles, I decided to stay away because I feared that the authorities might clean everybody off the streets. That actually happened. They put hundreds of "suspicious" people on ships and barges regardless of whether they were French citizens or not.

How did you develop such survival instincts?

FEUER: The people in Luchon were very astute politically. Most of them hated Pétain. I remember a poor farmer, living in a dilapidated house in the mountains. He told me he used to have a picture of Pétain, but he took it down. He was so outraged over the marshal's behavior.

But Pétain supposedly had great appeal in such rural areas.

FEUER: Not in Luchon. There they considered him a traitor for negotiating with the Nazis. But you have to understand, that place was far away from Paris. Also they were still influenced by what happened in Spain during the Civil War. Luchon had a lot of Republican refugees.

Before General Francisco Franco's victorious Nationalist armies closed the border in their final defeat of the Spanish Republic in March 1939, as many as 400,000 Spaniards and International Brigade volunteers had streamed across the Catalonian border into France. The swamped French authorities hastily set up a series of internment camps in the Lower Pyrenees to feed and house this panicked and exhausted mass of humanity. The cost on a treasury already short of money was enormous and further eroded French sympathy for the plight of refugees.

How did you finally arrange passage to the United States?

FEUER: After I got my visa [in May 1940], I found out that the only way to get to the United States was to embark on a French ship bound for Martinique. There was no direct line from Marseilles to any place in the United States. So I booked passage on a ship called the *Winnipeg,* a French ship despite its name.[17] When I got to Martinique, I would see about getting to the United States.

The circumstances under which the French lived when the Germans began controlling their national priorities and eventually their destiny were not calculated to bring out the best in people. After the German victory, antisemitism gradually became more à la mode, especially for those in government, who saw in it the key to advancement. Popular outbursts against the Jews, however, remained scattered and sporadic. The armistice contained a clause which obliged the French to surrender those Jews the Reich demanded — for the most part important enemies of the Reich who had fled to avoid arrest. But the age of mass roundups, deportation, and extermination of Jews was still in the future. Until then the Nazis were content that the Jews live anyplace but in Germany. Vichy was eager to get rid of its foreigners and did not care where they went as long as they left. Therefore they could not have been more delighted when the *Winnipeg* sailed away with its unwanted cargo.

FEUER: I left France in May 1941. Gestapo agents were checking papers at the dock when I boarded the ship. I recognized them immediately because they spoke French with a German accent.

And they looked at your passport?

FEUER: Yes, yes, sure. A German passport with a "J" on it.

But weren't they interested in detaining you?

FEUER: No, apparently not. I was just lucky. Perhaps they were only looking for certain people.

Were your fellow passengers mostly Jewish?

FEUER: The ones I knew, but there were all kinds of people on board. The ship was small, about 15,000 tons, and crowded; the accommodations were very primitive. We stopped at Casablanca, and I remember going up to the bridge and taking a picture of the harbor. A man came and took my camera and took the film out and destroyed it, but he gave me back the camera. I was lucky—he could have arrested me.

I never made it to Martinique. Two days before we were to land, a Dutch gunboat captured the *Winnipeg,* and we were diverted to Trinidad and put into a camp. We could only circulate with a police escort, but we had all the food we wanted, and we were treated very well. It was quite a change, coming from a war-torn continent.

Feuer was in the camp on Trinidad for about a month until he could arrange for passage to the United States. He was able to get in touch with his American "relations," and with the money they sent him, he arranged passage to New York City on the SS *Uruguay,* a Gracemoore Line passenger ship coming from South America.

FEUER: The incredible thing was the amount of food available. What was not eaten was thrown overboard. You come from years of deprivation and you see this happening. It was a shame, a pretty disconcerting experience.

The Earth Is Round: Anna Mandler Akeley

"And when Hitler spoke of the Ostmark, they suddenly felt, 'My golly! We will be somebody.'"

Getting Rid of Jewish Influence

Many well-to-do Viennese Jews indeed had difficulty understanding the visceral, all-encompassing, no-holds-barred racism of the Nazis, which was more than excluding Jews from certain tony clubs. Some *Österreichjuden* found it wishful to believe that Hitler's persecution of the "good" Jews, those had lived in Austria for generations, would cease as soon as he realized that the *Ostjuden* were the real target. Failure to see immanent doom in the tea leaves of the future was especially true for those who had led a comfortable existence amid the baroque splendor, the intellectual fervor, and the Sachertorte brio of the Austrian capital.

ANNA AKELEY: The paper sellers shouted, "Extra! Extra! Extra! Hitler crosses the Austrian border with a German army!" The newspapers said that he would arrive in Vienna at 10 o'clock the next morning (March 13) to give a speech in the Heldenplatz, the big central square downtown. And everybody said, "My God. What will happen?" All businesses were to be shut, no schools would be open, and the streetcars would not run. Nothing. Everybody should go to the Heldenplatz. Well, I went to the Heldenplatz. I was some distance from Hitler, but I could see him standing in the car and then on the balcony of the chancellery. When he arrived, the people were jubilant, absolutely jubilant. The Heldenplatz held about 300,000 people and it was packed. I was amazed that the people were so jubilant.

Wasn't there a strong movement already to affiliate with Germany?

AKELEY: I thought that the thinking in Vienna was separated completely from the thinking in the hinterland. In Vienna, the capitalists and the burghers agreed on one thing: they did not like the Germans. The Viennese thought that dinner consisted of five courses, while the Germans thought that a Bismarck herring and a potato was a good meal. There was a joke that illustrated their difference in thinking:

Something happens to the Viennese tramway tracks, so the tramway company sends out workers to repair it. They work and work and nothing happens. Finally a German comes by, and he comes over and takes a heavy crowbar and with it he straightens out the tracks. And the Viennese look at the German and say, "Well, obviously you can do it if you use force."

German tourists came to Vienna for the *Sängerfest* (singing festival), crowding the Ring district stores and restaurants, and you had to translate the menus for them. Many Austrians refused to go downtown when the Germans had taken over.

Then how do you account for this enormous enthusiasm for Hitler at the Heldenplatz?

AKELEY: Hitler proved something when he took power in Germany by giving the people work. While the rate of unemployment dropped in Germany, it still stayed high in Austria, especially in Vienna, which had almost a third of the entire country's population. And therefore the workers were very excited about what Hitler had accomplished. I'm not sure they were for Hitler, but the promise of work was enormously attractive.

So the people were enthusiastic for Anschluss *because of the depression?*

AKELEY: They saw what Hitler had done in Germany.

And the great Viennese contempt for the Germans vanished?

AKELEY: Right. And when Hitler spoke of the Ostmark, they suddenly felt, "My golly! We will be somebody, not a nothing like Belgium, the Netherlands, or Liechtenstein."

Do you think that had anything to do with the fact that Hitler was an Austrian?

AKELEY: An Austrian in charge of Germany was the biggest thing that could happen to an Austrian, especially since he came from the lower classes; and when he promised something, he was seen to get it.

He also promised to get rid of Jewish influence. Wasn't part of the jubilation because the Austrians now believed that they could now go out and give it to the Jews?

AKELEY: Definitely. But this feeling was directed against the Polish Jews.

Well, maybe certain Austrians felt it was against the Polish Jews, but the Nazis themselves didn't make any such distinctions.

AKELEY: No. Because they didn't have the same experience.

This may be the perception of the social class from which you came — the older Austrian Jewish families may very well have felt that the Ostjuden *were an embarrassment — but I wonder whether antisemitism in Austria wasn't directed at all Austrian Jews.*

AKELEY: No, they didn't know enough about that. They had no experience.

Could this feeling have been prompted by a false belief on the part of the established Jewish community that the bulk of the Nazi antisemitic legislation would fall on the Ostjuden *rather than on them?*

AKELEY: I think so.

It seems that in your circles your Jewishness was defined more by others than by yourself.

AKELEY: That's right. When we were asked, we naturally said, "We are Jews," but we never talked about it.

After the demonstration for Hitler in the Heldenplatz, I walked back home, and when I got there, my sister and her husband, Otto Skall, were waiting. They had packed two suitcases and were leaving immediately for Prague. And my mother said, "But you need your jewelry." But my brother Kurt remarked, "The banks are closed. Besides, nobody should go to the safety deposit box and take things out, because people will get suspicious." They asked my mother how much money she had with her and how much my brother and I had. We gave it all to her — enough to live on for about two or three months. I was wearing a very beautiful ring, and I gave it to her. That was the only jewelry at home; the rest was at the bank. Then they said good-bye. There was no crying. My mother did not cry when any of us left. I remember my brother bit his lip; he was a crier even when he saw a sad movie. And so they left. They thought that they would be pretty safe in Czechoslovakia. Otto was from Prague. He was a first cousin of Stefan Zweig, the famous writer. And my sister didn't want to come to America. She said, "What immigrants do in America is become maids, and I'm not going to be a maid, not on my life." So they left, the two of them, and I never saw them again.

My brother left shortly after my sister. His wife had a first cousin living in Switzerland, and she was willing to guarantee them financially. At that time, I was engaged to a very nice man who was half-Jewish — his mother was a Gentile — and he called me the next day and said, "I have to talk to you." I said, "Naturally." So he came and said, "Look Anni, since I am a *Mischling* (half-breed),

I am not in direct danger. Whatever we had together will have to end. It doesn't help you, and it would only bring me into danger." I said, "Fine," and that was the end of that.

Did you still have your job?

AKELEY: The business opened the day after Hitler spoke in the Heldenplatz. When I arrived, the owner told me he was leaving the country. The Nazis were closing his business, and since they wouldn't let Christians work for Jews any longer, it was up to me to help with the liquidation. He told me that when the checks came in I was to divide them up, sending the ones with the large amounts to him, giving the ones with the small amounts to the Nazis. "And," he said, "buy yourself some gloves, do not leave fingerprints on any envelopes or checks." He instructed me to send the checks to a certain address in New York, and then he said good-bye.

Within a week the Nazis came and asked, "Where is the owner?" And I told them that he had left the country. They warned me not to send him any money, but I managed to do so anyhow. The Nazis, by the way, were not disagreeable, they were very businesslike. But they treated me like an underling who had to obey their orders. They continued to pay me the same wages, but I only made half of what I got before because I only worked from nine to one o'clock. This job lasted about four months, until the liquidation process was complete.

Shortly after, the new Nazi government told us that we could no longer live in our villa in the "Cottage" District. The Nineteenth District was to be "Jew-free." They gave us four months to find quarters in either the First or Second Districts, the only areas in Vienna where the Jews could live. That was not too bad for us, because my mother still had that house on the Salztorgasse. So she made arrangement to move back. Naturally we had to sell the furniture of the villa. We ended up giving most of it away. What we managed to sell brought less than one-tenth of what it was worth. The Nazis then confiscated that house and also our country residence at Altaussee.

The Nazi legislation gave your fellow Austrians an opportunity to take advantage of you?

AKELEY: Definitely. But none of our acquaintances. Mostly strangers. Our Christian friends, with one exception, behaved fabulously. And they ran a risk in helping us. And then came the law that Jews could buy in stores only after everybody else was served. Once when I went to the delicatessen, where we always shopped, there were about four people ahead of me, but while I was

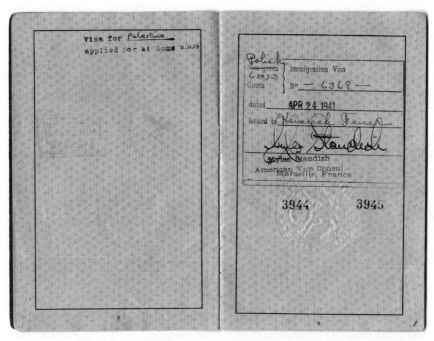

More than two years after Henry Feuer escaped from Austria, he was able to obtain an immigration visa to the United States. Note that he is included in the Polish quota.

Anna Mandler Akeley in 1931, enjoying the beautiful Alpine scenery.

waiting about six more people came. The daughter of the owner waited on the first four and then said out loud, "Mrs. Frost, you were here before those others, what would you like?" The greengrocer and the butcher were also extremely nice, going out of their way to serve me.

That's interesting, because the picture that has come across is that on the whole the Austrians behaved very badly.

AKELEY: Well, of course, all that changed completely when we moved to the First District, where we were not known. Then things became rather disagreeable. But to the Polish Jews they behaved horribly. And I mean horribly. They refused to sell to them.

Are you saying that the humiliations against the Jews were primarily, if not exclusively, against the Ostjuden?

AKELEY: Yes.

How onerous was your move back to the First District?

AKELEY: My mother and I were told that we could have two and a half rooms, one toilet, and one bathroom. Every other space had to be rented out to Jews who were also expelled. Therefore we had two other families (four other grown persons) living in our apartment. We were not accustomed to that, but they all behaved very well. I mean it was not a real hardship.

Did you ever remember thinking that being Jewish was a real pain in the neck? Since you didn't identify very strongly with being Jewish, did you see all this Jewishness as a burden that you would rather live without?

AKELEY: A terrible burden, you know. I never would have admitted it, because it was not proper to do so.

But if somebody by a magic wand had said, "You are no longer a Jew, but just an Austrian"—this would have been perfectly fine with you?

AKELEY: Perfectly.

Despite the worsening conditions for the Jews, the Mandlers struggled to maintain as much of their former life as they could. Anna still went skiing, her mother still held her *jour*, her open house, once a month on Sunday afternoon. To avoid the embarrassment of shopping in grocery stores, where they would be discriminated against, they relied on a family connection to obtain food. A sister of Anna's father had married a Gentile who owned a large grocery store, and he used to have food delivered to their apartment, including coffee and tea, which were otherwise virtually unobtainable. A family servant, who being Christian was no longer allowed to work for Jews, brought them weekly food parcels. Other friends provided similar assistance. When the Nazis decreed that the Jews should get no fuel, a friendly dealer loaded up 100 kilograms of coal in two suitcases for Anna to carry home. Anna refused to wear the yellow star, required of all Jews, though she would have been arrested had she been stopped and asked to show her identity card, which was stamped with a "J" for *Jude*. Walking around without the Star of David was especially risky during the time she had been engaged in the liquidation of the publishing business, since she had to report every day to police headquarters to deliver the incoming checks. The clerks, who were Austrians working for the Germans, knew she was Jewish but never reported her. Anna believed that this Viennese noblesse oblige came from the fact that she was from a prominent law-abiding family whose name had never been attached to scandal.

After the publishing business was liquidated, Anna was without work until the end of the year, when she was told to report to the Vienna General Hospital, where she was put to work shaving wounded soldiers. Since the Second World War had not yet started, the origin of these wounds remained a mystery, and Anna was instructed not to ask any questions. She was only on the shaving detail a short time before she was transferred to the X-ray unit and allowed to practice a skill in which she had earned a degree. In July 1939, she met Edward Stowe Akeley, an assistant professor at Purdue University, who would be her husband. How Edward happened to be in Vienna is characteristic of the way many American Jews sought to maintain contact with families and friends during the Nazi period:

> The wife of the head of the Purdue physics department had a
> sister who had lived in Vienna and had come to Lafayette
> shortly after the *Anschluss*. The sister was a friend of Anna's sister,
> Auguste, now living in Prague. When the Nazis invaded the

rest of Czechoslovakia on March 15, 1939, creating the satellite state of Bohemia and Moravia under Reichsprotektor Konstantin von Neurath, contact to the outside world almost ceased. Knowing that Edward planned to go to Europe for the summer, the department head asked him to go to Prague to look up Auguste Skall, since his sister had not been heard from since the German takeover. Edward did so. Auguste then asked Edward if he could go to Vienna, since she could no longer communicate with her mother and her sister. Again Edward complied. His first meeting with Anna in her First District apartment was tense, because Anna thought he might be a Gestapo agent masquerading as an American. She avoided saying anything pejorative about the Nazis, and his admission that he considered Hitler the curse of the world only put her more on guard.

AKELEY: We found out that we rather liked each other. And he said, "Anni, you have to get out of the country. I have already given two affidavits to Berlin Jews. But since I am only an assistant professor with $1,800 a year, they won't let me give any more affidavits. I will try, however, to find somebody who will give you an affidavit. Get out, get out, it is crazy to stay. It will have a terrible ending." And when he left, I took him to the airport and I thought that I would never see him again. And I was very sad and said, "Now Edward, that's good-bye." He said, "I hope not, I will try everything I can. Anyhow, get out, wherever you can go, get out."

He went off to his plane, and I was standing to take the bus back to town when an open-top car with some SS officers stopped, and one of them asked me, "Fräulein, could we give you a ride?" I thought, what am I going to do? If I refuse I will offend them, so I accepted. On the way back, we talked small talk, the flooding of the Danube etc., nothing concerning Nazism and nothing concerning the Jews. They let me off near St. Stephen's Cathedral because I did not want to be let off at my home. I said, "Thank you very much for the ride." They said, "It was our pleasure, good-bye and *auf Wiedersehen.*" I got off, thinking that was a close call, and when I got home I was determined to do something to get out of Austria.

Getting an affidavit to enter the United States could be a simple formality for some but an insurmountable obstacle for others.

Those with family members already in the United States had relatively little trouble, but those without such connections often had a desperate search ahead. Success often depended on sheer luck.

Shortly after the *Anschluss,* Anna had gone to the Jüdische Kultusgemeinde for assistance. The Nazis used the Jewish Religious Community to promote its policy of forced emigration. According to the project worked out by SS chief Reinhardt Heydrich, rich Jews would be forced to pay for the emigration of the "Jewish rabble." However, the officials at the Kultusgemeinde considered Anna Mandler Frost a Christian because of that "conversion" of her father, and they told her to "go somewhere else."

AKELEY: I had no resentment, because I understand that they could help only the people who were members of a congregation and who went to synagogue. People like that were not in our circle. Although I have no resentment, I didn't feel very happy about it. But I understood their way of acting.

A Thirty-Thousand-Dollar Passport

The incident with the SS officers underlined the extreme precariousness of her existence and prompted her to write to friends in New York City to ask if they could get her an affidavit. The friends succeeded in a roundabout, unexpected way.

Once as the friends were standing in a queue at the Metropolitan Opera to buy tickets for a performance, they happened to be discussing the problem of getting an affidavit for their friend with other people in the same line. An eavesdropper joined the conversation and asked them to give him the name of their friend. About a month later, Anna received a letter from Washington, D.C, written by a Jewish bureaucrat, who asked for the details of her situation. The man promised to see what he could do. About two months later, at the end of 1939, the affidavit arrived. The affidavit came with a note: "I wish you luck, but don't come to me expecting that I will help you further."[18] By then the Germans had already invaded Poland, touching off the European War.

Anna still needed two more important documents: a passport to leave Austria and a visa to enter the United States. To get the German passport she turned to the Quakers for help. The Quakers did not have an office in Vienna, which was now a mere provincial capital, and Anna had to go to Berlin. It was the first time she had been in the German capital. She was impressed by its cleanliness, beauty, and power. She also noticed that fewer Nazi flags flew there than in Vienna, and nobody asked her if she was Jewish—the National Socialist regime was so well-established that no special point had to be made.

AKELEY: They didn't seem to even try to find out who I was. You know, they had that famous attitude that "business is business."

Didn't your papers state that you were a Jew?

AKELEY: I carried my Austrian birth certificate, which did not have the "J" stamped on it, so there was no way they could tell. When I originally went to the Society of Friends, they asked me how much money I had, and when they found out, they told me that a passport would cost me $30,000.

I was already aware of the amount, and my mother had agreed to sell some of her stock to cover it. I stayed in Berlin three days, because it took me two days to get the money transferred.

On January 24, 1939, the Germans established a central emigration office for Jews within the finance ministry. However, the SS was the agency really responsible for solving the Jewish question by emigration and evacuation in a way that was most favorable under present conditions. Since the Nazis always intended their anti-semitic policy to be a paying proposition, they issued passports strictly on the basis of what the market would bear. Anna would have been forced to pay a large sum for her exit visa, even if she had been able to use the offices of the Jewish Kultusgemeinde. All agencies that acted as go-betweens had to turn over most of the proceeds to the Reich treasury and were allowed to keep only a small amount for expenses.

How did you learn that the Quakers might help you?

AKELEY: The moment the Nazis came, the Jews who could get no help from the Jewish organizations discovered that the Quakers might be of assistance. It was understood that, unless you had a special prominence, you needed money to get out. But I had jobs and had not done anything special. The Quakers behaved very well.

After I got my passport, I had to go to the American consulate in Vienna. I thought that would be a very simple procedure, but at the consulate I was told I had to go to a doctor and prove that I did not have TB. So I got X rays and returned to the consulate. It was located in the former embassy building, a gorgeous old palace with furniture in real Maria Theresian style. The consul sat at a beautiful rococo desk inlaid with three different types of wood. When I came in, he had both his feet on that desk. I said, "Good afternoon," but he hardly said anything. He was not incorrect, but he made no attempt to be polite. He made me swear that I would not overthrow the government of the United States. I didn't know which hand I was supposed to use, but I saw that he had put up his left hand, and so I did the same. But he didn't even look up. He told me to come back in a month.

How long was it from when you first went to the consulate until the time they told you could go?

AKELEY: About six weeks. Then I booked a first-class train ticket to Trieste and bought a first-class boat ticket from Trieste to New York. It was the first time I would travel first class. The Jewish upper classes never went first class. They considered first class only fit for the employees of the railroad or steamship companies, for aristocrats—and for Americans.

Why didn't those people go first class?

AKELEY: It was not done. It was too ostentatious. But I wanted to go out in style. I was allowed to take out a steamer trunk with my possessions. I got a lot into that: most of my clothes, including three dirndls and three ski outfits, some porcelain, and a few Persian rugs, one a silk prayer rug. But no silver, nothing like that. I was supposed to leave Trieste on June 28, 1940. But by then Italy had entered the war, and the whole Adriatic was closed for passenger travel.

After the stunning German offensive in the west in the spring of 1940, topped off by the humiliating retreat of the French army, Mussolini feared that he had to get into the war before Hitler took all the glory. He said he needed several thousand dead to be able to take his place at the peace table. Therefore, on June 10, 1940, he declared war on France and launched a westward offensive into the lower Alps. The Italian army was ill-prepared for operations and made little headway against French resistance. But the Duce's move did come in time for him to claim a share of the spoils after the armistice was signed at Compiègne on June 22, 1940.

AKELEY: I sent Edward a telegram: "Can't come, Adriatic is closed." And he sent me a telegram that said, "The earth is round." At first I thought the message was crazy, but finally I understood what it meant. Edward wanted me to go east. So I had to go to Berlin again to get a ticket and the necessary permissions to travel through the Soviet Union.

I came back to Vienna, and I left in July. But this time I was allowed to take with me only two little suitcases and money equal to three American dollars. I packed some clothes, some perfume, and other personal effects—things like that. I was, however, warned not to take any valuable collector stamps, because they would find them. Well, like many others, I did take some stamps, and they never found them. But one year after I came to America, I gave my old clothes to the Salvation Army, forgetting that I had sewn the stamps inside the linings.

When you left, you knew the situation was not going to get any better for your mother.

AKELEY: I cried terribly; my mother did not cry at all. She said, "I hope to hear from you, and take care." And that was it. I was in a complete sort of desperation. I feared leaving my mother alone, but I thought I would be able to get her out of Austria as soon as I arrived in the United States and found work.

Two army officers were in the same train compartment with me, and they asked me where I was going. "Well, I'm going to Berlin." "What for?" "Then I want to go to Moscow." "Oh, are you one of the people who leave Germany on their own free will?" I said, "It is not on my own free will. I have to leave." And they said, "Prove it." And I said, "I cannot prove that I'm in danger." And they started saying, "That's not true. You might not be in an agreeable position, but it's not true that you are in danger." And I got very upset, because they kept insisting that I was leaving on my own free will. So finally I said, "Yes, I'm leaving on my own free will." What else could I have said?

Akeley took the Moscow-Express from Berlin, changing at Minsk for a train with the wider, Russian gauge. The German-Soviet Treaty of Nonaggression of August 23, 1939, together with its secret protocols, had prepared for the partition of Poland, which, once accomplished, allowed Hitler to fight a one-front war against France. A further "friendly agreement" between the two countries provided for mutual political and economic cooperation, including exchanges of raw materials. Therefore, until the Germans invaded the Soviet Union in June 1941, civilian passage was allowed between the two countries. The journey through occupied Poland passed through the battlefields of the previous fall, with their burned-out villages and sites of violent death. Warsaw was a city in ruins, a foretaste of what Hitler had in mind for other enemy capitals. When the fighting had stopped, the conquerors had rapidly repaired the destroyed infrastructure, so rail traffic was back to normal.

From Moscow, Akeley took the Trans-Siberian Railroad east, a trip of nearly 6,250 miles, lasting seven days and seven nights, across the Urals, around the southern tip of Lake Baikal, through six time zones and fourteen major cities. She was confined to the train during the whole journey, forbidden to get off even when it stopped briefly at a station. In that closed atmosphere, she had little rapport with fellow passengers, some of whom she suspected might be informants. From Chita a branchline headed southeast to Harbin and from there to Pusan in Korea, where she boarded a ship for Kobe, Japan.

When she arrived in Kobe, the local office of the Quakers told her that the ship on which she was booked for passage to the United States had been held up in the Philippines because of a typhoon. They could give her no idea of when her trip might be resumed, but in the meantime they arranged for her to be lodged in a room with three Japanese working girls, all sleeping on bedrolls. The Quakers also gave her a daily allowance in order to buy a bowl of curried rice twice a day.

With her visa permitting entry into the United States running out, Akeley booked passage on the *Hikawa Maru,* which sailed from Yokohama on September 3, 1940.[19]

AKELEY: I had accommodations in the hold of the ship. There were thirty people, men and women, in this one room with rows of bunks stacked in threes. I had the lowest one, which had advantages and disadvantages: the advantage was that one could get up right away, the disadvantage was that people woke you up when they climbed up and down the ladders for the upper bunks.

Leaving Yokohama was very touching. The people on land and the passengers held on to either end of paper streamers until they broke. The people were all Asiatic—I was one of the few Caucasians. And I was seasick for the entire seventeen-day trip.

Notes

1. *Documents of British Foreign Policy,* series 2, 6:751.

2. *Mein Kampf* (Boston: Houghton Mifflin, 1971), 655.

3. Ibid., 3.

4. Friedelind Wagner, *Heritage of Fire* (New York: Harper), 109.

5. Ibid., 124. The dumplings perhaps, but the liver, no. Hitler was a vegetarian.

6. Albert Speer, *Inside the Third Reich* (New York: Macmillan, 1970), 131.

7. Ibid., 105–6.

8. Ibid., 857.

9. Ibid., 101.

10. *Documents of German Foreign Policy,* series D, 1:43–45.

11. The letter, dated June 8, 1938, was addressed to "Dr. Heinrich Feuer, in Schutzhaft, Landesgericht für Strafsachen, Wien I." It generously made Feuer's discharge effective three and half months hence, on 30 September. Ironically, the announcement was written on the official business stationary of the Firma Jacob Feuer.

12. Trieste had one of the highest ratios of intermarriage between Jews and Christians. In 1927, out of 355 marriages involving Jews, in only 100 were both partners Jewish.

13. The social legislation was, for example, quite detailed. Forbidden were marriages between Jews and non-Jews (this included converted Jews but excluded marriages for the purpose of legitimizing offspring); employment of Jews in Gentile households; and Jewish adoption of non-Jewish children. An additional decree provided for the expulsion of Jewish children from the state schools.

14. John Cornwell, *Hitler's Pope: The Secret History of Pius XII* (New York: Viking, 1999).

15. This proved to be an extremely wise decision, as much of the popular resentment against the flood of refugees that inundated France from 1938 to 1940 was directed against those people who spoke French unintelligibly or not at all.

16. Had Feuer stuck around Nantes a few more days, the German military advance might have cut off his avenue of escape. When the armistice was signed on June 22, the German advance had reached the confluence of the Garonne and Dordogne Rivers, where they pour into the Gironde estuary, just north of Bordeaux.

17. In service since 1918, the one-funnel *Winnipeg* of the French Line was 9,802 tons and measured 473 by 59 feet. It was sunk by a submarine on October 22, 1942.

18. She would meet the man who had given her the affidavit briefly in San Francisco and did not hear from him again until after the war, when he was working for the American government in Germany. He wrote a letter to her in West Lafayette, asking her to supply an affidavit for someone he had met in Germany and enclosed a

photograph of a young, very pretty woman—obviously his girlfriend. Since the man was already married with a family in Washington, Anna was reluctant to comply. Yet her sense of obligation to the one who had helped save her life compelled her to honor his request and she furnished the affidavit.

19. This 11, 622 ton (511′ × 66′) one-stacker of the Nippon Ysen Kaisha Line was the only Japanese passenger ship to survive the Second World War. Commissioned in 1930, it was withdrawn from service three decades later.

7

A Determination to Succeed

Severed Connections with the Past: Henry Feuer

"I think they were just too tired to move again . . . they had already fled from their homes during World War I. I think it was more, more or less, *que sera, sera,* whatever fate would bring."

From the Window of a Bus

Feuer arrived in Manhattan at the end of June 1941. He had financed his flight from Austria through France to the United States with no help other than what was provided for him by his family and himself.

HENRY FEUER: The day I landed was a very beautiful day, and my relatives—my brother and an aunt of mine—were all waiting for me. They knew I was coming.

Do you remember how you felt when you saw the Statue of Liberty?

FEUER: Considering what I had been through, I wasn't that easily, how shall I say, influenced by a statue or . . .

Or easily moved?

FEUER: Yes, I wasn't that naive anymore and probably a little bit cynical. Then, I didn't even know where my parents were. I knew that they could go to Palestine and that they had left Austria, but I didn't know about their condition or whether they had survived. Not until the end of the war did I find out that they were still alive. But many of my close relatives were killed, some of them very young people. I thought that they would have been able to leave as well.

Why didn't they?

FEUER: Some because of their own stubbornness. They could see what was happening, but they didn't want to leave. And that's something I couldn't understand. It wasn't as if they couldn't get out, because at first you were not really marked by the Nazis as an enemy, really an enemy. Then you could have managed to escape, as I did. But they just didn't. They were well-educated people. I mean, one was a lawyer, and another one was a pharmacist. Especially the lawyer. He had lived in Germany for a while. He knew what went on much better than we did.

To what do you attribute this?

FEUER: I think they were just too tired to move again. See, they were about the same age as my father, and they had already fled from their homes during World War I. I think it was more, more or less, *que sera, sera,* whatever fate would bring.

Obviously they didn't think that their fate was destruction.

FEUER: No, of course not. But I don't know, because I never discussed it with them, because to me it was clear.

They were also people of property. It's sometimes difficult to leave property.

FEUER: Yes, it would have been rather difficult. They were not flexible anymore. But the bad thing was that they also influenced their children, and some were killed with them.

Feuer lived with his brother in Manhattan for about three weeks. He wanted to find employment as soon as possible, but the prospect of getting a job locally seemed remote. Besides, the hustle and bustle of the New York metropolitan area overwhelmed him—in Luchon there had hardly been any cars. Those at the local Jewish agency thought the best chance for work lay in the Midwest, and they suggested going to Toledo. They even agreed to make arrangements for him to live there temporarily with a Jewish family. Feuer bought a Greyhound Line ticket and headed west, seeing the American continent for the first time from the window of a bus.

He found Toledo a very pleasant town. There were even some refugees there from Vienna. He had not known them before, but they became very good friends. With help from the local Jewish agency, he found work as an apprentice pharmacist in a local hospital. He needed a state license to advance any higher. This involved taking remedial high-school courses, his advanced chemistry degree notwithstanding. He avoided this by going to Chicago to take the pharmacy board exams of the State of Illinois.

But Feuer had not gone to the university to become a pharmacist, and even before he got notification that he had passed the Illinois exams, he had obtained a postdoctoral research fellowship in the chemistry department of Purdue University. He had read about the position in the *Chemical Engineering News,* a copy of which he had obtained from the University of Toledo library. Feuer had never heard of Purdue University.

Feuer worked under the direction of the head of the department, Henry B. Hass, who had a contract with the Vicks Corporation (of cough drop and VapoRub fame), for research on a synthesis for menthol. Feuer was lucky to get the job, considering the prejudice against Jews in industry and academia. Purdue was no exception.

FEUER: Hass was a remarkable man, one of the few people who wasn't prejudiced. He had a number of Jewish graduate students, whom many other professors here would not have accepted at that time. He hired other Jewish professors, like Nathan Kornblum and Herbert Brown, who later won the Nobel Prize in chemistry. I think that many faculty members in the chemistry department didn't approve of it, but he didn't ask for their opinion. This prejudice against hiring Jews has now changed, of course.

Aside from a certain amount of such antisemitism, did you have any difficulty in adjusting to the small-town atmosphere of West Lafayette?

After all, you had come from a world that, to put it mildly, was consider-ably more cosmopolitan than this particular community.

FEUER: It was very difficult. I used to go quite often to Chicago. There were very good train connections. On the other hand, Indianapolis was nothing but bars and burlesque shows.

How did you get into teaching?

FEUER: Hass indicated that they were looking for somebody who would teach general chemistry three days a week in Indianapolis—a joint Purdue-Indiana University undertaking—and I applied for the job. I had never really taught be-fore. I had given talks at professional meetings, but had never been before a class.

I got the job and commuted to Indianapolis three times a week. I didn't have a car, so I went by bus or by train. After one semester, I got a tenure-track position as assistant professor.

What was your relationship to the Lafayette community?

FEUER: All my acquaintances were in the university, not only in chemistry. I par-ticipated in discussion groups with all kinds of historians, political scientists, and English professors.

What is your relationship to the Jewish community in Lafayette?

FEUER: I had a few friends, but I'm not very close to them, because when I really needed them, when I came here, they didn't do anything.

To reach out to you?

FEUER: That's right. I'm not a religious person. I don't have to go to the temple to pray.

When did you become an American citizen?

FEUER: I got my citizenship as soon as possible, in 1946. The same year I got married.[1]

In View of What Had Happened

Did you ever entertain any thoughts of reclaiming your Austrian citizenship?

FEUER: I thought about it, but why should I? What's the point? Basically, I don't think that the Austrians have changed. When I went back, I didn't feel that welcome. I still resent how they behaved. That is the big disappointment, which I have all the time. My connection with the past was severed. The people my age that I knew, either Jewish or non-Jewish, have mostly died.

Once I met a former classmate when my wife and I were in Gmünden, a resort in Upper Austria. He used to live in Vienna, and we went to the same Gymnasium. It was an incredible coincidence. We were walking across a bridge, and a man came toward us. He looked at me. I looked at him. He yelled out my name. I yelled out his name. I knew him very well. He was a socialist; we went on hikes together. He was non-Jewish.

What was the nature of your conversation?

FEUER: Oh, the pranks we did. (Laughing.) Pretty superficial stuff.

Did you talk about what happened after 1938?

FEUER: There was no point to it, I mean, we were getting along very well.

You didn't want to return permanently, but you were not like some people who never wanted to set foot on German soil again because of what happened.

FEUER: I had some reason to go back. My parents went back to Vienna, and I had seen them on visits between 1948 and 1953. After my father returned, he got compensation from the person who had taken over his business, although he had to go to court. He was able to live very well. And my sister and brother-in-law went back. He was a sales representative of Spanish and Italian firms, and he sold merchandise mostly to non-Jews for the simple reason that there were very few Jewish companies left. And he also did very well. He had been born there, he was a real Viennese. He said to us very often, "If you retire, why don't you come back to Vienna?" I replied, "I'll see." I didn't want to argue with him. But in view of what had happened, I wouldn't have felt very comfortable living there.

Did you ever talk to your father about how he felt going back to Austria?

FEUER: (Laughing.) I never asked him.

The Austrians never appeared to have assumed responsibility for their actions, and they consider themselves to be victims.

FEUER: Well, you really cannot believe them. If you know or had seen how they behaved, it's ridiculous that they now consider themselves victims. And they know it. That is why they don't want to discuss these things.

*Do you feel that if there were a change in circumstances what happened
in the Nazi period could happen again?*

FEUER: The economic situation is pretty good, much better than it was before
World War II. And you don't have too many unemployed people. I don't know
what one can expect from the young generation. It has been over fifty years
now.

In order to answer I would have to live there for a while. You have to go to
bars and inns, et cetera, and listen to people; then you could draw a conclusion.
There is a neo-Nazi movement. But it does not seem to have much popular support.[2]

*Do you have uneasy feelings about the antisemitism that currently exists
in the United States?*

FEUER: After what I have experienced, where can it go? It doesn't affect me the
way it did in Europe.

What sort of feeling do you have when you think of Israel or Zionism?

FEUER: I spent about a half a year in Israel in 1964 as a visiting professor. I did
some research, and my wife, Paula, taught at the university. At that time my sister still lived in Tel Aviv, but we stayed in Jerusalem and had a beautiful home.
We had many, many friends, and we visited many kibbutzim, and I was very
much impressed with what went on. So I supported them, and I still do.

But your Jewish identity is not religious.

FEUER: That's right. I don't like the influence of Orthodoxy in religion or politics.

*How would you react if somebody were to say to you that the Jews as a
people would disappear through assimilation?*

FEUER: I wouldn't feel one way or the other. You already have over 50 percent
intermarriages in this country. I'm not against it at all. I pity the religious and
Orthodox families who couldn't influence their offspring. You have to ask yourself why that happens. You might think that the Jewish people would avoid intermarriage and really stick together. My parents kept an Orthodox household,
but my father never tried to force his lifestyle on me. Had he seen me in an inn
or restaurant eating nonkosher food, I don't think he would have said anything.

What elements of your past helped shape your academic values?

FEUER: As I told you, my education was very strict, but that was very good for
me. I don't think I was a particularly good student, but I learned how to do

different things in a short time. The languages I learned, whether classical or modern, helped to widen my horizon. I read a lot in German and other languages, and that helped me to understand things and get along with people. At the university, I had the freedom to make my own decisions and I could proceed at my own pace. I wasn't, as is the case here, required to finish a course of study or research in a semester. I could do it faster if I wanted to. That flexibility served me tremendously in making decisions.

What about your determination to excel?

FEUER: I think I always wanted to learn new things and to find out new things.

Can you relate the effect of the Nazi period to the formation of your values?

FEUER: I learned to evaluate very carefully what people tell me. During the whole escapade, this helped me to survive. But it also carried over into my research. I'd read something, and if it didn't sound plausible, I would be very careful in accepting its truth. This has led me to search for things that have not been done before.

In other words, you have tended to develop confidence in your own judgment, whether in research or survival?

FEUER: I also learned how to get along with people from all over the country and the world. I learned you have to be very careful how you treat them and have to know how to evaluate what they tell you. It's all connected.

Was there a price to pay for this?

FEUER: The price is that you have a hard time getting close to people, because the ones I really was close to, and I don't mean my family, all perished. You see, if you lose people with whom you have spent days and days mountain climbing together, it's a very big loss.

You meet people who have a completely different background. They haven't gone through the same experiences; they haven't seen what you have seen. What is important to them isn't important to you. So it is very difficult to get close to them. I might like them, but I don't feel that they really know me at all.

Because you fear that if you get too close, and something happens, you're getting more pain.

FEUER: What I said has happened many times.

Also the pain of betrayal?

FEUER: That has happened too, yes.

Are you, in essence, optimistic or pessimistic?

FEUER: At my age I don't know quite what you mean by optimism or pessimism. But I must be some sort of an optimist. I wouldn't be here if I hadn't been.

Survivorship Makes No Sense: Anna Mandler Akeley

"It was terrible to know that my mother had all the necessary papers but couldn't leave. It was too late, and that was that."

Short-Term Employment

Anna Akeley landed in Seattle, Washington, on September 20, 1940. During the crossing she had lost so much weight from not eating that she was down to eighty-three pounds. The immigration officer suspected that she might have tuberculosis and might have refused her entry had the Quakers, who had been expecting her arrival, not again taken her in charge and agreed to look after her room and board until she recuperated.

Apparently the Quakers had a tremendous organization.

ANNA AKELEY: Unbelievable, fantastic. And they didn't ask me to join the Quakers, nothing like that. I had to sign that I owed them $242, the money they had advanced to me during my trip.

Akeley didn't want to get married with debts. She therefore postponed moving to West Lafayette to be with Edward and went instead to San Francisco to find work. She held a variety of service jobs: bus girl in a restaurant at the Top of the Mark, a general maid and cook for a private family, a dental assistant, and a secretary for a mentally incapacitated Dutch meat importer with whom she spoke German. Having escaped the dangerous world of reality, she now entered one of make-believe.

AKELEY: The man's wife was a doctor, and they had two boys, one eight, the other one ten. The job paid eighty dollars a month plus room and board. So I went there, and his wife said, "I don't know what's wrong with my husband, but he doesn't function anymore. Although he is retired, he still thinks that he is a meat importer and tries to make phone calls, and he wants a secretary. So you make the phone calls, but don't worry, because the phone is disconnected. Don't be afraid of him. He is not dangerous at all." He was a small man, fifty-two years old, and rather weak. So I took the job.

When he met me, he shook my hand and said in good German, "I'm so glad, you know. I have trouble with another language." I said, "But you know Dutch." "Oh," he said, "Dutch is my mother language, but I cannot use it in business." So I arrived the next morning, and he said, "Please make a phone call to this firm and tell them that I want two and a half tons of their product." So I made the call. And then he said to me, "And now write a letter to that company, demanding that they send me the money they owe." So I typed the letter, and then he said to me, "It's bad with the situation as it is." And I asked him, "Sir, what situation?" And he said, "Oh, you know. The situation." He never knew what was going on.

And then he asked me, "Can you take shorthand?" I had learned very little German shorthand, and I couldn't do English shorthand at all. So he complained to his wife that I was not a good secretary. I should at least know English shorthand. But she said, "Look. She's a refugee. We cannot dismiss her."

But the day came when I couldn't stand this pretend world any longer. I wanted to scream at him and tell him what nonsense it was. Also, I was unhappy speaking German all day, because I wanted to speak English. However, I took it for about six weeks, and then I told his wife that I wanted to quit. She started to cry and said, "That's the trouble. I have had other people, and nobody can stand it. I understand. This is an impossible situation for me. He is demented. I will have to put him in an institution." And I said, "Because of me?" And she said, "Yes. Because I can't find anybody better than you." I told her I would stay on for another two weeks. And the last day I was there, I told him, "I have to go away because of family affairs." And he said, "It's better this way, you don't know shorthand, anyhow."

Akeley was still in San Francisco at the time of the attack on Pearl Harbor (December 7, 1940), and within days the United States was officially at war with Japan, Germany, and Italy.

While Henry Feuer was living in Luchon, he had to have his passport renewed every six months. Note that the renewals are issued by the Swedish consulate, which acted for Germany in France since the declaration of war.

One of a number of transit visas required for Anna Akeley's eastward voyage from Austria to the United States.

AKELEY: There was an international center that I used to go to on weekends where I made friends. The first time I went there after the Pearl Harbor attack, some agents of the FBI were sorting out the people into groups. They put Germans in one group and "neutrals" into another group. The Japanese did not go to that international center; I don't know where they went. I was put with the Poles and the Belgians, because the Austrians were also considered conquered people. They said, "All you who were overrun by Hitler are freed. But if you leave San Francisco, you have to let us know where you are going." I was extremely shaken.

Were you still in contact with your mother?

AKELEY: There were no longer any direct communications with Vienna. Even before, it was not as easy to telephone, and it was very expensive, but until the war we could correspond. She would write about the crowded conditions in which she lived, and how the people she was living with would get along. She was a great reader, and she told me I should read this or that book.

Did she convey any sense that she was in danger?

AKELEY: The only thing she would say was that things were complicated. She didn't dare go into details. She didn't know if her letters would be opened or not. It was very difficult for her, with all her children gone.

After my brother and I got to the United States, we hocked all the jewelry we had managed to get out and used it to get an affidavit for our mother. She already had a passport, and in November 1941 she received the affidavit. But because of her "agitated depression" she could not leave immediately, and by the time she was ready to travel, the Germans and the Americans were at war, and she couldn't go. It was terrible to know that my mother had all the necessary papers but couldn't leave. It was too late, and that was that.

When her debt to the Society of Friends was reduced to a mere three dollars, Akeley wrote to Edward and told him she would come in two weeks. He had been visiting her in San Francisco during his vacation periods.

AKELEY: I asked, "Well, Edward. How is Lafayette?" And he replied, "It's flat and the corn grows there." Still, I outfitted myself completely, even buying a silver fox stole. And I bought a typewriter. Edward said he would pick me up in Chicago. As I rode the train east, I looked out the window at America. We went through Nebraska and Iowa, and there was nothing to see, just like going through Siberia. But on the Trans-Siberian the towns were one day apart, while here they were just a few miles. I thought the big silos were enormous bird feeders. When Edward picked me up in Chicago, he shook my hand. "Hello, how are you?" he said. He wasn't very demonstrative. And then he looked at me and said, "Why do you have dead animals around your neck?" It was those silver foxes. He never told me that the temperature could be ninety degrees. We were married on May 28, 1942.

The Introductory Courses

Did you feel completely secure in this country?

AKELEY: I didn't know then that deep down Franklin D. Roosevelt did not want so many Jews coming in. We thought he was a great rescuer.

On the whole, you felt very positive about living here?

AKELEY: I felt that here I can make a living.

How did you make that living?

AKELEY: The second day I was in West Lafayette, Edward introduced me to Karl Lark-Horowitz, the head of the physics department. I had known his sister in Vienna. When Horowitz had come to Purdue in 1928, the physics department was only a service department, so he went to President Edward Elliot to get it turned into a graduate department. Elliot, despite his antisemitism, recognized Horowitz's genius and gave him the money.[3]

What did you and Lark-Horowitz talk about when you met? Your Austrian background?

AKELEY: He asked me about my education. And that evening he called and asked me to send my credentials to him the next day. Edward took them over, and four hours later he called again and offered me a visiting instructorship teaching the introductory laboratory course in physics during the fall semester.

The scarcity of qualified teachers during the war prompted the offer, and also considerable anxiety in the one to whom it was made. Akeley had not studied physics since her days at the Roentgen Institute, sixteen years before. But her husband agreed to help refresh her knowledge by tutoring her every night after he had finished his own teaching. Still, such help did not prepare her for the rigors of appearing before a class.

AKELEY: In my class, the shortest student was six feet tall, and when all five feet of me came in, they got up. They addressed me as "Madam," and I said, "Thank you, gentlemen. Please sit down." So far so good. But then on the first experiment I referred to "induced electrical current" as "seduced current." And they started to howl. Now, shy I was not, and I asked, "What's wrong?" And a 6'7" guy by the name of Bell, who was in the first row, stood up and looked down at me and asked, "Does Madam want a theoretical or experimental explanation?" Then somebody else corrected me, and I started to explain the principles of "induced" current. I taught five sections of that same course for two semesters, twenty-four hours a week, a full wartime load.

And I stood there and I had the feeling, "My God. I teach here some kids who really want to learn this. And some of them will not come back from the war." And I felt horrible about that.

Later Akeley was asked to develop a special physics course for physical education majors and one for home economics majors. Her husband was working on a secret army project to develop a system to trick the Germans into believing that they had been able to ascertain the wavelengths of the American radar system. When the war ended in 1945, the scarcity of professors, upon which circumstance Akeley's teaching position depended, also ended. Horowitz told her he could not ensure her tenure unless she got a Ph.D. He proposed arranging a special course of study, with himself and her husband as mentors. But this proved impractical, to say nothing of unethical, and she continued on a year-to-year contract. She continued working under this "temporary" arrangement until 1959, when finally at the age of fifty-five, she was rewarded with tenure, one of the few people in the science department to receive it without having a doctor's degree.[4] She continued in the rank of instructor until she retired twelve years later, in 1971. She had taught for twenty-nine years, winning a teaching award in the School of Science and special recognition by the university in the form of an official medal. These achievements she recalls with particular pride and satisfaction.

A Fantastic Opportunity

You have gone through many changes in your life. Did you ever have much opportunity to talk to people about your experiences?

AKELEY: I did not like to speak about the tragedy of my mother or the fate of my sister and my cousins. Once Rabbi Gedalyah Engel, who organizes the Holocaust Conference here, wanted me to come to the remembrance service, but I refused. I said, "I cannot. I do not want to. I don't need any remembrance day."

Did you also sense any reluctance in other people to hear accounts of survivors?

AKELEY: Yes, definitely.

What did you find out about your mother's and sister's disappearance?

AKELEY: After the war we hired a private investigator and found out that my mother had been deported to Theresienstadt in June 1942, and there she disappeared. We don't know what happened to her. She was probably sent from Theresienstadt to Auschwitz, where she perished. My only hope was that she managed to kill herself rather than being led to her death, and that she was glad that it was going to be over.

What did you find out about your sister?

AKELEY: We got a letter telling us that on the day she and her husband were going to be deported, they turned on their gas stove. It's a terrible burden, and I try not to think about it, because if I do, I have to take antidepressants.

Do you ever dream about it?

AKELEY: Not at all. I dream more about Edward and sometimes my brother, but never about my mother or my sister and my cousins.
Never.

Aside from you and your brother, none of your family survived?

AKELEY: I, for some unknown reason, am the last one alive. That is very disagreeable, I assure you.

Why is that?

AKELEY: When I was younger, I thought death was bad, but I pushed the thought of it away. But somebody calls me from Vienna and says, "By the way, I'm coming to visit you. I would like to see you a last time." And then my lawyer tells me, "You have to make arrangements in case you are totally incapacitated." And I have those memories of my father, who was so sick and in such pain that I couldn't stand it. That follows me now. If I get a pain, I go to three different emergency rooms. I am scared of pain because of my father.

Now I'm not much good for anything. When I taught, I got a "best teacher" award, that's true, but I really didn't do much for the students. I only understood that they didn't understand. However, coming to the United States gave me a fantastic opportunity to become a teacher, something that would never have happened had I stayed in Vienna.

Did you ever feel that you would like to go back to Vienna?

AKELEY: I never wanted to go back. Outside of my mother, I had nothing there. I was so sure when I arrived in this country that my brother and I would be able to get her out. I am offended by Vienna. I sure was kicked out. And when I'm thrown out, I stay out. I was never thrown out anywhere. I was always accepted. They rejected me, and, if I'm rejected, I go. I was shocked that the Viennese people would have gone for a thing like National Socialism, that it would become so fashionable to be antisemitic.

But it became fashionable all over Europe.

AKELEY: Naturally, it was catastrophic to be a Jew.

We're talking about more than just a fashion. Isn't this so-called "change" merely a revelation of what had been there all along?

AKELEY: Yes. But I prefer to think of those many who helped us.

But you still harbor tremendous resentment over how the society as a whole turned on you.

AKELEY: I was terribly bitter and I have never forgiven them.

Despite your feelings, did you ever go back?

AKELEY: Yes, with Edward. The houses we owned in Vienna were taken away, but I wanted to see if that villa we had in the country was still recorded in the name of Paul Mandler. I remember going to Altaussee and asking the mayor if I could see the books of ownership prior to 1938. And he said, "All those have disappeared." Naturally he was lying. But I asked a lawyer in the next-larger town, and he said, "Do not waste your money with me. I cannot do a thing about it." He was not unfriendly, but brusque.

Did Austria pay restitution?

AKELEY: The Germans gave money to both my brother and me. The Austrians had little money to give, but they put us on social security, paying us as if we had continued to work from 1938 to 1958. I now get eight hundred dollars a month. And my brother, who was higher-paid than I, got twelve hundred a month.

Did you get restitution for the property you lost?

AKELEY: We got only $60,000 for the villa in the Nineteenth District, a ridiculous price, because it eventually sold for $700,000. But the house was in bad shape. During the occupation, the property was in the American sector, and the officers quartered there tore the wooden wainscoting off the walls to use in those big ceramic stoves that were in every room. They offered to pay for that damage, but Kurt and I wrote back that we were taken in by America, and we were very happy that they were there, and that we didn't want to be paid. They replied, insisting that we please accept payment. They found it very difficult to understand how we could refuse payment. But Kurt and I persisted; and that idiotic thing went on until they gave up.[5] Our house in the First District was bombed very badly. It wasn't clear who hit it, but we never asked the Americans for restitution. We got very little for what was left—I think ten thousand dollars each.

The nice thing about my trip there was that it gave me the opportunity to thank some of the people who had been so nice to us and to give them presents for their kindness. For example, we had given our silver candelabra to the tailor, and now he wanted to give them back. But I told him that I no longer had any use for such things and that he should keep them or sell them. Also, I had brought with me some jewelry, which I distributed to those people who were nice. I was glad to see them. But I did not enjoy one moment in Vienna.

Didn't you miss the luxurious lifestyle you once had? In West Lafayette you live rather modestly by comparison.

AKELEY: I was dumb to think once that everybody needed at least five servants.

Weren't you angry about the style of life that was taken away?

AKELEY: Not as much angry as deeply offended. I was fourth-generation Viennese.

Your family was destroyed because you were Jewish. How do you see yourself now in terms of any Jewish persona?

AKELEY: I was punished for something when I had nothing done wrong. My family was treated unfairly, although I do not remember that we were ourselves unfair. My father and mother always had an open pocketbook for charitable causes. They contributed, for example, to the repair of the Mariakirche-am-Gestade.

Your father also helped the Jewish community.

AKELEY: And how!

There must have been in him a certain identity with the Jewish community.

AKELEY: Definitely. Only he did not go to synagogue or anything. I mentioned that the only thing he did was to insist that my brother became bar mitzvahed.

Do you have any regrets about your Jewish identity?

AKELEY: No. No regrets. But in Vienna I never belonged to the Jews, nor did I belong to the Gentiles, most of whom were to a certain point antisemitic, saying such things as, "What do you expect? He's a Jew."

Did you ever regret not having children?

AKELEY: I never wanted children. That is very strange, because I'm not an ogre. I find children very nice. But Sigmund Freud said that people want to have children so they can avoid a concrete ending to their life, and I have to reply that I never had the feeling that one has to conquer death.

You think of yourself as Jewish one way or the other?

AKELEY: I was born a Jew, and therefore I am a Jew. Period. But I always objected to that Judeo-Christian combination when their concepts of God are so different. The Christian God is an all-forgiving God, an all-loving God.

Except he is also the God who eternally damns anybody who doesn't believe in Him.

AKELEY: On the other hand, the Jewish God punishes people unto the seventh generation. That is not a very friendly God.

Did you ever think about why you escaped extermination and others didn't?

AKELEY: Survivorship doesn't make sense. To say that somehow I was protected by God doesn't make any sense.

It's not uncommon for people consciously or subconsciously to feel a certain sense of guilt because just by chance they made it. You feel the same way?

AKELEY: Absolutely.

What do you feel gave you the ability to survive?

AKELEY: Luck. I was lucky. There is no other explanation.

Notes

1. Paula Feuer was born in Manhattan (New York City). She got her master's degree and Ph.D. at Purdue, where Henry met her. She was in the engineering science department, from which she retired as a full professor.

2. This interview was conducted before the success of the far right Freedom Party of Austria in the October 1999 national elections. The FPO won 27 percent of the votes, which, in the Austrian government formed on February 4, 2000, earned it half of the cabinet posts, including the deputy chancellorship. Party leader Jörg Haider, the head of the state government of Carinthia, had pandered to the Austrian electorate with a clearly xenophobic and volkish campaign. Although Haider had once called Hitler's government a heinous criminal regime, he came from a Nazi family and was proud of it, and he was constantly willing to play on Nazi and racist themes if it served his purpose. In 1995, he praised a group of Wehrmacht and Waffen SS veterans for having "risked their lives so that the younger generation should have a future in which order, justice, and decency are still principles." On another occasion, he said that "Vienna must not become Chicago," meaning a city of mixed-race gangsterism. Some doubt whether Haider believed his own rhetoric—he would readily pull in his horns when pinned down—but there was no question that his disturbing message fell on fertile ground. Many Austrians, like people in other countries, were alarmed at the increased immigration from eastern, mostly Moslem countries, and they were disturbed that European multiculturalism would destroy their national integrity.

   The Austrians have also had difficulty reconciling themselves with their Nazi past. On the one hand, they could look upon themselves as victims of the *Anschluss;* on the other, they could view the Nazi period without shame and even with a certain amount of admiration. *Wir brauchen einen kleinen Hilter* (we need a little Hilter) goes a popular slogan.

3. Once at a faculty reception Elliot said to Edward Akeley, "I heard that you married a Jewish refugee. She didn't seem to me to be either Jewish or a refugee when you

introduced her to me." And Edward replied, "President Elliot, since when are you a connoisseur of Jewish refugees?"

4. Another was Anna Whitehouse Berkovitz, also featured in this book.

5. Later, when she was making out her will, she asked her lawyer whether she could leave some money to the United States "to show America that I appreciate that they took me in." And he advised her to consider instead making a bequest to some particular institution, for example, the Smithsonian. In the end, though, she decided to favor the local community, particularly Purdue University and the Lafayette Art Museum, both of which shared in a valuable collection of Mexican and South American art that she and her husband had collected over the years.

Part Three
Czechoslovakia
and
Poland
and
Hungary

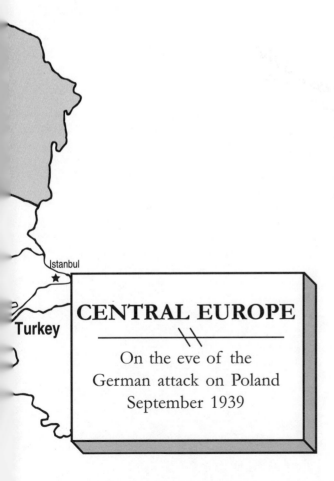

● Smolensk

sk

● Kiev

U.S.S.R.

Istanbul

Turkey

CENTRAL EUROPE

On the eve of the
German attack on Poland
September 1939

8
The Exploitation of Weakness

For most of the First World War, the Allies believed that the Austro-Hungarian Empire would survive and remain a force for stability in Eastern Europe, perhaps as some sort of federated union. But this vision was not shared by the state's various national groups, who had little desire to preserve the integrity of the Habsburg Monarchy. These ethnic demands merged with considerations of security, economic viability, and the Great Powers' interests to create a series of new states, which had little experience in self-rule.

At the Paris Peace Conference, Edvard Beneš, chief spokesman for the Czechs and Slovaks, laid claim to all the homelands that stretched from Bohemia east to the Carpathians and the Ukraine. To the north he wanted the historic Polish-Hungarian frontier and to the south all the territory down to Yugoslavia and the lands of the Danube. Beneš also demanded all of Ruthenia, claiming that the Slavic peoples who lived there would be happier associated with the Czechs and Slovaks than with the Hungarians.

The Treaty of St. Germain with Austria and the Treaty of the Trianon with Hungary gave this new Czechoslovakian state everything Beneš had demanded except for the Yugoslav corridor. Its diverse population included 8.7 million Czecho-Slovaks, 3.1 million Germans, 745 thousand Magyars, 462 thousand Ruthenians, 180 thousand Jews, and 75 thousand Poles—a total of 13.4 million.[1]

In such a conglomeration, nationality was determined principally by language. However, the Jews, whatever their language, could choose any nationality. Almost half of the 354,000 Jews living in the new state officially chose to be considered something other than Jewish.

Under the obligatory "protection of minorities" treaty signed at the peace table, the new state was obliged to accord to the one-third of the citizens who were not part of the state's two main national groups full protection of the law without distinction of birth, nationality, language, race, or religion—an obligation that was incorporated into the new state's constitution. The dominant Czechs, however, tended to look on the other nationalities as incapable of handling their own affairs. Thus Czecho-Slovakia became an unstable concoction of ethnic resentment, threatened by separatism from within and by German revisionism and Polish and Hungarian irredentism from abroad.

The German takeover of Austria in March 1938 had increased the tension. It had significantly altered the balance of power in Eastern Europe, giving Germany a common frontier with Italy, Yugoslavia, and Hungary with control of most of the Upper Danube, including direct access to Czechoslovakia's central plateau. Czechoslovakia, however, seemed a more difficult target than Austria. The country had a good army and a defensive system that was reputedly comparable to France's Maginot Line. Furthermore, it had treaties with both France and the Soviet Union.[2] Hitler recognized that the subjugation of Czechoslovakia would involve more careful planning than his slapdash operation against Austria.

However, Czechoslovakia had an exploitable weakness in its 3.25 million Sudeten Germans, who were living in the mountains of northwestern Bohemia, many of whom wanted to join the Reich. In his closing speech at the Nazi Party Congress at Nürnberg, Hitler denounced the Czechs for oppressing the Sudeten Germans and pledged "that if these tortured Sudeten creatures can of themselves find no justice and no help they will get both from us."[3]

The fear of a German invasion and the resultant French intervention, with the likelihood of a general war, prompted British Prime Minister Neville Chamberlain to try to resolve the crisis in face-to-face talks with Hitler. Chamberlain had been a businessman before he entered politics, and seeking agreement through appeasement was the way he learned to settle outstanding differences.

Chamberlain met with the Führer on three occasions, the last at Munich on September 29–30. German demands for the immediate surrender of the Sudetenland were confirmed during the first hour of the talks, and the rest of the time was spent working out details. An agreement was signed just before 2 A.M. on September 30, and a copy immediately transmitted to the waiting Czechoslovak representatives, who had not been allowed to participate in the discussions.

Hitler confessed that he could not understand why the British and French would go to war over an issue in which they had no direct national interest. The British and French agreed. The Munich Agreement was a stunning reminder that the nations that had helped to create Czechoslovakia at Paris in 1919 believed they now had a right to decide its fate. Chamberlain genuinely believed that he had brought "peace in our time." The Czechs were not so sure, but being isolated, they had no alternative but to go along. Czechoslovakia was too divided and its birth too painless for it to have developed a life-or-death commitment to its own survival. The Czechs monopolized most of the important positions in the central government and had failed to create a genuine Czechoslovak nationalism. Surrender to Nazi demands cost them dearly: 40 percent of their heavy chemical industry, 55 percent of their bituminous coal reserves, 63 percent of their paper production, 68 percent of their copper, 97 percent of their lignite, and all of their graphite and zinc. The agreement avoided bloodshed, but the Czechs ceded to a mortal enemy territory that contained their most important military defenses. They thus prepared the way for the dismemberment of their entire state and the servitude of their people. Czechoslovakia's neighbors, Poland and Hungary, who had both coveted Czechoslovakian territory, now took advantage of the country's isolation to press their own claims for chunks of the weakened state.

Songs of Derogation: Anna Whitehouse Berkovitz

"I always felt, especially after the war, a terrific pressure to make up for everything that [my mother] had lost."

A Ruthenian Community

Anna Weiszhausz was born in Munkács in Ruthenia (now Mukachevo, Ukraine), which before the creation of Czechoslovakia had been in the Hungarian part of the Dual Monarchy. The city had been one of the most thoroughly Jewish cities of the empire, a formidable center of Hasidim. After the First World War, its Jewish population continued to grow, although many families were in the process of abandoning or had already abandoned traditional Orthodox beliefs and ways of life. Many were sympathetic to Zionism. By 1930, the year Anna Berkovitz was born (as Anikó Weiszhausz), Jews comprised over 40 percent of the Munkács population. The city had five yeshivas, a Hebrew press, and thirty synagogues, most of which were Orthodox.

Anna's parents, Eugene and Elizabeth,[4] did not keep kosher, observe Jewish holidays, or go to the synagogue. They had been part of a Magyarized middle class and no longer spoke Yiddish at home or associated only with Jews. Anna's father was the son of a wine merchant who had sent all of his six sons to the university. Eugene graduated from the University of Vienna with a degree in engineering and spoke Hungarian, German, and Czech fluently.

His wife, Elizabeth Friedman, was the daughter of a lumber merchant and the granddaughter of an officer in the Hungarian army. The family "owned" the local salt concession, a monopoly that made the local population refer to them as the "Salty Friedmans."

Anna's grandparents were not as secularized as her parents. They kept the Sabbath and a kosher household. But, in a nod to progress, Anna's maternal grandmother permitted her children to eat ham and kielbasa, as long as they did so outside the house.

ANNA BERKOVITZ: My mother's parents, with whom I lived for several years, probably had as much effect on the formation of my own values and character as did my parents. They were "progressive" in the sense that they were tolerant of other religions; they believed in secular education, they had liberal social attitudes, and they dressed fashionably. But they defiantly adhered to and kept up Jewish traditions, although not within the narrow tenets of Orthodoxy. In the United States they might be termed "liberal Orthodox" or "Conservative." My grandfather attended synagogue every week as well as on all the Jewish holidays, when my grandmother also went. They were realists to the extent that they knew that if they didn't allow their children to eat nonkosher food on the terrace at home, the children would probably go to the local tavern and eat it nonetheless.

A great deal of what I know about Jewishness I ascribe to these grandparents. My fondest and most happy childhood memories are of the traditional Sabbath dinners, the holiday festivities, and the interminable seders at their house. The warmth of these celebrations has remained with me throughout my life.

Anna attended a Zionist school, one with no special religious classes. Hebrew, though, was the main language of instruction, established in order to prepare the younger generation for settlement in Palestine.

BERKOVITZ: Education meant an awful lot to my parents. From the time I was born, I knew that I had to excel in school. I just knew that getting a B was not acceptable. Everybody told me that my mother was the best in school and that my father was the best in school and that I had to follow their footsteps. The question of my not going to university was never brought up, because it was always assumed that I would go either to the University of Prague or to Budapest or Vienna, and I would become a professional. There was absolutely no other possibility.

How did you react to that pressure?

BERKOVITZ: I was bothered that I might not be able to live up to those expectations. But there was no alternative. My mother never taught me any of the household arts, like how to cook and how to sew. She prepared me to be a professional.

Was your mother a graduate from a university?

BERKOVITZ: She went to a *Bürgerschule,* sort of a middle school, and she was very proud that she had been a good student, but when she was sixteen her parents didn't allow her to go on to the Gymnasium because they needed her to supervise their household and servants. My mother passed away five years ago, when she was eighty-two years old, and when she was dying she told me that although she admired her parents, she always resented the fact that they had taken her out of school.

Your mother was, then, the driving force for going to the university?

BERKOVITZ: My mother was a very strong person. In fact, I put that on her gravestone: "Elizabeth Whitehouse, a woman of character and principle." When she died, I was close to sixty, but until her end I still was her little girl, and I always felt, especially after the war, a terrific pressure to make up for everything that she had lost.

O n October 8, 1938, following the Munich Agreement, which had cleared the way for the dismemberment of Czechoslovakia, Ruthenia became part of the Autonomous Republic of the Carpatho-Ukraine, a satellite of Germany. This arrangement lasted until March 15, 1939, when the region became a province of Hungary. All these political changes affected Anna's education. While still in primary school, she would change schools and languages of instruction four times: from Hebrew to Czech to Russian to Hungarian and finally back to Hebrew.

BERKOVITZ: I wasn't through yet, because then after all that, I came to the United States and learned another language. That was probably as traumatic as any, because at that time I was a teenager.

Such rapid changes were very traumatic and even years later affected me, when I had children of my own. When the question of a sabbatical came up and my husband wanted to go to France or to Israel, I wouldn't go. I did not want to subject my children to what I went through, having to go to different schools, where you felt a complete outsider, a stranger, and you didn't understand the language.

W hen Ruthenia became part of Hungary, the position of the Jews became more precarious. Antisemitic legislation, inspired by the Nürnberg Laws of National Socialism, limited Jewish participation in the liberal professions to 20 percent and in the administration to 5 percent. Jewish economic activity was also restricted, resulting in a loss of livelihood for a quarter of a million people. New racial laws defined a Jew as a person whose two parents were considered Jewish when the new state of Hungary had been created in 1919, whether or not they actually practiced the Jewish religion. This qualifier added 100,000 Christians to the category of Jew.

Anna's father had been a reserve officer in the Czechoslovakian army, and when Ruthenia became part of Hungary, he received a commission in the Hungarian army. But no sooner given than taken away: he was demoted to the ranks and assigned to a special Jewish labor battalion. Two younger brothers of Anna's mother were also in the labor battalions. When Hungary joined the war against the Soviet Union on June 27, 1941, five days after the German invasion, Eugene's detachment was sent to Russia. These army auxiliaries were divided into ten to twelve units of about 14,000 men each. The men wore uniforms but had no rank and were expected to do all the dirty and dangerous work: dig trenches, handle the dead, and march in front of the regular troops across mine fields. Most of the Jews who thus served on the eastern front never returned.

No Place to Go

From 1940 to 1944, Anna lived in Munkács with her grandparents while her mother remained in Bustahaza (now Bustino, Ukraine), a small village in the Carpathian Mountains, where her husband had worked as a supervisor for a Swiss lumber company. He had become a victim of the Jewish quotas and was out of work when the war began, but the company he had worked for still allowed him and his wife to stay in the house it owned.

BERKOVITZ: I would wake up in the morning, hearing the Hungarian soldiers sing derogatory songs about Jews. In one of them, the words went something like this:

> Kis kertemben zsidó magot ültettem
> Minden reggel puska bottal ütöttem
> Mégis ki nöt keze, lába, szakálla
> Kötelet a büdös zsidó nyakára![5]

Were these soldiers from the Munkács community?

BERKOVITZ: Probably not. There was a military post there, and the soldiers would sing as they marched through town. Then because of the quotas, my grandfather lost his wholesale coal license, and he had to go into the retail business. Where once he sold carloads of coal, he now had to measure it out in bundles or individual charcoal briquettes. Hardly the type of business that he was used to. In my grandfather's house also lived two of his daughters and two of his sons, my younger aunts and uncles, and some Hungarian soldiers.

My grandfather's income was diminished, but we were home and we were getting along. We thought we were relatively safe. The Hungarians were rounding up German, Czech, and Polish Jewish refugees, but we thought the same thing couldn't happen to us because the Hungarians would not let it happen. After all, we were integrated into the professional, political, and mercantile life of Hungarian society.

What did you hear about the progress of the war?

BERKOVITZ: We knew a lot of what was going on. We listened to the radio. My grandfather's office had big maps on the walls, and every day he followed the military campaigns with pins. We were politically very aware and were hoping that eventually this monster [Hitler] would be stopped. But we did not know about the extermination of the Jews. We knew about concentration camps, we knew about ghettos, but we really did not know about the Final Solution.

What broadcasts were you listening to?

BERKOVITZ: Before our radios were confiscated around 1943, we were getting it from the BBC. We were aware of the Blitz, the course of the struggle in North Africa, the battles in the Soviet Union. But there was also a grapevine: so-and-so talking to so-and-so, and someone who talked to a guy who was there, and this and that. There were also the Polish, German, and Czech refugees who had a sort of information underground. People would come and go. They would come to our house collecting money for this or that, dropping bits of news.

Just after the war with Russia began, the police started rounding up people who did not have legitimate Hungarian citizenship or people whose parents were foreign-born. They didn't touch us, but my grandfather had a cousin who was a chemical engineer and had been born in Poland, as was his wife. The couple had an eighteen-year-old son who had been born in Munkács, but that didn't save him. One day the police picked him up and put him across the border into Poland. He was eventually shot, but we didn't know that at the time.

The deportations of foreign Jews began in July 1941, when the Hungarian Office for Alien Control expelled about 20,000 Jews to German-conquered Galicia. These people had, for the most part, come from areas that had once been part of Czechoslovakia. They were sent to the Kamenets-Podolski area of the General Government,[6] where German and Hungarian army units massacred them.

BERKOVITZ: People came and promised to get these deportees back for a certain amount of pengös [the basic Hungarian currency unit]. The grandparents of that boy I told you about went through the horrible, terrible agony of spending all their money to get him back. "Yes," they were told, "we know where the guy is; we know where he's being kept; yes, he's there; well, he wasn't there, but he'll be there tomorrow. Next week we will bring him home." But he never returned.

After our radio was confiscated, we no longer knew what was happening. We lived only with rumors, hopes, and fears. But compared with what happened later, when the Nazis came, we seemed to lead a rather normal life. We had enough food, we had enough clothing, and I still went to school.

Was there antisemitism in that school?

BERKOVITZ: Up until the time the Nazis came, there was no overt antisemitism. We still had religious instruction. The Catholics would stay in the homeroom, the Protestants would go down the hall, and the Jews would go down to the basement.

Other than the fact than you got the basement, were there any stumbling blocks put in the way of this religious instruction?

BERKOVITZ: No, and I continued to have girlfriends who were non-Jewish as well as Jewish. The only overt harassment I ever experienced was when I would go to school on Saturday, and the religious kids, the Jewish kids, would stone me.

It seems kind of remarkable that there was no "official" prejudice, considering that Hungary was an ally of Nazi Germany.

BERKOVITZ: In fact, there was. My father lost his job. My grandfather lost his wholesale business. I was not allowed to attend the Hungarian Gymnasium because of quota restrictions. I was made to feel that I was different, that I was part of an unacceptable minority. Consequently, I never felt completely secure.

But most of the people that we dealt with in Munkács were Jewish: the doctor, the dentist, schoolteachers, and merchants. I wasn't the one who came in contact with the officials, who were non-Jewish, so I don't know how unpleasant things were for my grandfather, for example. What he had to go through to get his licenses renewed, or if he was hassled when our radios were taken away.

Hungarian army officers took over two of the five bedrooms in my grandparents' house. I had to sleep in my grandfather's room because my old room was now occupied by an officer. They lived there free of change, but they were always very polite and very nice. They thanked us and would even flirt with my aunt. But you had to be very careful what you talked about.

That civilian society in which you lived was largely devoid of men in their active years?

BERKOVITZ: The same in the Gentile community. Only older men and boys. The others were in the regular army. I always felt very bad that my father wasn't around. One of the happiest moments in our life was when my father made it home. His whole battalion walked home from Kiev and he was discharged. When he came back, we were very happy, even though he had lost his job.

These anti-Jewish policies begin to affect you as soon as Ruthenia was annexed by Hungary. Didn't you have any premonition that very bad things were going to happen?

BERKOVITZ: My father was very pessimistic, but even so, there was no place to go. In 1939, he had gotten in touch with some people in England through his firm, and he was given a visa to go to London, a visa only for himself, not for his family. And he decided that he didn't want to go alone. My grandfather's sister lived in Los Angeles, and she sent affidavits to the two young boys, my young uncles—they were twenty and twenty-seven—so they could come to the United States. They made preparations to go—this was around 1939—but my grandparents decided that it would be too difficult to conduct the business without them and decided they shouldn't leave.

Of course, very few people could know where these anti-Jewish measures would lead.

BERKOVITZ: The first inkling I had was when my father walked home from the Ukraine in a Hungarian labor battalion in January 1944. He came back with stories about people having to dig their own graves before they were shot. He told this to my grandfather. I wasn't supposed to hear, but my bedroom was next to the room in which these conversations took place. When I think of it now, I just remember how scared I was. And I remember my grandfather saying that such things could not happen in Hungary.

Did the Jews believe that [the regent Admiral Miklós] Horthy would protect them?

BERKOVITZ: Well, they believed that the whole infrastructure would protect them. And apparently they were not that wrong, at least until March 1944.

A Majority Ate Pork: Gavriel Salvendy

"My mother's family, like that of my father, looked to Budapest for civilization."

A Magyarized Family

Rimavska Sobota, where Gavriel Salvendy grew up, had been part of the Kingdom of Hungary under the Dual Monarchy. Its population was a mixture of Hungarians, Slovaks, Jews, and gypsies. Although located in one of the realm's most remote areas, the town's upper crust took their political and cultural direction from Budapest.

GAVRIEL SALVENDY: My parents were strictly Hungarian; their parents were Hungarian. They had all been educated in Hungarian schools. They spoke Hungarian at home. Although they became Czecho-Slovak citizens in 1919, they continued to identify with the Magyar culture of the old Austro-Hungarian Empire. Rimavska Sobota became part of the Slovakian half of Czechoslovakia, but the majority of its seven to eight thousand people spoke Hungarian and still looked to Budapest rather than Bratislava. As a matter of fact, both my older brother and I were born in the main hospital in Budapest. My parents moved to the capital a couple of weeks before we were delivered. So, actually, we were Hungarian by birth. Budapest was written on my passport. When I was a couple of weeks old, they brought me back to Rimavska Sobota, where I grew up. So I was Hungarian by virtue of birth, and Czechoslovakian by virtue of the fact that I lived in Rimavska Sobota.

The Jewish community in Rimavska Sobota was very small, perhaps one hundred families, and very close-knit. Maybe 80 to 90 percent married within the community or the immediately surrounding area.

When did the Salvendys settle there?

SALVENDY: They were part of the banishment of the Jews from Spain in 1492. One branch went to Germany, another group went to Slovenia, and some ended up in northern Hungary. At the time of my parents' wedding, over sixty years ago, we still had distant relations living in Germany. The name "Salvendy" is unique; there are no others by that name in the United States, for example.

And your mother?

SALVENDY: Probably German or Austrian. Her name was Braun. My mother's family, like that of my father, looked to Budapest for civilization. Even after the First World War, my mother's father refused to invest his assets in Czechoslovakia. He would go to Budapest and buy apartment buildings. He also purchased Hungarian farmland.

What was the source of his wealth?

SALVENDY: From the wine and alcohol business. He owned wineries and distilleries. My mother's family was one of the wealthiest in the area, more prosperous than my father's, whose wealth came from farming. My father's family owned between ten to twelve thousand acres of land. My paternal grandfather was considered an "elder" of the region, very much respected by the Gentiles.

N on-Hungarians were frequently accorded positions of prominence, provided they were sufficiently Magyarized and wealthy. In Slovakia, such people, no matter what their religion or ethnic background, became the instruments of Budapest's policy to create a Hungarian national state at the expense of Slovak home rule. Full emancipation had been granted to Hungary's Jews in 1867. The Budapest government encouraged assimilation and promoted Jewish participation in the country's economic development.

Was your family religious?

SALVENDY: My mother's parents were not religious at all. I think they hardly ever went to synagogue, if at all. My father's parents were not Orthodox, they didn't keep kosher, but they kind of went to the synagogue. They followed the holidays and were strong contributors to the Jewish community. Nearly all their friends were Jewish.

But I think my parents were more Jewish when they lived in Czechoslovakia than when they went to Israel. In Czechoslovakia, they felt a tremendous need to go to synagogue every Saturday. But in Israel they had a greater sense of fulfillment and never went.

Did they take you to synagogue when you were a child?

SALVENDY: Together with my brother. It was an Orthodox synagogue, where the women sat separately from the men. I wanted to sit with my female cousin, but

Gavriel Salvendy, right, with his brother Jancsi. Photo taken in front of their house in Rimavska Sobota.

Anna Weiszhauz Berkovitz (standing) with her parents in Bustahaza, 1939. (The two on the left are family friends.)

they were so strict that they wouldn't even let the little girls and boys sit together. But there was no other synagogue. You couldn't say "I'm more liberal.
Therefore, I don't want to worship with the Orthodox."

I think it was funny and strange that there was separation of the men and
the women, because I don't think that many of the Jewish people there kept kosher. A lot of them—I would say the majority of them—would eat pork.

Your parents didn't dress in a way that would define them as Jewish?

SALVENDY: No. My father always wore a suit and tie and always seemed better-
dressed than the others.

Did they speak Yiddish?

SALVENDY: They didn't know Yiddish.

What was the education of your parents?

SALVENDY: My father had a Ph.D. in agronomy from Prague. He also went there
for his undergraduate degree. He got the doctorate in 1933, when he was only
twenty-two years old, very young. He finished it in one and a half years, graduating with distinction—an achievement of which he was very proud. His thesis was on how to grow better tobacco for cigars. He patented the process and
sold the patent to the Germans after Hitler came to power. He didn't sell it to
the Czechs or the Hungarians. But the Germans bought it. Imagine, a process
invented by a Jew is being bought by the Germans.

And your mother's education?

SALVENDY: When she was sixteen, her parents sent her to a finishing school in
Vienna, where she learned to behave like a lady, discuss art and books, speak
several languages, and how to make her way in society. Her mother had probably done the same, because the Braun household always got daily newspapers
in Hungarian, German, and French.

*Your father also must have spoken fluent Czech if he went to the Univer-
sity of Prague.*

SALVENDY: And German and Russian.

How did they live?

SALVENDY: Their house was completely different from those here in the United
States. The bedrooms were very, very small, even the master bedroom. Also, the
bathrooms were small. But the living room was enormous. I mean, incredible. It

was something like eighty feet long and thirty-five feet wide. The dining area was also phenomenal. My father was very modern and had electric doors installed. Then he had an orangerie built as an extension of the living room in which to grow oranges, lemons, and other sorts of citrus fruits. All in climatically controlled conditions. One of the earliest things I remember about the house was this big radio. I was about three or four years old. And I always wanted to go inside and see the man who was talking inside.

How many servants did they have?

SALVENDY: Two full-time servants: a cook and a butler. The butler looked after the house but also ran errands, like taking my mother's dress to the dressmaker and making trips to the bank. Then they had three part-time helpers: a washing woman, a housecleaner, and gardener. When my brother and I were born, they hired a live-in nanny.

A Change of Government

Salvendy was born in Budapest on the final day of the Munich Conference. He was just a few weeks old when his mother brought him back to Rimavska Sobota, which was no longer part of Czechoslovakia. No sooner had Hitler returned to Berlin after the Munich Conference than the Hungarians reminded him of a protocol in the agreement in which he promised to settle "the problems" of the Hungarian minorities within three months.[7] The Führer suggested they first try to negotiate with Prague. But these negotiations failed to produce the desired result, and the Hungarians asked for German arbitration.

In the Vienna Award of November 2, 1938, Hitler allowed Hungary to annex the southern areas of Czechoslovakia, which contained large Magyar populations. Thus Czechoslovakia lost the cities of Nové Zámky, Šurany, Leviče, Lučenec, Rožňava, Košice (Kassa), Ungvar, Munkács, and Rimavska Sobota. Now instead of Magyars living in Czechoslovakia, Czechs, Slovaks, and Ruthenians (plus some Germans and Jews) were living in Hungary—43 percent of the "liberated" territory's total population of 1,041,494 people.

One issue on which almost all Hungarians could agree was the destruction of the Treaty of the Trianon. They greeted the Vienna Award with great jubilation and were encouraged to demand more.

The Hungarian government wanted immediate military occupation of the rest of Ruthenia. But the Germans were not ready to let them have it until after they had completed the destruction of Czechoslovakia. In March 1939 they occupied the rest of Bohemia and Moravia and recognized the creation of a separate Slovakian Republic. The following year, the Hungarians were finally allowed to take Ruthenia, and also the Romanian province of Transylvania. Hungary, now inextricably enmeshed in the Nazi web, could not assert its hegemony in the Danubian basin and maintain its independence at the same time. Hitler expected Hungary to join his war against the Soviet Union. On June 27, 1941, five days after the German attack, Hungary obediently complied. Hitler also wanted Hungarian participation in "the Final Solution of the Jewish question."

SALVENDY: My father had been a captain in the Czech army, skipping the rank of lieutenant. In 1942, though, the Hungarian army drafted him as an auxiliary, put him in a labor battalion, and sent him to the Ukraine.

At that time Hungarian soldiers were living in part of our house, and we kids began to be teased as Jews. We'd go out on to the street and the Gentile kids would point at us and chant, "Hey, Jew, Jew, Jew." Later they began to hit us.

My father came back from Russia at the end of 1943. And when he arrived, I couldn't recognize him. He was unshaven and had a big mustache, and his appearance scared us.[8]

The prewar Hungarian governments were a restless coalition of conservatives and right-wing radicals, of which the most prominent and energetically pro-Nazi and antisemitic was the Arrow Cross Party, which after 1939 controlled the second largest bloc of votes in the parliament. Its leader, Ferenc Szálasi, believed that the Hungarians, the Germans, and the Japanese were the world's chosen people. Already in 1938, the Hungarian parliament began passing laws which defined Jews on a "racial" basis and curtailed their participation in business and in the professions. In 1942, Jews were ordered to wear a yellow Star of David on their clothes.

Such measures made life increasingly disagreeable for the Hungarian Jews, but many believed the repression would not last. They took heart that they had not been deprived of their citizenship and had the government's explanation that Jewish labor was essential for the economic health of the country. Furthermore, the antisemitic legislation was not rigidly enforced and was full of exemptions.

SALVENDY: The Salvendys were basically exempt from wearing the yellow badge. We got the exception because of my grandfather's status of elder. I remember my father trying to get the exemption extended to relatives on my mother's side of the family. She, of course, had it because she was married to my father, but her sister, for example, didn't. So my father went to Budapest to make special arrangements. And he succeeded. For her alone. Her father never got it. However, all this changed when the Germans occupied the country.

Always in the Middle of Change: Robert Melson

"[My parents] were in a dynamic middling, they were moving from Jewish community into the non-Jewish community. They were somewhere in the middle."

Degrees of Assimilation

The Polish cardinal August Hlond wanted it both ways. He denounced racist ideology as contrary to Christianity, but called the Jews "Bolsheviks and free thinkers" who spread pornographic literature, practiced usury, and promoted white slavery. This instruction, intended to be read from all the pulpits of the Warsaw diocese, added weight to an already existent antisemitic campaign, which had grown in intensity since the death of Marshal Josef Piłsudski in 1934. Piłsudski, who had taken charge of the Polish government in 1926, had refused to allow antisemitism to become an instrument of policy in his government. But his successors had no such reservations. They branded Jews as unreliable and unsuitable for inclusion in Polish society.

No sooner had Piłsudski been buried than the government, in September 1934, renounced the 1919 treaty, which had obligated the state to protect its minorities. The following year, the Sejm, the parliament, restricted the right of opposition and minority parties to participate in the government. Agents provocateurs staged riots against the Jews, trying to frighten them into leaving the country.

These acts were followed by demands that Jewish influence be eradicated from the nation's cultural and economic life, and that Polish commerce be "Polonized." The ministry of education decreed that Jewish students sit on "ghetto benches" in university classrooms. Professional organizations inserted restrictive covenants in their membership bylaws.

Such radical measures were aimed directly at Jews like Melson's parents, both of whom came from the upper middle class and had thoroughly assimilated into Polish culture. Neither looked or acted particularly Jewish, and when they met, neither was sure of the other's religion.

ROBERT MELSON: My mother was born in Warsaw in 1912, when the city was part of the Russian Empire, but she never thought of herself as anything but Polish. Her father was a famous tea merchant. The family spoke Polish at home. She spoke it perfectly, with no Yiddish accent.

For my mother, Chopin was god. She read me [Adam] Mickiewicz, the great Polish national poet; she knew his poems by heart. She studied voice at the Warsaw Conservatory of Music. But since her voice wasn't strong enough for an opera singer, she did operetta. When the depression hit in 1929, she tried to help out at home by singing in the nightclub called the Audriel. She was a young woman, very pretty. Very Polish looking. And she had this flair, she was attractive, she was sexy, but she was not an intellectual woman in any sense of the word. Sometimes, when I look at these pretty cheerleaders at Purdue and the kind of mentality they have about life, I see my mother. She was not a complicated woman; she was straightforward. She loved music, she loved dancing, she loved acting. She had a ready laugh, and was a terrific, terrific lady.

Melson's father, Wulf Mendelssohn, had come from Stanislav, in Galicia, where his father, Julius Mendelssohn, owned a kilim rug factory. Grandfather Julius had been an officer in the Austrian army during the First World War, a time when the family had lived in Vienna. After the war, he sent Wulf to a *Handelshochschule* (business college) in Berlin, where the son joined a Zionist fraternity that fought duels with non-Jewish fraternities.

MELSON: My father spoke fluent German, was black-haired, with a strong nose and large brown eyes, a very handsome guy, kind of a dashing guy. A real ladies' man. Now, if he would walk into the room, you would say, "Yes, I can see he's Jewish," but the term "Jewish" meant not just looks, it meant accent, it meant bearing. There was a kind of Jewish stereotype of what it meant to be Jewish — that is, the stereotype the Jews had about each other — and if you didn't fit that Jewish stereotype, you confused the issue.

My father was an elegantly dressed guy, athletic, spoke with a heavy German accent, but not a Yiddish accent, and had a certain kind of upper-class, German kind of arrogance to him. It never occurred to my mother that he was Jewish, because everyone had the stereotype of what a Jew was supposed to look like and how he was supposed to act. He was well-traveled. Before he made his way to Warsaw, he had lived in Vienna, Berlin, and Paris, where he worked as an assistant producer to a Hungarian movie producer. His job was to round up the scorecards [bums] for a battle scene of a Napoleonic war.

In Warsaw, he opened a wholesale stationery business. He met my mother at a *café-dansant*. She was dancing with somebody else, and, as he described it, they looked at each other and fell in love. Shortly afterwards, they started living together. And she told her parents, "You know, I've fallen in love with this guy and he calls himself William Melson." And my grandfather said, "William Melson, that sounds Swedish. He is obviously not Jewish." And my grandmother said, "It doesn't matter to me, but your father, forget it." My mother, who was very attached to my grandfather, was very, very troubled by this.

My grandfather was an observant Jew, in fact he was a Hasidic Jew, but not any kind of Hasidic Jew that you can think of, he was modern-dressed and so on. He was a follower of the rabbi of Gur, one of the most famous rabbis of the time.[9] His wife — my grandmother, Stephanie Bethsheba Grumpf Ponchek — was a very assimilated modern woman. In fact, my grandmother had an affair all during their marriage, hardly the usual notion of *shtetl* family life in the backwoods of Poland praying in the local *schtiepl.*

Was that the first time the issue of your father's religion came up?

MELSON: Yes, but let's set the context. This was Poland of 1936, steeped in antisemitism. People were afraid to admit that they were Jewish when they were in public, especially in those circles. As my mother said, "You never discussed origins, social or religious origins, with anybody when you first met them." They were simply afraid to raise the subject, because they had fallen in love with each other. And they were afraid of what they were going to hear, both of them. My father, too, was concerned.

That reluctance wouldn't have come up in nonassimilated circles?

MELSON: Right. In nonassimilated circles you probably wouldn't have met anybody romantically who wasn't Jewish.

That reflects your parents' high degree of assimilation.

MELSON: Exactly. In traditional circles you would have been paired off, and in Warsaw, the probability of meeting somebody who was non-Jewish was very, very low.

Did your parents do anything Jewish? For example, did they go to the synagogue on Yom Kippur?

MELSON: My mother did. She learned Hebrew as a child because of her father. She went to synagogue on all the high holidays, went to Hebrew school, all the rest of it. It was a school where the rabbi and the teachers were brought in.

My father was not observant. His father had already broken with Judaism. So with him we are talking about the second or third generation of assimilation.

He had no bar mitzvah?

MELSON: He was bar mitzvah. Again, this shouldn't be seen as black or white. That people have assimilated doesn't mean they have converted or were denying their Jewishness. Coming from Jewish backgrounds, they were in kind of a middle ground or gray ground. My father was bar mitzvah but never went to *schul.* My mother came from this assimilated background, but she did go to the synagogue with my grandfather. However, my grandmother was reluctant to go.

For example, my grandfather would be praying on Saturday morning, my grandmother would be smoking cigarettes on Saturday or going out to visit friends, going to a coffee shop in downtown Warsaw. It was that kind of background. And, I think, in a sense, it was very contemporary. They were in some kind of a transitional phase.

Who knows where it would have taken them, had there been no Holocaust? Maybe toward conversion, maybe not. Maybe the next generations, meaning me and my children, would have reacted against it. I don't know. They were in a dynamic middling, they were moving from Jewish community into the non-Jewish community. They were somewhere in the middle, that's where they were.

The name Melson is not at all a Jewish name. My father changed it before the war. He couldn't do it legally, but he listed himself in the phone book as Melson. He started calling himself Melson. Privately he still considered himself Jewish, but publicly he impersonated a non-Jew. Not only because of the social or cultural antisemitism, but also because of the economic antisemitism. In his business, he was dealing with the army and with the government. In 1936 Jews were prohibited from dealing with either the army or the government, and he had huge contracts with both. So he hired a Polish go-between to be the so-called official head of the business, and he called himself Melson.

Therefore you have two people: one who calls himself by a non-Jewish name and is acting as if he is not a Jew; the other looking very, very Polish, speaking fluent Polish. It's important to understand this background to understand what happens next.

When did your parents find out they were both Jews?

MELSON: According to my mother, they went to a café one night and she was going to have it out, and she said to him, "You come from Stanislav in Galicia?" He answered, "Yes." And she said, "Well, I spoke to my parents and they have some very good friends, the Horowitzes, in Stanislav. Do you know them?" And he replied, "No, I can't say that I do." She said, "Well, there was a Dr. Rappaport, whom my father also knew from Stanislav, do you know him?" "No, can't say that I've ever met him." And finally she said, "How many Jews would you say live in Stanislav?" He said, "I have no idea." Telling me this story later, my mother said: "I got really angry, I got pissed. I stood up and I said, 'Willie, are you or are you not Jewish?' And he said, 'I am.' And then, she said, they embraced, and she took him home to meet her father. And like her father, he wore a *kipah* [skullcap] at dinner, something he would never have done otherwise, but he did so out of respect for my grandfather. A few weeks later they were married.

Your father considered himself Jewish by tradition rather than by religion?

MELSON: I would say Jewish by nationality. He was a Zionist, not the kind of Zionist that runs Palestine, but a Zionist assimilated Jew, with mildly socialist political views, on which he never acted because he was a capitalist businessman.

Did their friends share their values?

MELSON: Yes.

Did they have any friends in the Orthodox community?

MELSON: None really.

Did they have any good Polish friends?

MELSON: No, that's what is interesting. They really didn't. They were in a sub-group of the Jewish community in Poland. They felt comfortable with that group of people, and they had no non-Jewish friends before the war.

When Melson's mother first saw Robert after his birth, her reaction was: "My God, this kid looks just like me! Same blond hair, same blue eyes, same pug nose." This resemblance would be more important than the mere delight in seeing physical characteristics replicated. For the Melsons, appearances became vital to their survival.

Many assimilated Poles, Melson's parents included, tried to ignore the ominous implications of a mounting antisemitism. They missed the connection between Polish antisemitism and National Socialist antisemitism and tended to downplay the possibility of war.

MELSON: There were articles in the paper about the Nazi war threats, but they were mostly dismissed as not being terribly important. My father especially tended to do this because he really saw himself as coming from a German cultural background. He said, "I was in Berlin in the 1930s. I saw the Brown Shirts. I was at a swimming pool once when they came and started beating people up. But I thought this was just part of the craziness of the times and that it didn't mean anything."

More for economic reasons than because of growing antisemitism or fear of war, Melson's father moved his family to Stanislav in the spring of 1939 to work in the Mendelssohn family's rug factory. They were there when the war began.

Under Soviet Occupation

Despite his triumph at Munich, Hitler was dissatisfied. He felt that he had wrongfully been persuaded to solve the crisis peacefully. "It was a moment of weakness. There was Chamberlain's pleading, there were the fears of the German people, there were the doubts of my generals. I gave way. But no longer. I return to my original plan."[10] The Führer was convinced that he had wide latitude to redraw the map of Eastern Europe without fear of French or British intervention. In March 1939, the Germans smashed the Munich Agreement by occupying the rest of Bohemia and establishing a protectorate over Slovakia.

Chamberlain was dismayed at Hitler's unreliability, but not

angry enough to abandon the policy of appeasement. However, to quiet his critics, he made a tough speech at Birmingham on March 17. "Is this the last attack upon a small state or is it to be followed by another?" he asked, indignant that Hitler had broken his word. "Is this in fact a step in the direction of an attempt to dominate the world by force?"[11] He warned that Britain would resist such a challenge to the limits of its power.

Like many German nationalists, Hitler found the Polish Corridor and the loss of Danzig intolerable. On October 24, 1938, he had promised Poland that he would respect its western frontiers if Germany were given Danzig and had an access strip across the Polish Corridor. The offer was, of course, insincere.

In the spring of 1939, mounting fears that Germany would soon attack Poland prompted Britain to promise to protect the country's independence. Hitler dismissed the guarantee as meant for domestic consumption. "The campaign of antagonism against Germany," he remarked, "was organized by Churchill on the orders of his Jewish paymasters, and . . . any and every nation which fails to eliminate the Jews in its midst will sooner or later finish by being itself devoured by them."[12]

On April 3, 1939, he ordered plans drafted for the invasion of Poland (Operation White) to begin on September 1 at the earliest. Since such an attack could touch off a struggle with Great Britain and France, Hitler moved to protect his rear through an agreement with Soviet Russia. Negotiations lasted four months, resulting in a nonaggression treaty, which was signed on August 23, 1939.

The Nazi-Soviet Pact divided Poland into German and Soviet spheres of influence. Poland was partitioned about midcountry, the line running along the Narev, Vistula, and San Rivers. The signatories promised to decide in the future "whether the interests of both parties make the maintenance of an independent Polish state appear desirable."[13] Hitler now had the carte blanche he wanted to attack Poland. But unlike the Czechs, the Poles had decided to fight. Their determination did them little good.

On Friday, September 1, at 4:45 in the morning, Wehrmacht Panzer units rolled across the Polish frontier. Within a week, the Germans had destroyed the bulk of the western Polish army, smashed the Polish air force on the ground, and were poised to capture Warsaw. The blitzkrieg was so effective that Stalin feared that unless he entered the war at once, he would not get what he was owed. He ordered the offensive to begin on September 17. The Soviets claimed that the disintegration of Poland had forced them to act to protect their Ukrainian and White Russian brothers.

The attack from the east caught the demoralized Polish defenders completely off guard, and by the end of the month they had surrendered. Soviet troops rolled into Stanislav on the second day of the attack. In their vanguard came the apparatchiks to begin the process of Stalinization, which was naturally based on the power of the secret police. Rubber-stamp people's assemblies were "elected" in the western Ukraine and in the western Belorussian districts to vote on the formal incorporation of the territory into the Soviet Union. They were dissolved after they had served their purpose.

The inhabitants in the annexed territories were given Soviet citizenship and a curriculum of Marxism-Leninism. Free trade was outlawed; the ruble replaced the zloty; businesses, farms, and natural resources were nationalized; political, social, and religious organizations were disbanded or driven underground; and savings accounts were confiscated. Soviet bureaucrats moved into confiscated apartments and houses, and they took the middle- and upper-management jobs. They became the teachers and professors. Russian became compulsory in the schools. Polish street names disappeared. The ringing of church bells was outlawed. But the Soviets were equal-opportunity oppressors and, unlike the Germans, did not specifically target the Jews for persecution, concentrating on merchants, community leaders, and intellectuals. Those suspected of being "enemies of socialism" were deported. As a favor to the Nazis, political refugees from the German part of Poland were hunted down and handed over to the Gestapo.

MELSON: One day the Communist authorities announced that they were offering employment to people with degrees. If these intellectuals would only show up at the railroad station, they would be relocated and given jobs. My uncle Tadjo (Tadeusz Ponchek) read this announcement, packed his bags, and went to the railroad station to volunteer. As he was walking to the railroad station (as he told the story) one of the Jewish workers from my father's factory who knew the family ran into him just as my uncle was trying to get into line to get

Demeter Pista and Kati, Gentiles who were instrumental in saving the lives of Gavriel Salvendy and his family. Pista died in 1976, and Salvendy last visited Kati in 1999, when she was ninety-two years old. Photo taken in 1964.

Group of survivors, July/August 1945, Sweden.
Anna Berkovitz stands, 3rd from right in the 4th row.

onto this wonderful train, which was going to take him to be relocated to give him a job, and the worker said to him in Yiddish, "Get the hell out of here. Just get out." And my uncle was smart enough to turn around and go. It turned out that the train was a sealed train, and that the people who got on stayed on the siding for three days without food or water, and then they were all shipped to Siberia. These were the intelligentsia who volunteered, and they were just shipped out.

A particularly brutal example of this Soviet drive to eliminate the Polish elites occurred at Katyn Forest, near Smolensk, when in April and early May 1940, secret police death squads murdered 4,400 Polish army officers who had been captured by the Red Army the previous September. All of the victims had their hands wired behind their backs and had been shot in the back of the head. The Soviets blamed the atrocity on the Germans and broke off relations with the London-based Polish government in exile when it requested an inquiry. Not until 1990 did the Russians confirm that Stalin had ordered the executions.

When the Soviets confiscated the Mendelssohn family's rug factory, Melson's grandfather naively thought he could strike a deal with the new Communist masters.

MELSON: He went to the local commissar. "Look," he said, "I'm not interested in the money, but I love the factory, I built the factory. I know how to run the factory. Let me stay as the manager. Take the money, take the factory, but let me continue running the factory." For his troubles he was arrested by the secret police and placed in a concentration camp. He was badly beaten, so severely that he lost one eye, but he somehow managed to survive.

My parents were issued identity cards that said "Social background: Capitalist." The Communists confiscated their home, but they managed to rent another house and have a maid named Hella, a Ukrainian girl who used to work for the family. I remember her vaguely, because she was very fond of me, and I used to chase her around the kitchen table trying to raise up her long peasant skirts and see what was underneath. Hella used to turn around and lift me up. It was a happy moment.

Anyway, we were staying with Hella, and my father decided he had to do something to earn a living. As he explained it: "There were two powers: the commissars in the government power and the secret police in the NKVD. Once the secret police gets ahold of you and finds out about your social background, they will send you off either to prison or to the gulag. As long as you keep out of their way, you can deal with the commissars. Now, what do the commissars want? They want production, any kind of production."

So my father went to one of the commissars and asked him, without showing him his papers, what he needed. And the guy said to him, "We need everything, anything." My father asked, "Could you use some ink?" And the guy answered, "Sure, we could use some ink." So then my father went out and with some other Jews, classified as capitalists, formed an *artil,* which was a collective for producing things, with my father at the head, and it produced ink. And then it produced candles and lamp oil. As long as it produced something, the workers got some food. [Usually bread and some kind of soup, once a day.]

Another memory I have of those days is waiting for my father to come home on his bicycle. He would be holding the daily loaf of bread, and he would grab me and put me on the bar of the bicycle, which would hurt, but it would be fun.

About that same time, this would be late 1940 or so, my mother started getting letters from my grandparents, who had been sent to the Warsaw ghetto. The letters described the very harsh conditions there: people dying of typhus, lack of food. My mother sent packages of food. And in one letter, her mother wrote, "We are really in bad shape. In fact, I had to hide the last package you sent me from other people because we are simply beginning to starve to death." At that point my mother took her winter coat and sold it. She would have done anything to help.

On October 3, 1940, the Germans ordered the 150,00 Jews who lived throughout Warsaw to move to the old Jewish quarter of the city. The Jews could bring with them only those possessions they could carry or pull on handcarts. Similarly, the 80,000 Gentiles forced out to give way to the new inhabitants had to leave most of their possessions behind. Later, the Warsaw Jews were joined with other Jews from towns throughout the region, 72,000 in the first months of 1941 alone.

The Germans sealed the Warsaw ghetto behind a wall. Henceforth any Jew caught outside without permission was liable to be shot. Starvation was commonplace, climbing to about 5,000 victims a month. The amount of food one obtained (much of it smuggled in) usually depended on the amount of money a person or family had. The poorest of the population survived on begging, stealing, or on soup kitchens. There were recorded cases of cannibalism. However the overcrowding (in 1941 the population was 470,000), lack of medical care, proper hygiene, heat, and sanitation produced epidemics of typhus, whose ravages spared few. But whatever the cause of death, the amount was never high enough for the German authorities.

The establishment of the Jewish ghetto in Warsaw was part of an overall Nazi policy to concentrate all the Polish Jews in ghettos, usually in the rundown and neglected parts of cities. The first of these had been established at Piotrkow on October 28, 1939.

Do you remember anything about your sense of being Jewish in those years of Soviet occupation?

MELSON: I don't know where it came from, but my very first memory was that I was in a room, there was sunlight, the windows were open, there were some long curtains billowing from the breeze that came up through the window. I was in the middle of this room, and I had a little shovel and a little brush, and I was trying to find all sorts of *chometz* bread particles. There was a maid there, and my mother was there, and they were trying to explain to me why I should be doing this, and it looked like a lot of fun trying to find pieces of grain or bread any place in the house. And I was supposed to shovel it and put it in a pile in the middle of the room.

This must be near Passover? But why would you be doing that if your family was assimilated and these things didn't mean very much to them?

MELSON: Well, it did and it didn't have meaning. You shouldn't stereotype so much. You shouldn't see things in a binary way with the religious Orthodox Jews on the one hand and the assimilated on the other. It wasn't that way.

There were certain customs that you celebrated en famille, and there was another persona when it came to the rest of the world?

MELSON: That's a good way of putting it, but it's still more complicated. When I read about historians' conceptions of what Jews were like during this period, I get a sense that they are always trying to put things into categories. But life at the time was a process, something dynamic, people were always changing in various ways. Some were becoming Zionists, some were becoming socialists, some were becoming more orthodox, and some were becoming less orthodox. People were always in the middle of change.

Notes

1. As recorded by the 1921 census.
2. In the treaty signed on May 16, 1936, the Soviets had made their commitment to defend the Czechs against aggression contingent on the French acting first.
3. *Survey of International Affairs* (London: Royal Institute of International Affairs, 1938), 2:261.
4. Eugene and Elizabeth were popular names in the Austro-Hungarian Empire because of their association with the Habsburgs, as were Franz, Karl, Augusta, and Anna.
5. "I planted a Jew seed in my little garden / Every morning I beat it with my rifle butt / In spite of that it grew hands and feet and a beard / So let's put a rope around the neck of the stinking Jew!"
6. In September 1939, the Germans and the Soviets partitioned Poland. The Germans split their section into two roughly equal parts: the western and northern areas were annexed directly to the Reich and settled with Germans; the eastern, central part, including the cities of Warsaw, Lubin, and Kracow, became the General Government and was to be used as a labor colony. In this 37,000-square-mile area lived 12 million people. Hans Frank, a principal creator of the Nazi legal system, became its governor, with his capital in Kracow. The General Government gained more territory after the German invasion of the Soviet Union, when all of prewar Poland came under Nazi rule. Hitler now decided to expel all Poles from the area and liquidate its entire Jewish population.
7. If not, they would form the subject of another meeting of the heads of the governments of the four Munich Powers. At the same time, under the same clause, the Poles presented their demands for the part of Teschen awarded to Czechoslovakia in 1919. Hitler let them have it.
8. He was one of the lucky ones, considering that as many as 43,000 labor battalion Jews (out of 50,0000) perished in the general retreat of the disintegrating Second Hungarian Army following the defeat of the German army at Stalingrad in January 1943.
9. Abraham Mordechai Alter (Gerer Rebbe).
10. Leonard Mosley, *On Borrowed Time* (New York: Random House, 1969), 98.
11. Neville Chamberlain, *In Search of Peace* (New York: G. P. Putnam, 1939), 275.
12. Adolf Hitler, *Secret Conversations* (New York: Farrar, Strauss, and Young, 1953), 338.
13. Under the agreement the Germans also accorded the Soviets a free hand in determining the fate of Finland, Estonia, Latvia, and the Romanian territory of Bessarabia. *Documents of German Foreign Policy,* series D, 7:227.

9

Within Hitler's Empire

Operation Barbarossa, Hitler's attack on the Soviet Union, began on June 22, 1941, with a three-pronged blitz: across the Baltic states, through eastern Poland, and down into Bessarabia—a broad front extending from the Baltic Sea to the Black Sea.

On July 2, units of the Hungarian army, part of the Wehrmacht's Army Group South commanded by Fieldmarshal Gerd von Rundstedt, entered Stanislav. The Hungarians wasted no time in using the region as a dumping ground for the Jews they had expelled from Ruthenia, the former Czechoslovakian province that they had acquired, with Hitler's permission, in 1939. With the addition of these deportees and those refugees who had fled before the advancing Germans in 1939, the Jewish population of Stanislav was now 10,000 more than its prewar figure of 30,000.

Eastern Galicia became part of the General Government, which the Germans had established in 1940 as a giant labor colony. From his capital in Krakow, Governor-General Hans Frank, former legal advisor to the Nazi Party, set out to destroy the Polish nation through economic exploitation and eventual starvation. The Nazis singled out the Jews for particularly brutal treatment; some half million more (added to the previous two and a half million) were now at their mercy.

False Papers: Robert Melson

"Throughout this story is the recurring theme of tremendous chutzpah and resourcefulness, and extraordinarily good luck. These were the essence of our survival."

A Red Tricycle

On July 26, the Germans assumed civil administration of Stanislav and here, as elsewhere in the former Soviet sector, went on an antisemitic rampage. The first *Aktion* in Stanislav took place on August 2, when one thousand Jewish leaders and professionals were taken to a nearby forest and shot.

ROBERT MELSON: I asked my father what was going on, and he was reluctant to talk. Finally, he said, "Very unpleasant things are happening." I said, "Dad, what do you mean by very unpleasant things?" He said, "Well, very unpleasant." And I said, "You mean you would walk down the street and you would see some religious Jews being humiliated, beaten up?" He said, "Yes, this kind of thing."

And then he said that one day there was an announcement that people with degrees were supposed to show up at the local Gestapo station. And he turned to my mother and said, "You know, I have a degree, maybe I should go." And my mother said, "Don't go." And he didn't go, but his uncle and some of the people he knew, some of the Melson family, the cousins, they went, because they had degrees. One was an engineer and another was a lawyer; and they all went and they were never seen again.

But the largest *Aktion,* and the most bloodthirsty to date, took place in Stanislav on October 12, when over 10,000 Jews were murdered in the local Jewish cemetery.

MELSON: In early October, there were announcements all through town, posted on churches and other buildings, that all Jews were to come to the center of

town, one valise per person, and that they were going to be relocated somewhere to the east to relieve the population pressure. My parents were going to
go, because there were threats that if you didn't show up you would be shot.

However, the night before they were supposed to go, my mother had a
dream. And in the dream her father came to her, he was carrying a placard and
it said October 12 on it, and he showed her the placard and warned, "Danger."
She tried to reach for him, and he disappeared. She woke up in the middle of
the night and told my father that they had to flee. So they came to get me, and
together we left town and fled to the home of some friends who were Jewish
converts from Catholicism. My parents figured they would be safe with them.
(They did not know then that these people would also perish.) But they stayed
with these friends until they decided it was safe to return to their rented house
with their Ukrainian maid. It was when they returned that they found out what
had happened.

A former girlfriend of my father's had survived the massacre by hiding under the bodies. The shootings continued from morning till evening, till 6:30 in
the evening. Then as it got dark, the shootings continued under the lights of
trucks. This young woman managed to survive by being buried under the bodies, digging herself out later that night. She made it out, saw my father, and told
him what had happened.

A few days later, there was an announcement that a few streets in Stanislav
were going to be converted into a ghetto for those who had remained, and that
the remaining Jews should go to this ghetto. People came to my parents — Jewish friends of theirs — and said, "Why don't we stick together and go and find
an apartment together in the ghetto? We will take care of each other, we will
help each other out." At which point my father said, "No, I'm not going to go,"
because he now realized that the Germans really wanted to kill all Jews. "Outside the ghetto, at least I have some chance. But going to the ghetto means that
I will die."

*What indication did you have of what was going on? Were your parents
keeping all this from you?*

MELSON: I remember going to the countryside to these Catholic converts. I remember they put us up in the basement and there was straw on the floor. And
I thought this was really exciting. Who would think that you could actually
sleep in the straw in the basement of a house, whereas I had always slept in a
bed? So now we're sleeping on straw.

That was an adventure for you?

MELSON: An adventure, but without any connection to the larger outside world. When my parents returned home, and my mother opened the door, there was a party going on. Hella had invited in some of her Ukrainian friends, and they were drinking and having a great time. Hella was wearing my mother's red dress, and when she saw my mother, she said, "I'm very sorry, I'm very sorry. I thought you'd be dead by now." And she chased all her friends off, took off her dress, and went back to being our maid. In the meantime, she helped protect us.

In retrospect, we're talking about righteous Gentiles. Hella definitely fit that category; she was a terrific girl. But she was also realistic: You were dead now, so I'll take your dress.

Knowing that they could not continue life as before and that their days might be numbered, with half of the Jewish population of Stanislav already massacred, Melson's mother had a bright idea.

Before the German invasion, during the "Russian period," she and her husband had met a non-Jewish couple at a café near the railroad station. Jan and Janina Zamoyski were about the same age as Melson's parents. They came from similar social and educational backgrounds, and both couples had sons about four years old. They hit it off, visited each other's houses, and went out together. The Zamoyskis were from a very aristocratic Polish family; he was a count, but like the Melsons, he had been impoverished by the Soviet occupation.

Melson's mother now went to the Zamoyskis and asked them for help.

MELSON: "My dear friends," she said, "you know our situation. You know that they are killing Jews. Our only chance is if you will give us your papers of identity. You can always get other papers of identity. You can say you lost them. You were baptized at the local church; your birth certificate is at the local church. You can go back and get your birth certificates. We, with our papers, if we are found, will be killed." The Zamoyskis were cordial and sympathetic. They thought about it a while, and they came back to her and said, "We are willing to do that, but on one condition. We are totally broke. We are living from day to day. We need money. And for 20,000 zlotys [about $5,000] we will do this."

My mother went back to my father and said, "For 20,000 zlotys they will do it." My father said, "After the Russians got through with us, who in the hell has 20,000 zlotys? We have nothing except a couple of bicycles, a typewriter, and some old suits. That's it." And he said, "It's really impossible. We don't have 20,000 zlotys." At which point my mother simply broke down crying. She realized they were trapped.

But the next day, she had another idea, which she didn't reveal to my father. She went back to the Zamoyskis and said, "We're getting the money together. The problem is I really need to see the papers before I turn it over. Could you show me the papers, because now we are talking about a business transaction? And I really need to know what it is that you have."

They brought out the papers: birth certificates, marriage certificate, all the rest. Then while they were making a little tea to serve her, they left her alone to examine them. About five minutes.

My mother was not intellectual, but being an actress, she could memorize lines quickly. And she looked at those papers, scratched some numbers and dates on her handbag with her fingernail, and tried to memorize the rest. And then she said, "Fine, thank you very much. I'll soon be coming up with the money," and she went home.

The next day she went to the local church and was introduced to the priest. "Father," she said, "don't you recognize me?" And he said, "No, I don't. I cannot. I don't know you." And she said, "Why, I'm Janina Zamoyska." And he said, "Oh, my God, I'm sorry, Countess Zamoyska! Please sit down. Can I get something for you"? He was very, very impressed. And they chatted for a while, and she said to him, "During the Soviet occupation they took everything we had, including our papers of identity. Now the Germans are here, and we desperately need these papers. We need the birth certificates and the marriage certificate. Could you get them for me?"

He called her into his study and began to question her: What was her mother's name, what was her father's name, and where were they born, the date and the week. Then he asked where she was born, what was her husband's name, and so on. Later she told me, "I remembered all of it and I made no mistake. I never faltered." And he gave her the birth certificates and the marriage certificate. And she put them into her bag. She walked out and went home.

In retrospect she remembered, "You think such stupid things when things like that happen in your life. My one thought was: Would Willie be impressed with me?" And she went home and she told him, "This is what is going to save our life." And he looked at the papers and he embraced her, and that was the beginning of our impersonation. From then on he was going to be Count Jan Zamoyski and she was going to be Countess Janina Zamoyska and their son was Babusla Zamoyski, whose nickname was Bobby. So I became Bobby, later

Robert. My birth name was Silvio, after my grandmother, whose first name was Silvia.

What was really quite incredible about the story was not only the sheer luck of it, but that the priest did not really know the Count and Countess Zamoyski. The normal thing for him to have said was, "My dear young lady, I don't know who in the hell you are. I was with the Zamoyskis last week. You are not Countess Zamoyska." Then the next thing he would have done was call the Polish or Ukrainian police or the Gestapo and be done with it. But he didn't know.

Throughout this story is the recurring theme of tremendous chutzpah and resourcefulness, and extraordinarily good luck. These were the essence of our survival. Talk about women's rights or women's power, or whatever. This is a story of the capacity of women.

In Stanislav it would have been impossible for the Melsons to use their false papers to get new identity cards, but leaving the city was no easy task. Nobody could travel without special permission — not on trains, not on highways. So Melson's mother went to a local garage and found a man and, putting on her best Marlene Dietrich manner, asked him for help. Fortunately the man was about to go to Krakow with a truckload of goods that Obersturmbannführer (SS-Lieutenant-Colonel) Wilhelm Krüger, the local Gestapo commander in Stanislav, had looted from dead Jews. The driver said he was willing to take her, but she had to pay for it.

MELSON: She said, "I have no money." He said, "Okay, but you understand you will have to pay in some other way." She said, "Fine, I understand, no problem." He said, "Okay, on Thursday I'll come over and pick you up."

He was as good as his word, and on Thursday he came over to pick us up. He had a bottle of vodka and my mother got into the cab with him in the front of the truck, and they began kissing and hugging and drinking vodka. In the meantime, my father opened the door in back of the truck and ten people were sitting there — all Poles or Ukrainians, none of them Jewish. He said it was amazing that no one recognized him, because he came from a fairly well-known family, but no one did.

I used to have a red tricycle. And I used to ride it down a hill behind our house. The tricycle attracted the attention of all the kids in the neighborhood and gave me tremendous status. When we were about to leave, I was holding that tricycle with my right hand and my mother was dragging me by my left hand. I knew that unless I held on to that tricycle, it was going to be left behind. My mother was dragging me to the truck to get in front with her, and I was trying to pull the tricycle up into the cab with me. She finally said, "You've got to leave the tricycle here, there's no room." I got hysterical, screaming until I was weak, and she yanked the tricycle out of my hand and plopped me into the truck. The truck took off. I looked back and saw Hella. She was waving back at me and at her feet was my red tricycle.

A few miles from town, the truck was halted at a checkpoint policed by German and Ukrainian guards. They were looking for Jews.

MELSON: They asked my mother and the driver to get out of the truck. They looked at the driver's papers, and my mother said, "You're looking for Jews, do you take me to be a Jew? Do you want to see my papers?" She's holding me in her arms. And the guy manning the roadblock looks at her and said to her in German, "Oh no, you keep your papers. You look like the Virgin Mary holding the little Jesus in your arms."

The Germans were suckers for blonde hair.

MELSON: Yeah, blonde hair, blue eyes, and pug noses. And the soldiers didn't bother them any further. And the truck drove off again. I still don't know what to make of it: my mother and myself in the cab of this truck, with ten Ukrainians and Poles and my father in the back, surrounded by the stuff Krüger had ripped off from the Jews. It was winter and I got under this huge comforter we brought with us and fell asleep.

Killing Jews Is Hard Work

Getting *kenkarta* (identity cards) proved relatively simple because the Melsons were not known in Krakow the way they were in Stanislav. Melson's father found employment as a salesman for the yellow pages of the local Krakow telephone directory. Making use of his German accent when he spoke Polish, he had no difficulty signing up customers, often for the most expensive ads.

MELSON: My father recalled, "I came home and I realized they were taking me for a German. They thought I was some kind of an official from some kind of a ministry. I was intimidating them." He said he went out the next day and got himself a Tyrolean hat with a shaving-type brush in it and then got himself a black leather coat. "I went dressed like that, and I didn't ask from then on what ad they wanted to buy, I said, 'You'll buy such and such an ad for this business.' And they signed on the dotted line, and I started making a lot of money."

At this time, late 1941–early 1942, Poland had a variety of Schindler-type businesses, run by German profiteers who went there to make as much money as they could. Goods, any kind of goods, were very scarce, but Melson's father came upon a company based in Warsaw, run by a certain Walter Bonaburger, which sold plastic raincoats and plastic aprons. His father told Bonaburger that he was a free-lance salesman who wanted to expand his market to Krakow. Bonaburger agreed to sell him raincoats at twenty-five zlotys per coat. Melson's father next went to the German supply ministry for the General Government, where he talked with Herr Siegel, the minister-director himself.

MELSON: My father said to him, "I want to do a business with you." And the guy said, "I've got nothing to sell." So my father said, "I don't want to buy anything, I want to sell you something." The guy asked, "Yeah, what do you have to sell?" My father told him that he had raincoats. Siegel replied, "How did you get raincoats? This is impossible." When my father told him that he got raincoats from Bonaburger in Warsaw, Siegel asked him how many raincoats he was talking about. My father said, "How many do you want to buy?" Siegel said, "I can buy forty thousand raincoats." And my father said, "Each raincoat costs forty zlotys." And the guy said, "It's too much." My father said, "Mr. Siegel, I'll tell you what: whatever money I make, I can do what I want with. I can buy my wife a new silver fox, I can get a girlfriend, or we can share it. It's up to you." That was the way my father talked. And Mr. Siegel said, "Well, let me think about it."

The next day, when they had coffee together, my father had a thousand zlotys in an envelope and he said, "Mr. Siegel, before you even start telling me anything, here is a thousand zlotys. Put it in your pocket, and then we will talk." Mr. Siegel took the thousand zlotys, put it in his pocket, and as my father said, they were in business.

The guy bought the forty thousand raincoats at forty zlotys each. My father had fifteen zlotys per coat, not counting the "profit" he shared with Siegel, and he made a hell of a lot of money. And he was making a lot of money for Walter Bonaburger at the same time.

This new affluence, and his contacts with Bonaburger, allowed the Melsons to move from the Polish area of Krakow into the restricted German area. Not only was it a more affluent district, but it also was, ironically, a safer area, since Poles were more likely to discover who was and who was not a Jew or to become suspicious of somebody with such an aristocratic name.

The apartment the Melsons inhabited in this area was brand new. So was the furniture. They had a telephone and a maid. And next door was SS Standartenführer (Colonel) Kruk, a short, fat man whose job it was to kill Jews!

MELSON: Colonel Kruk came in one day, and he said to my mother, "My wife is coming next week. You will come and clean my apartment," and then he left. When my father came back from the office and heard the story, he was outraged. He went over to Colonel Kruk's apartment and said, "I am Count Zamoyski. You will never to speak to my wife like this." And then he said, "But here is a bottle of schnapps, let's have a drink. I have a maid, so if you need help cleaning your house, she'll come and help you." And they finished the bottle of schnapps together.

Colonel Kruk became so friendly with us that he wouldn't leave us alone. He was at our place almost every night, telling my parents how hard his work was, how many Poles he had to hang that day, how many Jews he had to kill, how terribly difficult the work was. And my parents were sympathizing with him.

What was your relationship to Kruk?

MELSON: In the back of this apartment house was a construction site. There were planks and holes and machinery. It was a great playground and the neighborhood kids loved it. One of the games we had was "King of the Mountain." And one day, I happened to be at the top of this heap and another little kid came up, trying to get to the top, and I pushed him off. The kid rolled down and scratched himself a little bit and he began crying. So then I walked down the hill, and I started for home.

This little kid waited for me and threw a rock, which hit me on the side of the head, and I had blood pouring into my eyes. I rushed home crying, and my mother got terribly upset, and without thinking, she went to Colonel Kruk to get a doctor. Colonel Kruk came out in his jodhpurs and his undershirt, his hair uncombed. He was very fond of me, and he was outraged. He got his gun, started waving it around, and swore he was going to kill the little kid who had hit me. My mother got ahold of him and said, "That's okay. You don't need to do that. Bobby will be okay." And she calmed him down. I was lying there seeing this guy waving his gun around. I didn't care if he was going to kill anybody or not. But I found it strange.

Was your cover ever blown?

MELSON: Two or three times my parents got calls. "Come to the Gestapo, we need to talk to you." They would hide and wouldn't know what to do. But then they would go back to the apartment, and the Gestapo didn't come.

They didn't know what it was about?

MELSON: They didn't know. They'd simply get a call, come to the Gestapo on such and such a day. After the second call, we stayed with a Polish family we knew who realized that we were Jews. The woman said to my mother, "You don't have to play this charade; we know who you are." My mother said, "How do you know?" The woman replied, "We can sense it. We know what you are doing, but we'll help you."

Another couple that helped us out was a German couple, the Turmans. Her name was Greta Turman. Her husband, whose name my mother doesn't remember, was an older man who was head of the forestry department in the General Government. My father wanted to sell him these plastic industrial aprons that Bonaburger had, and they hit if off tremendously and became great buddies. Again, when the Gestapo came looking for us, my parents went to the Turmans and said, "The Gestapo is looking for us."

They knew we were Polish. But what would a family like the Zamoyskis be doing trying to hide from the Gestapo in the middle of the night? The Turmans said, "Come and stay with us." Then one of them turned to my mother and said, "You are not Jewish, but your husband is." And my mother said, "Of course not, how could you possibly think that?" And they said, "Well, I may be wrong." But in any case, here were two couples who were willing to help.

You were circumcised. If that were discovered, you certainly would be in deep trouble. Did your parents alert you to the danger?

MELSON: Exactly. I was told never, ever to pee in the street, never whip it out, but go behind a bush or a car. Never, ever, do that. One of the big beatings I got from my father was because of that. I was coming home from a movie with some friends and I peed in the street. When my father got wind of that, he gave me a real beating. But I just assumed that it was impolite to pee in the street. All of my other friends were peeing in the street, but I wasn't supposed to do that.

So you didn't know you shouldn't do it because you were Jewish?

MELSON: Of course not. I had no idea I was Jewish until the end of the war, when my parents told me.

What did you think you were?

MELSON: During the war, I got the sense that we were in constant danger. There was a constant sense of tension, a constant sense of danger, a constant sense that something was terribly wrong. A constant sense that secrets were going on that they were not telling me. I had a sense of being excluded in some peculiar way that I didn't understand.

Did you go to church?

MELSON: Of course we went to church. We celebrated Christmas.

So you gave every appearance of being observant, upper-class Polish Catholics?

MELSON: Either upper-class Polish Catholics, or possibly *Volksdeutsche* (ethnically German). A lot of people who thought that Poles were not allowed to live in the area where we were living assumed that we were really German.

How did your parents acquire the worship practices of Catholics?

MELSON: The Polish couple who hid us and discovered we were Jews helped us out. They essentially taught my parents how to go through the motions of being Catholic. I remember going to confession, and I would go to mass and take the Eucharist.

In trying to convert some of the zlotys he made into dollars, a hard currency, or jewelry, Melson's father came into contact with black marketers, some of whom either discovered or suspected that he was Jewish and began to blackmail him. So the father bribed a certain

Captain Godfried, who was connected to the economics ministry and had business in Bohemia, to take him and his family to Prague. Godfried did not suspect the Melsons were Jewish; he took them for upper-class Polish Catholics.

A Feeling of Being Abandoned

The father went first. He had letters from Captain Godfried and Bonaburger and others signifying that he was *kriegswichtig,* important to the war effort. There were many more goods in Bohemia than in Poland, and he set up shop and began supplying his Polish business associates with everything he could get, making more money than before. When he was established, he arranged papers *(Ausweise)* for his wife and son to come to Prague. They were escorted by Captain Godfried.

MELSON: My mother posed as Godfried's girlfriend. My mother put a bandana around my face, because I was not supposed to speak Polish on the train. I wasn't supposed to say anything, and if someone asked me what my name was or anything, I was supposed to indicate that I had a toothache and couldn't speak by pointing to my face. I remember the train and how scary it was to go through a tunnel and come out on the other side. I remember my mother saying, "Don't put your hand out the window because the telephone pole is going to knock it off." Then we came to the Prague station and my father was waiting for us. And I remember with him was a very pretty young woman, his "business partner." Her name was Rhea. She was a Czech woman whose husband was a customs inspector. My father needed somebody like that to facilitate his shipments back to Poland. And he started an affair with Rhea.

You are not supposed to do things like that during uncertain times. Not only was it dangerous because he was circumcised, but such an entanglement could be enormously risky. It was one of those crazy things. I mean, here we were fleeing from the Nazis, and my father was having an affair with Rhea. But that's the reality of things.

For me, in addition to the wartime tensions, there were now these family tensions. My mother and me against my father and Rhea. And my father was wheeling and dealing and making money, and anybody who was suspicious, he bribed them off. As he later told me, "Money was the oxygen that kept us going. Without it we would have been in a lot of trouble."

The Melsons lived to the east of Prague in the resort town of Poděbrady. They had a maid and a governess for Robert—a fanatical Catholic named Bertha who rapped his knuckles whenever he made a mistake in his arithmetic and drilled into him the notion that he should become a Roman Catholic priest. Robert never took off his clothes in front of Miss Bertha, so she never discovered he was circumcised. In fact, she was impressed by his modesty. Robert's best friend was Freddy, the son of one of his father's business associates.

MELSON: We went to birthday parties, we went to Christmas parties, we decorated the tree together, we played together with little German and Swiss friends downstairs. Because I was supposed to be Polish, I was always stuck together with the Czech kids. We were always playing war. We were always the Russians, they were always the Germans. We always lost, and we always understood that we were supposed to lose, because if we didn't lose, we might get into trouble.

I also remember a Jewish woman walking by once, and some of these kids taunted her. At Eastertime, my governess took me to the old town in Prague to a passion play. And I saw Jesus carrying a cross and he was surrounded by people in hideous masks who were whipping him. And I said to Miss Bertha, "Who are these people, who are these?" She said to me, "They're Jews!" obviously outraged at these horrible creatures who were whipping our savior, our sweet Jesus.

It was now 1944. One day, word came from Prague that his father had been arrested. He had been suspected of helping a Jewish woman. Melson's mother feared that it would only be a matter of time before they discovered her husband's true identity. Finally, she got a notice to appear before a certain Standartenführer Bartelt of the Yiddische Abteilung at Gestapo headquarters. She could not take her son with her, because if they discovered he was circumcised, that would be the end. To get him out of the way, she therefore made arrangements with a Mrs. Vasseli to look after him until the end of the war. She had met Mrs. Vasseli by chance in the park of the Poděbrady hospital, to which Mrs. Vasseli had come from her home in Slovakia to receive fertility drugs. Mrs. Vassili had no children of her own and willingly agreed.

MELSON: So one evening we went to the railroad station and Mrs. Vassili was there. And my mother said, "We will be seeing each other soon, don't worry. Be a good boy and don't show your private parts to anybody and be polite. And don't forget your name is Zamoyski." And I had this feeling that I was being abandoned. My father had been arrested by the Gestapo, my mother was going to try to get him out, and I was going with a stranger. I had been conditioned to always look different from the way I felt. And I knew that I now had to look cheerful and happy and cute.

Sitting next to Mrs. Vassili, with the train pulling off, I saw my mother running behind the train and waving to me. I waved back while Mrs. Vassili was telling me they had a farm and what animals they had and how happy I would be and how wonderful it would be. I was saying, "Yes. It will be nice, thank you very much," but I felt as if there were a pit in my stomach.

R obert lived with the Vassilis about four months, until he was sent back to his mother.

MELSON: I got off the train in Prague holding a bag and in the crush of people I saw a very thin man. He had an eye patch and he was trying to get to me. And I said to myself, "Who is this man who is trying to get to me?" And I tried to run away from him. I ran to the station's coffee shop, where Mrs. Vassili told me my mother would be waiting. I saw my mother there and she was drinking coffee, and this man was coming after me. And I went up to her, and she was laughing. I thought that she'd gone crazy. And I pulled at her and I said, "Mother, I think there is somebody chasing us." And she was laughing. And this guy came up and grabbed me and I looked at him and I realized he was my father. That must have been in March 1945, close to the end of the war.

But truly the most incredible part of the story was how my mother managed to get my father released.

After I was sent off with Mrs. Vassili, my mother went to Prague. She had been depressed, drinking and chain smoking, but she pulled herself together. She went to a beauty parlor, had her hair platinumed. In an overnight bag, she put some jewelry and the sexiest lingerie she could find, and trotted off to the Gestapo. As she said, "I was dressed to the teeth, the best clothes I had: a nutria coat and a hat. And wherever I went the people deferred to me."

However, she was full of apprehension and had fortified herself with a few swings of vodka. "They are probably going to kill me," she thought, "but this is not the time to be polite. I mean, what have I got to be polite for? I'm just going to tell him what I think."

So in this mood, she went to the Poncrats prison to see Colonel Bartelt. She entered and told the secretary, "I am Countess Zamoyska and I need to speak to Colonel Bartelt." Bartelt, who had sent her the summons, was the arresting officer and in charge of the case.

The secretary kept her waiting before she escorted her in to see Colonel Bartelt. When my mother entered his office, he was writing at his desk and didn't look up. And she said to him, "Hello, Colonel Bartelt. I'm Countess Zamoyska." And he said, "I know who you are." And she said to him, "I have difficulty talking to people who do not look at me." And he said, "I don't look at you, my dear lady, because you had a notice to come here two weeks ago and you disobeyed." And she said, "I disobeyed for a good reason."

He looked up at her, and said, "Why did you disobey?" And she said, "I hate the Gestapo, I think you are a pack of mad dogs!" He was taken aback. "How dare you speak to me like that?" he said, rising from his seat. And she replied, "I speak to you like that because that's the way it is. I think you are a bunch of rabid dogs. And that's why I was afraid to come." At which point he said, "Just wait a second," and he called out to an associate, "Kurt, come in here." When Kurt entered, Bartelt said to my mother, "Now, you tell him what you told me." And she repeated the same thing.

Kurt started laughing. They both started laughing. It was so ridiculous, just absurd. And she said to Bartelt, "I'm standing. If you were a gentleman, you would pull over a chair." And he did. He got up and fetched a chair, and she said, "Please hang up my coat." And he came over and hung up the coat, and she sat down and she said, "I didn't bring any cigarettes with me, could I have a cigarette?" And he told Kurt to get her a cigarette. And he said, "Okay, so why did you come?"

"Well, you've arrested my husband," she said. "I want to get him out of here." And he said, "Well, you are not going to get him out of here for free." She said, "I'm prepared for this." And she pulls out her underwear, her negligee, and she said, "There, I'm ready." He started laughing even more and he gave her clothes back to her.

He was totally taken with her. She was wearing this coat, and she was quite attractive, kind of sexy and kind of naive. And he thought she was a very charming and funny woman. (By then he had found the guy who had helped the Jewish woman escape and had him sent to Theresienstadt, but my mother only found out about that later.) And Bartelt said to her, "Look, you want to get your husband out. It will cost you something." He said, "I'll be through here in another hour. We will go out to dinner." And she said to him, "Look, I will be delighted to go out to dinner with you, but not tonight. I am not in the mood for it tonight. Make it the next time I come back to Prague." He said, "Fine."

She went back to Poděbrady and a while later got a call from Mrs. Bartelt, who happened to be her husband's secretary. And Mrs. Bartelt said, "Countess, the reason we haven't called you is because it would be dangerous for you to come to the Gestapo now. Wait a few more weeks and we will call you again. Then you can come and pick up your husband."

My mother waited a few more weeks. She got another phone call. She went back to Bartelt's office. The door opened and my father came in. He had lost thirty kilos (sixty-six pounds). He had been badly beaten and looked a mess.

And my father was raving and going on about German culture and that he was not a Jew and demanding to know how he could have been arrested and who was this woman. He was completely out of his mind. And Bartelt said to my mother, "Don't worry, most people who come from our prisons are slightly crazy at first."

My mother had brought some food for him and my father ate it and immediately threw up. Then he was returned to prison and my mother returned to Poděbrady.

Again, she waited for Bartelt's phone call. And the next time she came, my father was released. He was wearing an eye patch because he had been so badly beaten. That's why I didn't recognize him. I simply didn't recognize him. He looked like a scarecrow.

The Gestapo never discovered your father had been circumcised?

MELSON: No. A number of times we were in Gestapo custody, and my father was never asked to take down his pants to be checked for circumcision. He never knew why he wasn't.

An Instinct for Danger: Gavriel Salvendy

"Where are these bloody Jews? Have you seen any bloody Jews?"

Anything Could Happen

After the Wehrmacht's defeat in the Battle of Kursk in July 1943, the Hungarian government tried to distance itself from its German ally. Hitler allowed the Hungarian army to disengage from operations on the eastern front. It was no big loss from the German point of view, since Hungarian troops were not known for their discipline, bravery, or reliability, but the Führer continued to demand that the Hungarians furnish him with supplies and raw materials. He also pressed for the complete elimination of the Jewish presence in Hungary, demanding that the Jews be rounded up and handed over to the Reich for disposal. But the Hungarian government refused, claiming that any "final solution" of the Jews had to wait until after the war.

Although Hungarian conservatives were antisemitic, they were not inclined to mass murder. They regarded the "Jewish Problem" as a religious rather than a racial issue, agreeing with the position of the Hungarian Catholic Church that these "Christ killers" could be reformed through conversion. The conservatives also hated the Jews because they erroneously believed them to be politically subversive. However, although some Jews might be agents of Bolshevism, most feared revolution and actively opposed it.

In truth the Hungarian ruling classes had less to fear from any Jewish political or economic threat than they did from the pro-Nazi activists on their own radical Right. This collection of fascists and ultraradicals was not satisfied with just denigrating Jews. Rather, they wanted to move Hungary within the German orbit and were prepared to deliver up their country's Jews to Hitler as the price for his help in putting them in power. They seemed unaware that this strategy could result in a loss of their country's independence. Hitler wasted no time. Suspecting that the current Hungarian government of Miklós Kállay was negotiating with the Allies to change sides, he ordered his army to seize control of the country in Operation Margaret.

On March 19, 1944, units of the Wehrmacht invaded Hungary, overthrew the government, and installed a Reich plenipotentiary in Budapest. As German troops poured across the border, Hungarian fascists began arresting opposition politicians and started going after the country's 800,000 Jews, heretofore spared from destruction. Hitler's top priority was to end Hungary's mild treatment of its Jews, and he sent Adolf Eichmann to Budapest as head of a *Sondereinsatzkommando,* a special SS task force, to supervise his campaign of destruction.

Eichmann was amazed at the degree of acquiescence, support, and willing participation he received from the new Hungarian government and from a large part of the Hungarian people. Hungarian conservatives might not have pushed for the extermination of the Jews, but they nonetheless helped establish and reinforce the intolerance and bigotry on which the implementation of that policy was based. Eichmann even successfully co-opted local Jewish leaders into helping him with identification, classification, and assemblage. *Judenräte,* Jewish councils, were formed in Budapest and various provincial cities. Eichmann promised that if his orders were carried out obediently and peacefully, no harm would come to the Jews.

The new German puppet government gave Hungary a full set of Nürnberg Laws: all Jews were ordered to wear Stars of David, their assets and valuables worth over three thousand pengös (about three hundred dollars) were expropriated, they were excluded from public service and the professions, and their businesses were closed. Their bicycles, radios, telephones, and cars were confiscated. They were excluded from restaurants, hotels, cafés, and parks and forbidden to travel except by special permission. All the special exemptions and privileges certain Jews had received from previous Hungarian governments immediately disappeared. Henceforth, a Jew was a Jew, even those who had converted to Christianity, and all their property was forfeit.

GAVRIEL SALVENDY: Both my father and grandfather were tipped off when our family was targeted for deportation by a person from the city government who was concerned with Jewish affairs. He came to our house and told Father: "Get away quickly, because we are coming for you tomorrow morning, and I don't want to have to deport you." If that fellow hadn't come to warn us, we probably wouldn't be alive.

The family got together and decided to split up into smaller groups, so as not to attract attention, and go into hiding in the countryside. First, we found refuge in a house in a lower-class area of Rimavska Sobota. We were all there: my mother's father (her mother had died before), my grandparents from my father's side, my father, my mother, my brother, and I. It was crazy, because it wasn't really a hiding place.

Indeed, one morning the Hungarian gendarmerie came with an arrest warrant for my grandfather. My mother's father was about seventy-four at the time, and they dragged him in front of us and out the door. My mother got absolutely hysterical. That was a very dreadful experience, especially for a kid.

My grandfather was taken away because he was not a Salvendy. He was transported to Auschwitz, and all indications are that he was taken straight to the gas chamber.

Shortly afterwards, we took refuge in a farmhouse on a piece of property that my father had owned before it was confiscated. It had a one-bedroom house with an outside privy. My brother and I had the job of emptying the chamber pot, and sometimes we also went to a neighbor's house, maybe two hundred yards away, to get some food.

One time, when we were in the neighbor's house, three Hungarian policemen with dogs came to the door looking for Jews. The neighbor quickly hid us under the bed in the next room.

"Where are these bloody Jews? Have you seen any bloody Jews?" one of the gendarmes demanded.

The room where we were wasn't heated and the floor was very cold, and I wanted to cough. My brother put his hand over my mouth and held me so tight I thought I was going to suffocate. It was one of the scariest moments of my life. Even now I sometimes dream about it and wake up in fear. I thought we were going to die there, that any moment the door would open and we would be discovered. If they had just opened the door, they probably would have discovered us, and I wouldn't be sitting here talking to you now. After that experience, my father decided we were not safe there, and he sent someone he trusted to look for another farm where we could go.

Were these farmers protecting you because they were being paid, or were they "righteous Gentiles"?

SALVENDY: Righteous Gentiles. There was no question of payment. My parents had no money at that point. They simply had nothing.

But these were people your parents knew?

SALVENDY: They had worked for my parents. They were employees of the farm.

But they could just as well have betrayed you to the Germans.

SALVENDY: Yes. But they were willing to risk their lives to shelter us and bring us food. Actually, my grandfather and my father always had incredibly good relations with their workers. My grandfather would sit down with the lowest worker and eat dinner with him. He gave him as much respect as he would have given a professor, and people liked him for it. My father was the same way. They both were very generous to their employees. Always.

The Salvendys traveled in an ox cart by night to their new hiding place. Gavriel's father disguised himself as a woman in order to avoid questions about why he was not in the military. During the trip, the Hungarian police once stopped them and took them to their local headquarters. Salvendy still does not know why they were eventually allowed to go on their way—his mother and father both refused to talk about it afterwards. They had tremendously bad feelings about the experience and never clarified the mystery.

At their new place of refuge, Salvendy and his brother were almost discovered again. They were outside playing, acting like farm kids, when they saw four or five policemen approaching the farm, looking for Jews.

SALVENDY: We quickly burrowed into a huge haystack that was in the field, going so deep we nearly suffocated. While we were inside, some of these fellows began poking their bayonets into the straw, asking, "Is there anybody there?" We were really scared, my brother and I. Really scared. Today, I probably would have a heart attack. Fortunately, they did not hit either of us.

Where were your parents while this was going on?

SALVENDY: They were hiding in the farmer's house. But it's amazing how we had this intuition to dig into the haystack and hide.

You have had that automatic instinct for danger before. Where do you think it came from?

SALVENDY: I think it just came naturally. It was just one of those things. Nobody really said anything about it. I remember my mother always telling me to be quiet. Maybe that had an effect. My mother herself was always very quiet, but now she was really on the verge of hysteria. She was always cuddling us in her arms. "We just stick together," she said. "Let's just stick together. Wherever we go, we'll go together."

At some point, whether instinctively or not, you've developed a strong sense of survival.

SALVENDY: If you are a mature adult, you might be able to analyze it. But we were not smart enough to think about it at that age. After the haystack episode, things were quiet for several months, until the Russians liberated the area.

By the summer of 1944, the Soviet army was able to strike at will. With more than three hundred divisions and good lateral communications between northern and southern fronts, the Soviet offensive first attacked the Leningrad sector, securing the Baltic flank, then it drove into Belorussia. But by the end of July, most of Poland east of the Vistula had been liberated.

At the same time, Soviet forces smashed the German and Romanian armies in the southern Ukraine, opening up the lower Danube. The Soviets feared that a direct push toward Berlin without first securing the Balkans might allow the Bulgarians, Romanians, and Hungarians time to establish governments free from Communist influence, and consequently they kept their major effort here.

The offensive brought about the collapse of the pro-Nazi Hungarian government, but not an end to anti-Jewish savagery. Massacres, deportations, and evacuations of Jews continued until the spring of 1945, when the Red Army finally controlled the entire country.

SALVENDY: Toward the end of the war, anything could happen. The region around Rimavska Sobota became a major battleground between the Russians and the Germans. And the little farm where we had found asylum suddenly became a field hospital for the Soviet army. The kitchen became bloodstained, its table used for surgical operations. The whole room wasn't much bigger than my office and there was blood everywhere. Everywhere.

We were relieved when the Russians came. It was good that my father had been in the Ukraine for about a year and a half, because he picked up some Russian. He could talk to them and welcome them, and so they treated us very well. But it was still dangerous to be in a war zone. So we got a couple of horses and a cart and took off to another location, this time to hide in a small village.

Munkács was liberated on October 26, 1944, Košice on January 20, and Budapest on February 12. The Slovakian city of Bratislava fell on April 7, but not before the SS murdered all 497 members of a Hungarian Jewish labor battalion.

SALVENDY: Before we returned to Rimavska Sobota, we stayed in this small village for a few months so my father could make some money. With the cart and the horses we had, he started his own delivery business, and when he had earned enough, we returned home.

Anna Berkovitz
in Sweden,
July/August 1945.

William Melson, né Wulf Mendelssohn,
passing as Count Jan Zamoyski,
Prague, 1944.

Robert Melson and his mother
in Brussels, 1945 or 1946.

The house was ruined and badly needed repairs. All the furniture had disappeared. The Hungarian soldiers who had been garrisoned there had even found the jewelry, silver, and gold coins that had been buried in the basement. I guess my parents didn't do a very good job of hiding them.

For several months, all the family lived together in that house — parents, grandparents, and nieces — all those of us who had survived. We had no proper beds, furniture, or amenities, so it was rather uncomfortable.

My brother and I started to build our own little house out of the materials used to repair the larger dwelling. We found some old swords that had been hidden in the attic, and we took them to our house so that we would be able to protect ourselves against a German attack. Defending ourselves was a top priority.

After the war, we had no other Jewish boys to play with. They were all gone. Not one had returned. There were practically no Jewish people left in Rimavska Sobota. Most had been sent to Auschwitz, where they disappeared. Out of one hundred Jewish families existing in Rimavska Sobota before the war, I would estimate that only five survived.

The synagogue was gone. With Jewish life almost completely destroyed, my parents thought that the best thing for their children was to have them converted to Christianity. Our parents didn't want us to suffer anymore by being Jews, especially in school, where you had to attend religious class one hour a day. There were no Jewish classes because the total of all Jews could be counted on two hands. So my brother and I became Protestants and went to the Protestant church.

When we immigrated to Israel, we said, "The heck with Protestantism." Funny thing, though, we never got officially converted back, so I guess we're still technically Protestants.

You trace your own survival to righteous Gentiles?

SALVENDY: Definitely. We had help from the Gentile community, especially from the people who had worked for my father. But we also had incredible luck. Without both we could not have survived.

How many members of the immediate family didn't survive?

SALVENDY: My grandfather definitely died at Auschwitz. People we knew who were deported with him saw him selected for the line that went straight to the gas chambers. My mother's sister, who had been in a mental institution, was either deported or killed beforehand. We don't know her exact fate, but she also perished. But the others — my parents, my father's parents, my father's sister, my brother, and myself—we all made it. Seven out of nine. We were a fairly small family. Many of the Jewish families at that time had four, five, six, and seven children.

Given the circumstances, your family had a remarkable rate of survival.

SALVENDY: Absolutely. No question about it. Nobody, nobody came back the way we came back. Nobody. Nobody. Absolutely nobody.

The Camp of Death: Anna Berkovitz

"Even though Auschwitz was much more horrible than the ghetto, leaving home was the most traumatic thing."

Transportation to the North

With the Soviet armies driving headlong toward the Hungarian frontier, the Nazis made "cleansing" the Jews from Hungary's eastern provinces a top priority. Considering the high concentrations in Ruthenia, they had a field day. But the Germans did not have to act alone. Eichmann recalled that Hungary was the only country where the Germans could not keep up with the local authorities. He said that they got rid of their Jews like sour beer.

ANNA BERKOVITZ: As soon as the Germans arrived, all the Jews were required to wear yellow stars. You were immediately arrested if you were caught without one. I remember my aunt and my grandmother cutting out some materials and putting Jewish stars on the backs and fronts of our clothes. The new laws also decreed that the Jews could not leave town. But my grandfather thought I would be better off with my parents in the Carpathian village of Bustahaza, and he hired a taxicab to have me and two other children driven there. The ride through the mountains took about three hours.

When we got there, I was terribly upset because I was missing school. So after a week, I called my aunt in Munkács and told her to talk to the principal and tell him that I would be back soon and that he should get all my assignments from my teachers so I could make up the work I missed. I felt very upset because I was sitting around doing nothing.

On April 1, we were ordered to pack all the belongings we each could in two suitcases and report to the synagogue in the village at nine o'clock the next morning. My father came home with the news that the police would come for us, and then he ran into the bathroom and threw up. My father was, as I said, very pessimistic, and whenever he got very emotional, he got sick. My mother was better able to handle crises and was like a rock. She told him to calm down and assured him that we would get through this one.

We packed only as many clothes as we could carry. Since we couldn't take jewelry and silverware with us, we tried to hide it. We had a pantry above our basement, and we put some stuff in there. At night our neighbor Kleinmann brought over his wife's jewelry and their silverware, and we put it together with ours in that pantry, and my father and Mr. Kleinmann covered it up with a wall.

While they were working, there was a knock on the door, and I was sent to see who it was. It was the maid from one of our non-Jewish friends, whose Christmas tree I used to help decorate. We were often invited to some of their celebrations. The maid had a handful of pengös, and she said that her mistress felt that we wouldn't need our jewelry anymore, and she thought that maybe we would like to sell it. I slammed the door in her face.

The next morning, the police came, and we went to the synagogue, where we stayed all that day and night. That was the first time I had been to the synagogue. They said that all those who had served on the Russian front would be exempt, but that didn't happen. The only one who got excused was a next-door neighbor, a woman, who was the only pediatrician in the entire area. They also allowed a young woman to remain with her eighty-year-old grandmother, who was dying. But after a week, both the doctor and the granddaughter were taken to the ghetto.

We were put on trains, and after a three- or four-hour ride, arrived in Mátészalka, a collection point in eastern Hungary. When the woman whose grandmother died later joined us there, she told us that after we left, all our homes were immediately looted and were now completely empty.

Did you know what happened to the other Jews back in Munkács?

BERKOVITZ: Because Munkács had a sizeable Jewish population, they designated a whole section of the town as a ghetto. If you already didn't live in that area, you had to move there. My grandparents lived in a part of town that was not designated as a ghetto, so they had to leave their house. I never saw them again.

I still have nightmares about leaving home. Even though Auschwitz was much more horrible than the ghetto, leaving home was the most traumatic thing. I still have this dream in which I'm getting twenty-four hours' notice to pack and leave my home, not knowing where I'm going. I see my parents. I see the German soldiers. I see the Hungarian soldiers. And I'm saying, "I'm absolutely not going, I'm absolutely not going, I'm going to hide, I'm going to do this, I'm going to do that, but I'm absolutely not going." I see my old house. I see myself jumping out of the window. I'm trying to escape, but they are coming to get me.

I very seldom dream about the concentration camp. I very seldom dream about my family here in the United States. In my dreams I see my family in Hungary: my grandparents, my mother, my father. I'm reliving the time when we had to leave our home. I see other snatches. I see the German soldiers. I see the Hungarian soldiers. I don't make any distinction between them. I see my school. But now those memories are fading.

> *Why do you think you dream about these things rather than about Auschwitz?*

BERKOVITZ: I really don't know. Perhaps because the camp was so unique and so horrible that I'm blocking it out. Maybe because losing everything—home, family, identity—was such a basic trauma.

> *What consequences have these unpleasant memories had on your daily living?*

BERKOVITZ: No serious consequences. Perhaps I fear new situations more than other people. It's like I'm leading a double life. After I have one of these dreams I always wake and tell my husband. And he tells me one of his "bad dreams," which is such a mild dream that I say, "You consider this a bad dream? When I have a bad dream it really is a bad dream."

> *What were the conditions like in Mátészalka?*

BERKOVITZ: There were so many people who had already been put into the ghetto that they didn't have any more room, so they put the later arrivals in a Jewish cemetery, which had been fenced in. No tents, no facilities, nothing. We had to sit on the gravestones.

I remember going to sleep in that cemetery and looking up at the sky. This was the first time I noticed how beautiful the sky was. I felt I could reach up and touch the millions of stars. Every time I see a sky with stars, I think of this time.

The next morning, my father went into the village and ran into one of his buddies, who had been with him in the labor battalion. The guy was from this town, and he told my father that my father, his family, and friends could move into a big storage area they had under the roof of their house. This was one of those old-fashioned attics that could be reached only with a ladder from the outside. Eventually about fifty people came to live there.

Was there a shortage of food?

BERKOVITZ: I don't remember being hungry. We had beans, there was community cooking. People cooked outside on open stoves. Sometimes my father and his friend would bring greens and baked bread.

What did you do for sanitation?

BERKOVITZ: It was very primitive, but while we were there some Hungarian policemen came and said they needed a group of women to go and clean the houses that had been confiscated from the Jews. So we volunteered because these houses had bathrooms. But the experience was horrible, because the people who had lived there were now gone. It was spring, and the flowers were blooming, the gardens were beautiful. The houses that we were cleaning were absolutely empty. But I went there because I wanted to take a shower.

We were in that attic for about four weeks when word came that we were going farther into Hungary. They did not tell us that we were being deported to Auschwitz. We were taken in several groups. Since my father was a member of the Jewish council, we were not put on the first transport, but the third or fourth. We are talking about end of May 1944.

At this stage, people were beginning to form really close unions. Families bonding with other families. We had been the neighbors of the Kleinmanns', but hadn't been all that close. Now in the ghetto we became just like one family. Judith Kleinmann, their nine-year-old daughter, and I used to sleep together under one blanket in that attic. So we were planning to stick together with the Kleinmanns. However, Judith Kleinmann came down with the measles. So we had to separate. And that, of course, saved my life.

Had we stuck together, I would have been with my mother and Mrs. Kleinmann and nine-year-old Judith. At Auschwitz they separated the men from the women, and then they separated the women with children from the women without children. If you looked younger than sixteen or older than forty, you went with the women with children. This last group went directly to the gas chambers. If we had not been separated from the Kleinmanns, we would have all been put together and we would have all perished.

But people did not know what was waiting for them. My father's brother and his brother's wife, who lived in Czechoslovakia, had a six-year-old son, whom they had smuggled to his sister and her husband in Hungary. When my aunt was sent to Auschwitz, she had little Yanik with her, and both went directly to the gas chamber. People didn't give up their children. They naturally wanted to take care of them. But having children with you when you arrived at Auschwitz was a death sentence.

The Auschwitz-Birkenau death camp began before the war as a Polish labor exchange. Later the Polish army commandeered the facilities for soldiers' barracks. The Wehrmacht took over after the invasion of Poland in September, but on April 27, 1940, leased it to the SS for use as a holding pen for recalcitrant Poles pending their transfer to work camps. The new SS owners soon changed the temporary detention center into a permanent concentration camp. Materials at first were in such short supply that camp commander Rudolf Höss even had to scrounge around for enough barbed wire to secure the camp's perimeter. Höss also commissioned the camp's most lasting symbol: the forged-iron entrance gate with the infamous words "Arbeit macht frei" (Work leads to freedom)—a false promise, to be sure, but one that underlined the camp's initial purpose.

The Counting and the Selection

The Auschwitz area, which had not been part of the German Reich since 1457, now became part of the newly created province of Upper Silesia, an area to be cleared of its native inhabitants, exploited for its resources, and prepared for German "resettlement." The concentration camp became a center for the extraction of nearby sand and gravel, raw materials intended for Third Reich building projects. When I. G. Farben decided to build a synthetic rubber plant at nearby Monowitz, it became a major center of forced labor.

The high mortality rate among the slave labor population led to the building of Auschwitz's first crematorium, installed as a hygienic device, not a means of mass murder. The death toll kept pace with the increasing supply of forced labor, especially after the German attack on the Soviet Union brought forth a steady supply of captured Soviet soldiers. However, this source came to an end when

Hermann Göring, as head of the Four-Year Plan, gained control over the POWs. Himmler now had to concentrate on getting his labor from the Jews.

The Wannsee Conference of January 20, 1942, cleared the way for the development of an annihilation center, and on July 4, 1942, the first selection upon arrival was held. The annihilation of the Jews became Heinrich Himmler's supreme gift to the ideal of the "Master Race"—more intensely pursued after he was convinced Germany would lose the war. In achieving his goal, he was supported by countless Nazi ideologues, true believers, murderers, and thugs. But help also came from the ordinary people: the civil servants, architects, industrialists, agronomists, chemists, geologists, construction engineers, bookkeepers, and accountants—all those who could view this most horrendous enterprise as a technical problem.

The deportation of the Hungarian Jews to Auschwitz began on May 15, 1944. The railroad trip from Mátészalka first went west toward central Hungary then turned north, crossing Slovakia into Greater Germany. From Tarnow the train headed east again through Krakow and then on to Auschwitz. From sub-Carpathian Ruthenia and northern Transylvania 290,000 Jews were evacuated. Transports arrived daily, carrying between two to three thousand Jews, a hundred or more packed into each of the cars. There was only one water bucket and one waste bucket for the entire four-day trip. And no food, save what the deportees managed to bring themselves. The trains bore the deceptive inscription: "German Workers' Resettlement." Thousands died en route before reaching the final destination. Many of these were suicides.

BERKOVITZ: Our reception at Auschwitz [actually the Birkenau section of the camp] was just like the scene recreated in the film *Schinder's List*. It was an absolute insane asylum, an absolute madhouse. Dogs barking, people screaming, Germans shouting, people shoving. It was complete pandemonium. The only thing that we understood were the orders for the men to go in one line and the women in the other. My father looked at me and at my mother. She was wearing a black kerchief around her head, and my father ripped off the kerchief and told her to put it around my head. And that's the last time I ever saw my father. I had two long braids, and I put the kerchief over them, and the Germans never asked me how old I was.

It was around five o'clock. The sun was just going down, and we were marched down a road with barbed-wire fences on both sides. Behind the barbed wire were trees and people, weird-looking people with shaven heads and ill-fitting clothes. Aberrations. And they were screaming at us, "Throw us your purses, throw us your bundles." And I thought, "Who are these people? What are they? And why are they were asking us to give them the food that we might still be carrying?"

And then we went to the bath, which was adjacent to the crematorium. Two lines of men and women with hair clippers and razors were waiting for us, and we were immediately told to take off all our clothes and keep only our shoes. They even tore away our underwear and our socks. Everything. Then we joined one of these two lines and they shaved us. I turned to my mother and my mother turned me. And seeing my mother like that I burst into tears. That was the only time I cried in Auschwitz. Now I understand how it must have also felt for her to see me like that.

Then we were taken to the showers and locked in, and they turned on the water. A trickle of cold water, just enough to feel wet and sticky. There was no soap and no towels. Nothing. And when they opened the door and we came out, they handed us each a dress. A piece of cloth really. Some tall people got a tiny dress, some short people got something that hung down to their ankles. And that was what we wore from then on.

By this time it was night, and the glow from the flames climbing from the chimneys of the crematoria lit up the sky. The smell was awful. And we said, "It smells like garbage. They must be burning our suitcases and our clothes." But there was a Jewish Slovak girl, one of the *kapos* [prisoner section chiefs], who came to us and said, "Hungarian Jews, you ate chicken paprika while we were suffering. You came through the door, you'll go out through the chimney. You think they are baking bread over there? Those are your parents and your sisters burning."

Then they marched us to C-Lager [the women's section], but they had no room for us there, so they moved us into the latrines. The room had three long rows of cement seats, with between two to three hundred holes. That's where we sat all night. I spent my first night in the ghetto in a cemetery; I spent my first night in Auschwitz in a latrine.

The second night they divided us into groups and shoved us into various barracks, which housed between eight hundred to one thousand people. Twelve to sixteen women slept on bunk beds meant to hold only four. You couldn't stretch out and had to sleep on your side. If you got up at night to go to the *Scheisskübel* (shit bucket), you would not have a place when you returned.

What was your routine?

BERKOVITZ: They'd wake us every morning at about four o'clock, and we'd have about an hour of darkness in which to mill around and talk before we were lined up for counting. We then returned to the barracks and were locked up all day with nothing to do.

We got food once a day. We would sit on our cots, and they would dole it out from a cooking pot resting on a cart: one piece of bread per person and some watery brew, which sometimes contained bits of cabbage or turnips. People drank from the pot the best they could and passed it around. If you were the first one you got as much soup to drink as you could possibly slurp down in a hurry. If you were the last one, you might have received nothing.

The soup had a very chemical flavor, and it was rumored that they put something in it to stop the women from menstruating. So we were convinced that we were being sterilized. Nobody, in fact, menstruated at Auschwitz. I later learned that when people are starving, they stop menstruating because they lack the proper amount of body fat. Women need a certain amount of estrogen stored in body fat to menstruate. But not having periods at Auschwitz was really a blessing, because it would have been just awful as far as sanitation was concerned. When we were rescued and regained our normal body weight, we began menstruating again. Whatever happened was not permanent, but of course we did not know that at the time.

The first three or four days, I couldn't eat that food, that soup tasted so awful. But when people get really hungry, they can eat anything, even grass, if they can find any. If you lost too much weight, and your ribs started to show, you would get "selected out." They would have a "selection" two or three times a day. They would drive a truck up to the entry of the barracks, and the German guards would have you come forward and take off all of your clothes. They looked at you, and as soon as your bones started showing, you went straight onto the truck without any clothes. You just went. So you had to eat the food and try not to get diarrhea, because then you would become dehydrated and get emaciated much quicker. The prisoners called one who got emaciated "Musselman"[1] and stayed away. It was as if that person were a ghost, a living-dead person who would infect the others. If you started to get sick, they would send you to the infirmary, where your chances of survival decreased even more. So you avoided the infirmary at any cost.

You remember I told you that Judy Kleinmann had become infected with measles. Well, I got the measles in Auschwitz. I ran a very high fever and was very sick, but I didn't go to the infirmary. I stood for the counting and the selection, and I survived. I didn't even have an aspirin.

Death at Auschwitz was merely a question of time. Each day, day after day, you lived from one hour to the next. Luckily, when we were in C-Lager there was no epidemic, no typhus, as there was in other areas of the camp.

Did you ever look at people and speculate on their chances of survival?

BERKOVITZ: We were not speculating, but you could tell which people were determined to survive and which ones were lethargic and very depressed.

Was there any suicide?

BERKOVITZ: Maybe one or two occasions, but there wasn't much of it in C-Lager. Killing yourself, though, was very easy. All you had to do was to touch the wires. Generally, people did want to survive, but based on past experiences and personality you couldn't tell who. My mother, for example, was not terribly aggressive and had lived a very protected life. She was this old-fashioned European lady, very gentle and very delicate, a homemaker who had to be protected against the least little breeze. She was not the type of person that you would have suspected could have survived under such circumstances.

That there was a higher percentage of women who died in the camps than men has often been taken to suggest that the Nazis wanted to select out the women faster than men. Do you have any reflections on that?

BERKOVITZ: I really don't know whether that was true or not. But since the selection process was conditioned by the amount of calories given to us—I heard 600–700 calories a day—it would have been very easy to do. But I really don't know for sure. They also punished us for the slightest infractions. For example, when the count didn't tally, they would say, "no soup tonight."

Why would the count not check out? Were there any attempts to escape?

BERKOVITZ: Oh no, there were no attempts to escape, but people were going from one barracks to the next because they met somebody they knew or their partner was selected out, and they wanted to be with someone else. You were not registered in your block, and there was continuous fluctuation. Eventually, though, they would adjust the count within the whole camp, but that always took time.

Aside from being with your mother, and for a short time your mother's sister, you were surrounded entirely by strangers. How did you establish relationships with any of these people? Did you depend on any of them for survival?

BERKOVITZ: My biggest strength, the main reason for my survival, was my mother. She really protected me. We'd each get one slice of bread, but she would always give me some of hers. But people who were completely alone tended to form very close relationships with others. There were mother-daughter relationships with people who were not mother and daughter, or sister relationships with people who weren't sisters. It was very, very important to have these pseudo-families or replacement families, because if you were alone, you gave up very easily. It was extremely difficult not to give up.

Even given the horrible circumstances, you might say you were fortunate?

BERKOVITZ: That's right. We did not advertise the fact that we were mother and daughter. People near us knew, but the people in authority didn't know because they hadn't bothered to take our names.

Did these nuclear surrogate families ever branch out into extended surrogate families?

BERKOVITZ: No. People might know others from their same town, but they usually didn't make relationships with many strangers. People were so busy surviving that they really did not have excess energy to form new relationships. At Auschwitz people were coming and going all the time, and they just did not have the emotional strength to form an attachment and then see that person disappear.

Was there fear that if you didn't watch your bread very carefully, somebody would steal it?

BERKOVITZ: Yes, absolutely. We slept with the bread under our heads. People were surviving for themselves and stole all the time. We could constantly feel hands searching for our food to steal, but I never saw any physical fighting or pushing or shoving or real arguments. You would think that women would get nasty with their tongues and curse at each other, but I don't remember any of this.

Was there any organization or leadership among the prisoners?

BERKOVITZ: It was impossible. In Auschwitz you were shifted back and forth, and there was continuous coming and going and selection. The Germans determined the leaders. In each barrack there was a *Block Älteste Vertreterin* (senior block representative), who was usually a young Jewish Slovak woman. Some of these had been there two or three years prior to our arrival. They had managed to survive and achieve the exalted position of "head of the barracks."

They lived in an area separated from the rest of the barrack by a partition. They had beds with sheets, a table and chairs, a stove, and pots and pans and dishes. It was hardly a normal environment, but certainly a more "civilized" one than that of the rest of the people. They didn't eat the same food. Their food was delivered to them when the rest of us were supposed to be asleep. But if you weren't sleeping, you could smell the food cooking in their room.

Did the block representatives treat you badly?

BERKOVITZ: I cannot make a blanket statement; it depended on their personalities. Some of them just did their job like any might do under other very difficult circumstances, doing whatever had to be done. They got us up, chased us out for the count, and kept order. But others were extremely cruel, going around with rubber truncheons and beating people, making people afraid of them.

Did any of these block representatives get "selected"? They weren't really safe, were they?

BERKOVITZ: The plan was eventually to get rid of them too. Since there were thirty-two barracks, there were thirty-two *Block Älteste*. Some of them survived, some of them didn't. It depended on where they were sent after they closed down the C-Lager. I happened to know one of them who survived, but we thought that eventually, they would die with the rest of us.

Were there religious practices in the camp?

BERKOVITZ: I did see women praying alone, yes.

Nothing beyond the individual?

BERKOVITZ: No.

Not even two or three people praying together?

BERKOVITZ: No.

Usually people tend to get together to reaffirm their faith. You didn't see any of that?

BERKOVITZ: No, no.

Did the word get around when there was Yom Kippur?

BERKOVITZ: I tell you frankly, I don't remember.

Outside of possible religious and cultural differences, among the prisoners was there anything else that might have produced a feeling of separation?

BERKOVITZ: No.

What about class differences? You came from a very strong bourgeois environment. There were people in the camp who probably came from either higher or lower classes. How did that play itself out?

BERKOVITZ: People tended to make friends pretty much with people from their own class and with those of similar backgrounds. Formation of friendships was tenuous, considering their potential brevity, but there was constant networking. Somebody had a cousin who had a friend who came from a town near the town where one's mother was born, and so forth.

Given the horrors of the camp, would social class be something you noticed after a while?

BERKOVITZ: You couldn't tell by the way people looked, only by their behavior and the language they used.

Were there any political groupings, for example, among communists?

BERKOVITZ: I know what you are driving at, but there was really no sort of organized cohesion within the prison population. You just tried to survive. There was no organization where the strong people gave weaker people support or protection, or where some leaders would tell newcomers how to behave for their own good. There was none of that.

Women were probably more vulnerable than men, who had belonged to more organizations before they came to the camps.

BERKOVITZ: That's probably true, because most of these woman came from a very paternalistic society without any support groups. They were used to authority and not used to taking their lives into their own hands and making decisions. They were not used to standing up for their own rights or protecting or planning for themselves. At least that was true among the people I was near.

The Birkenau camp at which Anna and her mother were located served both as a *Vernichtung* (extermination) and a work center. At its peak in 1943, it held about 100,000 inmates. Most of the prisoners who were there were eventually gassed; the rest died from starvation, malnutrition, disease, infections, rat bites, infestations of lice, or battery. Nobody took Anna's or her mother's name or assigned them numbers. Why bother with people who would soon be dead? Survival, therefore, frequently depended on happenstance and unforeseen circumstance.

One autumn day, nearby air-raid sirens sounded.

At that period of the war, Allied activity in the sky above the Auschwitz area was not uncommon. About two and a half miles east of the death camp was the I. G. Farben synthetic oil and rubber plant at Monowitz. Auschwitz supplied it with prison labor, both male and female. On April 4, the pilot of a reconnaissance plane looking for industrial targets happened to capture the earliest aerial pictures of Auschwitz. A further surveillance flight on May 31 recorded frames of both Auschwitz and Birkenau. However, the photo evaluation experts were examining war production installations, not barracks, gas chambers, or crematoria. The Allies feared that the Monowitz factory might be producing synthetic fuel to compensate for the natural sources of petroleum lost to the advancing Soviet army. Therefore on August 20, Allied bombers paid the Monowitz complex a visit.

In a poem she wrote in 1996, Anna Berkovitz expressed the hope she had at the time that the planes had come to destroy the death camps.

On That Day in August 1944

It happened on a day in August,
Or so we thought,
As there are no calendars in Hell.
Time creeps interminably on
Blending the days of fear with
The night of flames.

But on that day, there came a glint of hope
As silver missiles streaked the sky
And as the sirens wailed
We huddled and prayed
That the bombs should fall

And after our deaths
The sign "This branch is out of business"
Would go up.

But, then, the sirens stopped
And the sky did not fall
And business in Auschwitz continued as usual.
And Satan laughed
As he re-kindled the flames,
Anticipating much more business yet to come.
"Mach schnell! Mach schnell," he roared,

And I always knew that
The world did not give a damn
On that day in August.

Five days after the initial strike on Monowitz, Allied aerial reconnaissance returned to survey the damage. The photo analysts concluded that further strikes were necessary. These occurred on December 18 and December 26. During that last attack, a number of bombs fell short and hit the SS sick bay at Auschwitz-Birkenau, killing five of the patients. This was the only time the death camp was bombed.

BERKOVITZ: One morning, as we were milling around waiting for roll call, we met some people from Munkács. We tried to find out news of my grandparents but were unsuccessful. But one woman told us that my mother's sister was in another barrack here at Auschwitz. So we met my mother's sister. She asked us to come and stay with her; and we moved from block 14, where we were first put, to block 9, where my mother's sister stayed. (I already told you that in that extermination camp people moved from one barrack to the next.) But every day there was still a selection.

One day the Germans came into our new barrack, and they said, "We need workers, do we have any volunteers?" Now, my mother's unspoken philosophy was to be as faceless as possible: try not to do anything to stand out, don't volunteer for anything. But my aunt had a different personality, and before we knew it, she jumped off her bunk and said, "I volunteer."

It happened that they were preparing the camp immediately adjacent to us for gypsies. And my aunt was put to work in the gypsy-camp kitchen. That was a good place to be. She got word to us where she was, and she made arrangements to meet us every morning to give us some scraps of food: a couple of potatoes, a couple of carrots, a turnip, whatever she could get. Sometimes she threw it to us, sometimes it got lost. But we got it enough times that all of a sudden we became healthier. And we also had a currency that we could use for barter.

We made a deal with a woman, actually a distant cousin, who was over in the workers' barracks. We would share our food with her, and she would arrange for us to get jobs and live in block 12, the workers' barracks. Consequently, we became *Scheisskommandos,* those people who went back and forth with buckets filled with human excrement from the latrines. This job meant that we were outside all day long and not in the barracks; and we therefore avoided the selections.

That's what saved our lives. When all the women in C-Lager were being exterminated, those in the workers' barracks managed to survive. When we arrived, that camp had about 34,000 women, who were constantly being replaced with new arrivals as they died or were killed off. But by November, when we left, there were only about 200 people left, mostly those in the workers' block 12.

And all the others had been murdered ?

BERKOVITZ: I would say 95 percent of them or more. [Of the approximately four million persons believed to have perished at Auschwitz, 400,000 were Hungarian Jews.] And so we stayed in the workers' barracks until all the prisoners in the rest of the camp were gone.

One night they backed up the truck to the entrance of our barracks, and we thought our time had come. We were marched down to the truck, and then they took us to another camp, right adjacent to the crematorium, and we got selected and selected and selected. This continued until the end of November 1944, when one day those who remained were put on a train which left Auschwitz. We didn't go to such a wonderful place, we went to Ravensbrück, but we had left Auschwitz and in a railroad car.

They Talked about Recipes

Ravensbrück, located about sixty miles north of Berlin on the shores of Lake Schwedt, near the small town of Fürstenberg, was the Third Reich's only camp exclusively for women. During its six years of operation, a total of 132,000 women and children passed through, of which 92,000 perished. The prisoners came from all occupied countries, the largest national group being 33,000 from Poland. The major labor activity was making SS uniforms, but the camp also provided slave labor for factories throughout Germany. Ravensbrück was also known for its sadistic medical experiments. At the end of 1944, the camp, already seriously overcrowded, burgeoned with new arrivals from the evacuated Polish camps. The rate of killing increased. New gassing equipment was installed and a third oven added to the crematorium. When this proved inadequate to handle the supply of corpses, they were trucked elsewhere or were burned alongside the road with flame throwers.

What happened to your aunt?

BERKOVITZ: My aunt stayed in Auschwitz. We didn't see her again until 1976, over thirty years later. She remained working in the kitchen until Auschwitz was liberated by the Russians on January 22, 1945.

On November 26, 1944, Reichsführer Heinrich Himmler had ordered the SS detachment at Auschwitz-Birkenau to begin the destruction of the gas chambers and crematoria in order to obliterate all the evidence of mass murder. The last of the crematoria, number 5, was blown up just two days before the Red Army arrived. By then, a policy of evacuation had replaced the one of mass murder. Some 60,000 inmates were sent west, mostly through forced marches, which for many became death marches. Even with the relentless advance of the Allied and Soviet armies, the Nazis continued to move the survivors of their prison camps around to prevent their enemies from liberating these witnesses of the Final Solution. Also, in these last months of the war, the need for slave labor increased. Convinced that the Jews were subhuman, the Nazis willingly implemented any policy that could prolong their suffering and further the war effort of the Third Reich.

When they liberated the camps, the Soviets found about 5,800 sick prisoners alive in the Birkenau compound; in Auschwitz, only 600; and at the satellite camp of Zazole, another 1,200. They also discovered the belongings of those who had perished: 348,820 men's suits, 38,00 pairs of men's shoes, 836,255 women's dresses, 5,525 women's shoes, vast quantities of eyeglasses and false teeth, and seven tons of human hair.

BERKOVITZ: We stayed at Ravensbrück for three weeks and underwent interminable selections. My mother was a frail little woman; I was a fourteen-year-old kid. I don't know how we ever passed through all these selections, but somehow we did.

Then we were sent to work in one of the Krupp/Essen factories in eastern Germany, near Magdeburg [eighty-five miles west of Berlin]. We were extremely lucky because we were among the few who didn't have to walk west on foot. Why they picked us to ride on trains, I don't know. You can interpret it any way you like: fate, God, whatever. The only thing that I can say is that if you gave up, you didn't survive. But that didn't mean that everybody who refused to give up survived.

Were the conditions better here than at Auschwitz?

BERKOVITZ: We were housed in a prison, which had about 300 or 400 German prisoners, 200 Polish women workers, and then about 200 Jews. We were in a concrete building that had bars on the windows and cells with doors that locked. It was a regular German prison. And we got the same treatment as the other prisoners. There were two people to a bunk rather than fourteen or sixteen. My mother and I got a bunk to ourselves. We were given a blanket for the two of us, and the bed had straw, which eventually filled with lice, but, anyway, it was our bunk and it was our blanket. There was also a stove in the cell, and we did have some wood.

All the overseers were Germans, of course. But there was no selection. You didn't sit around in the barracks all day waiting for a selection with this continuous fear of death, although we still dreaded being sent back to Auschwitz. We were told that we would never get out of there, and there was every evidence to support that.

You didn't know that Auschwitz was liberated?

BERKOVITZ: No. There were rumors that if you got sick they would send you back to Auschwitz. And once I did get sick, I had pneumonia, and I was put into the infirmary, where I had a bunk to myself and even some sheets on the bed. I was there for one day, when somebody told me that the next day they were going to empty the infirmary, so I insisted that I was ready to go back to work. "No, no," they told me, "you're too sick, you stay here." And I thought that meant that they were really going to empty the place, and I struggled back to work.

The factory was terrible and awful, but somehow you had the feeling that if you kept on going and did the work long enough, maybe the war would end and you would make it.

We were mixed in with the other prisoners and worked the same as they did. We worked all day, a twelve-hour shift. My mother and I ended up working in different areas of the factory, my mother on the day shift and I on the night shift. Lots of times we didn't see each other. When she was coming home, I was going to work. But we had Sunday off. That's when we saw each other.

We walked to work. The factory was an underground airplane factory, located in an old salt mine. It was a long march back and forth, and we went through tunnels and up and down the stairs when the elevators didn't work. But we were not beaten, and the work was not hard.

It was winter, and we got no warm clothes. We just had one dress, no sweater, and no underwear. The fact that it was underground saved our lives because we didn't march very long above ground; so it wasn't as cold as it could have been otherwise.

Every morning we would get up around 4:00 or 4:30, and then we were counted and the day shift started at 7:00. It was a long process. When we got back from the factory, we got our one meal of the day. Mostly watery soup, but there was more cabbage in the soup than at Auschwitz, and we got two slices of bread. Still, it was very little food, and eventually we would have starved to death. Fortunately we did not stay there long enough.

You were always very hungry?

BERKOVITZ: We were always very hungry, but a couple of times, I got a potato from the kitchen, and we would bake it on the stove in the cell. Those were probably the best meals I had during that year.

Did this increase your hope of survival?

BERKOVITZ: Yes.

How did your jailers distinguish among the different nationalities?

BERKOVITZ: Everybody had different stripes on their clothes running down the middle of their backs. The Jews had a yellow stripe. The Poles had a green stripe, and the Germans had a black stripe. The Germans were either criminals or political prisoners, mostly the latter. The Poles were forced labor, but they were not Jewish.

What kind of job were you doing?

BERKOVITZ: I was assigned to a French woman, a "civilian," who had volunteered to work in Germany. We sat at big table doing electronic wiring, winding thin copper wire on a spool for some part of an airplane. We would wind the wire with the help of a machine. We were communicating in German, and she wanted to hear my story. I told her about Auschwitz and everything. She was not mean or anything, but she never gave me anything, never a piece of bread or a cookie or anything, never any such help.

My mother was also assigned to a civilian, to an Italian who was really terrific. He would always bring my mother leftovers, some pieces of vegetables and bread and occasionally cake, and then my mother would bring it "home." Sometimes there was even a piece of chicken. So these "civilians" knew about what was happening to the Jews.

These "civilians" were quartered outside the prison?

BERKOVITZ: Yes, they could come and go. They were not prisoners like us.

Did you feel that this job was your key to survival, insofar as you were doing essential war work?

BERKOVITZ: Absolutely. In Auschwitz our hope was that we would be given some work which would make us useful so we wouldn't be killed.

Did working together reduce the sense of separation?

BERKOVITZ: In the factory there was more a sense of community than at Auschwitz. This particular prison had about one thousand people, but only two hundred of us were Jewish. All of a sudden, though, the Jews had a common identity. The people with the yellow stripes were my people, and we were a community.

There were no SS guards inside the factory. The guards who marched us to and from the factory were all former Wehrmacht soldiers; they were very benign. Occasionally, an SS-*Aufseherin* (overseer), a woman, would come in, but the German prisoners supervised the daily life. Some of them were actually nice.

Was there any kind of bonding, or did you still have this atomization?

BERKOVITZ: We made friends. There was a girl my age, and my mother sort of adopted her. She would come over to our bunk, and my mother would comfort her. She didn't survive, however.

What did the prisoners talk about?

BERKOVITZ: This is going to shock you. But the women talked about recipes. They would sit around and discuss menus and what they would eat and what they would cook. And people would tell what they had for Friday night dinners, and what it used to be like in their homes. And people would say, "On Saturday we had this and this and this." And they would tell how they prepared the food, down to listing all the ingredients.

You know what I would recall? Just before we were taken in January 1944, I visited my aunt and uncle in Budapest. I was a small-town girl, and I had never seen one of the capital's famous pastry shops. My aunt and uncle took me to one, and although we had very beautiful pastry shops in Munkács, they were nothing like those in Budapest. And my aunt said, "Pick out anything you want." So I picked out about ten different pastries, but I could only eat about two of them and had to leave the rest.

I would think about that tray of pastries over and over. I would remember each pastry and imagine what the ones I didn't eat might have tasted like. I told everybody this story, how I went to this pastry shop, and I had a plate full of pastries, and that I had left most of them there. I would dream about the pastries that I didn't eat.

Did the prisoners talk about family and friends?

BERKOVITZ: I would eavesdrop, and some of the women would talk about their dates, their romances, their boyfriends, their husbands, their weddings, their wedding nights.

Did they talk about sex?

BERKOVITZ: Yes. I was very naive. I wanted to listen to these things that I never heard before, because, you know, in the environment I grew up in, people didn't talk about sex.

Maybe in the environment they grew up in they also didn't talk about these things. Is it possible that the camps released their inhibitions?

BERKOVITZ: That is possible. Conversation went down to the primal things. But I don't remember them talking about their children. I think they were so hurting that they couldn't talk about them. I have to think what my reaction would have been had I been older, and if I had lost my children. I don't think I could have survived. I don't see how people who lost a child could have gotten through it. I think I was able to get through it because I was so immature and naive and hopeful for the future. Also, if I had not had my mother there, I would have been destroyed. But fortunately I had her there.

Do you think you were also the key to your mother's survival?

BERKOVITZ: Yes, our relationship was very important.

You mentioned your hope for the future. Did people ever talk about the future?

BERKOVITZ: I wish I had discussed that with my mother, what she thought and how she felt. But my mother refused to discuss anything with me after we were liberated. She said, "I don't want ever to talk about it again." And she didn't. She started to write a history of our family, but when she got to this period, she couldn't go on.

Was there a greater tendency to help each other in the prison work camp than in Auschwitz?

BERKOVITZ: Yes. For instance, when you washed your dress. You only had one dress, and until it dried you would have to sit inside naked. The only way to dry a dress was for a bunch of people to shake the clothes in the wind so the dampness would evaporate. You needed two friends for that—to take your dress outside and shake it up and down between them so that it could dry. People did that for each other. They might also cuddle each other when they were cold. And when one of the women was dying, my mother helped her, brought her water and so forth.

Did they share food?

BERKOVITZ: My mother did with me.

Did you see more expressions of religion in the work camp than at Auschwitz?

BERKOVITZ: Nothing organized. You knew who the religious people were because the religious people were praying, but that's about it.

When were you evacuated from this camp?

BERKOVITZ: One morning in early April 1945, we lined up to go to work. It was still dark and then it got light and became daytime. It wasn't Sunday, yet we weren't going to work. We didn't know what was going on. Then they said, "Take your blankets, you're going on a trip." We were utterly confused, we didn't know anything, except everybody was going on the trip, not only the Jews, but the Poles and the Germans as well. Had they taken only the Jews, we would have figured they were sending us back to a concentration camp. Then

the rumors started flying that the front was moving, and for the first time we realized that the Allied forces were in Europe and we were being evacuated.

They packed us into cattle wagons on a train. We began somewhere near
Magdeburg and went toward Hamburg. If you look at the map, you can see that
distance would be about a three-hour train trip, but we were on that train for ten
days. We were constantly moving, staying in railroad sideyards, moving an hour
or two and then standing still. With no water or food, people started dying.
And the stench was just awful. And when we finally stopped—I don't know
where—and they opened up the doors, my mother could not get up and had to
be lifted off the wagon.

We left the blankets in the car, and my mother was shivering, and I asked
the German *Aufseherin* [guard] if I could go back and get the blanket, and she
said, "Where you're going you won't need any blankets."

They led us to a clearing in the woods and made us stand there. We were
surrounded with machine guns. Some women were allowed to go with a guard
to get some water at a nearby well, and when they came back, they told us that
they saw piles of bodies in the nearby woods. Thousands of dead prisoners. We
were sure that they were going to shoot us right then and there.

That's the only time—coming back to your questions of organized religion—that's the only time I remember women getting together and saying a
prayer for the dead.

And then we saw a convoy coming, Germans on motorcycles and a couple
of trucks. And they lined us up. When the convoy arrived, they started giving us
handfuls of noodles and each person got a handful of sugar. I remember eating
the dry noodles and licking the sugar. And we got back on the train.

There was a woman about my mother's age who had a daughter about my
age. They were with us in the same wagon. And the girl had just died, and I remember the mother holding the body of her daughter, picking out and eating
the grains of sugar from the dead girl's hair.

Now, rumor had it—there were always rumors—that the commander who
was in charge of this transport had been given orders to shoot us, but he had refused to do so and went to the village to find food, and the only thing he could
find for us to eat was some noodles and some sugar, and he brought those back
and put us again on the trains. And we started moving again.

We ended up in Neuengamme, something like twenty miles from Hamburg,
where we were put into one of its concentration camps. It was night. We were
so hungry that we went around picking the buds from the trees to eat.

The concentration camp of Neuengamme had been established in 1940 as a forced labor camp for political prisoners primarily from France, Belgium, the Netherlands, Denmark, and Norway. About 90,000 passed through the camp; less than half survived. Neuengamme was also used for medical experiments, the most notorious of which was one carried out on twenty-five Jewish children between the ages of six and twelve who were transported there from Auschwitz. The children were injected with tubercular bacilli, purportedly to study the means of a cure. On April 20 (Hitler's birthday), with the British army a short distance away, the twenty survivors of this experiment were all given morphine shots and then hanged.

The camp was by then in the process of liquidation, with some of the prisoners allowed to return to Denmark and Norway. The deal was brokered by Count Folke Bernadotte with Heinrich Himmler. A last contingent of ten thousand regular prisoners was taken away just before the camp was liberated, loaded on three ships, and sent out to sea. On May 3 a squadron of RAF Typhoons mistakenly sunk all ships. Of the Neuengamme contingent, only two thousand survived.

BERKOVITZ: In the middle of the night, the SS came shouting, "Alle heraus, Juden heraus, nur Juden, Juden, Juden heraus, Juden heraus" (everybody out, Jews out, only Jews, Jews get out). They put us back on the train, just the Jews this time. Now we were sure we were going to be murdered, because our insurance policy—the Poles and the Germans—was no longer with us. Women prayed out loud. I fell asleep. Then I was suddenly awakened by a big commotion, and I heard languages I did not understand. I was sure I was back in a concentration camp, because there you heard every sort of language. And then they opened up the doors, and we saw ambulances and nurses and Red Cross signs all over. We were in Denmark. Folke Bernadotte had made a pact with the Germans to trade a wagonload of food for a wagonload of Jews. It was May 1, 1945.

The day before, just after three o'clock in the afternoon, Hitler had solemnly bid farewell to those still in his Berlin bunker. Then, accompanied by Eva Braun, whom he had married the previous day, he retired to his private quarters, where he bit into a glass ampoule of cyanide.[2] His wife then killed herself with the same poison. Earlier he had dictated his last will, in which he claimed that neither he nor anyone else in Germany had wanted the war against Britain and the United States.

"Centuries will pass away," he explained, "but out of the ruins of our towns and monuments hatred will grow against those finally responsible for everything, international Jewry and its helpers."[3] Hitler boasted that he had made these real culprits pay for their guilt "by more humane means than war."

On May 1, at 10 P.M., Radio Hamburg announced that Hitler had died "fighting against Bolshevism to his last breath." The formal surrender of the Third Reich now became the responsibility of Hitler's designated successor, Admiral Karl Dönitz.

On the morning of May 7, just past midnight, the instrument of capitulation (for all German forces either fighting or facing the Allies) was signed at a schoolhouse near General Eisenhower's headquarters in Rheims, France. It came into effect twenty hours later, and the members of the last Nazi government were arrested. In his testament Hitler had charged his successors with upholding "the race laws to the limit and to resist mercilessly the poisoner of all nations, International Jewry."

Notes

1. This death-camp expression meaning "Muslim" to describe a prisoner near death supposedly came from the stereotypical shaking hands and bent posture of Muslims at prayer.

2. The autopsy performed by the Soviets shortly after they captured the *Führerbunker* revealed the presence of a crushed ampoule of cyanide in the charred remains of Hitler's jaw. However, there is also evidence of a gunshot wound to his head. Perhaps Hitler shot himself while crunching down on the poison, or Eva Braun, no stranger to firearms, gave him the coup de grâce before her own suicide.

3. See Alan Bullock, *Hitler: A Study in Tyranny* (New York: Harper and Row, 1964), 794.

10
A Time for Renewal

After the formal capitulation of Germany, on May 8, 1945, the National Front government assumed control in Prague. As part of the political rehabilitation of Czechoslovakia, President Edvard Beneš wanted the pre-Munich character of the country restored. This meant the reestablishment of the association between the Czechs and the Slovaks and reacquisition of the lands annexed by Germany, Hungary, and Poland.[1]

The Allies allowed the reestablishment of the pre-1938 frontiers with the exception of Ruthenia, which the Soviet Union acquired. For the loss of this eastern tip of their country, the Czechoslovaks were compensated with territory around Bratislava, which had formerly belonged to Hungary.

Despite the establishment of a liberal, democratic system, toleration for the German and Hungarian minorities was in short supply as Prague began confiscating their property and expelled many from the country. In all, some 6,420,000 acres were appropriated and divided up into 270,000 new separate holdings. A concerted effort was made to destroy the German and Magyar culture in the vacated areas, including the suppression of the German and Hungarian languages. As victims of Nazi and fascist persecution, Jews were exempt from the expulsions.

Motivation, Desire, and Luck: Gavriel Salvendy

"I think my mother always felt a certain guilt for having survived."

The Children of Capitalists

In December 1945, the Red Army, which had liberated Czechoslovakia, was voluntarily withdrawn. Still, the danger of Soviet interference in the internal affairs of the state remained, and to maintain good relations with Moscow President Edvard Beneš had Communists included in the postwar coalition government. When the Communist Party received an impressive 38 percent of the vote in the elections of May 1946, Beneš invited its leader, Klement Gottwald, to form a government. The Communists took nine out of the seventeen positions in the government, including the prime ministry and the ministry of the interior.

In the Soviet-Czechoslovak Friendship Treaty signed during the war, the two states promised "to maintain close and friendly cooperation after the re-establishment of peace and to regulate their actions according to the principles of mutual respect of their independence and sovereignty and non-interference in the internal affairs of the other signatory."[2] The cornerstone of Czechoslovak foreign policy therefore became the maintenance of independence within the Soviet orbit, which was a realistic aim, considering the east-west distribution of military power in Europe following the collapse of Nazi Germany.

It took no great genius to figure out that the defeat of Nazi Germany would leave the Soviet Union the dominant power in Eastern and Central Europe. The Western Allies had not fought the kind of war that entitled them to determine the fate of that area, nor had they ever viewed their security in such way. Communism had not been an important force in Eastern Europe before the Second World War, but the presence of the Red Army more than compensated for that absence. Of all the communist parties in the area, the one in Czechoslovakia was the strongest and seemed to have the best chance of coming to power legally.

Stalin had his hands full elsewhere, especially in Germany, his main area of concern, and he apparently did not favor strongarm tactics against the Czechs as yet. Soon, however, the Soviet dictator would let the Czechs know that their optimism about his good intentions was misplaced.

Did antisemitism persist after the war?

GAVRIEL SALVENDY: Not in an overt way. But it was still there. There was one boy, about two years older than I, who came from a family of fascists and used to sing an awful song about the Jews every time he got near my brother and me. That was about the extent of the harassment I received. No physical abuse. He would just start singing that song about killing rabbis. That was his favorite song.

Our school was fairly near to our house and we could walk. But I had a rather difficult time there. The only language I knew was Hungarian. And I thought it was absolutely atrocious that I now had to learn Czech, which was completely new to me. I didn't know a word. I also had to learn Russian. Suddenly here I was a little young kid, having to face two new languages simultaneously. Of course with Russian I also had to learn a completely new alphabet.

In school you weren't allowed to speak Hungarian. Even in the street you were forbidden to speak Hungarian. If the authorities caught you, you would have an "X" shaved in your hair as a sign of betrayal, and therefore you would walk around showing everybody you had done something bad.

The teachers acted as if everybody knew Czech. They taught math in Czech, they taught history in Czech. It was very frustrating. My second-grade teacher broke his pipe on my head because he became annoyed at my slow progress.

With the heating up of the Cold War, the likelihood of Czechoslovakia acting as some sort of bridge between east and west became remote. The Soviets considered the country within their security zone and coveted its resources to help in the rebuilding of their own war-torn country.

SALVENDY: My father's land was restored to him. My mother's wine business prospered, and the family distillery became the largest in the region. It produced a whole range of spirits, from whiskey to slivovitz. So from a materialistic point of view, we were hardly suffering. For example, my father might take off three weeks to go skiing in the High Tatras. The family chauffeur would drive us there, and the nanny would come along to take care of us kids.

Your father had been a very strong Magyar nationalist, and yet Hungarian fascists were hunting you down. How did this change his sense of identity?

SALVENDY: He was a very proud person, and he always thought he could do the impossible, and outwardly it didn't seem to make a difference. But he must have been terribly hurt inside.

How did this period affect your Jewish identity?

SALVENDY: An interesting question, because my father had made a conscious decision to carry our assimilation to the point of conversion to Christianity to spare us from future suffering. Therefore, from 1945 to 1948, I basically lost my Jewish identity. I didn't think too much about it. At that age you do what your parents tell you to do. I even went to Protestant church and took religion classes.

Why Protestantism? Most of the people in that area are Catholics.

SALVENDY: My parents apparently chose Protestantism because they thought Catholicism was too religious. They just wanted a certificate that said we were Christian, not Jewish. I don't think they would have cared if I were a Muslim or whatever, if I could have claimed at that time that I was not a Jew. Because it wasn't as if I became a different person religiously. The important thing was to have the certificate of conversion.

So you still thought of yourself as Jewish?

SALVENDY: No question about it. I don't think of it as a change. It was all about getting the "paper."

Did your parents also convert?

SALVENDY: No. My parents really didn't have a religion. But all their close friends were Jewish. My mother had a weekly game of rummy and all the other women in it were Jewish. It included practically the entire female population of those who survived and had returned to Rimavska Sobota. And when my parents went skiing, all the couples that would come with them to the resort were Jewish.

*Did your parents ever talk about how they felt about being the remnants
of a once very prosperous and large Jewish community?*

SALVENDY: My mother always used to say in Hungarian the word for "terrible."
Her philosophy was: "either we all survive or we all perish together." I think my
mother always felt a certain guilt for having survived. She was very down-to-
earth and did not think we had done anything special for us to merit survival
and for the others to have perished.

By the end of 1947, Czechoslovakia and Yugoslavia were the
only states in Eastern Europe that had not become satellites of
the Soviet Union. Yugoslavia had a one-party Communist government, but at the beginning of 1948 Belgrade and Moscow were
headed for a major confrontation, which led to Yugoslav defection
from the Stalinist orbit. Stalin was determined that Czechoslovakia
would not follow suit.

No longer did it seem possible for the Czech Communists to
capture a majority of the votes in a free election. Stalin therefore decided to take control of the state in a coup d'état. Backed by the
threat of armed insurrection, Communist "action committees" and
trade union militias forced President Beneš to appoint a new Com-
munist-controlled government on February 25. Shortly afterwards
Beneš resigned, and Czech Communist Party boss Klement Gottwald took his place and began to impose Stalinism on the country.
Of all the Eastern European peoples, only the Czechs had managed
to create a functioning democratic system. But now, for the second
time in a decade, their free institutions fell under the heel of a total-
itarian dictatorship.

SALVENDY: The Communists told us that we no longer owned our house, and
that it would now be broken up into apartments. We were allowed to live in one
of the building's corners, separated from the rest by cement partitions. Our
farmlands and my father's business were also confiscated. They allowed him to
remain as manager, and he stayed in that capacity until just before we left for Israel. But when they found out we were leaving, they fired him, and even ordered us evicted from our apartment. That last order was never enforced,
though, and we stayed there until we left.

How else did your lives change?

SALVENDY: The Communists could be pretty ruthless. Shortly after they took over, the land around Rimavska Sobota was plagued by an infestation of caterpillars. And everybody was ordered to go out into the fields and pick the insects off the plants before the crops were destroyed. My mother was always petrified of bugs, even flies, and so the rest of the family decided that we would do twice the work to spare her from going into the fields. The Communists approved the idea that the rest of the family was willing to work harder, but they refused to excuse my mother. They insisted that she come too. They thought she was refusing to do such work because of her social standing.

When did you discover that you were going to Israel?

SALVENDY: About three months before we left, when these huge wooden boxes arrived at our home. They were enormous, as big as buildings. My parents then told me that we would be leaving.

Did your father decide to leave because the Communists had taken away all his property?

SALVENDY: That was certainly part of it. Things were bad and expected to get worse. But my father also discovered that the children of capitalists would not be allowed to attend the university. Only the working-class children could go. Besides, the Jewish community in Rimavska Sobota was practically nonexistent and getting smaller. Two of the remaining families had already decided to leave. One, with whom we were very close, lived across the street from us. Also, one aunt and one of my uncles were already living in Israel.

When that uncle visited us, he told everybody how great it was there. How the markets had these great vegetables and fruits, luscious pomegranates and oranges. And, of course, everybody there was Jewish. My uncle didn't mention the Muslims. To me it seemed like a very exciting place. But when we arrived, we discovered my uncle had not painted a true picture. He had only stressed those things that were positive.

And, of course, in Rimavska Sobota you had a lot of unpleasant memories.

SALVENDY: But my brother and I were reluctant to leave the little playhouse that we had built. We wanted to take it with us. I didn't overly care about the fact that I was leaving my friends behind.

So for you, it was a big adventure.

SALVENDY: It was exciting. We'd go by boat. I had never been on a ship before. And my grandmother would bake us a suitcase full of our favorite cakes and cookies. Hey, how could we go wrong?

It was tough for my parents, though. They really had to leave everything behind, walking out with only bits and pieces.

Pride of Ancestry

D avid Ben-Gurion had seen his lifelong ambition, the creation of a homeland for the Jews, fulfilled with the proclamation of the State of Israel on May 14, 1948. Ben-Gurion saw that the young state's continued existence, its security against its hostile Arab neighbors with which it had fought a bitter war of independence, depended on an immediate influx of new workers and soldiers, and the main aim of his foreign policy was to bring this about. All restrictions on immigration that the British had imposed were removed, and a worldwide effort was launched to bring Jews to Israel—as many and as soon as possible. Ben-Gurion was a Polish Jew and viewed the Jews of Europe, especially those of Eastern Europe, as the best source for Israeli citizens. He especially sought Holocaust survivors, beginning with those still in refugee camps in Germany, Austria, and Italy.

At the same time, the Israelis negotiated with the Communist bloc countries to obtain exit visas for their Jewish populations, even if this meant paying for their release. For Poland this meant a favorable trade agreement; for Bulgaria, Hungary, and Romania this meant cash, with prices ranging from eighty to three hundred dollars a head. The Czechs were less demanding, considering the Israelis had purchased large quantities of arms from the Skoda works to fight their war of independence. They even allowed the departing Jews to take along their personal property.

The tightening of Soviet control over Eastern Europe curtailed this emigration. However, by 1948 some 200,000 Holocaust survivors had left Europe for Palestine. The last significant year of this exodus was 1949, when 130,000 European Jews reached Israel, including 47,000 Polish Jews and 20,000 Bulgarian Jews. The influx of so many people in a relatively short period put enormous pressure on Israel's resources. Ben-Gurion, though, minimized the difficulties by reminding people that houses and jobs did not await the 600,000 Children of Israel when they started the Exodus from Egypt.

People came to Israel for religious and Zionist reasons, they came to escape further persecution, and they came because they feared that if they did not leave now it would be impossible later. But many simply joined the crowd, following members of their family or their friends who were going or who had already gone. Tales of a land of milk and honey undoubtedly encouraged some, but for others Israel was only a way station to somewhere else.

SALVENDY: We left Rimavska Sobota at the end of March 1949, went to Bratislava, and from there headed south toward Bari, Italy, where we boarded the boat for Haifa. Before we left Czechoslovakia, the police took some of our luggage away to "put into the baggage compartment," telling us that we would get it back as soon as we crossed the border. We never saw the stuff again. We were naive, but what could we do? Were we going to fight with the Communist police? My father also brought along about twenty cartons of cigarettes, which were also confiscated. However, they never did find my parents' jewelry, which was hidden in the thermos filled with coffee in the lunch basket.

In Bari we boarded this absolutely atrocious boat, hastily refitted to transport large numbers of people to Israel. No cabins, everybody sleeping in an open cargo hold lined with bunks three levels high. Forget about sleeping. People were crying, talking loudly, squabbling, constantly irritated. The air was foul. There were three shower stalls for a thousand people, and not enough benches for everybody to sit down.

The Exodus ships were old and rusty, mostly relics from the prewar days of illegal immigration which were even then barely seaworthy. These tubs were crammed with as many people as possible. Transportation arrangements were now made through Ships and Boats, Ltd., an enterprise of the Mossad Organization, which had before the war been involved with smuggling Jews out of Europe. Mossad (not to be confused with the Israeli secret service of the same name) was the travel agency of the World Zionist Federation and connected to the Israeli state.

SALVENDY: Most of the people on that trip were from Czechoslovakia. The food was served on long tables. There never was quite enough, and people had to fight like vultures for what there was. My grandmother, who was about four feet ten inches tall and weighed about 340 pounds, would push her way through the crowd to get food for the whole family. People were always screaming that she was taking it all. Yet there was practically no violence. The entire trip took a week: two days on the train and five days on the boat.

Describe the process of entering Israel.

SALVENDY: The customs and other formalities went quickly, very quickly. As fast as when you go through a passport check in the United States. There were no guards, just ordinary clerks.[3] Compared to the bureaucracy that came later, it was really simple, very informal and casual. My uncle met us and took us to a little, very cramped apartment.[4] We were there for about a month. Then we moved to a larger place in Tivon, a resort town about twenty miles from Haifa, where I attended school.

Adjustment to a new way of life was especially difficult for Gavriel's father. He had once owned and operated his own factory, but now he was reduced to a series of jobs that lacked prestige. His first was in a secondhand store handling the property of refugees who, like the Salvendys, had to sell their belongings to tide them over. Next Gavriel's father opened a clothes-cleaning factory, but after a year it went bankrupt. Finally he found employment in a business he knew something about, the making of wine, and he eventually rose to become a managing director. He never reached the level of control and fulfillment he had enjoyed in Europe, however. Understandably he expected his two young sons to enjoy the success he had not been able to recapture.

SALVENDY: We walked a couple of miles each way to school. In 1949, there was no public transportation. To this was added the difficulty of not knowing the language. They made us learn twenty new Hebrew words a day. We also had an assignment to get our parents to do the same. If we exceeded the twenty words we got extra credit. We were also taught Arabic. Two more new languages with two new alphabets.

How many does that make so far?

SALVENDY: Hungarian, Czech, and Russian. I also had some German. Now was added Hebrew and Arabic. Six languages and four different alphabets.

My studies were lopsided. I got As in math and physics. In those subjects either you understood it or you didn't, and I didn't have to put in too much time to get good grades. But in the humanities I didn't do so well. In humanities, understanding wasn't enough, you had to do the readings to get good grades, and I hated homework and skipped class. I was disruptive. My brother, on the other hand, was a star student. He was first in most subjects, while I was always somewhere toward the bottom.

As a result, when I was fourteen, they kicked me out and sent me to a trade school in Haifa. I was there two years, learning how to solder and weld and wire. I quit when I was sixteen and went to work in a machine shop. So I was the black sheep of the family, and my father was not too pleased. My parents, though, insisted I take night-school courses so I could get a high-school diploma.

You said that your Jewish persona was in a state of suspended animation during and after the war. What developed when you got to Israel?

SALVENDY: The school I attended was a Hillel school, so we had religious instruction one class period a day. With all that exposure, Judaism just flowed into me. I really didn't like Bible study, but I had an outstanding teacher for Jewish literature. In his class we delved into Jewish culture and Jewish identity. He used to have special discussion sessions at his house for about four or five students. Studying Jewish literature with that man was probably the strongest Jewish influence in my life.

The Israeli school system was supposed to create new citizens as fast as possible, teaching the resurrected Hebrew language and being the bridge between different cultures. However, the schools reflected the deep divisions already existent within Jewish society. In 1949, there were four official educational systems, two secular and two religious. With the massive new immigration these subsidiary systems were constantly accusing each other of stealing their students, sometimes with reason.

The Salvendys went to the general school system, founded in 1913, which provided a balanced education, promoting the nineteenth-century ideals of liberal nationalism and Jewish culture. About 44 percent of Israeli children, mostly the sons and daughters of merchants, teachers, clerks, craftsmen, and farmers, attended its classes.

Your school helped reaffirm a cultural identity that, ironically, you didn't have to begin with. But what about the religious component?

SALVENDY: I discovered you don't have to be religious to be Jewish. I became proud of being a Jewish person, but not a religious person. The Israelis aren't necessarily religious, but they are proud of their ancestry. Suddenly I could say, "Hey, I'm proud I am a Jew." But that didn't mean I was religious. In Israel I only went to the synagogue if there was a marriage or a bar mitzvah.

Did you have a bar mitzvah?

SALVENDY: No.

What were you learning in school about the Holocaust?

SALVENDY: At that time, nothing. We did learn about the pogroms and the Jewish experience in Russia compared to that in Israel, where the Jews could practice their religion openly and freely without fear. In this way they promoted pride in Israel. But I had zero exposure to the Holocaust in that school. Zero. Not even one lecture on the Holocaust. Now that you mention it, it's quite amazing there was no mention of the Holocaust. Of course, I knew about the Holocaust because of the personal experiences of the refugees.[5]

What about Israeli nationalism? Did you participate in patriotic demonstrations?

SALVENDY: There were parades and celebrations on Independence Day. I got to carry the Israeli flag in the local parade. There was singing and dancing in the streets.

I was very proud to work on a kibbutz for several weeks each summer. We'd get up about four o'clock in the morning and work in the fields for five hours. No pay, only food, and the work was hard. But I felt I was really serving my country. I also was happy to be in the Gadna, where we learned how to use weaponry, and do all kinds of exercise.[6] They gave us the notion that if all hell broke loose, we'd be called up to help defend the country.

Any unpleasant experiences?

SALVENDY: When I was eighteen, I was dating an Arab girl fairly seriously. And I found out how narrow the vision of my Jewish friends and their parents was. I judged her as a person, and I didn't care about her ethnic background. But they couldn't understand how I could go out with an Arab. Whether they had been victims of the Holocaust or not, they could not accept it. And many who

I thought were my friends simply disowned me. That was also the case with her family and friends, who didn't understand how she could go out with an Israeli Jew. Faced with such opposition we had to break it off. That was a very traumatic part of my life—the only time I became disillusioned with the people in Israel.

If you were disillusioned, it means you had illusions. What were these illusions?

SALVENDY: My point was that here are the Jewish people, who have themselves suffered from persecution, and now they are doing the same thing to the Arabs. They are judging them as a group, not on individual merit. I was disappointed in the Jewish people for being so prejudiced themselves.

To what do you attribute your sensitivity to such injustices?

SALVENDY: My parents were phenomenal. They said if she's nice, that's all that matters. My parents always taught me to judge people individually.

Did you bring her home?

SALVENDY: Oh, yeah. And my parents had absolutely no problem with it. You know, in those days in Israel you didn't bring people home for dinner, that wasn't the thing. But she would come home for coffee and cake. My uncle, however, thought it was atrocious and wanted to disown me. And when I began going out with her, the invitations I got from my friends and acquaintances for parties and dances suddenly fell to zero. They might say, "You come, but don't bring her."

Do you think this experience changed some of your attitudes about Israel and maybe Zionism?

SALVENDY: It gave me a feeling of regret that the people in Israel would be capable of the same attitude of which they themselves were victims. But, on the whole, my attitude toward Israel is very positive. In fact, when I finished my Ph.D. and then came to the United States, I felt guilty that I hadn't returned.

Even now, when I return, and I get off the plane and see the flag, I feel very emotional. "Hey," I say to myself, "these are my people." I can say the United States is my country, but I cannot say the Americans are my people. Because they come from all over. That doesn't mean that I'm not a good citizen, because I'm very proud to be an American, but it's not "my people" in this country.

Isn't that a tribal approach to nationality?

SALVENDY: Exactly.

Even assuming this "Israeli tribalism" is humanitarian and positive, you would still have to admit that the tribal experience of Nazi Germany led to things not so nice?

SALVENDY: That's true, but "my people," whom the Germans tried to eradicate, now live in their own state. Maybe the only reason we had achieved it was because of what happened in Nazi Germany.

But maybe the whole concept of Volk is inherently dangerous?

SALVENDY: No question of its danger when pushed to the point of fanaticism, as it was in Israel with the movement of Rabbi Kahane.[7]

In some sense, are you more Israeli than Jewish? I mean "Israeli" in a country or nation-state sense.

SALVENDY: The fact is, I'm not religious at all. But that does not make me any less of a Jewish/Israeli nationalist.

How did your experience in Israel help to shape your future career? Your choice of what and where to study?

SALVENDY: I was very much sports-oriented: the shot put, rowing team, weightlifting. When I was twenty, I broke the Israeli weight record in my class, and it lasted for about six years. But I was a beach bum. I wouldn't go to class. I didn't care for studying much. I was the family disappointment. So I ended up in trade school. And in the evening I worked in a warehouse packing things for the kibbutzim.

I never graduated, never got a high-school diploma, never took the national examination. I must be one of the few professors without a high-school diploma. I picked up some industrial engineering and accounting courses, but they were only one-year courses, not degree courses. And I worked for a time as an engineering technician.

Why didn't you finish?

SALVENDY: Because I didn't care for it. I didn't want to do it. I was more interested in the beautiful ladies on the beach and in my sport activities. My picture was in the newspapers for my athletic achievements.

Motivation and Desire

Salvendy left Israel in the spring of 1962 to tour Europe with his brother, who had just graduated from medical school at the University of Vienna. They ended up in London, and Gavriel liked it there so much that he decided to stay.

SALVENDY: I didn't have much money, so I started looking around for a job. I saw a sign in a window that they were looking for somebody to do ironing. I didn't know English very well, and I thought "ironing" meant "soldering." I had learned soldering in trade school, so I went in and applied. The place was a sweatshop with West Indian women cutting and pressing neckties. I immediately got a job ironing ties.

It was piece rate, nine pence per dozen, but by the second day, I was ironing two and a half times more ties than anybody else and making pretty good money. I stayed there about three months, until I found work in an industrial engineering firm, where my job was to help reduce costs by improving the use of production materials. I got an incentive package rather than a straight salary. My pay was determined by how much I saved the company. I was there two and a half years, and in that time I nearly tripled my salary.

Salvendy quit to study business at Brunel College (later Brunel University), which had just inaugurated an MBA program. Since Salvendy did not have a high-school degree, he doubted whether he would be allowed to work for a formal degree, but he performed so well that they awarded him a diploma, which became his ticket of entry into the production engineering program at the University of Birmingham.

Salvendy wrote a thesis that earned him a master's degree—the first degree he had received—and admission to the doctorate program. He completed the work in one and a half years instead of the normal two.

SALVENDY: I looked for a job in two places. I wanted either to teach at the Termyion, the Israeli Institute of Science and Technology, or at some university in the United States.

But I couldn't get anything in the Termyion, and began writing to every American university that had an industrial engineering department. I said in effect, "Hey, you can't do without me," and I was amazed that I began getting offers without interviews, mostly for one-year appointments. The University of Buffalo offered me a regular tenure-track position, and I decided to go there.

You characterized yourself as a sort of playboy, and now you reveal yourself as someone with tremendous dedication.

SALVENDY: I found that innate ability didn't guarantee success unless you had motivation and desire. Motivation and desire are critical.

In May 1971, Salvendy accepted an associate professorship at Purdue University, becoming full professor six years later, and then head of the Department of Industrial Management with an endowed chair. Election to the National Academy of Engineering came in 1990, followed by the Lomonsov Medal from the Soviet Academy of Sciences and an honorary doctorate from the Chinese Academy of Sciences.

SALVENDY: In my opinion, I got these awards from the Soviet and Chinese governments because they confused my area of human factors with that of human relations. Human factors is the science of designing systems for human use, nothing more. I got it in human factors because the USSR and the Chinese governments were always so criticized for their poor records in human relations that they desired to make a political statement, and human factors sounded close enough. If I had been in high-energy physics or in materials science, for example, I don't think I would have received these awards.

How do you think you managed to survive the Holocaust?

SALVENDY: At the time I wasn't sufficiently mature to reflect on what really happened. Let me tell you first of all that I do not have a sense of guilt that our family managed to make it. I have a great sense of admiration for my mother that she insisted the four of us should stick together. We either would survive together or perish together. She had a strong sense that the family was one unit. In retrospect I admire that attitude. It very much appeals to my spirit.

We know now, however, that had we been caught we would have all perished. Parents with young children, especially mothers, were almost always killed. We were practically the only ones from our village who made it; all the others perished in Auschwitz.

Why were you so fortunate?

SALVENDY: Three very simple reasons: one, my grandfather received special exemptions; two, people who worked for my father were willing to risk their lives to give us help—bringing us food when we were in hiding, warning us that the Hungarian fascists were coming; and three, sheer luck. Even though you may not like it, luck is always a contributing factor. Even with careful planning and help, without luck you were finished.

What about psychological explanations for survival?

SALVENDY: Obviously, we had to have a vital desire, because if we had stayed in our old house, we would have been deported. But I don't think that our determination was any stronger or different than what you would expect from normal human beings.

Was there also something that, in the American idiom, is called "smarts," a certain kind of intuitive feeling that a certain course of action is the best one? Could it be that certain instincts in a literal sense were more highly developed in you than in others?

SALVENDY: You raise a good point and that certainly was another contributing factor. But such instincts were developed mostly in my father; I certainly was too young. For example, when we were moving from one hiding place to another, we encountered a group of Hungarian Nazis whom my father immediately greeted with a "Heil Hitler." Had he not made such an approach, they might have stopped us and checked our papers. And who knows what would have happened then?

How about religion, how about God's grace? Some people might say they prayed and their prayers were answered.

SALVENDY: No, nothing like that. The whole family was not religious, not me, nobody.

So this experience didn't intensify your religious feeling.

SALVENDY: Not at all. It had no influence.

You don't feel that religious faith in any way contributed to your survival?

SALVENDY: No, because I really didn't have much religious training. In hindsight, my religious belief probably decreased, because I would say if there were a God, how could He have allowed all that to happen?

What do you consider yourself: agnostic, atheist, or what?

SALVENDY: I follow tradition but not religion.

What does that mean?

SALVENDY: We have a seder, but I do not go to the synagogue except on Yom Kippur.

So talk of God really does not interest you?

SALVENDY: No. I just don't relate to the phenomenon of belief. But I consider the tradition.

Why?

SALVENDY: I'm not sure. Maybe partly it's upbringing. My parents were not religious. My grandfather, my grandmother, my father's parents were religious, but my father wasn't.

Your wife, what does she feel about Judaism?

SALVENDY: Similar to me.

Is she Jewish?

SALVENDY: She was converted by a rabbi in London. But in Israel we have to watch it, because to be "fully recognized" there you have to be Orthodox. She knows more than I know of Judaism. She had to study it for about nine months.

When you came to West Lafayette, did you join the synagogue or the temple?

SALVENDY: Nothing at the beginning. We joined the *schul* later on, when my daughter began going to Sunday school. I was even president of the Sunday school. My wife is a member of the Jewish women's group Hadassah, but she never goes, just pays her dues.

Are your children practicing Jews?

SALVENDY: Laura, my daughter, yes; she had a bat mitzvah, but my son didn't want to do a bar mitzvah.

Have you been back to Slovakia?

SALVENDY: I went back once in 1969, exactly twenty years after I left. First, I had the obvious reaction that the sizes were completely different. As a kid, things seemed much bigger and much more glorified. In reality, my hometown was much more simple.

I went there to see our former head housekeeper, the person who was responsible for the total management and networking of our hiding. He was still alive, and I wanted to see him. And it was very interesting how grateful he was that I came, how delighted he was to see me. I never will forget that happiness and delight. It was as if I were his long-lost grandchild. The compassion and love that came from this person was magnificent. And then I met a number of other people there who knew my father. But they were very distant and gave me an extremely cool reception. Not hatred, but more like "so what."

How did you let your children know what happened to you?

SALVENDY: When they were smaller, I got a special book during Passover that talked about the Holocaust and about the Jewish holidays. And when they were young, as part of the seder, I always would discuss some of the things I had been through, increasingly adding details as they grew older. They became more and more interested. But I would say my daughter's probably more interested than my son.

So what does being a Jew mean to you?

SALVENDY: Oh, that's a long talk, that's a never-ending one. I don't think I'm going to touch that.

Today Is a Second Life: Anna Berkovitz

"I didn't talk about my past because my only wish was to be like everybody else."

Part of the Russian Quota

Members of the Red Cross took Anna and her mother and the convoy's other Jewish women by car and then by boat to Sweden. They arrived at the port of Malmö and were sent to a reception area, where they were showered, disinfected, given fresh clothes, and transferred to a sanitarium, where they stayed for about a month. They lived in a quarantined area and were nourished on special diets of oatmeal, chicken soup, applesauce, and toast.

ANNA BERKOVITZ: We were very upset about the bland food because we wanted to eat a lot of food that wasn't good for us at that time. A group of the women actually raided the kitchen, and the Swedes were absolutely shocked at their behavior. But our hosts were really wonderful. Groups of doctors came to the compound to examine people and ordered hospitalization for some of them. My mother still couldn't walk, but actually recovered quite well, as, indeed, did most of the rest of us.

We always felt that the Swedes would give us a permit to stay, but they certainly did not encourage us to do so and, in fact, facilitated our plans eventually to leave.

A bout two or three days after their arrival, Anna's mother wrote to an aunt who had lived in Los Angeles for the past thirty-six years. The aunt had been recently widowed and had no children; she believed that all her family in Czechoslovakia had perished in the Holocaust and was therefore excited to receive her niece's letter. She immediately wrote back. Anna's mother did not want to return to Czechoslovakia—the Ruthenian part had now been incorporated into the Soviet Union—and not being an ardent Zionist, she hesitated about going to Palestine. On the strength of this encouraging response from her aunt and on what she decided was best for her daughter, she decided to go to the United States.

BERKOVITZ: Life in Palestine was very insecure then, and I think that my mother was understandably tired of struggle and not ready for further hardships. It was not even clear at that time whether there would be an Israel. My mother had cousins in Israel who told her how difficult things were. I would probably have opted to go to Palestine because I felt that, having suffered as a Jew, I should fight to establish my Jewish identity and work for the creation of a Jewish state. And probably I would have been just as happy going there as to the United States. But my mother thought I would be better off in the United States, where I would have a better future and more opportunity. It was as simple as that.

By July 1945, we received our affidavits and applied for our visas. We were considered part of the Russian quota, which was then quite open. But we had to wait until my mother was strong enough to go to the American consulate in Göteborg for her interview and physical examination. When we finally did go, about five girls carried her up the stairs, and then she managed to walk from where they put her down into the immigration office. After the formalities were over, she walked out the door, and was carried back down the stairs and returned to the infirmary.

My aunt had sent us seven hundred dollars for transportation, and we waited until we got space on a ship to come over, which was scheduled to depart on March 26, 1946. By then my mother was well enough to walk. We landed at New York, where we were met by an uncle who lived in Cleveland.

Before we left we had gotten in touch with him and told him the time and date of our arrival and asked him to please come and pick us up. We did not realize that Cleveland was that far from New York, and that he would have to take off work to meet us. Anyway, he came and drove us back to Cleveland, where we stayed for about a week before catching the train for Los Angeles. We arrived in Los Angeles on April 8, 1946.

When we were in Europe, we thought that everybody in the United States was a millionaire. But when we moved here, we found out that everybody was not rich, especially my mother's aunt, who had very modest means. As a matter of fact, she was living alone in a hotel room and had no place to put us. She made arrangements for us to stay in the home of some relatives until my mother was able to get a job and could get an apartment of her own.

We arrived on a Saturday, and the next Monday my mother began looking for work. She had no profession and didn't speak the language, but she managed to find work in a Jewish bakery, where she worked for the next twenty-five years, eventually becoming its manager.

It became clear to me that you can lose everything, but the only thing that they cannot take away from you is a skill or profession. My mother had neither, but she was determined that I should get an education to prepare myself for a better life.

Anna's mother and aunt shared an apartment, while Anna became an au pair, helping to baby-sit a family friend's two small children. Sam Green, a friend of her great-aunt, registered her at the local high school and encouraged her academically. He became her surrogate father.

BERKOVITZ: I started in the ninth grade. I had just turned sixteen, so I was about a year older than the rest of the class. But I finished the ninth, tenth, eleventh, and twelfth grades in two years. I was practically a straight-A student; I got a B only in English literature.

It was awkward at first. The first day, we stood in line to sign up for classes, and a girl next to me asked, "Who's teaching the course?" And I thought that she was asking me, "Who's taking the course?" and I said, "I am." So she started

Anna Berkovitz and her mother, Sweden, January/February 1946.

Robert Melson's mother, Nina, Prague, 1944, after she had assumed the identity of Countess Janina Zomoyska.

Robert Melson and his family in Antwerp on the day they emigrated for the United States in 1947. From left, Willy, Nina, Richi, Bobi, and Ilona, a friend.

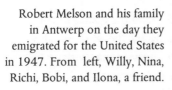

laughing. But she became one of my best friends, and I developed a circle of friends with the girls very easily. I had more difficulty with the boys, though.

I felt they were very immature and childish. So I didn't develop any relationship with any of the boys in school, only with the girls. As a matter of fact I have kept up with some of those girls throughout my adult life.

Were they curious about your past?

BERKOVITZ: I didn't talk about my past because my only wish was to be like everybody else. Nobody knew anything about my background. They just knew that I was from Czechoslovakia, that's all.

I pushed myself. I went to school during the day. I took night classes. I went to summer school, and then Sam tutored me in math, and I became a math major. High school was academically very rewarding. I was in the Honor Society. I don't think I was particularly smart, I just worked hard and I succeeded.

Did you already know English?

BERKOVITZ: I picked it up as I went along. But as you see, I haven't lost my accent, and I was only sixteen.

Socially I was not very happy because I was not part of the "in group." I didn't adjust particularly well to mixed company. I was very politically aware, and most of the girls and the boys only seemed interested in sports and silly things like that. I was interested in a career. Some of the girls who became my friends, though, were more serious, but serious girls in high school are not the popular girls.

That bothered you?

BERKOVITZ: More emotionally than intellectually. I wanted to graduate as fast as I could. My dream was to go to UCLA. My parents always wanted me to go to the university, and I always wanted to be a physician. But I started out studying pharmacy because you can always get a job as a pharmacist. I soon transferred to biology with a microbiology major, however.

It was difficult to get into UCLA; the competition was very stiff—at that time there was a huge influx of veterans—and the course of study was difficult. I was absolutely overwhelmed, especially by the impersonality of the place. There were five hundred people in a chemistry course, with no help sessions, no quizzes, and no homework. If you came to lecture, it was fine. If you didn't come to lecture, it was fine. But at exam time they expected you to know the material. I didn't know how to study, how to apportion my time, how to be a mature student. My first semester I got straight Cs, which completely devastated me.

Then I caught on, and from then on I got straight As. I made Phi Beta Kappa, and I graduated in three and a half years with highest honors. By the time I reached my junior year, I had only small classes, always with the same students, mostly microbiology majors. I began to know the professors, they knew me, and my classmates knew me. I really enjoyed my last two years, and I did phenomenally well. I would get something like 99 percent on a test, when the next-highest grade would be 65. I think I graduated number one in the class.

> *Do you think this success was due only to hard work? Many students who work hard don't have the success you did.*

BERKOVITZ: It was a constant struggle between the rational and the emotional. Between the things that you feel you want to do and those things you feel you have to do because it's in your long-range interest. Sometimes you don't want to stay home on a Saturday night and study, but you think that is the right thing to do because you have to do well on the test, and staying home is more important than going out and relaxing with a date. I gave you a trivial example, but the important thing is having a big goal in mind and working toward that goal.

> *Do you think the kind of success you demanded of yourself was related to the experiences that you had during the war?*

BERKOVITZ: No, it was directly related to my original upbringing, related to the values of my father and my mother, who expected me to be successful. When I was a little girl, I remember asking my mother: "Mother, what would you do if I couldn't possibly do all these things you want me to do?" And she just smiled and she said, "Well, you can do these things."

As far as my mother was concerned, getting a university education was the pinnacle. After that, the number-one thing was to get married and have a family. When I wanted to continue my education, she felt that there were other things besides studying.

Most of my classmates were in pre-med, and that was what I wanted to do also. But I felt that I could not put such a financial burden on my mother. And I followed the advice of my adviser, a female professor of microbiology, who told me that I should go out and get a job and save enough money to go to medical school later on. My mother agreed, but Sam Green was very, very upset. He thought I should stick with it and start going to medical school right then and there. In retrospect I should have done that.

> *That was a big mistake?*

BERKOVITZ: For my career? Oh, yes. Maybe for my life it wasn't, but for my career it was. Today I'm advising all my women students not to break their education. Once you leave school and get involved in other things, it's extremely difficult to go back.

While you were going to school in Los Angeles, were you in contact with the Jewish community there?

BERKOVITZ: No. We never became a member of a synagogue or anything.

Your mother wasn't very religious, was she?

BERKOVITZ: No, she wasn't, and she was, if anything, completely isolated. I think that being part of a Jewish community reminded her too much of the past.

When she finished UCLA in December 1951 (the B.S. degree was awarded the following June), Berkovitz got a job at the Cedars of Lebanon Medical Research Institute. The work on a cancer research project in the tissue culture laboratory was challenging, but she realized that if she were ever to be given real responsibility, she would have to go to graduate school. However, by then she had met Leonard, her future husband, who was doing a postdoctorate at the California Institute of Technology. After their marriage they lived in Santa Monica, where he had a job at the Rand Corporation. She continued doing tissue cultures until she started having children. She did not return to graduate school until after her youngest son began school. That was thirteen years after graduation from UCLA.

BERKOVITZ: Except for Sam Green, who wanted me to go right on to medical school, Leonard was the first person in my life who encouraged me to go to graduate school. But in those days, you were either a mother or you were a career person. Many women sacrificed careers in favor of motherhood. Most of my friends were mothers. After we were married, we waited almost four years to have our first child, a fact that prompted people to ask what we were waiting for. Even before my youngest son was in kindergarten and I returned to graduate school, I worked part-time, but my mother didn't like it. She thought that I should have subordinated myself completely to my children, which to her meant staying home all the time.

Did you feel somewhat betrayed?

BERKOVITZ: I thought she was very inconsistent, but I would not assert myself because after what we had gone through, I felt I had to do everything not to upset her. I thought that it was my responsibility to keep her happy, and I felt guilty that she hadn't made a life for herself. I resented the fact that she was living her life through me.

She first told me that she would begin dating when I graduated from high school, then she said, "I cannot date until you graduate from college," and then after I graduated from college, she said, "Well, I'm just too old now," which she wasn't. Later, when she was in her seventies, she told me that the reason she didn't remarry was because she had to take care of me. It was a very complex situation.

An Unlimited Capacity for Cruelty

The Berkovitzes came to West Lafayette in 1962, when Leonard accepted a professorship in the mathematics department. Returning to biology was especially difficult for Anna because the Watson-Crick discoveries had so completely changed the field. The genetics that she had learned was now so old-fashioned that she had to audit undergraduate classes to discover the basics of molecular biology. Accepted in the biology department at Purdue University, she began working on a Ph.D. but was ultimately faced with a problem not uncommon to women in general and to faculty wives in particular.

A university town such as West Lafayette provided few opportunities for faculty wives to find academic positions at the same institution as their husbands. Henry Koffler, head of biology, told her that after she got her Ph.D., the likelihood of her getting a tenure-track position in his department was "nil." However, he did offer her a temporary job as an instructor. She took it and decided to go no further than her master's degree.

BERKOVITZ: I enjoyed my job very much. I enjoyed teaching; I was teaching laboratories. My kids were still at home, and this was a very happy time of my life. And then after five years, Henry Koffler told me they were recommending me for tenure. Leonard said, "It will never happen, they don't have anybody tenured on the instructor level in the School of Science." But I got tenure, and Henry told me, "You will have to make a decision. If you take this tenured position, you will never be promoted; if you go back to graduate school, you won't get a job." So I took the job and then had the distinction of being the first tenured instructor in the School of Science who didn't have a Ph.D.[8] Not going on turned out to be a terrible mistake.

What happened to your sense of Jewish identity when you came to Lafayette?

BERKOVITZ: We were here less than twenty-four hours, and the rabbi from the Sons of Abraham congregation called on us. He was a very warm and hospitable guy, and the congregation engulfed us with love and attention, but we have actually not joined because they are too conservative for me. This has led to a mild disagreement between my husband and me, because he is more traditional than I am, and he has been supporting them. Our older son was bar-mitzvahed with the Sons of Abraham, but our younger son did not want to be bar-mitzvahed, and we did not insist. So we gave some support to the Sons of Abraham without actually belonging. Last year, though, we did make a decision to join the Reform Temple Israel.

What kind of experience was that?

BERKOVITZ: It's an affirmation of belonging to a Jewish community.

Do the Jewish religious services and prayers mean anything to you?

BERKOVITZ: No.

Would you consider yourself an agnostic?

BERKOVITZ: Probably, probably.

What about your affiliations or activities that relate to Jewish life?

BERKOVITZ: I'm a life member of Hadassah, but I'm not very active. I have a strong cultural identification with the Jewish people, but not as far as the religious ceremonies go.

You have also been active in Hillel and participated in a good number of their Holocaust remembrance conferences.

BERKOVITZ: I did particularly in the beginning, but sometimes the memorial service gets too diluted with other activities. I do certain things because I really feel these are the right things to do.

Recently a teacher called me up from Tecumseh Middle School and asked me if I could speak to an assembly of seventh and eighth graders, kids who are exactly the age I was when I was sent to Auschwitz. They did a unit on World War II, and they wanted a survivor to talk to them. These kids were completely unsophisticated, coming mostly from blue-collar neighborhoods, and they had never met a survivor, nor, indeed, any Jewish kids. I am glad that I talked to them.

I refused to prepare a speech and said I would respond to their questions. It was unbelievable. After an hour, there wasn't a kid who moved. They stayed throughout recess, asking one question after another. They wanted to know what my life was like before the Holocaust, what my school was like, everything that happened. Afterwards each kid wrote me a letter, which they probably did under duress, but it was really a fantastic collection of their reactions. I thought doing that was worthwhile because maybe the next time they hear somebody say the Holocaust never happened, they'll know better.

On the other hand, the Purdue alumni magazine wanted to write a big article about me, but I canceled the interview because I didn't see any purpose in spilling out my life to the alumni community. I didn't think it was appropriate or educational. They probably wouldn't have read it anyway.

Have you visited Israel?

BERKOVITZ: Yes, in 1969. We have cousins there, and we strongly support the state of Israel. But I think the experience did more to establish a Jewish identity in our sons than anything else.

What did you find out about your relatives who didn't survive?

BERKOVITZ: We hoped that my father would survive, but we don't know what happened to him. I assume he was not killed immediately, but I don't know. We don't know any specifics on the fate of the other members of our family either.

To what extent have you talked to your children about your experiences? Have they asked about it?

BERKOVITZ: I have taken great pains not to inflict the survivor syndrome upon my children. I have taken pains not to inflict them with my wounds. Until they grew up, they knew very little about my background. As far as their own identity is concerned, I prefer they do whatever they feel is comfortable.

What fundamental values would you extract out of your experiences?

BERKOVITZ: You can take anything out of them that you wish. But I don't know how you can really extract any good from the kind of experience I went through, because so many good, innocent, God-fearing religious people were wiped out. The Holocaust shows the absolutely unlimited capacity of man's cruelty to man.

How did you come to resolve your feelings?

BERKOVITZ: When I look at it rationally, the experience was a very bitter one. It's a lesson in mass inhumanity not covered up by any veneer of civilization. That's the basic lesson. But what I think the question should be is, What got me through? And the number-one thing that got me through was just sheer luck. Also, while I was in the camp, I had the attitude that this was an absolute, total aberration, and that if I survived, there would be this wonderful and just world out there. This attitude of some positive goodness kept me going.

So in order to survive, you had to be somewhat naive?

BERKOVITZ: That's right. You have to believe that there is a plan, and there is a basic good, and that once you overcome this temporary aberration, there is a righteous world there, because this is not really the way humanity is.

And from where did you get this feeling?

BERKOVITZ: I don't know. I just had this feeling of ultimate justice and ultimate goodness, that here was this evil that the whole world was fighting, and that this evil would eventually be overcome. Things were more black and white to me then than they are now. Things are not so clear to me anymore.

What happened to you was clear enough.

BERKOVITZ: But not clear as to whether it was an aberration or part of general humankind, whether this is the way people really are, whether we all are capable of such absolute evil.

During your experience, your positive idealistic side prevailed, but has your faith in human goodness subsequently been shattered?

BERKOVITZ: When I think back to those times, I say to myself, that was not me, that person in the camp, because I could not have gone through that. Now I don't see how I could have done it. This life today is my second life, a completely different life. But my survival shows you some of the strength of a human being and what can be endured.

If part of the reason for your getting through lay in a certain faith in a better world, how did a more traditional religious faith affect people's survival?

BERKOVITZ: I'm sure that a deep religious faith gave people a certain amount of strength. My mother and I didn't have it. The fact that we were being punished because we were Jewish made us more proud to be Jewish, so that if somebody had put a gun to our heads and said, "Deny your faith or die," we probably would have chosen death. This was our identity, and we were proud of that identity. But Auschwitz made us question the existence of God. How could a god let this thing go on?

Did you find that with certain people those experiences strengthened their religious faith?

BERKOVITZ: This question came up in a recent conversation I had with somebody who said to me, "You know, even under your terrible circumstances, there was a proof of God. While you were suffering, God showed his hand in the D-Day invasion. Had that not succeeded, the war would have lasted much longer and more millions of Jews would have perished."

Had the war lasted two or three months longer, both my mother and I would probably have been dead along with many more who managed to survive the camps. So in that sense you could say that it was God's will that the Normandy invasion succeeded. However, carrying this argument to its logical end, you would have to ask why God waited until six million Jews had been murdered before performing this miracle. Why didn't God make a miracle earlier?

On a personal level, though, you might say there is a god because that god was looking out for me.

And this has made you less religious?

BERKOVITZ: Less religiously Jewish while affirming my Jewish identity.

Did you ever go back to the place where you were born?

BERKOVITZ: No.

Do you have any desire to do that?

BERKOVITZ: No, I don't think I will ever go back.

But you've been back to Europe?

BERKOVITZ: I've been back to Europe, and I went as far as Budapest.

Have you ever been back to Germany?

BERKOVITZ: That was a very interesting experience. While we were on sabbatical in London in 1984, I decided that I wanted to go back to Hungary, to Budapest. And we agonized whether we should drive or fly, but we decided to drive, and of course, we had to drive through Germany. It was very difficult for me to set foot on German soil, so we pored over maps to see how we could go through Germany as quickly as possible. We spent the night right at the French border and planned to drive as fast as possible to Austria and then on to Hungary. But nevertheless, we had to spend at least one night in Germany. I was extremely, extremely upset. And then I had a very interesting emotional experience.

It was late May, early June. The same time of year when I had been taken in a cattle car from Hungary to Auschwitz forty years earlier. We had gone through Slovakia into Poland, through the high country. And I remember standing on a box looking through a little window at the beautiful scenery as we were passing through the High Tatras, seeing the pine woods and the spring flowers, and I thought how beautiful the world was with its blue skies and gorgeous mountains. And I was going to who knows where? I didn't know about Auschwitz, but I knew where we were going wasn't inviting.

Then, forty years later, almost to the day, again at the end of May, I was going through Germany in a car with my husband, going through beautiful scenery. Under very different circumstances. We were driving to Austria on the autobahn and the scenery was absolutely gorgeous, blue skies and pine trees on both sides, and I recalled this cattle car going to Auschwitz. I was very emotionally tense.

But I was fiddling around with the radio, and as we crossed a bridge I suddenly heard a prayer in Hebrew. Leonard said it was a prayer for the dead, a Kaddish, and it was being recited over a German station. And both Leonard and I started to cry, and I said, "Forty years ago I was going in a cattle car from Hungary to Auschwitz, and I was looking out that little window and seeing this beautiful scenery and the blue skies, and forty years later, I am going in Germany as a free person in a car with you, going over this bridge with the beautiful pine trees and the blue sky, and I'm a free person, and over a German radio station comes the Kaddish. If there is a miracle, this is a miracle. And maybe there is a God, after all."

And we both continued to cry, and after that, I felt better. I felt better, even though I was in Germany. I have had very few spiritual or religious experiences in my life, because as you can see, I'm not a religious person, but this I consider a religious experience. It was like a catharsis, and after that, I felt more comfortable being in that country, which had been the source of so much of my suffering.

When we got to Austria, we ended up staying in a castle that had become a bed and breakfast. The proprietress, the Countess von Augsburg herself, served breakfast. The countess's grandfather had once been a minister in the government of Emperor Francis Joseph. She did not know that she was serving the granddaughter of a Jewish coal merchant who had once been one of his subjects.

Security Is a Matter of Percentages: Robert Melson

"My God, what a crazy thing to have gone through and also, what a crazy thing to have asked a kid to go through."

A New Identity

After the end of the war, the Melsons moved to Brussels, where they lived for the next two years. It was there that Melson found out he was Jewish.

ROBERT MELSON: A day or two after we arrived in Brussels, I went with my parents to a club called the Shalom, a gathering place for fellow refugees and other displaced persons. My father started speaking Yiddish to the waiter, and my mother started to cry. And they're both embracing this waiter, and there are Yiddish songs being sung. They became part of this network, part of what we would today call a "support group." I felt tied to that. It felt Jewish to me. The other thing that was Jewish to me came from the stories my parents started telling me about what happened during the war. I was very close to my mother, and especially through her, through her sense of grief, I got this sense of Jewishness, although I really didn't know what being Jewish meant. I knew my parents were connected to this group of people who had survived the war and a lot of our family had been killed. That's it, I thought, that's what it means to be Jewish.

Melson's father, unable to obtain a regular work permit, engaged in black market operations. He did so well that he was able to send his son to Le Rosay, a fashionable boarding school in Switzerland. He was enrolled there under the old identity of Zamoyski.

You found out that you were Jewish, but then your father told you to pretend that you were non-Jewish. How did you feel about that?

MELSON: Well, first of all, when you are nine years old, you don't challenge what your parents say, you try to go along with what they are asking you to do. Moreover, during the war, I had a sense that life was like being in the army. There were tough things you had to do to get through, and you didn't ask too many questions. I had been told many things, like not peeing outdoors, about not playing in certain places and not saying certain things. And my father had been arrested by the Gestapo; I had seen that happen. So I thought this was just another thing one had to go through, and it was important for me to do it as best as I could.

The experience at that Swiss school was confusing and hard to bear—not that every day was unpleasant, but that it was just tense, enervating. I couldn't be honest with my roommates—one of them was a Muslim and the other was a Swiss kid who was Christian. I had the constant sense that I was living a lie, especially as I had to continue the charade of acting like a count, going to confession, going to catechism lessons, going to mass. I had to constantly listen to all that Christian kind of antisemitism, a continuation of the anti-Jewish lessons I had learned as a Catholic kid, going to church with my governess: that the Jews had crucified Christ, that the Jews were this and the Jews were that. That stuff was part of the climate. Only now, it got tedious and unpleasant because I knew I was not that person. And I started getting all sorts of psychological ailments.

Toward the end of my career in that Swiss school, I was constantly in the infirmary for one undiagnosed thing after another. And then at the beginning of the new term, after I had been there about a year and a half, my mother came one day and took me out of there. We went back to Brussels, and about two months later we were on a boat going to America.

And it really wasn't until later in life that I thought about it. I said, "My God, what a crazy thing to have gone through and also, what a crazy thing to have asked a kid to go through." And I don't know why my parents did it. Neither of them was a deep thinker, certainly not a deep thinker as far as kids were concerned.

We are much more sensitive to our kids' needs now. I guess we are the post-Freudian or something generation. We realize that kids and other people have an internal life. I don't think my parents thought of me that way. It was just, "Bobby will just do what he's supposed to do," and that's that.

I finally started to get content with my Jewish identity when we came to New York, in November 1947.

Why did you go to America?

MELSON: My father had this image, this vision, of what America was like. America to him was freewheeling. He was an operator, a hustler; he was a dreamer. He wanted to be a millionaire. He wanted to live big, to make it big in America. This was his conception. We had relatives in Brazil, and some in Australia, and we could have gone there. But my father was intent on coming to the States. He had this vision. He really fell for the romance of America, hook, line, and sinker. He saw himself as a Humphrey Bogart character. He *was* in some ways a Humphrey Bogart character. He loved America, the image of America. That is what drew him.

My mother found a distant cousin living in New York, living in Brooklyn, cousin David Ruben, and through him we got this affidavit to go to New York. David Ruben picked us up at the boat, and that was it. I think we had dinner with him once, and we never saw him again.

You must have had enormous adjustment problems. You started out as Polish, then all of a sudden you became Czech, and then the Czech identity went, followed by the French or Franco-Swiss identity. And then you became an American. How did these radical changes affect your sense of identity?

MELSON: I never would have put it the way you put it. I was my parents' kid, and we were living in a very dangerous time, and somehow I had to do whatever they were asking me to do, because we could all be killed. So all this business of learning Czech and French, and doing this and that, had nothing to do with identity. It had to do with survival.

The real change for me came when I arrived in America. I had the sense that here was where normal life was going to start. Before that it was all craziness. Whatever happened in Europe was insane.

I wouldn't have known what the term "identity" meant. There was chaos before, but here there was normal life.

What language did you speak with your parents when you were at home?

MELSON: Polish with my parents, and Czech outside of the home, then later French, but still Polish with my parents. But the big change was coming to America. I mean, this was the traditional living-room story. I've heard this story being told by Italian immigrants about coming to America. We had been here about a month or two, and my dad said, "I don't want to speak Polish to you anymore at all. We'll speak English at home." But my mother and I still spoke Polish, because it was just closer. It was easier.

Always?

MELSON: Yeah, it was kind of Polish-English. You know, if you needed a word that was Polish, you pulled out a word. If you needed a word that was English, you pulled out a word. But with my dad, very soon it became English, even though he spoke halting English, and I could hardly speak English when I came. But I picked it up within five months, and at six months I was rattling on in English. He was a pretty smart guy and he picked it up. And he and I always spoke English. My mother and I spoke Polish, so that is very significant. But for the rest, no more Polish at all. A new life, a new start. Everything. America was real life.

Then how does this kid who is raised as a Polish Catholic and speaks three different languages before he even comes to America start to become a Jewish-American kid?

MELSON: My mother enrolled me in this Jewish Center on 86th Street, run by Rabbi Midsenki, and I started learning about what it meant to be a Jew. Few kids that I know who are that age like Hebrew school—my own kids hated it—but I kind of lapped it up. To me it was another thing to do, but it was something I enjoyed.

One of the early memories of that school indicates how I thought of myself in terms of being a Jew. I remember being in Rabbi Midsenski's office. The door was open and I looked through the hall and saw some kids playing basketball. And I said to him, "Who are those boys?" And he said, "They belong here. They belong to the Jewish Center, they're kids who come here after school and they shoot baskets." And I said, "Are they Jewish?" And he looked at me surprised and he said, "Yes, of course!" And I remember being so amazed that there could be Jewish kids who would be playing basketball, because to me being Jewish meant you were fleeing, you were making believe you were somebody else, you were being despised by the Christians, or you were dead! That's what being Jewish meant. I couldn't understand that being Jewish meant wearing shorts and shooting baskets, because the notion of Jewishness was so fraught with disaster and tragedy for me that to associate it with something less disastrous was unthinkable.

Now it was associated with not being in danger.

MELSON: You didn't have to be in danger, you didn't have to be dead, you didn't have to be lying and living on false papers.

Then with the establishment of Israel, I saw Jews fighting and winning. My God! Such a revelation! My thought was that Jews were cadavers. These were not cadavers. These people were actually surviving, fighting, winning.

Your experiences certainly cut you off from your fellow students.

MELSON: Yeah, they did. And I'm sure that will affect me for the rest of my life. I've always been good at very close friendships, but not terribly good at mingling and being relaxed in large groups. I always feel a little tense about it.

What connection did your former life have in conditioning your values?

MELSON: My sense is that all of us who came here as immigrants, as refugees after the war, the parents as well as the children, launched into making America the best they could—taking the opportunities and overcoming the obstacles—and trying to make this country as homelike as possible. It was a kind of rejection of the European past, and that meant setting aside the war years, not thinking about it, and not dealing with the past.

I did not want to study Europe. I did not want to have anything to do with Germany. Certainly nothing to do with Poland. Just the thought of Europe was chilling. The whole place was a graveyard! I avoided studying the Holocaust. I worked hard in making myself a so-called "normal American young college kid." I knew the Jews had this past, and I knew it was important, and we talked about it in the family, and sometimes I would talk about it to my friends, just in passing. And I knew that history was something important to deal with. But I didn't have the courage to deal with it. This was also in the 1950s, when I was going to college, and there was no academic framework, no courses on the Holocaust, nothing. If it was mentioned at all, it was in the context of those nasty things the Nazis did to the Jews, and now let's go on to more serious things, like the Battle of the Bulge. And I was always shocked by that. I said, "Now wait a minute! Wait a minute. Isn't there something more?" But there was no moral or intellectual framework to deal with this issue. And so I didn't deal with it. Besides, it was frightening to deal with.

I had heard of Elie Wiesel's book *Night,* which came out by then. But I did not have the courage to read it. I had held it in my hands, looked at the first page, and put it aside. So I did not want to have anything to do with Europe.

How did you end up being a political scientist?

MELSON: I clearly wanted to go to college. There was never any question in my mind that was what I wanted to do. And I don't think that it had very much to do with being Jewish or not being Jewish or with the war. It had to do mostly with my class background, the context of the people I knew, my family. My father had gone to graduate business school; my mother had gone to the conservatory. People always assumed that their kids and the kids of their friends would go to college, in fact, to good schools. The funny thing was, it wasn't even a question of which college I would go to. I was told which college I would go to. It was going to be MIT, because my father had learned that one of the best engineering schools in the United States was MIT, and he had me apply. But I wasn't particularly good in math or science, and within a year at MIT I quickly discovered that I was in over my head. MIT luckily had a program for wishy-washy people like me who were interested in history, philosophy, and literature, and I transferred to that program, and I did okay.

Refining the Options

Melson first majored in anthropology, but then switched to political science at MIT, majoring in African studies, which was more psychologically neutral. After passing his preliminary examinations in 1964, he got Carnegie and Ford Foundation grants to go to Nigeria to do a study on the labor movement. By then he had met his future wife, Gail, who was studying at Harvard. She joined him in Nigeria, and they got married there. On the way back, they stopped off in Europe to visit his parents, who were then living in Munich. While he was there he decided to return to Warsaw.

MELSON: I tried to find the places my parents had talked about, the streets my mother remembered from her childhood. The ghetto was gone, replaced by Stalinist workers' quarters. But in 1965 there were still areas of Warsaw not yet rebuilt, something I found comforting, because it reminded me that there had been a war, that something had happened here.

We stayed with a Polish graduate student who took us around, and told us that five nuns had been shot here and the professors at the University of Warsaw had been killed, and that the underground had assassinated a Gestapo officer. He showed us the bullet marks at the university where people were shot. All these stories I found very comforting, because that was what I was looking for. But the graduate student was totally unconscious of antisemitism. I told him I was Jewish. It didn't register. To him I was simply a Pole from America. He couldn't understand why I wanted to visit the ghetto. In that respect, the trip was kind of demented.

Munich, on the other hand, was unreal. The beer gardens, the sunny weather, and the people who looked as if there never had been a war.

Melson's first university teaching post was at Michigan State. While there, he heard about the war in Biafra, whose massacres triggered a strong response.

MELSON: Most of the victims were Ebos, and to me the Ebos were the Jews. And in a peculiar way, the Ebos saw themselves as Jews. This was not just my invention. They had been the successful, enterprising, upwardly mobile people in Biafra and Nigeria. When Nigeria began to collapse, they got it in the neck. And they seceded and called themselves Biafra. Then massacres started all over the country. Against them. And I totally identified with their predicament. I tried to write about it, and for the first time I began to think about something called the Holocaust as a historical event that might have some parallels to what happened in Nigeria. Somehow this Nigerian experience, the reports from some of the people I had interviewed, made me confront the reality of brutality that connected with my own experience.

This process of association and identity was intensified when I went to Israel in 1968. It was a very emotional experience for me. And then I realized why it was such an emotional experience: we arrived in Israel, we went up to Jerusalem. I went up to the Wall, to the Western Wall—and as I've told you, I do not come from an Orthodox family or a religious family. Whatever religion I have, I picked up by myself—and I went up, like all Jewish pilgrims, and I had a vision of my grandfather. And I remember it was such a strong feeling. Going to Israel was psychologically, somehow emotionally, tied into his death. And somehow touching the wall was touching him.

After that, I began to realize that I had exhausted my interest in Africa, and that I would try to deal with my own experiences during the war.

Melson came to Purdue in August 1971. It was there that he began seriously to concern himself with the Holocaust. First he wrote about what he had seen in a novelistic form, then he focused directly on these events by introducing a specific seminar on the Holocaust. This course was the beginning of the Purdue Jewish Studies Program, launched with the inaugural participation of Walter Hirsch [also a subject of this book] and Larry Axel, from the philosophy department. The program received little support or encouragement from the university administration, but through the assemblage and development of an appropriate array of relevant courses, mainly in history, political science, and language, it did attain the status of a minor. After a second trip to Israel, Melson began work on a study comparing the Holocaust and the Armenian massacres.

MELSON: I was reading all of this Holocaust-related stuff, but I did not want to be a person whose Jewish identity was solely linked to the Holocaust and to the history of victimization. I wanted a Jewish identity that was filled with Judaism, that was filled with Hebrew, that was filled with Jewish literature, Hebrew literature, Israeli literature—things that were positive.

How did this relate to your involvement in the creation of Jewish studies?

MELSON: The idea behind the Jewish Studies Program was in part selfish. If I was going to speak and teach about the Holocaust, I wanted a support group. I wanted a network, a context, where we could be talking about other things. It was a kind of an attempt to surround myself with a Jewish content that in a way would protect me from the Holocaust. It would allow me to study the Holocaust without getting sucked into it and getting depressed by it and thinking that's all there was. I've spent twenty years thinking about the Holocaust and twelve years writing a book on the Holocaust. I'm getting a little tired of the topic. But what I'm not tired of is the other side of it, namely, Judaism and the Jewish content.

So at this point you obviously have a very strong Jewish identity.

MELSON: Sure.

To what extent is it cultural and to what extent is it religious?

MELSON: It's primarily cultural. I have my own kind of private Judaism. I pray, but I don't think that an Orthodox Jew or a Reformed Jew would much recognize what that prayer is. It has a lot to do with my grandparents. You might say I have my own peasant religion. Judaism is a religion that I find interesting, intellectually and culturally. Unfortunately, I was not brought up in a religious environment. My mother would light Friday night candles once we came to America, but she never did that in Europe. And she would go to high holiday services, but not my father. I regret that I don't come from a richer Jewish experience. I wish I had more of a feeling for the Jewish service.

I have a very good friend in Israel who is a professor and happens to be an Orthodox Jew. He goes to services every Saturday and Friday night and takes it very seriously. I asked him once, "Barry, why do you do that? I mean, what do you get out of it?" And he said, "Oh, when I was a little boy my grandfather used to take me every Saturday down to the synagogue, and he was a respected man and I'd walk down the aisle with him holding his hand, and all the men would pinch my cheek. And he would sit me down next to him, and we would go through the service, and I loved it. And I've loved it ever since."

Believe me, I envied him that experience. I wish I had that experience. If my grandfather had lived, I probably would have had that experience, because he was a Hasidic Jew.

> *It's intensely ironic that had you had that kind of experience and come from that kind of a family, you would have been more identifiable as a Jew, and you might not have survived.*

MELSON: Exactly, of course, of course.

> *In what ways were you influenced in your Jewish identity by your wife, Gail?*

MELSON: Gail is a kind of ego ideal of what it means to have a Jewish education. Her Jewishness is so natural to her that she has no conception of what I crave. Her grandfather was a practicing rabbi in New York. Her mother was a Hebrew teacher. Gail speaks fluent Hebrew. She knows much more about Judaism than I do, than I'll ever know. She imbibed it with her mother's milk, to put it simply.

> *What sort of experience, religion, and tradition do you want your children to have? What do you want to leave them of your experiences and your traditions?*

MELSON: I'd like them to be comfortably Jewish and proud of and sensitive to their Jewish heritage. I'd also like them to be free men and women and make the kind of choices they want to make. I want them to combine Jewish tradition and Jewish culture with a kind of optimism and the kind of openness that is the American part of me. We've talked a lot about the Judaism part, but I take my American part seriously, too. I mean, I came here as a little kid, and I identified as an American. That, to me, is important. I'd like them to be open to the world, looking to the future, stand up for their rights, be individualists—all that which is the best of the American experience.

But also I want them to be secure and proud and firm in their Jewishness. I think both of my kids have the kind of natural ease with their Jewishness that Gail has. That's one thing I've really admired in Gail all the years. I look at her with amazement. She is the least troubled with her Jewishness of anyone I know. She just takes it, it's just a nice thing.

What about your own sense of security?

MELSON: I wish I felt more secure. Sometimes I feel 72.5 percent safe, but 27.5 percent not safe. For example, one thing that makes me uncomfortable with Jewish studies is that it makes me too visible as a Jew. We survived the war on false papers, by denying that we were Jews. And it percolated into my bones that it is not physically secure to be a Jew. And I've reacted two ways, sometimes with a kind of "in your face" attitude and sometimes with withdrawal. Part of the Jewish studies business is "in your face." But the other part of it brings a kind of insecurity, a kind of nervousness.

You know, there would be a comfort in teaching something like political parties in Nebraska. I don't identify myself with political parties in Nebraska. But as a Jew teaching Jewish studies, I lose privacy. I find myself dealing with things that personally energize me. Jewish studies energizes me. But it is also exhausting.

You have quite an incredible story.

MELSON: To survive you had to have an incredible story. The credible story was that you went to the ghetto and then you were shipped out to Auschwitz and then you died. If you did not have an incredible story, you were dead.

Notes

1. Poland had wanted to hang on to Teschen, which they had grabbed after the Munich agreement with Hitler's permission.
2. Edvard Beneš, *Memoirs* (Boston: Houghton Mifflin, 1954), 285.
3. Since the Salvendys had a relative on the spot to vouch for them and take charge of their welfare, they were spared the grueling process of entry reserved for others less fortunate. The border control officials had established an assembly-line procedure to handle documentation, luggage inspection, medical examination, disinfection, inoculation and so forth. From the gate of immigration many of the recent arrivals, having no place to go, were sent to various overcrowded camps and remained there for many months.

4. The ministry of labor had sponsored the construction of two-story concrete dwellings, each apartment consisting of very small one- or two-room units with a kitchenette and a lavatory. The buildings were located in practically every town and city. The head of this ministry at the time the Salvendys came to Israel was Golda Meir.

5. The Holocaust really came to the forefront only in 1962, after the Eichmann trial. One of the reasons the government shied away from it was through a sense of shame that the Jews hadn't fought harder against their enemies. Later on, when Israel became strong, the use of the Holocaust became very important in Israeli life and Jewish identity.

6. The Youth Corps (Gedudei Noar) of the Israeli Defense Forces, administered by the ministry of education and culture, was obligatory for most students in secondary schools. Aside from its militaristic and physical fitness aspects, its purpose was to help turn recent immigrants into future Israeli citizens.

7. American-born Meir Kahane was the leader of the ultranationalist Kach Party, which advocated the forceful expulsion of all Arabs from Israeli-controlled territory. The Kach sponsored terrorist attacks against Arabs, including, in one famous incident, the blowing up of a bus on Mount Hebron. In 1988, the government passed a law empowering the Central Elections Board to bar all candidates who advocated racism from election to the Knesset.

8. Actually there were two, the other being Anna Mandler Akeley, who is also included in this study.

Part Four
The United States

11

A Sense of Service

S hortly after World War II, a group of American citizens sued the German government for having imprisoned them in concentration camps during the war. Their case dragged on for nearly forty years and was finally settled in 1995, with $2.1 million being divided among eleven of the aged plaintiffs. Most of the other litigants had since died. The case prompted U.S. Attorney General Janet Reno to ask the Justice Department's Foreign Claims Settlement Commission to conduct a review to determine the extent to which other Americans might also be eligible for such reparations. Eventually more than two hundred Americans were deemed eligible for compensation. This settlement only affected those American citizens who had been imprisoned in "recognized" concentration camps, a distinction that effectively excluded many other American citizens who had been imprisoned elsewhere but forced to work as slave laborers. This omission was rectified in a subsequent settlement. However, recognition of these claims still did not close the historical chapter on those American citizens, mostly Jewish, who were direct victims of Nazi racial politics. Still mostly unknown are those cases of hundreds of American prisoners of war who had been selected for the special treatment usually reserved for undesirables, especially the Jews.

The 1929 Geneva Convention stated that prisoners of war should at all times be treated humanely and protected against "acts of violence, from insults and from public curiosity" (part 1, article 2).[1] The agreement only allowed different treatment of prisoners if such differences were beneficial and based on military rank, physical and mental health, professional abilities, or gender (part 1, article 4). It forbade the employment of "prisoners of war on unhealthy or dangerous work" and stated that the conditions of work should not be "rendered more arduous by disciplinary measures" (part 3, article 32). Furthermore, the POWs were to be lodged in "buildings or huts which afford all possible safeguards regarding hygiene and salubrity," the conditions being "the same for depot troops of the detaining power" (part 3, article 10). Food rations should also be equivalent to those received by the occupying power's garrison troops (part 3, article 11).

The enormity of the prisoner-of-war problem facing the Germans in the first years of the war overwhelmed all available resources. On the Russian front the Germans had captured almost five million soldiers. Since the Germans considered the eastern war a war against racial inferiors, the conquerors herded their prisoners into compounds, provided them with little food and water, and let them slowly starve to death or perish by disease. Those deemed worthy of "special measures" had a more sudden death.

In July 1941, Reinhard Heydrich, chief of the Reich Security Head Office (Reichssicherheitshauptamt), or RSHA, began to exterminate all Soviet prisoners of war who his Einsatzgruppen (mobile execution squads) feared were carrying the contagion of Bolshevism. In this category were put "professional revolutionaries" (i.e., functionaries and party members), Red Army commissars, "fanatical" communists, intellectuals, agitators, thieves, troublemakers, and of course all Jews. The RSHA established screening centers and dispatched screening teams, usually consisting of one officer and four to six men, into the prisoner-of-war camps to select those who would be taken away and shot. The executions frequently took place in concentration camps, where secrecy could be ensured.

However, in terms of treatment the Germans usually distinguished between their western-front prisoners and those from the eastern front. They shot Jews who were formerly of German nationality now serving in foreign armies, if they could identify them, but other Jewish POWs were rarely executed. They could, though, be separated from the other prisoners and assigned to special work camps, where many of them ultimately perished. This is the story of one of the survivors.

Other Ways to Skin a Cat: Leon Trachtman

"I really do think that people of my generation had a sense of community purpose, which was developed in response to the challenges of the Great Depression—a feeling which manifested itself in the arts, in music, in philosophy, and especially in politics."

A Son of Immigrants

Leon Trachtman's paternal grandfather had left Russia for the United States just before the start of the First World War. He brought with him his wife, his three sons, and a daughter. In Odessa, where they had lived, he had been a professional temple scribe. But while the profession of copying Torah scrolls was respectable, it was hardly lucrative, and the grandfather tried to augment his meager salary with other, secular work. However, he once lost a job working on a road crew because his determination to keep kosher reduced him to eating crackers and water, a diet hardly adequate for one doing manual labor. The family's straitened circumstances dictated early employment for the sons, who were apprenticed to local jewelers even before they became teenagers. This proved to be a wise choice, since with this "portable" profession they eventually established a successful jewelry manufacturing business when they came to the United States.

The Trachtman family's motives for emigration were familiar ones: the United States held the prospect for economic improvement and the promise of escape from the menace of antisemitism, which in Imperial Russia often resulted in individual attacks and organized pogroms.

Leon's father, Max Trachtman, was fifteen years old when he arrived. He met his wife, Annette, in New York City, where she was a secretary for a diamond dealer with whom her future husband did business. Her parents were also immigrants, having arrived in New York around the turn of the century. She had come from a family of amber merchants who lived in Palanga, a Baltic Sea resort town in Lithuania, then part of the Russian Empire. In a sense Leon's parents had come from different worlds: she from a quite highly Europeanized community, he from a provincial seaport. Though both had Orthodox backgrounds, her family was far more cosmopolitan than his. She spoke of uncles and cousins who would travel regularly to Saint Petersburg to go to the opera and to art galleries. Some of her family's limited discretionary monies were used to purchase a piano and a wind-up phonograph and Caruso records — things that would have been out of the question in her husband's family. They were married in 1923.

LEON TRACHTMAN: My father was essentially a nonobserving Jew and an agnostic. He had reacted very negatively to his father's extreme Orthodoxy and lost his religious commitment to Orthodox Judaism when he was ten years old. The family was very poor, and my father told me of times that neighbors would offer him and his brothers something to eat. But his father wouldn't let them accept it because it wasn't kosher. My father became embittered from what he considered the imposition of meaningless and pointless rules in the name of nothing at all. He couldn't figure out why God would care whether or not he ate a piece of nonkosher bread. If, indeed, it did matter to God, it was not a God he was much interested in worshiping. But while he rejected the system of rules that his father imposed, he did love his father, and he lived in his father's house as an adult until he married.

My mother also seemed to have puzzled over the nature of God's existence and religiously was not very observant, although from time to time she would light the Sabbath candles. When I was a youngster I was rarely taken to the synagogue, even on high holidays, but when I was nine years old, my parents felt it was necessary to start preparing me for my bar mitzvah, so I began studying Hebrew in after-school Hebrew schools.

I never threw myself wholeheartedly into the Jewish educational experience, as some of my classmates did, but I learned what I had to learn and did quite well. My parents, much to their credit, began celebrating some of the holidays as a model for my sister and me. We began to have seders. However, when I was in my thirteenth year, I began to entertain serious doubts about religion.

I can't exactly tease out what I was thinking at that young age, but I think I must have picked up some of my father's attitudes, although he made no special effort to wean me away from the practice of Judaism. In retrospect, I think I must have decided that there were lots of other things I could study which would give me a more satisfying view of the universe than the Hebrew scriptures—a pretty arrogant attitude for a kid to have. I therefore began to invest my reading time in a wider range of literature.

I went to a school whose enrollment was probably 70 percent Jewish, and on the Jewish holidays a large majority of the kids would stay home. Out of a class of twenty-five, only about seven or eight kids would still attend. When I was in the seventh or eighth grade, I would argue with myself as to whether I should stay home on the Jewish holidays or go to school. Since I didn't celebrate those holidays and didn't feel any special commitment to them, it seemed wrong for me to get a day off from school just to stay home and read or play. On the other hand, I was obviously a member of the Jewish community, and it would have looked funny for me to go to school. So, at different times I did different things: sometimes I stayed home and felt guilty because I was not observing the holidays, and other times I would go to school, but I felt funny doing that too.

My mother, I think, was happier when I stayed home, but my father was completely neutral. He didn't feel it was a betrayal of the Jewish tradition if I went to school on a Jewish holiday, nor did he feel it was a personal betrayal if I stayed home without observing the holiday. He took me to the synagogue while I was enrolled in Hebrew school, but after I expressed my feelings neither of us went.

At any rate, I continued to prepare for my bar mitzvah. A matter of weeks before the ceremony I told the rabbi that I wanted to write my own now-I-am-a-man speech. But he insisted that I give one of the several canned speeches that they had already prepared. So I said, "Well, if this is your planned performance, then I'm not going to say anything at all." I left and never went back.

What was your father's reaction?

TRACHTMAN: He and my mother were supportive of my wishes to speak for myself. Still, both believed that I should be bar mitzvahed, but my father said that there was more than one way to skin a cat—other ways to get the job done, so he arranged that I would have the ceremony at one of the little storefront Orthodox synagogues in the neighborhood. It took place at 6:00 in the morning. My mother wasn't there, but my father was. I went there, said my piece, was congratulated by some of the men who were there, and that was the end of it.

No big party, no speeches, no receptions, no gifts. But it was a perfectly legitimate bar mitzvah.

Although your father came from a very traditional background, it seems he developed into a fairly liberal individual in matters of religion.

TRACHTMAN: Absolutely. But there was no question that culturally he identified himself as Jewish. My father was the kind of person who, when he met some of my friends, would immediately want to know if they were Jewish or non-Jewish. I surmise that his confidence in his relationship with others depended in part on a person's being Jewish or non-Jewish. My mother, on the other hand, did not share his rebellious attitudes in matters of religion, but she felt much more comfortable with a wide circle of acquaintances and was not so culturally bound as he was.

I think my father had the potential to operate on a much higher intellectual level than he did, but his lack of a secular education prevented him from following intellectual pursuits. He did read a lot, but was truly self-educated. His being apprenticed out at the age of eleven simply limited his opportunities. I never sensed any bitterness on his part, though, or ever got a sense of any profound unhappiness or hostility because of his circumstances.

Leon's father worked at the jeweler's trade most of his adult life, save for a few years during the Depression when his jewelry business failed and he simply scratched away to keep the family housed and fed. During those years there was little discretionary income for anything beyond bare necessities. The four Trachtmans (Leon, his father, mother, and sister) lived in the Crown Heights area of Brooklyn, then probably about three-quarters Jewish. This preponderance was reflected in the student bodies of the local elementary school, many of whose pupils were the children of first- or second-generation immigrants. The teachers, though, were mostly non-Jews who came from that breed of tough-minded Irish women who made you learn, or else!

Although neither of Leon's parents had an academic background or, indeed, much formal education, they both prized intellectual achievement and assumed that their children would get a formal education, including college.

TRACHTMAN: I had some absolutely superior teachers in elementary school and, especially, in high school. This was during the thirties, the era of the Depression, and people who had earned their college degrees then simply couldn't get jobs in higher education. Therefore, they went into the public school system, and I had some wonderful teachers who had Ph.D.s and were well enough prepared to teach at the university level.

As a Jew in a Jewish neighborhood, do you remember any antisemitism?

TRACHTMAN: I can remember that when my parents looked in the classified ads for apartments, some of the ads said "restricted"—an obvious code word for "no Jews." My mother was very upset, and I felt upset because that was not the way people were supposed to behave. Although in this modest way my life had been affected by institutional antisemitism, I never really bore the brunt of personal antisemitic sentiments. My mother would tell me that when she was a young girl, she and her sisters would come home from school through some non-Jewish neighborhoods and might be chased and occasionally have stones thrown at them. I never had anything like that happen to me. And the fact that Jews were not welcome in certain restricted housing was an abstract notion to me, and made no special mark as far as I can tell.

There was no question that you would get a higher education?

TRACHTMAN: Not really, though I don't understand why we didn't make a lot of preparations in my family for me to go to college. There was never any exploration of alternatives. Some kids from my neighborhood went to Ivy League schools. Norman Mailer lived in my neighborhood, and he went to Harvard. But there was never any hope of my going to an expensive university, nor were the possibilities of scholarships investigated, so I simply applied to Brooklyn College, where tuition was free. I must say I experienced a decline in teaching quality at Brooklyn College from that at my high school. But I went there for only one year, from 1942 to 1943.

Did you ever get involved in any of the radical movements which were then part of the college scene: socialist, Marxist, Zionist?

TRACHTMAN: My family was politically liberal. I had some cousins who seem to have gotten slightly involved in some leftist causes, but throughout high school and during that one year at college, I became wary of such wholehearted commitments. Maybe I felt that there was no cause that could be so correct and pure as to command my unstinting loyalty. Political extremism simply did not represent the kind of values that appealed to me. It may be a matter of temperament that attracts people to some place on the political spectrum. It's revealing that today we see many of the left-wing radicals of the 1930s making a 180-degree shift in their politics, moving from the left to the right. I haven't shifted that much from my original moderate liberal views and orientation.

After two semesters at Brooklyn College, Trachtman volunteered for the army. He was just three months shy of his eighteenth birthday. He could have waited to be drafted, but he felt that by joining up early might he might be able to choose his assignment (an assumption which turned out not to be the case). But more importantly, he believed that all able-bodied people should make a direct contribution to the war, to which he was fully committed. One of his acquaintances exaggerated a medical condition to get a deferment. Trachtman found this behavior shoddy.

TRACHTMAN: The Second World War has been characterized as "the last good war," perhaps more in retrospect than while it was being waged. Though they certainly had a wide range of solutions—from state socialism to libertarianism, I really do think that people of my generation had a sense of common purpose, which had been developed in response to the challenges of the Great Depression—a feeling that was present in the arts, in music, in philosophy, and especially in politics. People recognized then an obligation to the whole of society to find solutions to the Depression and related problems.

War on the Alsatian Front

Trachtman completed basic training at Fort Benning, Georgia. He was first sent to the 87th Division, where he stayed for a month or so. Then he was assigned to a special military police detachment at Fort Jackson, South Carolina. Here he learned about traffic control, mob control, and other security procedures. In May 1944, he was transferred to an antitank platoon in the 100th Infantry Division.

TRACHTMAN: The 100th Division was not one of those great army divisions that dated back to the Civil War. The 100th was initiated during the war and was recruited mostly from West Virginia, western Pennsylvania, and western Virginia.

I don't suppose it contained many Jews. Did you feel in any sense an outsider?

TRACHTMAN: Not really. As in any group, there were people I liked and some that I didn't. My best friend in my platoon was Stanley Sherman, a rough-hewn scion of an Irish family in Detroit, a man twice my age who was an ex-bartender and true man of the world. Our backgrounds were as different as could be.

What was your reaction to the Allied invasion of France on June 6, 1944?

TRACHTMAN: I remember sitting in the barracks in Fort Bragg, listening to the radio. By this time we had learned something about the destructive power of rifle, machine-gun, and artillery fire, and we were probably not quite so gung-ho about going over and joining the fray. We had mixed feelings: on the one hand, we thought that it was great that the Normandy invasion was taking place, and we were prepared and even eager to follow. On the other hand, we had increased feelings of trepidation. We knew that in the very near future we were also going to face enemy fire.

In August we got our orders to pack, but we didn't know whether we would be sent to Europe or to the Pacific. Only when we arrived at Camp Kilmer in New Jersey did we figure it would be Europe.

The convoy left in September, heading east, zig-zagging across the Atlantic to frustrate German U-boats. The seas were rough and the crossing took over two weeks. Trachtman was on board the *George Washington,* a former German luxury liner that the United States had confiscated during the First World War.[2] As a troopship, its third-class passenger and cargo areas had been converted into huge open bays with rows of iron-railed bunk beds three cots high, accommodating hundreds of men, with resultant stench. The convoy steamed through the Straits of Gibraltar then turned north toward the port of Marseilles.

General Dwight Eisenhower had insisted the Allies make a landing on the French Riviera to gain ports to funnel through to Europe the forty divisions still in the United States. The invasion, originally code-named Anvil, then changed to Dragoon, had begun two months after D-Day. Preceded by heavy air attacks and naval bombardment, an American-French assault force, on August 15, 1944, hit the small beaches that stretched along the rocky Riviera coast from Port Nègre to St. Tropez. Compared to the landings on Omaha Beach, opposition was surprisingly light, and after four days the Germans were retreating northward. Hitler did not think a do-or-die defense of southern France essential to the protection of the Reich.

Units of the French First Army, commanded by Jean Joseph de Lattre de Tassigny, captured Toulon on August 27 and entered Marseilles the next day. Meanwhile the divisions of the American Seventh Army under General Alexander Patch carried out a two-pronged attack up the Rhône River valley and over the mountainous Route Napoléon. The Americans seized Lyons on September 3, Besançon on September 7, and Dijon on September 11. By then the Seventh Army and the Third Army, coming from the west, had become part of the Sixth Army Group under the operational control of General Eisenhower for the drive into Germany.

Marseilles became a main port of supply for the Allied Armies fighting in northern France. Before the end of the war, almost four million tons of supplies and nearly a million men had landed there. Trachtman's division arrived before the port of Marseilles had resumed its deep-water capacity and was therefore brought ashore at night in smaller landing craft.

The soldiers were formed into marching units on the quays and headed through the darkened city toward Aix-en-Provence. In an open field about twelve miles away, they pitched pup tents and began unloading their jeeps, artillery, and ammunition. Provence was entering its rainy season. It was very muddy and chilly.

TRACHTMAN: We did get some eight-hour passes, and I made it to Marseilles a couple of times from our camp area. I stumbled by with my high-school French. The people were very warm and welcoming. Although we certainly were not the first American soldiers they had seen, our presence was still pretty new. Two friends and I managed to meet a French girl somewhere along the Canebière, and she invited us to have dinner with her family at her parents' apartment. The family was of Greek extraction. Food was very scarce at that time, but with some greens, a few olives, and bread, they fixed us a really wonderful gourmet dinner. The mystery of Mediterranean food. It was a very pleasant, an outstanding experience.

After a couple of weeks, we loaded up our trucks, and we moved up the Rhône valley, each squad in my platoon having a small truck to pull its 57mm cannon. We went through Lyons and past Dijon and arrived at the end of October at Baccarat.[3] Outside the city we got our first baptism of fire, then we liberated Raon-l'Étape—the first city we captured. I remember marching through the center of the town and feeling some sense of achievement. It was not a terribly bloody fight.

At Moyenmoutier, we met a brother and sister and once more were invited for dinner. They lived in a farmhouse with parents and grandparents. They kept rabbits, so we had roast rabbit for dinner. When we sat down to eat, the grandfather ran down to the basement with a pick and shovel and came up with two bottles of wine, which he said he had buried when the Germans came. He had sworn that he would not dig them up until they were liberated, and now this was the time. The girl was very pretty; her name was Jeannine.

From Moyenmoutier we moved east into Alsace. We went from town to town: Rohrbach, Bettviller, Reyersviller, Bitche. While I knew generally what area we were in, I couldn't keep up with all our moving east and west, and north and south. You'd fight on one front, then be pulled out and put in reserve on another. The weather was turning cold; it would be a very cold winter. My recollection of those weeks is of fighting our way into towns, exploring basements and back alleys to be sure the Germans were gone, settling in, taking over, and a day or two later, moving on. We had no sense of just where the front lines were. We never saw a map, but were simply told to get in the trucks; we'd drive for two or three hours, then we'd disembark and fight someplace. We'd be told to stay there and start digging foxholes, never quite knowing precisely where we were.

We rarely saw Germans, and there were few face-to-face encounters. We'd fire our weapons and sometimes see Germans disappearing. After some heavy shelling, we'd move into an area and find some Germans who wanted to surrender.

We were really scared when the German 88s were firing,[4] and they would for hours. Two or three of us would huddle in a very shallow foxhole. In December, the ground was so frozen that we could hack out only a little depression and keep trying to make it deeper. If we were going to stay where we were for any length of time, we would cut some small trees and lay them over the top of the foxhole to deflect shrapnel and put them on mounded-up earth to protect against the rain and melting snow. It was always cold and wet and you never had a chance to dry out your boots.

Camped outside of Bitche, we were under a very, very heavy artillery pounding. We huddled in some Maginot Line blockhouses at Fort Schirmeck. I particularly remember one of our antitank squads being bogged down in their truck in the woods and having a shell explode above their heads, showering the shrapnel down on top of them. Three of the seven were killed, another two wounded. It was the first time I had seen death really so close.

T rachtman was outside Bitche on December 16, 1944, when the Germans launched their great western counterattack, known, because of American resistance, as the Battle of the Bulge. On the eve of this last great German offensive of the war, Hitler had told his generals that if Germany lost, it would have forfeited its right to exist. The Führer had gambled all his reserves in an attempt to move northwest through Belgium and capture the port of Antwerp. He believed that this strike would split the American and British forces, thereby shaking the Allied faith in victory and leading to the conclusion of an armistice.

The offensive caught the Allies off guard, but resistance soon stiffened, and at Bastogne the Americans forced the Germans to fight a time-consuming war of siege. With clearing weather, the American air force was able to slow the German advance to a halt, enabling a counterattack.

By then, all of Lorraine had been liberated. But in Alsace the Germans still held a salient, the so-called Colmar Pocket, anchored in the south on Mulhouse, and they still occupied a thin strip of territory in the north along the German frontier where the 100th Division was deployed.

TRACHTMAN: It was very cold and snowy. Units of the Seventh Army were being dispatched north to help check the German advance in the Ardennes. We who stayed found ourselves covering much larger areas of the front. Battalions now guarded areas normally covered by an entire division. We moved away from Bitche and headed west back toward Rohrbach. On Christmas Eve, we stopped in a small one-street village.

I was ordered to take a message to another squad at the end of the town, a distance of about a quarter of a mile. A light snow was falling. It was absolutely quiet, no artillery or small-arms fire, and I was walking down the middle of the main street. I didn't see anybody; it felt eerie walking all by myself. It was suspected that some Germans were still in the town. As I walked all alone, I thought, "Wouldn't it be strange and ironic if some sniper would shoot me in this seemingly peaceful and deserted village?" I had this sense that I was walking in a completely unreal world.

Capture

On December 31 Hitler pushed two army corps and one SS division into Alsace through the Saverne Gap in an attempt to link up with the German forces in the Colmar Pocket. The attack quickly plowed through the thinly stretched forces of the American Seventh Army. Eisenhower first considered withdrawing the Allied forces from Alsace, then organized a counterattack that blunted the Germans.

TRACHTMAN: On January 6, my unit moved into the town of Rimling, where we were attacked by a Waffen-SS force, commanded by a certain Major Wilhelm Krelle. The Germans made two major and noisy night attacks, which we repulsed. Firefights continued over a two-day period, our guns moving from one end of Rimling to the other. We'd capture snipers, knock out tanks, and keep the area secured. It was at this time that my platoon sergeant, Charles Cary, took actions that culminated in his being awarded the Congressional Medal of Honor, posthumously.

On the third night the Germans began infiltrating certain areas of the town. I was attached to F Company, and we had established a defensive line along a row of houses. The house we occupied was built on a slope—it was a kind of split-level dwelling with the main floor at street level in front and the rear of the house with an exit at a lower level, sloping off in the back. Several of us were off watch, and we went into this basement, taking our turn to get some rest. There were some sheep down in there with us on a dirt floor.

We were dozing and were suddenly awakened by noises upstairs. It was clear that German was being spoken. It seemed that after failing to take the village in two night attacks, the enemy had begun trying to capture the town house by house. Those in our company who had remained upstairs on guard duty had apparently left without having a chance to warn us. We opened the back door to try to get out, but a concussion grenade dropped from a window above knocked us back. We were ordered up through the trap door, and marched out the front door toward the German lines.

The road lead out of town in a gentle curve. It about 5:00 A.M. and still very dark. It would be some time before we could see the first vague signs of daylight. We came in the sights of some American machine-gun nests down the road, and they fired at us. They couldn't tell in the dark that we were prisoners. Ironically, we could have been killed by our own fire.

The Germans marched us to their battalion headquarters, where we were interrogated. Not very searching questions. Then we moved on and were eventually locked up in one of the upstairs bedrooms of a large farmhouse. The place had been stripped and was left with just some bedsprings and a few pieces of wooden furniture. There were about fifteen of us, all captured at about the same time in a couple of different places. We were each questioned again. The standard sorts of questions: names of units, positions of troops, that sort of stuff. One of the Germans obviously found one of my answers unsatisfactory, because he leaned over my shoulder from the rear and warned me of the dire consequences of refusing to give information. "By the way," he said, "would you rather be shot or hanged?" I interpreted that as a threat, Geneva Convention or not. The interrogators were all very fluent in English. One told me he had a degree from Princeton University.

Those days were very confused. We were held in a couple of places close to the battle line, but at some point, we were herded onto a train and sent to a prisoner-of-war camp in Germany. The trip took a couple of days. We crossed the Rhine at Ludwigshafen, where the train stopped in the middle of the bridge. We heard air-raid sirens. The horrible question was, "What if the train were hit, since bridges were logical targets? Wouldn't it be hideous to be hit by American bombs and drowned in a locked boxcar?" But eventually we reached our destination at the town of Bad Orb, just northeast of Frankfurt am Main.

Did the prisoners discuss the situation with each other?

TRACHTMAN: We mostly posed unanswerable questions: "What's going to happen now?" "Do Germans keep prisoners?" "Where are they taking us?"

What were the conditions at the Bad Orb prisoner-of-war camp?

TRACHTMAN: Very bad. The camp had been a military training area. It had permanent, obviously well-constructed barracks. When I was there the camp had perhaps a thousand or more American prisoners, and there was another area, separated from us by barbed wire, in which there were Russian prisoners.

We slept on the floor in a large, cavernous room. We had no beds, no showers, no opportunity to clean up, no clean or dry clothing. The food was bad. Apparently there was a standard soup for prisoners—we called it grass soup—which was essentially a kind of broth with a few greens floating around in it, and occasionally some turnips. That, plus a bit of bread, was all our daily food. I don't recall any incidents of serious abuse, but it was a pretty miserable place. However, as bad as it was, it was far better than the place where some of us were to go shortly.

After some weeks, an announcement was made that all Jewish prisoners were to report to another barracks by a certain date and time. This was the first time I had ever thought about what it might mean to be Jewish in a German prison camp. It had not occurred to me that I would be treated any differently from the other American soldiers. I knew of no other Jewish prisoners in our immediate group.

I had been spending most of my time with my friend Stan Sherman, who had been captured with me, and together we tried to evaluate what the announcement meant—specifically what would happen if I didn't report as ordered.

We all got German identification tags when we were captured, but they only had numbers on them; religion was not noted. Yet I could be easily identified, since religion was marked on my American dog tags. We figured that there would probably be dozens of Jewish prisoners out of the hundreds and hundreds of others who were there, and that it was unlikely that they would line us up as a group and shoot us. But on the other hand, if I didn't join the group and later the Germans discovered my identity, they might not have so hard a time disposing of a single person. We were aware of the hostile attitude of the regime toward the Jews, but we didn't know about the death camps or about mass murders. We were thinking like combat soldiers. So Stan reluctantly advised me to go, and I did. That's the last time I ever saw him.

I reported to another barracks in the Bad Orb camp area. It was not a permanent barracks like the one I had left, but rather more an American-style wood-frame barracks with a concrete floor. I was there about three days and then was marched with the others out to a railroad siding, put in boxcars, and headed to the east.

Notes

1. Schindler and Toman, *The Laws of Armed Conflicts,* 275–88. At the outbreak of the European war in 1939, forty-three countries had officially pledged to abide by the

provisions of the convention. All of the European states, including Germany, with the exception of the Soviet Union, signed. Also joining were the United States and Canada.

2. President Woodrow Wilson had used the ship to come to France for the Paris Peace Conference in 1919. Afterwards it was mothballed with other ex-German steamers (*Kaiser Wilhelm II, Kronprinzessin-Cecilie,* and *Amerika*) in the Chesapeake.

3. Baccarat in Lorraine, home of the famous crystal manufacture, between Nancy and Colmar, had recently been cleared of Germans.

4. Originally designed as an antiaircraft gun, this weapon was later adapted, supposedly on Hitler's initiative, into a field piece for destroying enemy tanks.

Leon Trachtman, August 1944.

At the conclusion of basic training, Fort Benning, Georgia, c. March 1944.
Leon Trachtman is in the back row, 5th from the right.

12
Two Kinds of Time

The Personality of Endurance: Leon Trachtman

> "As you sat in the barracks or walked around the compound, you would see a soldier whose face developed a certain yellowish pallor, and somehow you knew that in a matter of days that person would die."

The Concentration Camp at Berga

There were 350 American prisoners of war in the group now headed east. At this stage of the war, the Germans had decided to fill their forced-labor quotas with labor heretofore considered off-limits. The use of prisoners of war to further the war effort was not only a violation of the Geneva Convention but also a departure from previous German practice concerning their enemies in the west. German treatment of Russian prisoners of war was another matter. The USSR had not ratified the Geneva Convention—as if the Germans needed any excuses for their actions. The policy to screen captured American soldiers bears the mark of Heinrich Himmler, who by the fall of 1944 had eclipsed Hermann Göring as the one chiefly responsible for the care and treatment of the prisoners of war.

The Bad Orb selection process began with the identification and separation of all the Jews, about eighty in all. Then it moved to other undesirables: misfits, troublemakers, those who had served time in the stockade, those who had been fingered through interrogation, denunciation, intimidation, observation, or impression. This yielded an additional sixty or seventy soldiers. The screening team was still about two hundred short. The rest of the quota was probably achieved through arbitrary choice or through identifying an ability to sustain hard work.

LEON TRACHTMAN: The boxcars taking us to the forced-labor camp were the same kind that had been used in the First World War: the old 40-and-8s, designed for forty men or eight horses. We were sixty to a car. You either stood or squatted. It was not possible to lie down, even if you wanted to.

The trip was a wretched and miserable experience. It lasted four days. I don't think the doors were opened more than two or three times, so as a result the car became awash in urine and feces. We were each given one can of food for the whole trip, meat of some sort, resembling spoiled dog food. We got water on the few occasions that we stopped and were permitted out. It was difficult to see out through the razor-thin slits in the side of the car. We could only tell when it was day and when it was night. By the time we got to Berga, our uniforms were so greasy, filthy, soiled, and muddy that we certainly did not look like uniformed soldiers. We were unloaded and marched to the barracks.

Our section of the camp was really quite small, with not much distance between the barracks and the barbed-wire fence, barely enough space for us to line up for roll call. There were six buildings, each containing ten triple-deck bunks wide enough for two people. We slept two people below, two in the middle, and two up on top—thus six soldiers to each bunk, sixty in each barracks. We slept on burlap ticks filled with straw on top of wooden slats. We were given no blankets. The room had only a little pot-bellied wood-burning stove in the center of the room. We wore the clothes we were captured in. Everybody was covered with lice.

You had been classed as an undesirable because you were Jewish. Did there exist any special camaraderie because of this?

TRACHTMAN: The Jews were not isolated, but rather intermingled with the others. We were part of a unit of 350, not a special subunit of 80. There was a strong sense of unity among the whole group, with no visible distinction between Jew and non-Jew. We were quite simply a slightly skewed cross-section of American soldiers.

What was your daily routine?

TRACHTMAN: A couple of days after we arrived, we were introduced to our jobs. The Berga camp was near a granite mountain, into which a dozen parallel tunnels were being dug to create an underground arms factory. The excavating went on around the clock, in three shifts: I estimate they ran from 7 in the morning to 3 in the afternoon, 3 until 11, and then from 11 until 7.

In addition to the camp of American prisoners, there were two other camps: one for Yugoslav partisans and another for nonmilitary prisoners from various places. There were some French, some Danes, some Dutch, and many other nationalities. These were, I think, preponderantly Jewish, but with many non-Jews among them.

The Americans all worked as a group. On the day shift, we would be roused at about 5:30 in the morning then assembled outside for a roll call. The Germans were very precise. A guard would have us count off by numbers, and if the count didn't tally, we stood there, for hours if necessary, until the numbers were right. Then we would have breakfast, such as it was: just hot water or tea.

The breakfast doesn't seem to be loaded with calories. Were the other
meals any better?

TRACHTMAN: No. At noon we typically had a bowl of soup with essentially nothing nutritious in it except for some stringy leafy vegetables floating around. Maybe once a week the soup would have some cubed turnips in it. In the evening, we would get a little chunk of dried ersatz bread, occasionally with a pat of butter or a tiny cube of cheese. And very, very, *very* occasionally a tiny little piece of some sort of wurst. That was it. Many of us broke the bread in half and ate half in the evening and saved the other half for breakfast, spacing it out.

We were always hungry, but we so adjusted to our minimal diet that as time passed the pangs of hunger seemed less. But people constantly thought about food. Some could think of nothing but steak. I thought of baked things. I wanted bread and rolls, muffins, things like that.

After breakfast we were marched off to work. It was pretty dank in the tunnels. We were surrounded by all this scaffolding and water was constantly dripping down. We were given pneumatic drills that were run by air compressors, and with them we would drill holes about five or six feet deep into the rock face. Then we would go outside while dynamite was packed in the holes, and the charges exploded, blasting the rock face down in chunks. We would then reenter the tunnels, pushing narrow-gauge cars on rails that had been laid, and shovel up all of the debris. When the little cars were filled, we would push them back outside and down to the edge of the Elster River, where we dumped them. Then we would go back inside, move the scaffolding forward, and start drilling the next five or six feet. So there we were, working eight-hour shifts, drilling, blasting, shoveling, drilling, blasting shoveling. It was hard work, very heavy work. We had old-time air compressor drills that made one's whole body vibrate.

German miners set the charges. They were not guards, but rather specialists, some coming from near Dresden, where they had been civilian coal miners. They told us how to construct the scaffolding and where to drill. They seemed to be volunteers, but I'm not sure about that, since their attitudes varied greatly. One of them communicated quite clearly to us that the game was up for Germany and that they were just going through the motions until the war ended. But others seemed convinced that Hitler's secret weapons would have the desired effect in sustaining the war effort and that they indeed would succeed in building a productive arms factory. We were convinced that the whole project was a crazy idea. At the rate we were going, it would have been two or three years before any kind of factory installations could possibly have been created.

After our shift we would walk back to the barracks by the same route we came. Going and coming, we would pass the other groups coming on or off shifts. As we passed we would whisper to each other. Some had been prisoners for a long time, and they had little shortwave radios and other means of getting news. They would tell us of the progress of the American armies.

Considering the harsh conditions, it was evident that you were being worked to death.

TRACHTMAN: Certainly if we had stayed there long enough. Medical care was nonexistent. Not even an aspirin. On one or two occasions someone who we assumed was a doctor went through the barracks. But I don't know what effect that person had. There certainly was no sick call. On occasions when our guards thought that the people who were truly ill were malingering, they might throw a bucket of cold water on them.

Everybody was getting thinner and thinner. My normal weight then was about 165 pounds, and at the time I was liberated I was down to about 110. This was true of everybody. I think we all harbored infections of various sorts: hepatitis, upper-respiratory diseases, dysentery, diarrhea. We were all likely targets of death. In the two months we were there, I figure that between thirty and forty Americans died.

This might sound metaphysical, but as you sat in the barracks or walked around the compound, you would see a soldier whose face developed a certain yellowish pallor, and somehow you knew that in a matter of days that person would die. And not of a particular identifiable disease. I became convinced (and, of course, I don't know how valid this observation is) that this process involved a kind of psychological surrender. People who gave up tended to succumb more easily to whatever proximate cause. Also I had the impression that the older prisoners tended to survive better than the younger ones. When I say "older," I mean the thirty-year-olds as opposed to the eighteen- or nineteen-year-olds.

Why was that?

TRACHTMAN: I'm not sure I can properly articulate it, but it might have had something to do with the fact that many of these older soldiers had come from depressed regions of western Virginia, western Pennsylvania, and West Virginia and had lived through hard times before they entered the army. They had been born around 1918 and were adolescents or young adults between 1932 and 1937—the worst years of the Great Depression. Lots of them had come from very poor homes where they had to struggle for existence. Some had worked in CCC camps. Many of them had already experienced profound social and economic trauma, they had seen really hard times. Therefore, before their baptism of fire in the war, they had already built up an ability to survive. This was in contrast to the nineteen-year-olds, who had been only six or seven or eight years old during the Depression and had not yet built up comparable survival skills.

> *That's not so strange a notion. During the First World War those who survived best in the trenches usually came from the lower classes, those who had known deprivation. The soldiers from more affluent households had a terrible time. If you had lived in the London slums, the trenches in France would have been a less devastating culture shock than for those from middle-class households.*

TRACHTMAN: Yes, for many of the older soldiers the tough times of the Depression were a real challenge, and they had developed their survival skills physically and psychologically more fully than had the nineteen-year-olds.

How did you manage to survive?

TRACHTMAN: I really don't know. Like most of my fellow prisoners, I lived one day at a time. Goals were short term: Get through today's work shift. Get through the night. Survive a two-hour roll call in twenty-degree weather. But mostly it was matching the guards' survival with my survival. They had to stand around to guard us for eight hours in the freezing cold, the snow, and the wind. If they could do it, I was determined I could do it also. Of course, we were working and they were not. On the other hand, working probably kept us a little warmer during those winter days and nights.

What was the mood of the workers during each shift?

TRACHTMAN: That question reminds me of a wonderful old *New Yorker* cartoon from a couple of generations ago. It was in Egypt, and you see the sands stretching for miles. One overseer is talking to another about the thousands of Hebrews building the pyramids. One of the Egyptians says to the other, "Many hands make light the work."

We Americans all worked on the same shift. The tunnels were very narrow and did not afford much room for maneuvering, so everybody couldn't work at the same time. So I think what helped survival was that we had too many workers for the job. Had we had equipment and space for everybody so we could all work at once, it would have been more strenuous. Even so, by the time we got back to the barracks, we were so exhausted that we went to bed and fell asleep as soon as we hit the straw ticking.

You hear that in the prisoner-of-war camps there were organized efforts or acts of resistance or subtle sabotage. Did that sort of thing go on?

TRACHTMAN: There was a moderate amount of malingering, taking longer to drill a hole than necessary, that sort of thing. And there were a number of escape attempts, probably fifteen to eighteen in the course of a couple of months. To my knowledge, all of them failed. Either the people were shot or brought back alive. The ones brought back alive were very badly treated. They were given the rankest and dirtiest jobs, like emptying out slip trenches. Standing around in all this accumulation of human waste increased the likelihood of disease. Most of these men didn't survive.

How easy was it to escape?

TRACHTMAN: It was very difficult from the barbed-wire enclosure. But every day we were on the road, walking to and from the job site. In the dark of early morning, we had to have three or four people hauling what they called the "tea wagon" from Berga to the camp. For those hauling the tea wagon, it was possible for two to slip away in the dark.

Another way was to walk away from the work site pushing one of the wheelbarrows. The guards would assume that you were on some special detail, and when you got around the bend to a wooded area you'd just take off.

Slipping away was really the easy part. The problem was, what did you do in the middle of Germany, where everyone who saw you was likely to inform the local authorities? Altogether there were probably fifteen attempts. All except one were recaptured in a short time and severely punished.

Did you feel that the Jewish prisoners of war were more picked on than the others?

TRACHTMAN: By and large our treatment was no different from that meted out to the large majority, which was not Jewish. We all had the same rations, did the same work, and had the same sense of solidarity as American soldiers. We were pushed around a little bit, shoved and cuffed from time to time, but this mostly had to do with individual behavior. If somebody was slow a guard might shove him. The guards really had no idea who was Jewish and who wasn't.

I did not see anything done to any member of our group comparable to what I saw being done to the nonmilitary slave laborers. For example, one day as we were going to work and were passing another group coming off, one of those other workers fell out of line and collapsed, whereupon one of our guards gratuitously stepped over to where the man was lying, took his rifle butt, and battered the man's head. Nobody did anything so brutal to us, as far as I could tell. I think a little deference was made because we were both American and military. But still we could be struck, shoved, and knocked down.

So you didn't fear for your life because of some brutality?

TRACHTMAN: I don't think anyone felt that he might get a bullet in the head or that he would be beaten to death. But having icy water tossed on you when you had pneumonia was certainly likely to precipitate death.

Who were the guards?

TRACHTMAN: Mostly men in their forties, too old for military service. I sensed that they were pulled off other civilian jobs for this duty. They didn't wear the green uniforms of the Wehrmacht [regular army]; they had blue uniforms, most likely those of the Volkssturm [home defense force].

How about their general attitude?

TRACHTMAN: Most were hostile, but except for a few cases, rarely did they demonstrate overt brutality. One guard even gave us bread surreptitiously. At what risk to himself, I don't know, but he obviously was sympathetic and did what he could.

What sort of organization existed among the American prisoners? Did you have camp leaders, and how were they chosen?

TRACHTMAN: I can't remember whether we chose barracks leaders formally or whether they just emerged. But we had a couple of guys who were dominant.

Based on rank?

TRACHTMAN: No, based on personality, the ability to assume a leadership role.

Can you give an example?

TRACHTMAN: We had a case when a young man was caught stealing bread. People who had saved half of their rations of bread from the evening meal usually slept with that chunk of bread under their straw ticks. And when someone discovered in the morning that his food was gone, he was naturally outraged. So the informal leader of our barracks worked out a watch system so that somebody would be awake all the time to see who was sneaking out of bed in the middle of the night and stealing the bread. And in fact, somebody was apprehended: a nineteen-year-old from a pretty well-to-do family.

There was a lot of sentiment that he should be killed. After all, he was stealing our lives by taking our bread. But an older man—one, in fact, with a criminal past—stood up and said, "Guys, don't do this. It'll always be on your conscience. Now that you've caught him, he will never do it again. And remember, he never had tough times to live through like some of the rest of us. He's never learned to handle deprivation." So we scared the hell out of him and warned him never to steal again. And he didn't.

I always thought it ironic that a guy who never had to sweat and worry about where his next meal was coming from would go into stealing and that his defender, the one who really saved his life, was a man with a really shady past. Our group did not accept the stealing of bread because it violated their norms of behavior. But there were also norms of forgiveness and mercy in not killing the thief.

What about religion in your camp? Did many people conduct services or pray?

TRACHTMAN: We had one soldier on the train who recited a perpetual rosary, repeated Hail Marys and Our Fathers all day long. But I really wasn't aware of anything going on besides a very basic kind of petitionary prayer. I observed nothing that was collectively organized.

Rescue and Repatriation

On February 6, the Allies launched a major offensive into the Ruhr, driving east from the Dutch city of Nijmegen into the Reichswald. By the end of the month, the British and Americans occupied all cities west of the Rhine after some of the bitterest fighting of the war. The American First Army began crossing the Rhine on March 7 after the Ludendorff bridge at Remagen was captured. On March 2 units of the Third Army had made unopposed crossings at Mainz and Worms, and a day later, the British Twenty-first Army Group gained the Rhine's eastern shore further downstream, near the Dutch frontier. In a classic double envelopment, the two branches of the Allied armies now swung around the Ruhr, trapping 400,000 German troops.

Meanwhile the Soviets were preparing their final assault in the east. At the beginning of April, their troops swarmed across the Oder with more than seventy armored brigades, and soon after they put Berlin under direct attack. The Germans were now squeezed into an ever-narrowing strip of territory from Denmark south to Austria.

On Easter Sunday, April 3, 1945, roughly three hundred American survivors of the forced-labor compound at Berga were lined up and told they were leaving the camp.

TRACHTMAN: It was a beautiful day—one of the first that had a little smell of spring. We headed southeast. The first town we went through was Greiz, a gray city, a grim-looking city, with grim-looking people who gave us lots of very cold and unfriendly looks. I suspect they didn't even know who we were, other than obvious enemies of the Reich, but they regarded us with hostility.

We would march twelve to fifteen miles a day. One or two of the guards would go ahead and find a place down the road for us to sleep, usually in a barn. Every night when we finished walking we would get our cup of tea or bowl of soup or hunk of bread and lie down in the hayloft. Sleeping in nice clean straw was a terrific and delightful contrast to life in the camp.

The next morning we were on the march again. Not a very orderly column, not military at all; we just straggled along by ones and by twos, usually talking together. I told myself that as long as any German guard was able to march, I was going to march. I was not going to drop out. I was determined to keep in step with any German guard who kept going.

We didn't know why or where we were going except that we were heading south into Bavaria. Every day was pretty much like another, marching, eating, and sleeping. But virtually every day somebody died; death on the march became pretty commonplace. My guess is that we lost another fifty or more. They just dropped from exhaustion and were left at the side of the road. I don't know what happened to the ones who were ill and could not go on and were left in the barns, but I don't have any recollection that any of us were shot, which was quite a different story from the slave laborers we encountered heading in the same direction. They came perhaps from Buchenwald or other camps and were almost without exception dressed in striped uniforms. I saw many of them shot. If any fell out of the march through exhaustion or perhaps to relieve themselves, one of their SS guards would come up and simply shoot them in the back of the head. At one point, in a space of a couple of miles, I counted as many as two hundred bodies lying in the ditch. Most of those who had been shot were pathetic, beaten-down figures. But I recall one seventeen- or eighteen-year-old who had been shot in the back of the head and had fallen backwards so he was spread-eagled on the ground. His face wore an expression of total contempt. Of course, you can't really tell what a facial expression on a corpse means, but the set of his features struck me as defiant and contemptuous. I had real admiration for him.

On the morning of April 13 a remarkable thing happened. After we had been roused for roll call, we saw a squad of eight or ten German soldiers approaching our guards and then coming over to talk to us. They spoke a little English, and some of us could speak German. They told us that they were in a detachment that was encamped some ten miles away and that they had been told by some civilians that a group of American prisoners was in the vicinity. So before dawn they marched over to where we were to find us because they wanted to express their condolences at the death of our president. That was the first time we knew that President Roosevelt had died.

That enemy soldiers would walk twenty miles to express their sympathy struck me as a totally anachronistic, almost chivalric kind of behavior. It was an expression of honor among combat soldiers that seemed like a throwback to the nineteenth century and earlier. It was such an incredible anomaly, happening at such a time and in such a place. After they paid their respects and expressed their sympathy, they simply turned and marched back.

As we got further into Bavaria we passed some farms where imported workers, mostly Polish and Russian, were at work planting root crops. From time to time some of them would throw us some turnips or a rutabaga or even a seed potato. Somehow the Bavarian people we occasionally ran into seemed more kindly disposed to us than had the people in the city of Greiz and elsewhere in

Thuringia. Maybe this was because in Bavaria we went mostly through villages and small towns rather than more urban areas.

In one village, some of the German townswomen insisted that the sick soldiers be brought to the town hall rather than a barn with the rest of us because they wanted to nurse them. They brought cots and gave them some nourishing soup, not our thin grass variety. Our guards protested. But these women were very strong-minded. One of them was the mayor's wife and a take-charge sort of person. The women kept two boys to care for while the rest of us were marched off to sleep in the barn overnight. I don't know what eventually happened to them.

The concern of these ladies, the tossed turnips and potatoes from the Russian and Polish workers, and the behavior of that squad of German soldiers who expressed condolences about Roosevelt's death seemed to cast a tiny, tiny, tiny glimmer of light at the end of a very long, dark tunnel in those dreadful days.

Were there any attempts to escape from that column?

TRACHTMAN: We did have roll call every morning, but it was not very exacting. You'd get up in the morning, you'd have roll call. That's the way life was. On the march I doubt, though, if there were escape attempts because it was clear that something very significant was taking shape, and it was going to happen soon. It seemed we were not going to be shot as a group, and the probability of surviving seemed greater if we stayed together than if we ran off by ones and twos. It was clear that the war was almost over. From time to time, far, far, far in the distance we could hear artillery fire. The idea at this point was to stick together as the best plan for survival.

How about your own physical condition?

TRACHTMAN: If anything, I was feeling better on the march. Pleasant weather came with April. There was no more work in the icy cold tunnels. We had a little extra food from the potatoes, carrots, and turnips; and walking along at the rate of twelve to fifteen miles a day was pretty easy compared to drilling holes and shoveling rocks.

I get a picture of six people trying to get the food when it was thrown to you.

TRACHTMAN: We didn't scramble after it like uncivilized people. If we got two or three potatoes, the people who got them would share them with their immediate neighbors. I guess the assumption was that this would even itself out over time. I think we had too much respect for each other to fight.

Did you feel anger or rage or hatred toward this enemy who was singling you out for repression?

TRACHTMAN: Well, I think rage is an expensive luxury. Obviously we were well aware that this was not the way people were supposed to be treated. On the other hand, I personally don't recall being furious at the guards. The only time I felt deep anger was when I saw one of our guards kill one of the slave laborers who fell out of line. The guard quite methodically took his rifle butt and crushed the prisoner's skull. I was appalled and horrified and furious.

The column of Americans moved almost due south, using mostly the small back roads, avoiding population centers, and staying out of the way of possible attack. The prisoners bypassed such cities as Plauen, Hof, and Bayreuth. No one was ever sure of the eventual destination or indeed found out whether there was one. Although it might seem that these prisoners were headed for more war work, in the closing days of the war, forced laborers frequently marched or were transported around for no apparent reason, as if their continued status as prisoners was reason enough to confirm that the Germans still had faith in victory.

After three and a half weeks on the road, the American prisoners had walked two hundred miles or more. On April 25, the American and Russian armies met at Torgau, on the Elbe River. Meanwhile, units of the American Seventh army continued to sweep into Bavaria, where German resistance, unlike the life-or-death struggle going on in Berlin, was scattered and sporadic, but nonetheless actual.

TRACHTMAN: On April 26 we were about twenty kilometers [twelve and a half miles] north of the city of Amberg. We slept in a barn as usual, and in the morning the guards lined us up for roll call. Artillery fire was much closer than it had been, and we could hear tank motors in the distance. Our guards gathered behind the barn, and then, without warning, suddenly took off over a hill, just leaving us there. As the tanks came closer and closer, we retreated back into the barn.

When we looked down the road, we could see the white American star painted on the sides of the tanks. Some of the guys ran out of the barn waving their hands, but were so unrecognizable that the American tanks fired at them. I don't think anybody was hit. But one person did collapse and died either from exhaustion or a heart attack. In any event, we were finally recognized as American soldiers, and the guys in the tank column showered us with food. A terrible mistake. Eating all that rich food, C-rations and K-rations, after semistarvation caused all sorts of stomach and liver torments. I soon developed hepatitis, but it was not clear whether it was an infectious hepatitis or whether my system just rebelled against all that rich food, causing jaundice.

The tanks moved on, and in a couple of hours some trucks and an ambulance or two came and picked us up and took us to a hospital in Amberg. They let us take hot showers and made us shave every place. We were just covered with lice, so the hair under our arms, our pubic hair, and the hair on our heads had to be removed. It was our first shower in six months. Then they gave us clean clothes.

I was moved to several other hospitals in Bavaria before being airlifted to a hospital in Rheims, France. I was there on May 8, the day of the official end of the war in Europe, and I remember hearing the church bells ringing in celebration.

T he instrument of surrender was signed in a schoolhouse at Eisenhower's headquarters near Rheims at 1:41 A.M. on May 7, 1945. Prior to the capitulation, Admiral Karl Dönitz, the new head of the German state following Hitler's suicide, had tried to surrender only to the Western Allies because, he claimed, the Russians were savages. Eisenhower informed him that unless he surrendered immediately, the entire Allied front would be closed to prevent any more German refugees from entering the British and American zones and the Germans would have to deal with the Russians alone. Dönitz gave way. Eisenhower refused to attend the Rheims ceremony, sending instead his chief of staff, Lt. General Walter Bedell Smith, and other Allied officers of similar rank. Thus the Allied representatives intentionally and insultingly held lesser rank than their German opposite number, Colonel-General Alfred Jodl. The surrender was to take effect one minute after 11 P.M. on May 8, the day that Truman and Churchill officially declared V-E Day. However, Stalin refused to accept the Rheims signing as final and demanded another formal surrender. This took place in Berlin twenty-nine minutes after the Rheims surrender had officially come into effect.

Trachtman remained at Rheims for about a week, and then he

was transferred to a hospital at Saint-Denis in the Paris suburbs, where he was put on a special low-fat diet.

TRACHTMAN: I was at that big French hospital in Saint-Denis about the time when the dramatic news appeared about the existence of Auschwitz and the other camps. I overheard two French maids at the French hospital talking, and they were discussing the news about the death camps, and one of the French women said to the other, "Too bad Hitler didn't finish the job." Appalled is a modest way to describe my reaction.

Trachtman's group had not remained together. Its soldiers were gradually dispersed to different hospitals and medical facilities. After two weeks in Paris, Trachtman was sent to Cherbourg and within a day or two was on board the hospital ship *Arcadia,* bound for New York.

Discharge from the army followed a military "points system" whereby the date of separation was based on how long one had been in the service, how long had one had served overseas, how long one had been in combat, and so forth. Trachtman had to wait until December 1945 until he had accumulated enough points to be eligible for processing out. He spent the first months upon returning to the United States in military hospitals, initially at Halloran Hospital in New York's Staten Island and then at Fort Oglethorpe in Georgia. Then, when his turn came for discharge, he was sent to Fort Dix in New Jersey.

Putting Things in Perspective

Trachtman had already decided to finish his university education, although the thought of doing so was not something that had sustained him while he was in the prison camp.

TRACHTMAN: Only after I came back and was feeling reasonably well did I consider what I was going to do with my life. I didn't think there was a lot of use for an antitank gunner in civilian life. But it never really occurred to me that I wouldn't go back to school, and my parents, who assumed that I would get a higher education, were gratified that I decided to continue. I was the first member of my immediate family to attend college. I think my parents thought of college as a destination and didn't really understand the nature of faculty life or of scholarship and research. Nonetheless, as I went along, they were very supportive. I don't think it ever occurred to either of them that I would end up as an academic type.

I enrolled for the spring semester, beginning February 1946, at Hamilton College, near Utica, New York. Having a scholarship from the State of New York and support from the G.I. Bill enabled me to attend that little Ivy League–type place. I sent my trunk on ahead and, with only one suitcase, boarded the New York Central train without so much as a by your leave. I had never visited Hamilton and knew little about the school or its surroundings. It did not seem like a very adventurous thing to go there alone after what I had been through. But it was quite a contrast to today's students, who arrive at college in the company of their bedraggled parents, bearing TVs, CD players, computers, and Lord knows what else.

After you left the army did you experience anything like what today is called post-traumatic stress syndrome?

TRACHTMAN: I didn't have time to.

T rachtman was at Hamilton for two and a half years. He graduated in June 1948 with a major in English literature and a minor in history, then went on for graduate work at Johns Hopkins in Maryland. In September 1951, having finished his prelims and started writing his dissertation, he joined the faculty of Hood College, in Frederick, Maryland, teaching English and speech. At Hood he met his future wife, Marguerite, and they were married in September 1952.[1]

He stayed at Hood College for five years, then worked two years as a science writer for the National Institutes of Health in Bethesda, Maryland. He came to Purdue University in September 1958, starting as a science writer for the Purdue Research Foundation and working in grants and contracts administration. In 1965, he became a member of the Purdue English department. He taught courses in literature and science writing and participated in the establishment of an interdisciplinary program in science and culture. Later he joined the Department of Communication. In addition to teaching and writing, at various times he served as an administrator:

executive secretary of the Office of Research Contracts and Grants; and assistant, associate, and acting dean of the School of Humanities, Social Studies and Education.

What effect did your life-threatening experiences in the concentration camp have on your character?

TRACHTMAN: I think it made me more sensitive to the response of people in highly stressful situations, and maybe a little bit more insightful. But I didn't have any one peak moment, an epiphany or revelation, when some great truth burst upon me about the way people were, how the world was, or how cosmic justice operated. I can't reconstruct my train of thought, but in a crazy sort of way, the threat of death may have made me more understanding of why people act as they do.

Didn't being put in a situation of extraordinary injustice and brutality make you a more angry person?

TRACHTMAN: In February 1946, about the time I reentered college, I heard from some fellow prisoners who were organizing a movement to try to capture and bring to trial the commander of our camp. I remember writing back to the organizers that I really didn't want to do it. I did not want to hound this guy and pursue him. I wrote that it behooved us to put that time behind us, and that I didn't want to make it one of my missions in life to track down an individual and see that he was hanged or imprisoned. I guess that ran counter to the spirit of the Nürnberg trials. [The first trial of the Nazi war criminals had begun in Nürnberg in November 1945.]

Colonel Hess was certainly not an admirable sort, and ultimately he was, of course, responsible for his actions, but he was a rather low-level functionary who, I felt, was trapped in a horrifying system that shaped the way he behaved. I don't know whether he ever personally killed or did physical violence to anyone. Maybe if I had I actually seen him bludgeon somebody to death, I would have felt very differently. But I just felt that I had more important things to do than to try to hunt him down.

Did the fact that you were singled out for persecution because you were Jewish reinforce your sense of being Jewish?

TRACHTMAN: I don't think it reinforced it particularly.

Did it in any way give you the impression that being Jewish was a burden?

TRACHTMAN: I don't think I ever felt that being Jewish was a burden. It was quite clear why I and eighty or so others had been singled out, but I always had before me the picture of two hundred and seventy non-Jews who had been singled out for precisely the same treatment.

Did you consider yourself Jewish?

TRACHTMAN: All of my life. In the years before my concentration camp experience I had arrived at a very secular position in terms of my own religious beliefs, but that didn't alter the fact that I had been born into and brought up in a Jewish culture. My parents didn't saturate me with a sense of Jewishness by constantly telling me to be aware that I was a Jew, but I certainly knew who we were. Besides, it was hard to grow up in New York in the 1930s in a Jewish family in a largely Jewish neighborhood and not consider yourself Jewish. Neighborhoods were identified ethnically: Jewish neighborhoods or Italian neighborhoods or Irish neighborhoods—the three great ethnic groups in New York.

How did your camp experiences affect the Judeo-Christian belief in an omnipotent, omniscient, and benevolent God?

TRACHTMAN: I had established a perspective on that issue before I ever went into the military service. I had concluded that, given the state of the world, there was no way that one God could have all three characteristics, and if an all-powerful God played these grim jokes on human beings, it was not a God I cared to worship.

Did the notion of God make any sense to you?

TRACHTMAN: When we were under artillery fire, many of my platoon mates engaged in serious prayer that they be saved. Under those circumstances, the impulse to pray is very powerful. The sheer terror of being in combat was worse than being in prison. In prison there was a constant abrasiveness, the work and inadequate nutrition steadily wearing you down, but basically one day was like another. But having shells exploding all around you is sheer terror.

Even in those very difficult circumstances, I remember saying things like, "If there is a God, why doesn't he stop this?" rather than, "God, please put an end to this." By then, I had reached an agnostic point of view. I had pretty much decided that a truly benevolent God who knew everything could obviously not be all-powerful, or he would stop these dreadful happenings. If God were omnipotent and saw these happenings and let them go on, then he was really not benevolent. So it's not a question of my faith in God either being deepened or shaken by my experiences.

At what point in your life did you start to reflect on your experiences?

TRACHTMAN: For decades I can't remember spending a lot of time worrying about why people perpetrate such evil acts on others or whether people are sinful by nature or simply weak. The answers to questions of whether some people are more likely than others to behave in a certain way have been sought throughout history. They certainly have been posed in my reading of and teaching about English literature. Yet these are questions I rarely considered in terms of my own experiences until about eight years ago, when I was asked to speak of my experiences at one of the Holocaust conferences here on campus.

Curiously, a lot of what I have done in my writing has been responsive to such external stimuli rather than the product of my own introspection. I never felt that I had some sort of special message for the world, but if somebody commissions me to think about something and to produce something, I can usually pretty well do it. After that first speech, I started thinking about such issues more deeply than I had for the many intervening years. I tried to organize my ideas about what impelled Germany to behave the way it did.

Was there something unique about the German nation, the German people, or the German culture? Could anybody be capable of these outrages? Had I been in the same position as some of my guards, how might I have behaved? I never could emerge with a clear-cut answer to these questions. My mother was a very virtuous person, and when she saw some kind of despicable act being performed, she tended to say, "Oh, I could never do that." But I could not absolutely convince myself about the roots of behavior of individual guards, and I could never be sure that I could not have behaved in such a fashion, that I was not capable of inflicting pain upon a fellow human being.

It's in recent years that I've come to some conclusions about the wellsprings of this sort of human behavior, about why some cultural groups seem more capable than others of committing such crimes.

Recent studies suggest that people with generally decent backgrounds are capable of the most heinous crimes.

TRACHTMAN: I'm not sure that we can escape the attitudes and pressures imposed on us by our culture. I think people are powerfully socialized into their patterns of behavior. One hears of episodes of Germans shooting American prisoners, and it makes Americans feel good to say, "Boy, we would never do that to German prisoners." But I know differently, I know that some Americans have done it.

*Perhaps it's possible for someone like yourself to do something odious
under certain circumstances. But isn't it a sort of rationalization to assert
that because I might do something under similar circumstances, I therefore
should not judge too harshly those who do?*

TRACHTMAN: No. Even if I were to conclude that almost anybody, under the
right pressure and in the right environment, were capable of this kind of behavior, I don't think one can be exculpated. I think the Nürnberg trials were
absolutely justified to set a necessary standard for the world community on
genocidal behavior. I say this even though I did not want to participate in hunting down one specific individual.

*But you certainly would make a distinction between the organizers of the
machinery of destruction and its small-cog perpetrators?*

TRACHTMAN: I started thinking about other groups who had done essentially
the same thing as the Nazis, although not on the same order of magnitude. For
example, the Hutus' brutal massacre of Tutsis in Rwanda didn't quite reach 6
million, but not for want of trying. Then there were the widespread mutual massacres between the Muslims and the Hindus after Indian independence; more
recently there were the Islamic terrorists in Algeria, who would go into a village
and kill and decapitate thirty or forty people, and there was the Serbian policy
of ethnic cleansing in Kosovo.

One of my sons has a good friend whose mother was born in Serbia. When
she heard about the Serbs going into Bosnia and killing unarmed Muslims, her
reaction was, "Those Muslims—always getting into trouble." When I think of
such attitudes—blaming the victims—I think of the environment in which the
guards in our prison were brought up and how Hitler told them the Jews were
to blame for everything that was wrong with Germany.

I asked myself what kind of environment I would have had to live in to
make it possible for me to beat somebody to death. Quite honestly I can't conceive of myself ever doing that, but every time I say I could never do something,
there's a haunting voice that says maybe I could. That maybe I don't know myself all that well.

One would certainly have hoped that the middle-aged Germans who grew
up in the years before Hitler would have had the benefit of living in a more cosmopolitan European culture than those brought up in the more constricted,
narrower, more hating environment of Nazism. But as you know, you didn't
have to go to Germany to find antisemitism. It was endemic throughout Europe.

Before Hitler, Germany was a country of refuge.

TRACHTMAN: Many Eastern European Jews were thankful to get to Germany, where they didn't have people pursuing them, as was common, say, in Russia. In order to make people behave the way the Nazis did, they had to have pounded into them relentless messages of hate: in schools, in churches, and in the public square. There had to have been a need for scapegoats and a militaristic environment that dehumanized the objects of hate. Remember, American blacks in both antebellum and postbellum United States were not really viewed as humans. So the lynching of a black in South Carolina was not truly considered murder, as the killing of a white person would have been.

Or when you kill a Bosnian Muslim because "they are always getting in trouble."

TRACHTMAN: That's right, exactly. Having a culture that dehumanizes the "other" people is essential. Another thing the Germans did was use the principles of scientific management to do their job of killing. Mechanizing and technologizing and dividing the labor of killing made it easy for individual perpetrators to escape personal responsibility. "Were you responsible for the killing of the Jews?" "Oh no, all I did was make them take off their rings and earrings and necklaces and put them in a pile, and then I collected the jewelry." Or: "All I did was to march these one hundred people from this barrack to that building, that's all I did." And: "All I did was to press these buttons and turn this handle."

The Germans arranged the procedure of killing to minimize the sense of individual responsibility by breaking the task of killing and repression into many discrete parts. When you begin to look at the process as technical problems rather than as murder, it puts it in a different light. Of course, this is not true of the hundreds of thousands of cases of shooting and bludgeoning.

Joe Weizenbaum at MIT once compared the technological cast of mind with a human orientation.[2] For example, if you went to a doctor and asked him to amputate your thumb, the first and obvious question the doctor might ask is, "Why?" However, he said, the technologists don't think that way. They would say, "Well, let's see, do we have the instrumentation available? Do you have enough money to pay the fee? Is the procedure technically feasible?" Weizenbaum said that one of the problems with contemporary society is that in the public arena we may have too much of a tendency to ask "how?" and too little of one to ask "why?"

Another ingredient of genocide is a deep respect for authority. Germany had a culture of obedience. After all, one of Immanuel Kant's best positions was, "Argue all you want about whatever you want, but obey!" That was part of German culture. People might have sweated and squirmed about doing something despicable, but in the end they went along. But as to the general question of who is capable of this sort of behavior, I guess I came most reluctantly and hesitatingly to the conclusion that virtually anybody, given the right circumstances, the right situation, and the right manipulations, was capable of perpetrating such despicable acts. But then I always reflect on those who displayed high courage and simply refused. So I am left with a degree of ambivalence.

> *That's not necessarily ambivalence. What you are saying is that there are a lot of people who are capable of evil, but there are still those who would refuse. Furthermore, in the case of Germany you had lots of rescuers, those who seriously risked their own and their family's lives. Theirs was not a cost-benefit analysis; when a moment of truth came, they simply helped save Jews. Certainly, the number of the rescuers was not large, but there was a significant number in Germany, Poland, and elsewhere. So we should be studying why certain kinds of people are rescuers and certain kinds are perpetrators, with the rest inclined to mind their own business and indifferently look the other way. That was probably what most people did.*

TRACHTMAN: One would expect that certain numbers of people in any culture or any nation would respond the way you described: a certain number of eager perpetrators, large numbers of semiwilling or semiunwilling perpetrators, and probably a small number of those who adamantly refuse. But another good question is why such barbarity erupts in a particular place at a particular time.

Consider the Vikings, for example. In the ninth and tenth centuries they were the scourge of Europe, pillaging, raping, burning, destroying. What has happened to their descendants? Today you can't pick a fight with a Norwegian—they are the quintessential preservers of peace. What has happened culturally to make the Nazi kind of behavior so improbable in areas like Scandinavia, considering their history?

> *This suggests that while people are capable of being absorbed into a brutal system, they are also capable of moving in the opposite direction. There is the Talmudic notion that different impulses exist in human beings: bad impulses are rage, anger, and envy; good impulses are kindness, generosity, and forgiveness. Therefore, the task of civilized society is to build fences around the bad impulses, to prevent people from doing evil*

things. Do you conclude that people, no matter what their background, are basically alike in their capacity to create mischief?

TRACHTMAN: One hates to flatter oneself, because ultimately you don't really know how you would behave in a full range of circumstances. But deep down something tells me that I could not have behaved that way. I have never felt the impulse to deliberately cause hurt and pain. But as I suggested, I may just be kidding myself.

> *But on the other hand, if you encountered some situation in an institution like Purdue where some people were committing either morally or legally reprehensible acts, would you report them? Would you say, "Well this is bad, but there's not much I can do about it," and look the other way? Whistle-blowing is a little different from not being able to hit or verbally abuse somebody. The question is, then, "Under what kind of conditions would you become a whistle-blower, if at all?"*

TRACHTMAN: I have no answer to that. Whistle-blowers usually pay a high price for their deeds. Obviously there are things that I would not do, but to what degree I would interfere if I saw these things happening — I just can't say.

> *You've separated yourself from Judaism in terms of religion, but what values do you retain from your Jewish background?*

TRACHTMAN: I don't know how much of me is the product of the Jewish influences of my grandparents and parents or of my environment as a child. It may well be that some of my attitudes and thoughts, the ways I question and analyze issues, bear an imprint from the kind of thinking I did and the kind of conversations I had as a child. I suspect that even though I paid no particular price as a child for being Jewish — I wasn't beaten up, I wasn't chased home from school, I wasn't reviled — my initial acquaintance with people who had suffered came from the stories my father told me about his experiences of growing up in Odessa. My knowledge of Judaism has perhaps made me a more sensitive person to the rights of others, to the needs of others, and to the importance of defending the fundamental civil rights of all people.

I have been active in politics all these years, and I have always felt the obligation of the majority to defend the rights of the minorities to work and live in peace. I think the culture of my background probably predisposed me against political extremism. I've taken positions on issues, but I think I have never violated the rights of people who disagreed with me.

Notes

1. They have four children: Daniel, born 1953; Susan, born 1956; William, born 1960; and James, born 1963.
2. See Joseph Weizenbaum, *Computer Power and Human Reason: From Judgment to Calculation* (San Francisco: W. H. Freeman, 1976).

Epilogue

Individual experience is the brick and mortar of history. Every human being forms part of an overall structure that contains the meaning and importance of an age. Thus, both the particular and the general are material for reflection, interpretation, and analysis. However, because people constantly change, modern historical interpretation tends to prefer the great movements rather than individual lives which are the essence of history, unless those lives are the lives of the rich and famous.

Academics like predictability. They search for meaning and value in the things they can understand and discover. This proved particularly true for the survivors in this book when it came to examining their own lives and trying to sort out the relevance of their earlier experiences with Nazi persecution.

Order is a necessary part of explanation. Putting human behavior in an understandable framework—whether political, psychological, social, or moral—helps shape peoples' comprehension. This is certainly true in Holocaust studies, where there is a propensity to make distinctions among perpetrators, bystanders, rescuers, and victims. But all of these come in many colors. Perpetrators, for example, can be divided into categories of those who took pleasure in butchering people, those who became instruments of such action, those who acted to advance their careers, and those who acted out of ideological commitment. These distinctions are by no means exhaustive and by no means mutually exclusive.

Rescuers also come in many forms. There are those who truly risk their lives to help other people and those who merely look the other way or decline to report a critical piece of information to the authorities. The truly righteous Gentiles act out of a genuine willingness to give assistance without doing a cost/benefit analysis. Ironically, though, the most trivial, random act of kindness might make all the difference in the cruel game of survival — at least this proved to be the case for the survivors in this book. A good turn from a stranger, no matter how casual, could prove crucial.

Survival was clearly not something that could be learned from books. It was not something that prayer could guarantee. It was "on-the-job" training, with often uncertain consequences. If it became a matter of faith, then faith in the God of Luck was often more important than faith in a Lord of Creation.

All the academics in this oral history were persecuted for their connection to the Jewish faith, a connection that Nazi bigotry translated into a malignant theory of racial inferiority. Yet none had come from a particularly strong religious environment. Their families had been mildly to strongly assimilationist, both in orientation and practice. Most had been exposed to traditional religious practices, such as attendance at a seder, visits to a synagogue, and religious instruction; but this exposure did not leave an indelible imprint on their lives. The Jewish bourgeoisie of which they were a part had been profoundly influenced by the ideas of the Enlightenment, which attenuated their Jewishness in favor of so-called secular values and practices.

Their lives followed the general pattern of such assimilation, which was well advanced in continental Europe, especially in Germany, France, and Austria, as well as in certain communities in Eastern Europe. Gone almost entirely were those customs and routines that traditionally made Jews stand out from their non-Jewish neighbors and that now had become obstructive to success in modern society, or were at least perceived as such. The survivors in this history had given little special consideration to their Jewishness before the Nazis made them aware of it. Neither did the trauma of Nazi persecution translate into a strong religious identity. (On the other hand, a large survivor literature from Hasidic Jews shows that those with a strong religious identity emerged from their ordeal with their faith intact, although perhaps battered.)

Indeed, assimilation enhanced the chance of escape. Had those in this book been part of a strong traditional community, they might not have felt so vulnerable and made plans to escape; instead, they might have been disposed to hunker down and weather the storm, as people had done in past pogroms.

Ultimately, however, no matter what the state of assimilation, or the extent to which people abandoned the faith of their forbears, Nazi persecution made it impossible for those persecuted not to consider their Jewish heritage for the rest of their lives. If the religious aspect was not heightened, at least the cultural aspect was. At the same time, though, their direct experience with Nazi racial politics often heightened their suspicion of any kind of strongly held beliefs.

Great trauma often heightens a need for transcendence. For those in this book this did not come from any single experience but rather was a continuous process occurring in various stages and at various times, even, to some extent, achieved through their university careers. It came through a belief in humanitarian values that found new expression in their private and professional lives. It came in their careers of study, teaching, and writing, through the satisfaction that they were helping to enrich the world of their adopted country, community, and university. Rather than feeling victimized, these survivors retained the feelings for compassion and good works which had been part of their common Jewish cultural identity. Having seen the ability of government to do harm, they believed that it should be used to serve the people, not become their master.

Selected Bibliography

The literature on the Nazi persecution of the Jews is too vast to attempt anything near a complete bibliography. These are some of the works that I found helpful in my research.

Documents, Memoirs, Speeches

Abzug, Robert H. *America Views the Holocaust, 1933–1945: A Brief Documentary History.* Boston: Bedford/St. Martin's, 1999.

Auerbach, Frank Ludwig. *Immigration Laws of the United States.* Indianapolis: Bobbs-Merrill, 1961.

Baynes, Norman H., ed. *Speeches of Adolf Hitler.* London: Oxford University Press, 1942.

Benes, Edvard. *Memoirs.* Boston: Houghton Mifflin, 1954.

Chamberlain, Neville. *In Search of Peace.* New York: G.P. Putnam, 1939.

Documents on British Foreign Policy. London: Her Majesty's Stationary Office, 1972– .

Documents on German Foreign Policy. Washington, D.C.: U.S. Government Printing Office, 1949– .

Eichmann, Adolf. *The Trial of Adolf Eichmann.* Tel Aviv: Israel State Archives, 1992– .

Freemantle, Anne, ed. *The Papal Encyclicals.* New York: Mentor, 1956.

Gilbert, G. M. *The Psychology of Dictatorship.* New York: Ronald Press, 1950.

Goebbels, Joseph. *The Goebbels Diaries, 1942–1943.* Garden City, N.Y.: Doubleday, 1948.

Hilberg, Raul, ed. *Documents of Destruction, Germany and Jewry, 1933–1945.* Chicago: University of Chicago Press, 1971.

Hitler, Adolf. *Mein Kampf.* Boston: Houghton Mifflin, 1943.

———. *My New Order.* New York: Reynal and Hitchcock, 1941.

Hitler, Adolf. *Secret Conversations.* New York: Farrar, Strauss, and Young, 1953.

Höss, Rudolf. *Commandant of Auschwitz.* Cleveland: World Publishing, 1959.

Klemperer, Victor. *I Will Bear Witness: A Diary of the Nazi Years, 1933–1941.* New York: Random House, 1999.

The Laws of Armed Conflicts: A Collection of Conventions, Resolutions and Other Documents. Edited by Dietrich Schindler and Jiri Toman. Geneva: Henri Dunant Institute, 1981.

Mendelsohn, John, ed. *The Holocaust: Selected Documents.* New York: Garland Publishing.

Nazi Conspiracy and Aggression. Washington, D.C.: U.S Government Printing Office, 1946.

Riefenstahl, Leni. *Triumph of the Will.* Universum Film Aktiengellschaft (UFA), 1935.

Schellenberg, Walter. *Hitler's Secret Service.* New York: Harper and Row, 1957.

Speer, Albert. *Inside the Third Reich.* New York: Macmillan, 1970.

Wagner, Friedelind. *Heritage of Fire.* New York: Harper, 1945.

Whom We Shall Welcome: Report of the President's Commission on Immigration and Naturalization. Washington, D.C.: U.S. Government Printing Office, 1953.

General Histories and Encyclopedias

Arendt, Hannah. *The Jew as Pariah: Jewish Identity and Politics in the Modern Age.* New York: Grove Press, 1978.

Dear, I. C. B., ed. *The Oxford Companion to World War II.* Oxford: Oxford University Press, 1995.

Encyclopaedia Judaica. New York: Macmillan, 1971– .

Flower, Desmond, and James Reeves, eds. *The War, 1939–1945: A Documentary History.* New York: Da Capo Press, 1997.

Gilbert, Martin. *The Second World War: A Complete History.* New York: Henry Holt, 1989.

Katz, Jacob. *Toward Modernity: The European Jewish Model.* New Brunswick: Rutgers University Press, 1987.

Kleine-Ahlbrandt, W. Laird. *Twentieth Century European History.* Saint Paul, Minn.: West Publishing Company, 1993.

Mosley, Leonard. *On Borrowed Time.* New York: Random House, 1969.

Pinson, Koppel S. *Modern Germany: Its History and Civilization.* New York: Macmillan Company, 1966.

Rothschild, Joseph. *East Central Europe between the Two World Wars.* Seattle: University of Washington Press, 1974.

Runes, Dagobert D. *Concise Dictionary of Judaism.* New York: Philosophical Library, 1959.

Snyder, Louis L. *Encyclopedia of the Third Reich.* McGraw-Hill, 1976.

Survey of International Affairs. London: Royal Institute of International Affairs, 1938– .

Taylor, James, and Warren Shaw. *The Third Reich Almanac.* New York: World Almanac, 1987.

Wehl, Elizabeth-Anne, Stephen Pope, and James Taylor. *Encyclopedia of the Second World War.* Edison, N.J.: Castle Books, 1989.

Wistrich, Robert S. *Who's Who in Nazi Germany.* London: Routledge, 1995.

Zentner, Christian, and Friedemann Bedürftig, eds. *The Encyclopedia of the Third Reich.* New York: Macmillan, 1991.

Atlases

Cram, George F. *Cram's Modern Atlas*. New York: Cram, 1904.

Gilbert, Martin. *The Macmillan Atlas of the Holocaust*. New York: Macmillan Publishing Co., 1982.

Hammond's Home and Office Atlas of the World. New York: Hammond and Company, 1944.

Freeman, Michael J. *Atlas of Nazi Germany*. New York: Macmillan, 1987.

Keegan, John, ed. *The Atlas of the Second World War*. London: Harper Collins, 1989.

Michelin. *France: Atlas Routier*. Paris: Michelin, 1992.

Natkiel, Richard. *Atlas of World War II*. New York: The Military Press, 1985.

Polish Army Topographical Service. *Pergamon World Atlas*. New York: Pergamon Press, 1968.

Stiedler, Adolf. *Hand Atlas: Über alle Theile der Erde und über das Weltgebäude*. Gotha: Justus Perthes, 1881.

National Histories and Monographs

Austria

Barker, Elizabeth. *Austria, 1918–1972*. New York: Praeger, 1971.

Brook-Shepherd, Gordon. *The Anschluss*. Philadelphia: Lippencott, 1963.

Clare, George. *Last Waltz in Vienna: The Rise and Destruction of a Family, 1842–1942*. New York: Holt, Rinehart and Winston, 1982.

Edmonsdson, C. Earl. *The Heimwehr and Austrian Politics, 1918–1936*. Athens, Ga.: University of Georgia Press, 1978.

Freidenreich, Harriet Pass. *Jewish Politics in Vienna, 1918–1938*. Bloomington: Indiana University Press, 1991.

Gellott, Laura S. *The Catholic Church and the Authoritarian Regime in Austria, 1933–1938*. New York: Garland Press, 1987.

Low, Alfred D. *The Anschluss Movement, 1931–1938, and the Great Powers*. New York: Columbia University Press, 1985.

Luza, Radomir. *Austro-German Relations in the Anschluss Era*. Princeton, N.J.: Princeton University Press, 1975.

Schneider, Gertrude. *Exile and Destruction: The Fate of Austrian Jews, 1938–1945*. Westport, Conn.: Praeger, 1995.

Stadler, Karl R. *Austria*. New York: Praeger, 1971.

Czechoslovakia

Cohen, Yohanan. *Small Nations in Times of Crisis and Confrontation*. Albany: State University of New York Press, 1989.

Douglas, Roy. *In the Year of Munich*. New York: St. Martin's Press, 1977.

The Jews of Czechoslovakia: Historical Studies and Surveys. Philadelphia: Jewish Publication Society of America, 1968– .

Kirshbaum, Stanislav J. *A History of Slovakia: A Struggle for Survival.* New York: St. Martin's Press, 1995.

Mamatey, Victor S., and Radomir Luza, eds. *A History of the Czechoslovak Republic, 1918–1948.* Princeton: Princeton University Press, 1973.

Wheeler-Bennett, John. *Munich: Prologue to Tragedy.* London: Macmillan, 1948.

France

Adamthwaite, Anthony. *France and the Coming of the Second World War, 1936–1939.* London: Frank Cass, 1977.

Adler, Jacques. *The Jews of Paris and the Final Solution: Common Response and the Internal Conflicts, 1940–1944.* New York: Oxford University Press, 1987.

Birnbaum, Pierre. *The Jews of the Republic: A Political History of State Jews in France from Gambetta to Vichy.* Stanford: Stanford University Press, 1996.

Brubaker, Rogers. *Citizenship and Nationhood in France and Germany.* Cambridge, Mass.: Harvard University Press, 1992.

Kleine-Ahlbrandt, Wm. Laird. *The Burden of Victory: France, Britain and the Enforcement of the Treaty of Versailles, 1919–1925.* New York: University Press of America, 1995.

Marrus, Michael R., and Robert O. Paxton. *Vichy France and the Jews.* New York: Schocken Books, 1983.

Paxton, Robert O. *Vichy France: Old Guard and New Order, 1940–1944.* New York: W.W. Norton, 1972.

Shrier, William L. *The Collapse of the Third Republic: An Inquiry into the Fall of France in 1940.* New York: Simon and Schuster, 1969.

Germany

Bezymenski, Lev. *The Death of Adolf Hitler.* New York: Harcourt, Brace and World, 1968.

Barkai, Avraham. *From Boycott to Annihilation: The Economic Struggle of German Jews, 1933–1943.* Hannover: University Press of New England, 1989.

Bullock, Alan. *Hitler: A Study in Tyranny.* New York: Harper and Row, 1964.

Burleigh, Michael. *The Racial State: Germany, 1933–1945.* New York: Cambridge University Press, 1991.

Cornwell, John. *Hitler's Pope: The Secret History of Pius XII.* New York: Viking, 1999.

Gay, Ruth. *The Jews of Germany: A Historical Portrait.* New Haven: Yale University Press, 1992.

Goldhagen, Daniel. *Hitler's Willing Executioners: Ordinary Germans and the Holocaust.* New York: Random House, 1997.

Höhne, Heinz. *The Order of the Death's Head: The Story of Hitler's SS.* London: Martin Secker and Warburg, 1969.

Feig, Konnilyn G. *Hitler's Death Camps: The Sanity of Madness.* New York: Holmes and Meier, 1981.

Kershaw, Ian. *Hitler.* London: Longman, 1991.

Malish, Bruce. *Psychoanalysis and History.* New York: Universal Library, 1971.

Manville, Roger. *SS and Gestapo: Rule by Terror.* New York: Ballantine Books, 1969.

Rosenbaum, Ron. *Explaining Hitler: The Search for the Origins of His Evil.* New York: Random House, 1998.

Sorkin, David Jan. *The Transformation of German Jewry, 1780–1840.* New York: Oxford University Press, 1987.

Toland, John. *Adolf Hitler.* New York: Anchor Books, 1992.

Taylor, Telford. *Nuremberg Trials: War Crimes and International Law.* New York: Carnegie Endowment for International Peace, 1949.

Thalmann, Rita, and Emmanuel Feinermann. *Crystal Night.* New York: Holocaust Library, 1974.

Turner, Henry Ashby. *German Big Business and the Rise of Hitler.* New York: Oxford University Press, 1985.

Waite, Robert G. L. *The Psychopathic God Adolf Hitler.* New York: Basic Books, 1977.

Hungary

Braham, Randolf L. *The Politics of Genocide: The Holocaust in Hungary.* New York: Columbia University Press, 1994.

Herczl, Moshe Y. *Christianity and the Holocaust of Hungarian Jewry.* New York: New York University Press, 1993.

Hoensch, Jörg K. *A History of Modern Hungary.* London: Longman, 1988.

Katzburg, Nathaniel. *Hungary and the Jews: Policy and Legislation, 1920–1943.* Ramat-Gan: Bar-Llan University Press, 1981.

Nagy-Talavera, Nicholas M. *Green Shirts and the Others: A History of Fascism in Hungary and Rumania.* Stanford, Calif.: Stanford University Press, 1970.

Ranki, Vera. *The Politics of Inclusion and Exclusion: Jews and Nationalism in Hungary.* New York: Holmes and Meier, 1999.

Rutter, Owen. *Regent of Hungary: The Authorized Life of Admiral Nicolas Horthy.* London: Rich and Cowen, 1938.

Sakmyster, Thomas L. *Hungary, the Great Powers, and the Danubian Crisis, 1936–1939.* Athens, Ga.: University of Georgia Press, 1980.

Stark, Tamás. *Hungarian Jews during the Holocaust and after the Second World War, 1939–1949: A Statistical Review.* New York: Columbia University Press, 2000.

Israel

Dan, Uri. *To the Promised Land: The Birth of Israel.* New York: Doubleday, 1988.

Halamish, Aviva. *The Exodus Affair: Holocaust Survivors and the Struggle for Palestine.* Syracuse, N.Y.: Syracuse University Press, 1998.

Metz, Helen Chapin, ed. *Israel: A Country Study.* Washington, D.C.: U.S. Government Printing Office, 1990.

Offer, Dalia. *Escaping the Holocaust: Illegal Immigration to the Land of Israel, 1939–1944.* New York: Oxford University Press, 1990.

Sachar, Howard M. *A History of Israel: From the Rise of Zionism to Our Time.* New York: Alfred A. Knopf, 1976.

Segev, Tom. *1949, The First Israelis.* New York: Free Press, 1986.

Szulc, Tad. *The Secret Alliance: The Extraordinary Story of the Rescue of the Jews since World War II.* New York: Farrar, Straus and Giroux, 1991.

Poland

Heller, Celia S. *On the Edge of Destruction: Jews of Poland between the Two World Wars.* Detroit: Wayne State University Press, 1994.

Hoffman, Eva. *Shtetl: The Life and Death of a Small Town and the World of Polish Jews.* Boston: Houghton Mifflin, 1997.

Fishman, Joshua A., ed. *Studies in Polish Jewry: The Interplay of Social, Economic, and Political Factors in the Struggle of a Minority for Its Existence.* New York: Yivo Institute for Jewish Research, 1974.

Garlinski, Józef. *Poland in the Second World War.* Basingstoke, Hampshire: Macmillan, 1985.

Korbo'nski, Stefan. *The Jews and the Poles in World War II.* New York: Hippocrene Books, 1989.

Melzer, Emanuel. *No Way Out: The Politics of Polish Jewry, 1936–1939.* Cincinnati: Hebrew Union College Press, 1997.

Roos, Hans. *A History of Modern Poland: From the Foundation of the State in the First World War to the Present Day.* New York: Knopf, 1966.

Steinlauf, Michael. *Bondage to the Dead: Poland and the Memory of the Holocaust.* Syracuse, N.Y.: Syracuse University Press, 1997.

Wiatr, Jerzy J. *The Soldier and the Nation: The Role of the Military in Polish Politics, 1918–1985.* Boulder, Colo.: Westview Press, 1988.

Watt, Richard M. *Bitter Glory: Poland and Its Fate, 1918–1939.* New York: Simon and Schuster, 1979.

United States

Bernard, William S., ed. *American Immigration Policy: A Reappraisal.* New York: Harper Brothers, 1950.

Davie, Maurice R. *World Immigration: With Special Reference to the United States.* New York: Macmillan, 1949.

Hutchinson, Edward Prince. *Legislative History of American Immigration Policy.* Philadelphia: University of Pennsylvania Press, 1981.

Morse, Arthur D. *While Six Million Died: A Chronicle of American Apathy.* New York: Random House, 1967.

Studies on the Final Solution

Bauer, Yehuda. *A History of the Holocaust.* New York: Franklin Watts, 1982.

Black, Peter R. *Ernst Kaltenbrünner, Ideological Soldier of the Third Reich.* Princeton, N.J., Princeton University Press, 1984.

Breitman, Richard. *The Architect of Genocide: Heinrich Himmler and the Final Solution.* New York. Knopf, 1991.

Browning, Christopher H. *Ordinary Men: Reserve Police Battalion 101 and the Final Solution in Poland.* New York: HarperCollins, 1992.

Calic, Edouard. *Reinhard Heydrich: The Chilling Story of the Man Who Masterminded the Nazi Death Camps.* New York: Morrow, 1985.

Dwórk, Deborah, and Robert Jan van Pelt. *Auschwitz, 1270 to the Present.* New York: W. W. Norton, 1996.

Feig, Konnilyn G. *Hitler's Death Camps: The Sanity of Madness.* New York: Holmes and Meier, 1981.

Fein, Helen. *Accounting for Genocide: National Responses and Jewish Victimization during the Holocaust.* New York: Free Press, 1979.

Fleming, Gerald. *Hitler and the Final Solution.* Berkeley: University of California Press, 1982.

Gilbert, Martin. *The Holocaust: A History of the Jews during the Second World War.* New York: Holt, Rinehart and Winston, 1985.

Hilberg, Raul. *The Destruction of the European Jews.* New York: Holmes and Meier, 1985.

Lederer, Zdenek. *Ghetto Theresienstadt.* New York: Fertig, 1983.

Levin, Nora. *The Holocaust Years: The Nazi Destruction of European Jewry, 1933–1945.* Malabar, Fla.: Robert E. Krieger Publishing Company, 1990.

Piotrowski, Tadeuz. *Poland's Holocaust: Ethnic Strife, Collaboration with Occupying Forces and Genocide in the Second Republic, 1918–1947.* Jefferson, N.C.: McFarland, 1998.

Reitlinger, Gerald. *The Final Solution: The Attempt to Exterminate the Jews of Europe, 1939–1945.* New York: A. S. Barnes and Company, 1961.

Weiss, John. *Ideology of Death: Why the Holocaust Happened in Germany.* Chicago: Ivan R. Dee, 1996.